CREATURES OF PROMETHEUS

CREATURES OF PROMETHEUS

Gender and the Politics of Technology

Timothy V. Kaufman-Osborn

ROWMAN & LITTLEFIELD PUBLISHERS, INC.
Lanham • Boulder • New York • Oxford

ROWMAN & LITTLEFIELD PUBLISHERS, INC.

Published in the United States of America
by Rowman & Littlefield Publishers, Inc.
4720 Boston Way, Lanham, Maryland 20706

12 Hid's Copse Road
Cummor Hill, Oxford OX2 9JJ, England

British Library Cataloguing in Publication Information Available

Library of Congress Cataloging-in-Publication Data

Kaufman-Osborn, Timothy V. (Timothy Vance), 1953-
    Creatures of Prometheus : gender and the politics of technology /
Timothy V. Kaufman-Osborn.
        p.   cm.
    Includes bibliographical references and index.

    1. Technology—Philosophy.   2. Technology—Social aspects.
I. Prometheus (Writer)   II. Title.
T14.K26   1997
306.4′6′082—dc21   97-17013
                                                        CIP

ISBN 0-8476-8564-0 (cloth : alk. paper)
ISBN 0-8476-8565-9 (pbk. : alk. paper)

Printed in the United States of America

♾™The paper used in this publication meets the minimum requirements of
American National Standards for Information Sciences—Permanence of Paper for printed Library Materials, ANSI Z39.48–1984.

CONTENTS

3
EXEMPLARY ARTIFACTS

PREFACE

A PREFACE IS A SORT OF CONFESSIONAL, A PLACE TO REVEAL MATTERS OTHERWISE private, to say things perhaps better left unsaid. Readers who find such disclosures embarrassing are invited to move on. Those given to the pleasures of voyeurism are welcome to remain.

Let me explain how I came to write this book or, more candidly, how I now reconstruct that history. Several years ago, I published a manuscript whose unlovely title was *Politics/Sense/Experience: A Pragmatic Inquiry into the Promise of Democracy*. One of the purposes of that work was to show how American pragmatism, especially the work of John Dewey, can explain the Western philosophical tradition's enduring hostility to everyday experience. That tradition, I argued, is defined by its chronic displacement of the search for temporally qualified and spatially situated meanings by the pursuit of axiomatic truths unsullied by the corruptions of ordinary life. Contemptuous of the ambiguous, the mutable, the sensual, Western philosophy has been marked by what Dewey called "the quest for certainty." That journey achieves its consummation when philosophy's metaphysical essences, characterized by the qualities of unity, simplicity, and transparency, are conflated with what is ultimately real; Plato's transformation of this world's fragile goods into the imperishable Form of the Good is the paradigmatic exemplar. Persuaded that cognition is the only authoritative mode of access to what is fully real, this brand of intellectual conceit transposes the modality of the ideal from the possible to the already achieved in reason. Doing so, it turns attention away from reconstruction of the conditions of collective existence and toward the sort of solace only a god can provide.

This was not a bad book, as first books go. If nothing else, it did what classical pragmatists never quite accomplished. That is, it demonstrated that it is indeed possible to fashion a comprehensive tale of the Western philosophical tradition, from its pre-Socratic origins to its Hegelian consummation, from a distinctively pragmatist point of view. In doing so, perhaps I persuaded a few that American pragmatism has something of value to contribute to contemporary debates most often confined to those speaking in European tongues (e.g., Habermas, Weber, Foucault, and Gadamer). And perhaps I persuaded a few that any effort to fulfill the promise of radical democratic politics is inseparable from a critique of Western rationalism. For so long as true being is identified with the cleaned-up products of abstractive thinking, so long as philosophy continues to commit what Dewey called the "intellectual fallacy," reason will sanction the subordination of everyday experience to authoritative ends formed in isolation from that experience. That in turn serves all too well the interests of those who would have us believe that democratic politics, in the absence of such subordination, cannot be other than anarchy.

In the closing chapters of that book, I indicated how we might begin to recover ordinary experience's sense-making capacity from institutional formations, such as the bureaucratic state, that are bent upon subjecting it to what I called "teleocratic rationalism." To do so, I proposed a pragmatist refashioning of a cluster of interrelated concepts; among others, these included nature, experience, meaning, art, and habit. Reworked so as to temper the foundationalism etched into their discursive history, these concepts can help us understand what we are doing when, always *in media res*, we occasionally fashion prosaic but sufficient sense from the events weaving in and out of our daily lives.

The argument of these last chapters, I now see, was not so much wrong as incomplete, and it was incomplete in a way that is peculiarly awkward for one claiming the mantle of pragmatism. Given my criticism of the intellectual fallacy, it was unwittingly ironic (or, less charitably, typically dense) to attempt to evoke the qualitative textures of sensible experience via a quasi-Hegelian history of ideas. My error, in retrospect, was to pay insufficient heed to a central postulate of pragmatism: a critique of the refined products of intellectual endeavor is never an end unto itself. This, I think, is what Dewey was getting at when, in the opening pages of *Experience and Nature*, he urged us to ask this of all philosophical speculation: does such thinking "end in conclusions which, when they are referred back to ordinary life-experiences and their predicaments, render them more significant, more luminous to us, and make our dealings with them more fruitful? Or does it terminate in rendering the things of ordinary experience more opaque than they were before, and in depriving them of having in 'reality' even the significance they had previously seemed to have?"[1]

Philosophical thinking, Dewey went on to explain, is one way of exploring the meanings of indeterminate situations that arise within the complex of relations that is culture. As such, it is inescapably "experiential." This is so in at least two senses. First, as is true of all thinking, philosophy is experiential in the sense that it takes its ultimate issue from qualitative matters that are "had" in ways other than or, at the very least, in addition to the cognitive. A problematic situation must be suffered and enjoyed, felt as a qualitative whole, as a condition of becoming the stuff of inquiry's explorations into the relations, the conditions and consequences, of its contextualized occurrence. Second, and again like all thinking, philosophy is experiential in the sense that the capacity of lived experience to bear enhanced significance, an embodied feel for the web of relations constitutive of it, is the ultimate arbiter of its sufficiency to the matters from which it emerges. To make these two claims is not to deny that experience is always saturated with the discursive fruits of inherited meanings. But it is to claim that there is a vital distinction to be made between having a baby and criticizing the contemporary institution of motherhood; between laughing at a clever pun and figuring out just why we did so; between savoring bouillabaisse and inquiring into the distinctive mix of its ingredients.

In any event, subjected to Dewey's test, did my first child measure up? When referred back to "ordinary life-experiences and their predicaments," did my reconstruction of the terms of sense-making help to render its conduct "more luminous"? I'm not sure it did. Or, rather, I failed to show how it might do so because I was not adequately attentive to the problematic situations that render the conduct of sense-making a perpetually unfinished and ever renewed enterprise. In saying this, I do not mean to reject the recondite exercises that define professional philosophical inquiry (including my own). But, unless these exercises are expressly related to the palpable perplexities of everyday experience, they will prove more partial than they need be. That explains why in parts 1 and 2 of the present work I show how the questions that occupy me emerge out of situated concerns, in this case, puzzles about the diverse ways made things participate in shaping and being shaped by gendered experience; and why in part 3 I indicate how my tentative responses to these questions might inform a reading of the struggles of specific women and men to fashion sense from the idiosyncratic situations they encounter in daily life.

On some level, when I completed *Politics/Sense/Experience*, I had a nagging sense that its form was not altogether congruent with its substantive argument. I did not really grasp the import of that sense, however, until I began to ask how I might wed the concerns of pragmatism to those of the feminist theory I had been reading for almost as long. Till that time, my consideration of pragmatism and feminism, like the rails of a track, had run parallel to one another and so never quite intersected. Now that they have done so, their points of correspondence seem almost too obvious to belabor.[2] Be that as it may, and although all "isms" are inherently problematic, it seems to me that the following generalizations are more true than false: Pragmatism and feminism share a mistrust of philosophical foundationalism and so call for a renewed appreciation of the quotidian, the contingent, the fluid, the ambiguous. Both affirm that the relationships in which a thing participates are constitutive of what it is, and hence that we must now rethink the liberal representation of the self as an autonomous and sovereign ego. Both regard with suspicion the interlocking gender-laden dualisms that define so much Western philosophical discourse: reason and emotion; public and private; nature and culture; form and matter; theory and practice; and so on. Finally, both insist on our need to explore the role of the sensuous body, not merely the immaterial intellect, in fashioning sense from what is given in experience. It would be wrong, though, to conclude that my aim in this work is to synthesize pragmatism and feminism within some more comprehensive theoretical framework. It is closer to the mark to say that my purpose is to weave their distinctive questions together, using the intuitions of each to complement those of the other, in an exploration of some of the "things of ordinary experience."

In addition to those whose texts have taught me these two idioms of political thinking, in addition to Sharon Kaufman-Osborn, who has shown me more about the true meaning of these idioms than has any text, in addition to my parents, who have lauded my work even when such praise was not altogether warranted, I want to express my gratitude to those who commented on portions of this manuscript prior to its final revision. These include Curtis Johnson, Christine DiStefano, Jennifer Becker, Patrick Peel, Tom Hawley, Peter Euben, Judith Grant, Tom Davis, Jane Bennett, Bill Chaloupka, and Bill Bogard. The assistance of Dennis Crockett and Dana Burgess was invaluable in locating the painting that appears on this book's cover. Also, I would be remiss if I were not to note my good fortune in finding an editor, Steve Wrinn, whose enthusiasm for this project often exceeded my own. Finally, I wish to acknowledge the students with whom I have worked over the course of the past fifteen years at Whitman College. In a way, this book is intended as a celebration of all who struggle to weave things not of their own making into enduring webs of significance. Predicated on a rejection of Hannah Arendt's claim that "the meaningfulness of everyday relationships is disclosed not in everyday life but in rare deeds,"[3] I mean this to be a distinctly democratic revel. To accept Arendt's aristocratic premise is to relegate most of us, unheroic mortals that we are, to a condition of perpetual non-sense. A refusal to be so relegated, an unwillingness to capitulate to the world's obdurate facticity, is the refusal I sense in those of my students who reject the predigested meanings relentlessly served up by the agencies of austere realism. Perhaps without reason, they insist on their right, as well as their capacity, to tease something other than pseudosense from the circumstances in which they are embedded. Doing so, they sustain me in my efforts to do the same.

While tending to the matter of acknowledgments, I should also indicate that earlier versions of two portions of part 2 have been published elsewhere. The first, under the title of "Teasing Feminist Sense from Experience," appeared in *Hypatia* 8, no. 2 (1993): 124-44. The second, under the title "Fashionable Subjects: Judith Butler and the Causal Idioms of Postmodern Feminist Theory," appeared in *Political Research Quarterly* 50, no. 3 (1997): 649–74.

My confession completed, I now leave what follows in the hands of those who must ultimately determine whether to absolve me for the sins to come.

Notes

1. John Dewey, "Experience and Nature," in *John Dewey: The Later Works*, vol. 1, ed. JoAnn Boydston (Carbondale: Southern Illinois University Press, 1981), 18.

2. In a 1918 essay titled "Philosophy and Democracy," in *Characters and Events*, vol. 2 (New York: Octagon, 1970), Dewey hinted at the possibility of an alliance between feminism and pragmatism: "Women have as yet made little contribution to philosophy. But when women who are not mere students of other persons' philosophy set out to write it, we cannot conceive that it will be the same in viewpoint or tenor as that composed from the standpoint of the different masculine experience of things" (846). Partly because Dewey himself never did anything with this insight, the possibility of such an alliance remained unexamined until recently. For the beginnings of such an exploration, see Lisa Heldke, "John Dewey and Evelyn Fox Keller: A Shared Epistemological Tradition," *Hypatia* 2, no. 3 (1987): 129-40; Nancy Fraser, "Solidarity or Singularity? Richard Rorty between Romanticism and Technocracy," in *Unruly Practices* (Minneapolis: University of Minnesota Press, 1989), 93-110; Margaret Jane Radin, "The Pragmatist and the Feminist," *Southern California Law Review* 63, no. 6 (1990): 1699-1726; Charlene Haddock Seigfried, "Where Are All the Pragmatist Feminists?" *Hypatia* 6, no. 2 (1991): 1-20; Richard Rorty, "Feminism and Pragmatism," *Michigan Quarterly Review* 30, no. 2 (1991): 231-58; and Timothy Kaufman-Osborn, "Teasing Feminist Sense from Experience," *Hypatia* 8, no. 2 (1993): 124-44. The entire issue of *Hypatia* in which this last essay appears is devoted to the question of the relationship between pragmatism and feminism.

3. Hannah Arendt, *The Human Condition* (Chicago: University of Chicago Press, 1958), 42.

FOUR PROPOSALS AND A WEDDING

After all, everything is a kind of poetry;
and so all the creations of every craft and
every profession are themselves a kind of poetry,
and everyone who practices a craft is a poet.

Plato

THE PROJECT OF THIS BOOK IS SITUATED AT THE INTERSECTION OF TWO CONCERNS. The first involves the relationship between human beings and the things they make, and the second the way gender informs and is informed by that relationship. For the sake of simplicity, it is tempting to treat these issues as if they were neatly distinguishable. That, however, is an enticement to be resisted. Matters of technology and gender are never unrelated in experience, and any argument that presupposes their isolability is sure to grasp the political import of neither.[1]

That technology and gender are altogether entangled is intimated by the West's archetypal account of craft's origins.[2] On Plato's telling, after fashioning all mortal creatures out of a mixture of earth and fire, the gods commanded Prometheus and his dim brother, Epimetheus, to equip each species with powers suitable to it. With more zeal than forethought, Epimetheus applied himself to the matter at hand:

> In his allotment he gave to some creatures strength without speed, and equipped the weaker kinds with speed. Some he armed with weapons, while to the unarmed he gave some other faculty and so contrived means for their preservation. To those that he endowed with smallness, he granted winged flight or a dwelling underground; to those which he increased in stature, their size itself was a protection. Thus he made his whole distribution on a principle of compensation, being careful by these devices that no species should be destroyed.[3]

The profligate Epimetheus, however, forgot to reserve any powers for the race of men, leaving them "naked, unshod, unbedded, and unarmed" (321c). Overcome by pity for these sorry creatures, the trickster Prometheus "stole from Hephaestus and Athena the gift of skill in the arts, together with fire—for without fire it was impossible for anyone to possess or use this skill—and bestowed it on man" (321d). So blessed, man promptly set about incorporating the labor of his hands within dozens of sturdy artifacts. Woven together, in time these things gave birth to a distinctively human world; and because that world endured long after its individual makers perished, its very existence sabotaged the strict distinction between beings mortal and immortal.

How shall Prometheus's beneficiaries be humbled? In his *Theogony*, Hesiod describes the "plague" Zeus inflicts upon these unworthy recipients of divine powers:

> At the orders of the son of Cronus, the famous lame smith-god [Hephaestus] shaped some clay in the image of a tender girl. The bright-eyed goddess Athena dressed and decked her in silvery clothes. A marvelous embroidered veil fell from her head and was held in her hands. Round her head the goddess tied a golden diadem on which the smith-god himself had exercised his skill, to please his father Zeus. When Zeus had completed this beautiful curse to go with the blessing of fire, he displayed the girl in an assembly of the gods and men, all decked out in the finery supplied by the bright-eyed daughter of the lord of hosts. Gods and men were speechless when they saw how deadly and how irresistible was the trick with which Zeus was going to catch mankind.[4]

The deception exercised by Prometheus is thus matched by the subterfuge that is the anonymous but "damnable race [genos] of women" (590-91). Objects of desire and desiring objects, these beings persistently lure men away from the task of building and sustaining the artifactual home with which they rival the gods. That women can exercise such seductive power is all the more remarkable given that they too are so many manufactured things, so many creatures who owe their being to the artisanal talents of Hephaestus and Athena.

If, as Plato's rendition suggests, men also are so many earthen works shaped to form by divine hands, then neither women nor men can claim to be somehow unmade, given in the nature of things. If these beings are dissimilar, accordingly, it is not because their origins differ. Rather, they become unlike insofar as they are absorbed within distinct domains of craft. While Athena's daughters come to be paradigmatically associated with the art of weaving, the sons of Hephaestus are identified with the work of the forge. Although both are artifacts busily engaged in the fabrication of still more artifacts, women and men become peculiarly gendered beings via their sustained implication in distinct ways of making and unmaking a world they inhabit in common.

If this work's first proposal affirms the impossibility of distinguishing issues of gender from those of technology, its second concerns our most familiar ways of thinking about the latter. By and large, I contend, our thinking about the gifts of Prometheus is structured by what I call the "Cartesian paradigm of use." (By the term "paradigm," I mean to refer to a loosely assembled cluster of conceptual habits, usually including unthematized metaphysical assumptions, characteristic questions, routine metaphorical extensions, conventional grammatical constructions, and so on; working together in ways too commonplace to be noticed as such, sense-making paradigms incline thinking in this way rather than that.) In a nutshell, the Cartesian paradigm of use affirms that human beings are so many discrete subjects whose autonomy is manifest in the choices they make concerning efficient use of the intrinsically neutral objects fashioned for their convenience. To crack that shell, consider the following claim, often advanced by my students: "Nuclear energy is neither intrinsically good nor evil. It all depends on the purposes for which we use it." Now consider the hackneyed slogan of the National Rifle Association: "Guns don't kill; people do." Each of these assertions presupposes that our technical instrumentalities are so many disinterested means whose value is determined by the interested ends to which they are put by freely willing human subjects; and, correlatively, each presupposes that the being, the identity, of these subjects is not essentially constituted by their engagement in a world of artifacts. In sum, the Cartesian paradigm of use assumes that human creators and manufactured creatures are in principle distinguishable, which in turn is the condition of the former's mastery over the latter.

For reasons explicated later, I believe that the Cartesian paradigm of use is ill-equipped to help us through the thickets of artifactually textured experience. In light of that incapacity, my third proposal is that we now need a more nuanced account of the relationship between the made things that are human beings and those that are not. To anticipate the account I offer in part 1, return for a moment to our divine upstart. Consider the speech delivered by Prometheus, as related by Aeschylus, after Hephaestus has secured the bronze manacles chaining him to a desolate crag in the Caucasus:

> For men at first had eyes but saw to no purpose; they had ears but did not hear. Like the shapes of dreams they dragged through their long lives and handled all things in bewilderment and confusion. They did not know of building houses with bricks to face the sun; they did not know how to work in wood. They lived like swarming ants in holes in the ground, in the sunless caves of the earth. . . . It was I who first yoked beasts for them in the yokes and made of those beasts the slaves of trace chain and pack saddle that they might be man's substitute in the hardest tasks. . . . Such were the contrivances that I discovered for men—alas for me! For I myself am without contrivance to rid myself of my present affliction.[5]

Prior to receipt of Prometheus's gift, just what were these beings? Should we assign them to the class of animals? Or perhaps to that of automatons? Or to that of monsters, beings for whom no class seems quite right? Apparently, they bore the visible shape of human beings; but it is not certain that this suffices to warrant calling them such. While their bodily capacities were perhaps adequate to ensure bare survival, those faculties were not yet human in any distinctive sense. Their ears detected the approach of prey, but they did not "hear." Their eyes watched the snow fall, but they did not "see." The fact of their embodiment was just that, a brute given, unable to participate in generating an articulated sense of the significance of things, of the relationship between the falling leaves and the approach of winter, between the sound of prey and the prospect of a feast.

What transforms these human shapes into beings worthy of the name is receipt of Prometheus's gifts. Through the appropriation of primitive tools, through the employment of fire to alter the form of things otherwise simply given, these protohumans begin to emerge from their "bewilderment and confusion." What were once mere "creatures of a day" (947) come to live into a meaningful future, as they grasp the relationship between present activities and future possibilities, between this crude blade and the prospect of skinning that deer to fashion something akin to a cloak. That cloak in turn tempers what is otherwise a warm-blooded body's unrelenting struggle to maintain a constant temperature. Just as the beast subdued by trace chain and packsaddle comes to "be man's substitute in the hardest tasks," so too does this cloak come to stand as surrogate for his native skin. Doing the work his body need no longer do, it is the indispensable condition of his song; only a body so protected can afford to let its imagination inch away from the immediacies of survival. Perhaps, therefore, instead of claiming that human beings make artifacts, we should say that artifacts make beings human.

If this be so, then the irony of Prometheus's present plight is acute. He who first delivered the fire that transformed mute beasts into beings capable of challenging divine prerogative is now deprived of that same gift. "I myself am without contrivance to rid myself of my present affliction." Like a prisoner tortured day after day within a cell no bigger than a broom closet, Prometheus is now a mere creature of his body's imperious cries, a thing who can no longer extend his being into a world of significant artifacts. "Tangled . . . in the net of ruin, past all hope of rescue" (1078-79), Prometheus bound must in time become a senseless brute.

The fate of Prometheus suggests an un-Cartesian way to think about the relationship between human beings and many (but not all) of the made things that jointly occupy the world. To get at that understanding, I appropriate the terms "projection" and "reciprocation" from Elaine Scarry's remarkable (but also flawed) book, *The Body in Pain*.[6] "Projection" suggests the capacity of human beings to relieve bodies of their more imperious demands by incorporating knowledge of human vulnerabilities into works of artisanal skill. "Reciprocation" suggests the ways artifacts remake agents by releasing potentialities that would remain untapped absent the work done by the fruits of fabrication. Via participation in the dialectic of projection and reciprocation, human beings keep at bay imperatives that would otherwise render them mere bodies in pain. We effectively disembody ourselves through artifacts that minister to needs we can now afford to forget.

To illustrate, consider once more that deerskin cloak: An understanding of a vital need of warm-blooded creatures is *projected* into that coat. This artifact *reciprocates* by freeing its wearer to take part in various activities, activities that would go unexplored were that body to remain naked. Or, to take a less obvious example, consider a simple tape recorder. An understanding of the capacity of human beings to remember is projected into this machine. The tape recorder reciprocates by freeing us from the burdens of immediate recall. Doing so, it counters memory's proclivity to recall only what it wishes; and that in turn bolsters the conceptualization of truthfulness as a virtue displayed by those whose recollections are congruent with the facts of the matter. Emergence of our modern notion of objectivity, consequently, is inseparable from invention of the artifacts that make it possible to check memory's flights of fancy. Or, think of René Descartes. When Descartes suffers his crisis of epistemological skepticism, he retreats to a bare room heated by a wood-burning stove. Into the ceiling above his head is projected the knowledge that human beings cannot be other than creatures of a day in the absence of shelter from the elements. If Descartes's room had neither roof nor stove, if he were not unreflectively situated in a world of hardy artifacts, he could never entertain the illusion that he is a being whose disembodied nature it is to think. The possibility of Descartes's philosophical practice presupposes the reciprocative work done by a host of mundane artifacts toward which he proves distinctly ungrateful, even oblivious.

The projection/reciprocation dialectic, incidentally, is what I mean to intimate via this work's title. That title is indeterminate in its simultaneous reference to the things human beings make and to human beings as made things. We are at one and the same time Promethean creators as well as creatures of Prometheus. Note, though, that in describing this dialectic I have made no reference to this work's subtitle and so to gender. In her *Body in Pain*, Scarry does not ask whether the projection/reciprocation dialectic is itself saturated with gender. Nor does she ask whether forms of creation in which women are especially implicated (most notably, reproduction) are well understood in terms of this dialectic. However, if I am to be true to my first proposal and if I am to avoid one of the defining errors of the Cartesian paradigm of use, these questions must be posed. However troubled, gender is a constitutive principle of all beings I am able to recognize as human. To presuppose a conception of the subject as a genderless being, to posit the existence of a generic human being, is to risk conflating a distinctively masculine subject with the subject per se.

How I mean to join my first and third proposal, that is, how I mean to think about the gendered dimension of the projection/reciprocation dialectic, was implicit in my earlier reference to Athena and Hephaestus. It is my contention that gender is well understood as a complex effect, an artifact, generated by differential participation in the dialectic of projection and reciprocation.

To become a woman, for example, is to be a creature of the dialectic of projection and reciprocation, as it is informed by gender-specific forms of divided labor. One does not rear babies because one is a woman; it is the conduct of rearing babies that makes one a woman. One does not clean house because one is a woman; it is sustained implication in such artifactually articulated practice that engenders a woman.

My fourth proposal, which perhaps should be my first, suggests that the present historical moment offers an unusually ripe opportunity to grasp the deficiencies of the Cartesian paradigm of use and, consequently, to make better sense of the relationship between gender and the world of made things. To see why this might be so, recall a claim Freud made in his *Introductory Lectures to Psychoanalysis*.[7] Writing in the midst of World War I, Freud argued that the twentieth century bears witness to the last of three shocks to humanity's accustomed sense of itself as the crown of creation. The first transpired when Copernicus displaced the earth from the center of the cosmos; the second when Darwin removed the human species from its privileged spot near the apex of God's creation; and the third now gains momentum, as the science of psychoanalysis challenges the Enlightenment's pretensions concerning the primacy of reason in directing conduct.

Each of these blows testifies to a border collapse, a disintegration of the demarcations customarily separating this from that sort of thing. Copernicus or, more precisely, Galileo contested the strict segregation of celestial from terrestrial spheres; Darwin demolished the wall separating human from animal; and Freud undid the distinction between reason and unreason. Building on Freud's argument, Bruce Mazlish recently contended that human beings are now struggling to come to grips with yet another shock, what he calls the "coevolution of humans and machines." As evidence, he cites the practices of biogenetic engineering, artificial insemination, and organ replacement, each of which mocks the distinction between persons, brought into being through the "natural" processes of biological gestation, and manufactured things, brought into being through the "artificial" work of fabrication.

"Postmodern" political and social theory, it seems to me, might be read as a response to the cumulative impact of these four shocks.[8] To see the point, recall Donna Haraway's argument in "A Manifesto for Cyborgs." There, in a variation on Mazlish's theme, Haraway argues that postmodern theorizing is made conceptually possible by the erosion of three once-fixed boundaries: between human and animal; between organism and machine; and, finally, between physical and nonphysical. Each of these once-naturalized distinctions has become questionable; all, to use Haraway's term, now "leak." What postmodern theory affirms in response is the centrality of the category of artifice; today, each of these distinctions appears to be a creature of contingent invention rather than of ontological necessity. This truth, she continues, is best exemplified by that "hybrid of machine and organism," that "creature of social reality as well as a creature of fiction," the essentially ambiguous cyborg.[9] Consistently eluding the border patrols deployed by the guardians of Western metaphysics, this impossible alien of uncertain gender unsettles our received taxonomy of existents. Profoundly disturbing the autonomous subject who must hold at arm's length the clear and distinct objects it means to master, the cyborg revels in its deliverance from the conceptual terrain mapped out by the Cartesian paradigm of use.

When familiar borders and accustomed distinctions come undone, the constructed character of reality becomes apparent. To date, I would argue, this recognition has been most fruitfully applied to the beings we call human. Think, for example, of the provocative work of Judith Butler. In *Gender Trouble* and, more recently, in *Bodies That Matter*, Butler upends our received notions of gender. To do so, she criticizes all efforts to naturalize the differences between men and women by rooting gender in the foundationalist category of sex. Gender, on her account, is a matter of performativity, of the ritualized expression of norm-governed conduct. To this argument, following Nietzsche, Butler adds the contention that there is no "I," no essential self, who stands outside or beyond the performances "it" enacts. What we call "I" is simply that which has been called into being within the discourses by which it is constituted, and so the apparently stable and self-identical ego is at bottom a manufactured appearance, a contingent artifact. The specifically gendered self, accordingly, is an ambiguous site of political conflict, of contest concerning the forms of identity that will be deemed real at any given historical moment.

As I will explain later, as with Scarry's, I have qualms about certain aspects of Butler's argument. Be that as it may, much of what I write here may be understood as an attempt to apply her contention concerning the contingent quality of gender identity to those things that appear most obdurately and self-evidently real: the prosaic instrumentalities we unreflectively "use" in our daily commerce with the world. In short, I mean to extend Butler's deconstruction of the subject to the tangible things we Cartesians are inclined to call "objects." But I also intend to arrest the disintegrative effects of that deconstruction by indicating how many of these "objects" ultimately respond to, and refer back to, the embodied imperatives of the creatures we call "human." In other words, and this is the wedding to which I refer in this section's title, I mean to marry Butler to Scarry and, in so doing, to call forth a theoretical child who, I suspect, will be found objectionable by both of its parents.

The provisions of this union are implicit in the most comprehensive theoretical term I employ in this work: "artifact." This term, which I employ in reference to human beings as well as to the things they make, to nonhuman beings as well as to the things they make human, locates its referents in an ambiguous conceptual space somewhere between that occupied by fixed Cartesian objects, on the one hand, and that occupied by utterly contingent creatures of a deconstructive day, on the other. To see the point, consider its etymology. "Art," from the Latin *artem*, refers to skill in the doing or making of something; as such, it reminds us that things made might be other than they are today. The infinitive *facere* means "to make" or "to do"; and *factum*, characteristically used to distinguish deeds from words, refers to a thing done or performed, an accomplished feat. Accordingly, to call some thing an "arti-fact" is to remind us of the artifice, the doing, contained within it; but it is also to remind us that this activity has now congealed into a thing done. To regard any given artifact merely as the consolidation of so much "art" is to forget how imperiously it resists efforts to make it something other than what it is now. But to regard that same artifact as a *factum*, as a thing whose nature is simply given, is to forget the etymological affinity between it and *fictum*, the domain of things that, because made, are always contestable and reformable.

It is tempting to respond to the erosion of accustomed sense-making borders by lumping together all hitherto distinguished things within some homogeneous postmodern soup, a nebulous broth labeled "the contingent" or, perhaps, "the discursively constructed." In a sense, my deployment of the term "artifact" does exactly that. But that alone will not suffice. While human beings may be kin to made things, and vice versa, our interest in sense-making is not well served by riding roughshod over their differences, by identifying kinship with identity. We may now be aware of the violence inherent in all efforts to articulate new terms of sense-making, of our inability to specify what is real without denying that same honorific to what is excluded from and by our categories, but violate we must. How, then, are we to distinguish between human and nonhuman artifacts without, in so doing, reinvoking all the unwanted conceptual baggage associated with the Cartesian paradigm of use and, more particularly, its construction of the binary opposition between subject and object?

To illustrate the dilemma here, consider my daughter (were I to have one). Is Rachael the same sort of thing as those more conventionally located in the class of artifacts (e.g., the Barbie doll given to her by a now suspect playmate)? So long as I find unproblematic the border separating human beings from nonhuman things, I will find it easy to distinguish my daughter from that plastic abomination. But does it complicate matters to know that Rachael emulates Barbie and, on occasion, has expressed a desire to make herself over in the image of this creature? Would it complicate matters still more if, subjecting herself to surgical reconstruction, or perhaps to the self-administered technology known as anorexia, she were to resculpt her body in the exact image of this ideal? What should I call her then? My daughter? A living doll? A pseudocyborg (whatever that oxymoron might mean)? A monster? If familiar Cartesian distinctions can no longer offer an adequate response to this question, nor will it do to render Rachael and Barbie one of a kind.

To ward off possible confusion, it should be understood that my aim in asking this question, in rethinking the relationship between human and nonhuman artifacts, is not to determine what Barbie or Rachael *really* is. Nor is it to stipulate whether someone in an irreversible coma, wholly sustained by medical hardware, is *really* a human being. Nor is it to determine whether a computer capable of artificial intelligence is *really* a machine. Such conundrums I will leave to members of the clergy, to attorneys, to professional epistemologists. For me, the term "reality" draws its force not from its implicit reference to the representational distinction between what is true and false, but rather from the distinction between what can and cannot appear in meaningful experience. The real is ultimately a complex political production. Consider, for example, what Adrienne Rich has dubbed "compulsory heterosexuality."[10] This historically specific way of producing, organizing, and regulating sexuality is an achievement whose ingredients include sexist language, sex-specific codes of conduct and dress, gendered ways of carving up space (e.g., the nuclear household), of dividing labor, and so on. So long as this complex of practices resides in the realm of the taken for granted, it elicits no defenders. Only when its reality begins to waver, only when it begins to shift from the realm of fact to that of fiction, will some feel called upon to accomplish with hateful words, with politically enforced sanctions, and, if necessary, with violence what its simple facticity can no longer secure. To find it necessary to stamp this contingent mode of sexuality "natural," to condemn as "abnormal" those who refuse or fail to abide by its dictates, to subject such problematic souls to the ministrations of priest, policeman, and psychiatrist, all testify to the precariousness of what was once self-evidently so.

When the order of things human and nonhuman comes unglued in this fashion, new political possibilities begin to appear real. Consider, for example, sexual harassment. Prior to the 1970s, what we now call "sexual harassment" did not appear in the realm of the real, at least in part because of the success of compulsory heterosexuality in defining women's bodies as commodities available to men on demand. Till then, should a woman claim that what her male employer considered so much harmless flirting was "really" the violation of a legally enforceable right, she would be greeted with derision or, if more fortunate, with uncomprehending stares. Such a claim would literally make no sense; it would be dismissed as the rantings of someone who was unbalanced, perhaps hysterical, clearly incapable of grasping what was truly going on. However, as compulsory heterosexuality began to appear questionable, as the law began to recognize a new category of justiciable offense, as courts began to impose tangible sanctions on those found guilty, sexual harassment began to be real-ized—made real. To ask whether sexual harassment "really" existed prior to this day, to play epistemologist, is to ask the wrong question. Better, I think, to ask how this reality was called into being and, given that "reality" is always a contested production, under what artifactual conditions it can sustain its appearance in time.

My aim, accordingly, is to explore the co-constitutive relationship between the class of artifacts I will call, for lack of a better term, "artisanal," and the class of artifacts we conventionally call "women" and "men," in fashioning what is real. As these quotation marks intimate, this effort necessarily involves reference to a third sort of artifact: the linguistic. No artifact ever appears as such; it always appears as an instance of one sort of thing as opposed to another. Indeed, the identification of any specific artifact as a member of this or that discursive class is essential to its intelligibility and so to its appearance as something real. To call what I sit on a "chair" is to render this concrete particular intelligible by designating the class to which it belongs, and the same is true of Rachael. The designation of a class as a class is, in turn, always a matter of drawing boundaries, of articulating the exclusionary differences between this sort of thing and that. That process proceeds more or less unproblematically so long as received discursive resources are adequate to felt sense-making needs. It proceeds less happily when things and their familiar names appear out of joint; and that, to return to my fourth proposal, is precisely where we stand today.

Several overlapping caveats must be introduced at this point. First, I will resist the temptation to elevate any one of these three artifactual forms (human, artisanal, and linguistic) above the others, to suggest that its participation is somehow more essential than the others in making real things what they are. Or, to reverse the spatial metaphor, I will resist the temptation to engage in reductionism, to argue that any two of these forms are merely epiphenomenal manifestations of some foundational third. I reject the sort of humanism that represents human beings as autonomous makers of the world they find themselves in. I reject the sort of determinism that represents human beings as mere creatures of their artisanal creators. And I reject the sort of discursive essentialism that contends that language alone makes things what they are. Each of these artifactual forms is irreducibly and simultaneously implicated in the making, unmaking, and remaking of the other two. I mean to disentangle the threads of these three participants in the constitution of real artifacts. I have no need for a red thread that aspires to supplant the work done by the others.

Second, no one of these participants in what I will call the "materialization" of real artifacts, that is, the conduct through which their taken-for-granted reality is secured, will ever be discovered in pure form, in perfect isolation from the others. Any materialized artifact represents a stabilization of the relations sustained between all three. Consider, for example, the reality of "the law." What sort of artifact is that? Is this an artisanal artifact, a human artifact, or a linguistic artifact? Clearly, "it" is all three. The law cannot be reductively equated with the persons whose conduct it regulates, for their identities cannot be intelligibly grasped apart from the linguistic artifacts that identify them as juridical subjects. But to consider the language of the law as its exclusive or essential constituent is to forget that the terms of this discourse are something less than fully real absent the palpable bodies they seize and shape. Finally, nor can the law be equated with the artisanal artifacts found in the courtroom, although clearly much of what the law is is vitally incorporated within the raised platform on which the judge sits, the text by which witnesses swear, the railing separating those more immediately caught up within the legal drama from those who are mere spectators, and so forth and so on. The reality that is the law, in sum, is nothing more and nothing less than a distinctive way of drawing together and sustaining the relationship between various human, artisanal, and linguistic artifacts.

Third, to draw out the obvious implication of the first two caveats, the conceptual distinction between artisanal, linguistic, and human artifacts is analytic rather than representational. When I treat these artifactual forms as distinct, I acknowledge that I am engaged in an act of intellectual simplification, an act that is never innocent. For the sake of fashioning the artifact that is sense, for the sake of contesting understandings I find politically pernicious and philosophically problematic, I tease these categories from the nexus of lived experience. But that nexus will never present us with the sort of self-contained categories and tidy distinctions we professional academics hold so dear. What is in experience always outstrips what is real.

When joined to my wedding of Butler and Scarry, my four proposals state an abridged version of the argument I advance in parts 1 and 2 of this work. The central purpose of part 1, titled "Artifacts As Agents," is to cast doubt on and then displace the Cartesian paradigm of use. I begin by offering a detailed exposition of this paradigm as well as an account of how it misshapes current debates about the political import of various technologies. Then, in order to indicate what sort of agency we should ascribe to artisanal artifacts, I advance a critical elaboration of Scarry's account of the projection/reciprocation dialectic, which in turn entails fuller specification of the metaphorical relationship between human bodies and the things they make and employ. Next, I ask whether the agency of artisanal artifacts renders them specifically political beings; and, as an extension of that question, I ask in what sense it is appropriate to claim that such artifacts are themselves gendered. Finally, with a little help from Aeschylus, I ask how it is that artisanal artifacts interact with linguistic artifacts and so come to acquire the referential stability that makes it so easy to think of them as inert "things," as neutral objects awaiting efficient use by so many autonomous Cartesian subjects.

Part 2 is titled "Agents As Artifacts." If part 1 asks how we might ascribe something akin to human agency to artisanal artifacts, part 2 reverses this question by asking how we might think of human beings as something akin to artisanal artifacts. To fashion a bridge between parts 1 and 2, I open the latter with a discussion of the distinction Hannah Arendt draws between the intangible "web" of human relationships, called into being by the form of agency she calls "action," and the tangible "world" of artifacts, produced by the form of agency she calls "work." Following that, principally through consideration of the work of Richard Rorty and Judith Butler, I propose a critical affirmation of the oft-repeated argument on behalf of the discursive and hence constructed character of all reality, including the reality that is human identity. The specifically critical dimension of this appropriation turns on the use I make of pragmatism's category of experience. This category, which I take (paradoxically) to be more comprehensive than that of reality, intimates that human bodies possess ways of participating in the project of making sense that are not reducible to the discursively intelligible. This affirmation of the sense-making import of what I call "embodied feelings" becomes crucial when I return to the artifact of gender. Gender, as I have already suggested, is a fiction made real, a materialized fact, and "women" and "men" are beings who are what they are by virtue of the diverse ways they participate in the dialectic of projection and reciprocation. But under what circumstances does the compulsory fact of gender become questionable, a problematic as opposed to a naturalized fact? In answering this question, what especially concerns me are those moments when, for one reason or another, artisanal artifacts outstrip received discursive resources and so provoke gender trouble. How such crises unfold cannot be understood absent consideration of the ways bodies, grasping far more than tongues can say, begin to tease sense from what is latent within pregnant experience.

(Here a quick caution about the relationship between parts 1 and 2 is in order. As is the case with my taxonomy of materialized artifacts, the distinction I draw between my principal concern in part 1, the agency of artisanal artifacts, and that of part 2, the artifacticity of human agency, is an analytic distinction. Given my belief that the relationship between the two concerns is essentially dialectical, that the being of each is constituted through its engagement with the other, the division of this work into two parts is necessary but also at odds with my substantive argument. I have elected to begin with the agency of artifacts rather than the artifact of agency for two reasons: First, this strikes me as a useful antidote to our accustomed Cartesian assumption concerning the priority of human beings to the things they make. Second, whatever contribution each of us makes to a remaking of the world is vastly overshadowed by the dense obduracy of the artifacts that precede our birth and endure long after we die; consequently, there is an important sense in which artisanal artifacts are existentially prior to the human beings they help to fashion.)

In part 3, I explore three situations in which specific women and men, some of whom are self-consciously fictional and some of whom are not, are discovered in the middle of working out their meaningful relations to each other, as these relations are mediated by a significant artisanal artifact. In each of these cases, I ask two questions: First, how does the artisanal artifact in question participate in shaping gender-specific modes of experience? How does "it," exceeding the intentions of its makers as well as those whose lives are touched by it, take part in fashioning a collective world, a world that consolidates structures of gender-saturated domination and subordination? And, second, how do the human agents implicated in each of these situations attempt to fashion meaning from the artifact in question? How, more generally, do the artifacts we call "persons" fashion the artifact we call "sense" from the artifacts we misleadingly call "objects?" Under what circumstances do those efforts disclose and sometimes invite subversion of oppressive relationships, and under what circumstances do they remain hidden from view?

The first of my three artisanal artifacts is the shield Hephaestus, the god of craft, fashions for Achilles, as described in book 18 of Homer's *Iliad*; here I contrast the meaning-making work of Hephaestus and Achilles with that of Thetis, Achilles' mother. The second is the creature who haunts Mary Shelley's *Frankenstein*; here, I oppose the interpretive practices of Victor Frankenstein to that of Elizabeth, his fiancée. The third is the nuclear plant at Chernobyl, which suffered more than a mishap in 1986; here I examine how Grigori Medvedev, a Soviet nuclear physicist, reads this "accident," and I contrast his reading with that offered by the protagonist of Christa Wolf's *Accident*, an East German woman whose knowledge of this incident is confined to what she hears on the radio. In each of these instances, fabricated artifacts that, only yesterday, seemed given in the nature of things suddenly proclaim their fictionality, their status as so many unstable creatures of artifice. And, in each case, it is the fiction of the law and, more specifically, the drama of a trial that shores up the meaning of a crumbling world and so reconsolidates the gendered relations that afford it determinate shape.

At first blush, the trio of artifacts I have elected to explore may seem peculiar. Their selection is not without reason, however. Return with me to Prometheus once more. Recall that, on Plato's account, Prometheus steals from Zeus "the gift of skill in the arts, together with fire—for without fire it was impossible for anyone to possess or use this skill." That flame is a sign of the power of human beings to compensate for their natural frailties by fashioning helpful things from materials offered in nature. In this book, I explore three of the key forms assumed by that power in the course of human history. In the first, the literal is identical to the symbolic, for the power Hephaestus draws on at his forge is that of flame itself. In the second, Prometheus's gift takes shape as the electricity with which Victor Frankenstein animates his creature. In the third, that power issues forth as so many radioactive particles that refuse to remain contained within the walls of Chernobyl's reactor #4. If the equation $E = mc^2$ suggests the general principle of the convertibility of matter into energy, then each of these three forms of Promethean power represents a distinct way of disclosing the reality that is energized mass. Each, that is, represents a specific way of bringing matter to life by releasing potentialities that would otherwise remain dormant; and, correlatively, each represents a specific way of bringing death to those whom Prometheus sought to benefit.

Because the legacy of Prometheus assumes so many guises, no unidimensional account of the relationship between human and artisanal artifacts will suffice. Persuaded that "(c)ommunications technologies and biotechnologies are the crucial tools in recrafting our bodies,"[11] Haraway offers the cyborg as the paradigmatic metaphor for the human condition within postmodernity. But, as with Descartes's illusion that he is a being whose essence is to think, the cyborg's existence presupposes the maintenance work accomplished by a host of humdrum artifacts. This exotic creature can afford to overlook that work precisely because these prosaic artifacts recede so completely into the domain of the taken for granted. I am wary of those who, in their infatuation with high-tech boy toys, seem to forget that women too have been praised most highly when their work in ministering to the elemental needs of others' bodies has been performed silently, invisibly. The parallel is not accidental, and it is one that should give feminists pause.

In any event, the complexity of our relationships to different kinds of artifacts drawn into the present from various historical eras demands a diverse kit of sense-making tools. In some situations, we remain akin to Hephaestus. Think, for example, of the work that goes into making a loaf of homemade rye bread. Here, our hands are immediately engaged in the qualitative transformation of materials into something that, although ultimately standing apart from its maker, palpably testifies to the human labor now incorporated beneath its still-warm crust. In other situations, we are more akin to Frankenstein's creature. Think, for example, of the replacement of flesh and bone limbs by their prosthetic equivalents. Or, less obviously, think of the disciplinary technologies analyzed by Foucault and others, ranging from the organization of living space within prisons to the system of grading that induces servility in most of my students. In such cases, work does not create a nonhuman thing standing apart from the company of its makers; here, the fashioned artifact is itself a human creature. In still other situations, we are more akin to the reactor operators on duty at Chernobyl. When two metal doors seal us within an Otis elevator, when I am lost once again within the bowels of Pennsylvania Station, when we board a Boeing 747, our lives are sustained by a host of technological artifacts, most of which we never know in any immediate sense.

In the first sort of situation, at least until we eat our daily bread, the visible artifact remains external to the body whose organs have shaped it. In the second, the organs of that same body invisibly articulate the work that has made them what they are. And, in the third, that body in its entirety disappears within a freestanding artisanal artifact, thus becoming something not unlike one of its internal organs.

My aim in this work is to suggest how we might begin to do justice to our standing as mutifaceted creatures of Prometheus. This does not involve offering solutions to concrete technological dilemmas, but it does involve affirming the ambiguities of things made, nonhuman as well as human. Only when artifacts assume the form of so many puzzles, of so many unsettled things whose meaning is available for renegotiation, only then can we begin to uncover their specifically political import. To make such import more apparent than it is at present is sufficient for my purposes. I leave to others the task of figuring out how to fashion artifacts whose entry into everyday experience does something other than consolidate established oppressions and ratify accustomed indignities.

Before I begin in earnest, one final preliminary about the artifact now in your hands: To ward off illegitimate appropriation, I would ask that you resist the temptation to assimilate this work's argument into an established academic discourse concerning technology. This is not a work of history aimed at delineating the causes of technological innovation and tracing its effects in other realms of culture. This is not a work of political science aimed at analyzing governmental programs that fund various forms of technological research. This is not a work of economics aimed at showing how cost/benefit analyses explain why some technological devices succeed in the marketplace, whereas others fail. This is not a work of philosophy aimed at clarifying the conceptual distinction between technology and science. This is not a work of sociology aimed at investigating the relationship between transformations in the class structure of industrialized societies and the adoption of specific technologies in the workplace.

From the perspective of any of these disciplines, it will appear inappropriate to rely, as I do throughout much of this work, on what are conventionally designated "literary" sources. I draw no categorical distinction between literary and more "theoretical" modes of analysis. To explain why I do not, I must return to my preface. There, I criticized my earlier work on the grounds that it did not adequately explicate the relationship between my pragmatist critique of the Western philosophical tradition, on the one hand, and the qualitative situations of ordinary experience, on the other. The advantage of literary sources, of course, is that they better enable me to examine (rather than ride roughshod over) the prosaic nuances, the subtle ambivalences, the unresolved conflicts, that endow everyday experience with its urgency as well as its bite. Recourse to the dilemmas of concrete characters, "fictional" as well as "nonfictional," does not signify a rejection of more conventional forms of theoretical analysis. Rather, it signifies my recognition that different languages disclose different things. While theoretical language is often better attuned to explicating the relations between this and that, literary language is often better at intimating the qualitative feel, the palpable presence, of things. Since both forms are irreducibly dependent on metaphor, since neither captures the reality of things-in-themselves, since each lets much of what enters experience slip through its discursive fingers, this distinction is more one of tone than of kind. Moving back and forth between the concrete and the abstract, I have tried to be true to the character of thinking, which, as I understand it, is similarly involved in shuttling between experience, as palpably suffered, and the sense-making work that unravels and reweaves its threads.

Notes

1. For an example of this mistake, see Bruce Mazlish, *The Fourth Discontinuity: The Co-evolution of Humans and Machines* (New Haven: Yale University Press, 1993). Explaining that his aim is to explore what he calls the "co-evolution of humans and machines," Mazlish writes: "Occasionally, I shall use the term *Man* capitalized, for linguistic convenience and out of historical tradition; in such cases, I mean by it a generic term, which includes both sexes equally of the human species" (5). With this claim, in addition to ignoring feminist arguments about the linguistic erasure of women, Mazlish asserts precisely what I deny.

2. For an exhaustive account of the historical twists and tales taken by the myth of Prometheus, see Hans Blumenberg, *Work on Myth*, trans. Robert Wallace (Cambridge, Mass: MIT Press, 1985).

3. Plato, "Protagoras," in *The Collected Dialogues of Plato*, ed. Edith Hamilton and Huntington Cairns, (Princeton, N.J.: Princeton University Press, 1961), 320d-e.

4. Hesiod, *Theogony*, trans. Norman O. Brown (New York: Macmillan, 1953), 577-89.

5. Aeschylus, "Prometheus Bound," in *The Lyrical Dramas of Aeschylus*, trans. J. S. Blackie (London: J. M. Dent, 1920): 444-50, 461-64, 469-71.

6. Elaine Scarry, *The Body in Pain* (New York: Oxford, 1985).

7. Sigmund Freud, "Introductory Lectures to Psychoanalysis," in *The Standard Edition of the Complete Works*, vol. 16, trans. James Strachey (London: Hogarth Press, 1953-74), 284-85.

8. Throughout the following pages, I use the term "postmodernism" and its derivatives with considerable reluctance. Arguably, to use this term is itself unpostmodern insofar as it implies an unproblematic periodization of history, its tidy divisibility into the modern and that which comes after. Its use is also unpostmodern insofar as this noun effectively fashions a fictitious unity from what are in fact quite heterogeneous philosophical positions. I employ the term nonetheless in order to gesture at those contemporary arguments whose convergence is principally a function of their common rejection of the foundationalist aspirations of the Western metaphysical tradition. Affirmatively, perhaps it is safe to say that the term "postmodern" refers to a philosophical temperament that prefers the unstable to the fixed, the open-ended to the closed, the ironic to the transparent, the accidental to the essential, the resistant to the hegemonic. But even these claims are hazardous and so, as a rule, I will try to avoid gratuitous generalizations about "postmodernism," speaking instead about specific authors and particular texts.

9. Donna Haraway, "A Manifesto for Cyborgs: Science, Technology, and Socialist Feminism in the 1980s," in *Feminism/Postmodernism*, ed. Linda Nicholson (New York: Routledge, 1990), 191.

10. Adrienne Rich, "Compulsory Heterosexuality and Lesbian Existence," in *Women: Sex and Sexuality*, ed. Catharine R. Stimpson and Ethel Spector Person (Chicago: University of Chicago Press, 1980).

11. Haraway, "Manifesto," 205.

1

ARTIFACTS AS AGENTS

i. *SpiderWeb*

LIKE PENELOPE, THE SPIDER IS SKILLED IN FORMS OF ARTIFICE PRACTICED AFTER DARK. Within her abdomen, each night she generates liquid silk. Squeezed from minute spinnerets, this sticky fluid congeals into so many elastic cords, and from these she fashions a web. Legs coated with oils teased from glands inside her mouth, she alone can dance without care atop this resilient wheel. When an unhappy victim is snared by its catching threads, all struggles to break free produce still more of a tangle. The vibrations provoked by this commotion, scurrying along radial threads from hub to margin, tell the orb's maker what is afoot. Casting freshly made strands to immobilize her prey, she withdraws its life-giving fluids, using a pair of poisonous fangs. As the web's damaged strands are snipped away, the carcass falls.

What is this thing? Is it an implement, or is it a weapon? A home or a trap? Is it inanimate, or is it alive? Manufactured or conceived? If this web's creator were schooled in the Cartesian paradigm of use, and if she were asked to describe her own creation, no doubt she would call it a tool. Pressed to be more specific, she might define it in terms of her subjective intent: "I designed it to catch bugs." Or she might define it in terms of its objective function: "Its purpose is to catch bugs." If required to restate these claims in the language of professional philosophy, she might suggest that her web is a material object whose relationship to its source is one of external causation, whose value-neutral nature is dictated by the intent of its maker, whose end is to trap mobile food particles in the most efficient manner possible, whose interaction with such particles is wholly mechanical, and whose deployment does not in any essential way remake its autonomous author.[1]

But this spider knows better than to be a Cartesian, and so she understands that no single noun will suffice to answer these questions. Besides a trap, her handiwork is an early-warning system against predators, a harp, a dance floor where she will entertain, a bed, a potential parachute (if she is a balloon spider), a source of liquid refreshment before the dew dries, a pharmacy storing the biological fungicides that protect her from disease, and many other things as well. Perhaps more important, she knows that none of these answers will prove adequate so long as it is predicated on a dualistic representation of the relationship between creator and creature. The world inhabited by this arachnid does not consist of a constellation of independent, inanimate, and neutral objects standing apart from her artful practice, and her body is not a self-contained subject clearly demarcated from those things. Through her craft, she fashions an enduring umbilical cord, linking inside to outside, and each sustains the other in time.

That cord performs its connective work in several ways. A spider's web is not created out of nothingness. It is the hardening into durable form of fluids originally internal. Indeed, if she is an orb weaver, the passage between within and without is subject to yet another twist; at the end of each day, she will consume her creation, only to recycle it as a newly fashioned artifact within an hour's time. In addition, a spiderweb is an objectified embodiment of its maker's intangible capacity to spin. Her craft(iness), for example, is embedded in the web's stabilimenti, the diagonal struts running from center to periphery. Because she relocates these thick strands each day, a victim who squirms loose today will find the lessons of experience foiled tomorrow. Still more artful are this web's visual signals, ranging from zigzag designs to floral colors, that dynamically mimic the leads insects employ in identifying possible sources of food. Should a species somehow learn that these cues are in fact so many clues indicating danger, its inability to distinguish what is real from what is not will soon bring its members to the edge of extinction.

The interweaving of internal and external, of body and world, has other dimensions as well. Consider how a web compensates for the incapacities of its maker's unaided appendages, their inability to snare and hold flying prey without assistance. Conceding this, our spider might grant some portion of the Cartesian characterization of her web. But were she to do so, no doubt she would be quick to remind us that this tool is not an optional means to be utilized or discarded at will. Securing the fluids that nourish her body's ongoing labors, this prosthetic device is the condition of her ability to weave, as indispensable to her as is her own heart. Indeed, and still more at odds with the Cartesian reading, her web is vital in the additional sense that it is quasi-alive. If she is a cribellate, as she draws each newly spun cord through the fine comb located on her hind legs, it becomes electrostatically charged. When jarred by an incoming insect, the spider responds by jerking the web's radial threads three or four times, and the oscillating currents transmitted by this organic telegraph pinpoint the exact location of her prospective meal. Like some odd contraption composed of so many elongated surrogate limbs, the web dramatically extends the reach of her otherwise circumscribed sensorium.

A spiderweb is continuous with its creator in these senses, and so it confuses the mutually exclusive distinction a Cartesian draws between tools and their users. However, as a freestanding creation, it also has a life of its own. As time passes, that web acquires a biography, and that history implicates its maker in ways it neither intended nor anticipated. As I feel its unseen strands caress the nape of my neck, I brush away this delicate handiwork. Demonstrating the error of all pretensions to sovereign mastery, I unwittingly thrust this creator back within the pinched confines of her immediate body; and it is from there that she must once more begin to fashion the chain of connections sustaining her place in the world.

Daughters of Arachne do not talk, and so cannot articulate the relationships joining their work to its conditions and consequences. Their existence, although not without sense, is without meaning. Children of Athena and Hephaestus, however, can explore these relations, and so can weave the spider's creation into a web of distinctively human significance. That work can be done well, or it can be done poorly. Should we think our task complete when we silently marvel at a spider's handiwork, our appreciation will remain partial. Should we think our work done when we discover the "right" name for this thing, we will have mistaken what it is. Should we think our labor finished when we specify this tool's instrumental efficacy to its creator, we will miss the ways its tentacles reach back within and so remake that maker. If we are to do justice to the wonder of this artifact, we must explore the relationship of it to the labors of her abdomen, to the killing that vitalizes the organs housed within that cavity, to the branches of an elm tree safeguarding her creature from the bluster of an unexpected storm, and much more. As painstakingly as the spider fashions lace from individual strands of silk must our sense making unravel and then, if only in thought, reweave those same fibers.

ii. *Disappearing Artifacts*

IMAGINE A COMMUNITY WHOSE MEMBERS NEVER ENGAGE IN ANY FORM OF CONDUCT aimed at removing stubborn food particles from between their teeth. Now imagine that, unbidden and absent an instruction manual, a cordless three-speed electric toothbrush, protected by an epidermis of white plastic, drops from the sky and lands at the feet of that community's elders. Within this context, altogether abstracted from the practices constitutive of toothbrushing, bearing no apparent relationship to any organ or felt need of the bodies amongst whom it has fallen, this thing is literally senseless. If the relationship between spider and web epitomizes the perfectly unproblematic integration of body, labor, and artifact, that between this nameless entity and these startled souls is its alienated antithesis.

For me, although I cannot begin to fathom its internal workings, this same artifact is intelligible because it implicates, and is implicated within, a relational web connecting it to the upwardly mobile standards of hygiene dictated by my mother, the habits of my right arm, a pair of receding gums, a current of cold water, a tube of mint toothpaste, a stained porcelain sink, a drain connected to the residential sewer line, and on and so forth. As one link within a more comprehensive chain of sense, this artifact dissolves within the streams of conduct it informs, and so effectively vanishes. Indeed, only should it dare to disrupt that conduct will I become aware of it *as* some-thing, as a thing distinguishable from its various partners. Until that time, my toothbrush remains effectively unknown; only an epistemologist would think otherwise.

Perhaps paradoxically, the ubiquity of what I am calling artisanal artifacts is a second cause of their daily disappearance. Think of the sheer multiplicity, the overwhelming proliferation, of devices we employ each day, from the moment we tumble from our beds to the moment we wearily return. Were I condemned to some lonely isle, were my artisanal artifacts confined to a coconut shell fashioned into an ill-formed cup, dried seaweed woven into a coarse blanket, and a willow branch sharpened at one end, the odds of my grasping these things as things worthy of inquiry would be far greater than is the case now. Precisely because we are so thoroughly immersed in a world of artisanal artifice, its particular fruits are no more apparent to us than is the water that sustains the red-tailed shark and the bottom-sucking loach in my aquarium. When things are never absent, nor are they ever present.

The artifactual texturing of everyday life is additionally occluded because so many of the instrumentalities that most profoundly shape specifically modern experience, at least in industrialized states, are quite literally hidden from view. Compare an early nineteenth-century log cabin in the rolling hills of southwestern Ohio with the house where I now write. In the former, a single visible artifact, the hearth, casts light on the pages of a leather-bound diary, softens the barley for soup, keeps at bay the chill of winter; if its needs are neglected, some-body will be reminded soon enough. In the latter, the sources of the heat warming my naked toes, the electricity illuminating my monochrome computer screen, the water poured into my unwashed coffee mug, are buried within the walls of this house. As with my toothbrush, these artifacts become objects of focal attention only when they break down, necessitating a call to one not so incompetent. In good repair, they stand as the conditions of my thinking rather than its object.

What might be called the "object-ivity" of artisanal artifacts, especially within a market economy, renders them resistant to reflective exploration in another and slightly different sense. In his *Material Culture and Mass Consumption*, Daniel Miller suggests that ordinary artifacts evince "a certain innocence of facticity," what he elsewhere calls an apparent "clarity of realism."[2] Although the familiar artifact presents itself as a self-contained whole bearing within its clear and distinct borders all that is necessary to know it, each purchased commodity contains traces left behind by hundreds of persons I will never meet. Concealed within the bar of soap that washed me this morning resides the sweat of the high school dropout who tends a hydrolyzer in Des Moines, the skill of the driver who each week escorts thousands of identical bars to a warehouse in Denver, the ill-paid labor of the clerk who placed this bar on a Safeway shelf in Walla Walla, and so forth and so on. Yet this artifact, sensually silent, speaks not a word about what is congealed within its confines. Its unblemished smoothness betrays nothing of the institutionalized relations of exploitation, the petty indignities, that went into its production and that now draw strength from my uncritical embrace of it as a finished object whose significance is exclusively a matter of present use.

One might expect those who inhabit the academy, committed to grasping the reality behind appearances, to challenge the artisanal artifact's various modes of disappearance. With certain notable exceptions, however, that would be a misguided anticipation. Again, Daniel Miller: "The deeply integrated place of the artefact in constituting culture and human relations has made discovery of it one of the most difficult of all areas to include in abstract academic discourse."[3] When the academy's disregard of artisanal artifacts is overcome within the fields in which I was primarily trained, political science and philosophy, more often than not the temptations of reification quickly take hold. Indeterminate generalizations concerning the totalitarianism of technological rationality (Herbert Marcuse), the ontological distinctions between labor, work, and action (Hannah Arendt), or the necessary opposition between instrumental and communicative action (Jürgen Habermas) supplant patient investigations into the ways human beings struggle to make sense of concrete things entering into the situated affairs of everyday life.[4]

Within the contemporary university, there is no established discipline expressly devoted to what I am calling artisanal artifacts. A partial exception, perhaps, is the subfield of anthropology known as "material culture studies." Yet even this enterprise, I would argue, is tainted by the Cartesian paradigm of use. To see how, consider its very name. To call a field of inquiry "material culture" studies is to demarcate it, at least tacitly, through reference to the distinction between that which is material and that which is not. It is to say that one's concern is with things that are not immaterial and that, in turn, is to say that one's concern is with things somehow more tangible than that paradigmatic exemplar of the immaterial, the idea. But does the distinction between material and immaterial do justice to the way things appear in experience? Is an epic poem, Homer's *Iliad*, for example, a material or an immaterial artifact? Is it a piece of material culture only when it assumes the form of a bound text? In order for something to qualify as a material artifact, must it be tangible in the literal sense that it can be touched? What if, recited by the bard, it can be heard but neither touched nor seen? Does it qualify as a material artifact then? If you answer no, I will ask why you think we should privilege certain of our embodied senses in determining what counts as a material artifact. Are not words so many vibrations of sound passing through the atmosphere? Is not my eardrum a material thing? If, on the basis of such questioning, you conclude that textual embodiment is not indeed requisite to its standing as a material artifact, I will ask you what you make of the fact that this thing has no determinate spatial location, that its "text" exists only in the memory of the story-teller. If that is where the poem "resides," is it not something immaterial? Or do you wish to argue that the poem is something material when recited, but immaterial when merely remembered? If you make that move, however, I will ask what this distinction is good for, since, apparently, it cannot definitively locate this thing in its own terms. In short, given that the category of "material culture" is parasitic on the distinction between material and immaterial, which is itself parasitic on a deeply problematic disjunction between mind and body, I cannot demarcate my inquiry in its terms.

In casting about for an explanation for the academy's disregard for artisanal artifacts, I cannot help but suspect that this represents yet another manifestation of Western intellectual culture's inveterate prejudice against the activity of making and the sphere of the material. Disparagement of work and its fruits is a recurrent strategy employed in class-divided cultures to discredit those who labor with their hands. To belittle those who are "unduly" preoccupied with the conditions of material existence is to deter members of exploited groups from inquiring too deeply into the relations of power dictating the current distribution of goods as well as the conditions of their production. The political import of this strategy was given its earliest philosophical expression in Plato's relegation of laborers to the lowest class of his republic, and its ethical import was implicit in the invidious distinction Aristotle drew between the merely productive and the genuinely good life. Such contempt was substantially reinforced by early Christianity's insistence on the triviality of this world's profane goods, its abhorrence of bodies and their desires, its construction of labor as the wage of sin. That we are inheritors of this Greco-Christian synthesis is confirmed every time my students speak the term "materialistic" with a sneer. That legacy is additionally confirmed each time a seventeen year old must choose, if indeed a real choice is available, between a liberal arts college and a vocational school. To be truly human, we have learned, is to rise above the grubby goods of the transient world. Beneath our dignity, such means do not merit the fastidious attention we devote to the ideas that are our professional bread and butter.

In sum, in ordinary experience, the question of artisanal artifacts is rarely posed because, unless calling attention to themselves as such, they are inseparable from the forms of conduct into which they are effortlessly integrated.

This phenomenological reality is given all the ideological support it needs by a metaphysical tradition that holds that material things are creatures of necessity, undignified particulars, that all too vigorously draw us back within the mundane world from which we essentially spiritual beings seek escape. When that tradition is given an additional Cartesian twist, when such beings become persuaded that, in order to ensure their spirituality, they must deny any kinship with things nonhuman, it is no wonder that artifacts routinely vanish without a trace.

iii. *The Cartesian Paradigm of Use*

TO SAY THAT ARTISANAL ARTIFACTS COMMONLY DISAPPEAR IS NOT TO SUGGEST THAT they do so because we never speak of them. Indeed, on my account, our vernacular ways of doing so are a vital cause of their resistance to critical inquiry. For the most part, at least in the contemporary West, when we talk of our relationship to artisanal artifacts, we speak of "technology," and our claims typically assume the following grammatical form: "I use X in order to achieve Y." How shall we describe the larger sense-making apparatus within which such speech fits all too neatly?

Embedded within the Cartesian paradigm of use is a set of fundamental premises concerning the nature of human beings and their relationship to the world. Although certain roots of this paradigm stretch back to classical Greek metaphysics, its present constitution is more immediately traceable to the decay of late medieval Catholic teleology, principally in the face of various challenges posed by early modern science. Because I have done so elsewhere, I will not trace that history here.[5] In this context, my aim is to offer an abbreviated account of this paradigm's specifically modern metaphysical postulates. The brevity of my account is justified, I assume, because Descartes has become such a popular whipping boy in recent years.

The Cartesian paradigm of use is mechanistic in its ontology, dualistic in its logic, and solipsistic in its epistemology. Descartes's *Principles of Philosophy* (1644) depicts the universe not as organism but as mechanism. That mechanism is composed of so many discrete corpuscles whose movements can be explained exclusively through reference to the workings of efficient causation. The force producing motion in the universe, although locating its ultimate origin in God's will, is not itself animate, spiritual, or inherent. Rather, what force exists is exclusively a function of the quantity of matter in motion, the speed with which that matter travels, and the reactions generated when one cold clod bangs into another. Nature, not surprisingly, operates on precisely the terms required by the new science of physics.

The human being, squarely situated within this carnival of careening bumper cars, cannot help but be a divided being. To the extent that he is a thing with a body, like all other animals, he is merely an automaton made of flesh.[6] That such a meat-contraption is possible, Descartes insists, "ought not seem strange to those who, cognizant of how many different automata or moving machines the ingenuity of men can devise . . . will consider this body like a machine, that, having been made by the hand of God, is incomparably better ordered and has within itself movements far more admirable than any of those machines that can be invented by men."[7] Working with this analogy, Descartes concludes that explanation of the human body's mechanistic motions requires no principles other than those necessary to account for planetary orbits or, for that matter, any being composed of matter. Muscles and tendons are so many springs; the heart is a fountain; human lungs are akin to the wheel of a mill. The essential difference between a living and a dead body, accordingly, is that between a clock that ticks and one that does not. In the former, the spring is wound; in the latter, it is either relaxed or broken.

However, insofar as man is a being capable of thinking, he must be something besides, in addition to, a mere soulless animal. Having expelled spirit from nature and hence from the human body as well, Descartes can only locate the soulful capacity to reason within the self-consciousness of the immaterial ego. Moreover, because his body (*res extensa*) has already been donated to the science of physics, Descartes must commit his self-consciousness (*res cogitans*) to some other discipline. And when that science, the enterprise of epistemology, turns to its true object, what it discovers is that the spiritual act of knowing is a matter of seeing with the eyes of the mind. Accordingly, the Cartesian "I" cannot help but conceive of itself as a being whose uniquely human relationship to the world is a matter of gazing outward via the lens of a disembodied and essentially private consciousness. Ontologically separated from the body's sensuous engagement in the alluring things of this world, the thinking ego is a monocular spectator, and the world a passing spectacle of objects in motion.[8]

What is the relationship between this cognitive onlooker and the external things it, via so many acts of disembodied seeing, comes to know? Finding incredible all teleological representations of nature, the Cartesian ego is persuaded that the neutered objects populating a Galilean universe can sustain no claim to intrinsic significance. Whatever value they come to bear they acquire only by being drawn within the projects of spiritual beings. The wood upon which I hammer, for example, is a means whose worth is exclusively a function of its instrumental contribution to the home whose conception I freely created in my spectatorial consciousness before I began to build. The world of nature, so construed, is defined exclusively as a heteronomous object of potential control. The independence of my essential self from the mechanically interacting corpuscles of that nature is manifest in the wholesale subordination of its inertial things to the dictates of my autonomous will.

In terms of this metaphysic, tools are the causal instruments through which man imposes his will on nature's inherently meaningless entities. Although made by human beings, tools bear no more intrinsic significance than do the things on which they work. Like the latter, these implements are so many amoral devices, mere means, whose value is exclusively a function of their efficacy in contributing to the accomplishment of ends posited prior to the initiation of making. That making, however, must not involve a remaking of these makers. Nature's resources, humanity's tools, and the things they fashion must remain so many lifeless servants who do their masters' bidding without talking back. Were they to do otherwise, were they to draw their animate partners into a conversation under the exclusive control of neither, then no longer could these smiling minigods remain confident that their soulful capacity to think unequivocally distinguishes them from watches, alligators, stars, and all other forms of stupid matter in motion.

Such, in brief, are the metaphysical underpinnings of the Cartesian paradigm of use. In my introduction, I noted that this paradigm is given familiar expression in the National Rifle Association's slogan concerning firearms. But it is not confined to such vernacular discourse. Listen to the professional philosopher, Joseph Pitt, in the closing paragraph of his essay titled "The Autonomy of Technology": "It is not the machine that is frightening, it is what other individuals do with the machine; or, given the machine, what we fail to do by way of assessment and planning. . . . There is no problem about the autonomy of technology. The problem is with individuals. The tools by themselves do nothing. That is the only significant sense of autonomy you can find for technology."[9] Alternatively, consider the standard textbook definition of technology as the sum total of tools and methods, devised by human beings, to control the environment for human benefit. Within this definition, one hears echoes of the Cartesian assumption that technology's relationship to the world is essentially instrumental; that human beings are technology's creators rather than its creatures; that technology is a morally neutral force; that the problem of technological misapplication can be checked by summoning the power of universal good will; and so forth and so on.

The Cartesian paradigm of use is also given expression in various forms of bureaucratic/economistic discourse, most notably in cost-benefit analyses and environmental impact statements. The American Office of Technology Assessment defines its task as "a comprehensive form of policy research that examines the technical, economic, and social consequences of technological applications. It is especially concerned with unintended, indirect, or delayed social impacts."[10] Note how the term "impacts," calling up images akin to that of a hammer striking a nail, suggests that the relationship between human beings and their technical conduct is mechanical and unidirectional rather than organic and dialectical. As so many discrete agents, we deploy various amoral instrumentalities to achieve our antecedently specified ends. That deployment, understood as cause, produces so many external effects. By calculating the scope of those externalities, we can determine whether the benefits occasioned by that use are outweighed by its costs. If so, we can then take steps to mitigate that impact, perhaps by swinging our hammer a bit more gently. Part and parcel of the discourses of management science, analytic tools such as these reassure us that, at least in principle, we remain masters of our fate.

Indeed, I would argue that traces of the Cartesian paradigm can be found in the English term "technology" itself.[11] First coined in the seventeenth century in reference to a treatise on the practical arts, within two centuries this term had been transferred to the arts themselves. By the nineteenth century, accordingly, it had become possible to ask: What is technology? Till then, while one might ask about this or that art, or even about the practical arts collectively, one could not think of all as so many manifestations of a single determinate essence: technology. Riding roughshod over the distinctions we might want to draw between manual tools (a loom and a screwdriver), ways of harnessing natural energies (a windmill and a nuclear reactor), means of altering human beings (the practice of tattooing and biogenetic engineering), ways of efficiently organizing action (a bureaucracy and orgasm-maximizing techniques), this ahistorical reification compromises our ability to explore the relationships between these diverse modes of making as well as between the matters of which they are made. More important, reduction of such modes to a singular noun encourages the representation of human beings as this entity's grammatical correlate, as a collective subject whose destiny is to secure autonomous mastery over the reified object we call nature. The very term "technology," in other words, reinforces the illusion that "it," like some enormous hammer, is subject to the rational control of an equally hyperextended agent. Although he would be horrified to hear it, the fact remains that Heidegger can ask "the question concerning technology" only because Descartes made it possible for him to do so.

iv. *Technophiles/Technophobes*

IN POPULAR AS WELL AS ACADEMIC DISCOURSE, THE CARTESIAN PARADIGM OF USE HAS NOT gone uncontested. Perhaps the most familiar challenge is represented by a position that, in order to indicate its opposition to the instrumentalism of the Cartesian paradigm, might be labeled "technological determinism." Such determinism is not new. "Things are in the saddle, and ride mankind."[12] So wrote Ralph Waldo Emerson in the mid-nineteenth century. Much the same sentiment was conveyed when the hapless Charlie Chaplin, in the silent film *Modern Times*, found himself literally caught within the cogs of an industrial machine grinding on without end.

Perhaps the most celebrated contemporary exponent of the sentiment shared by Emerson and Chaplin is Jacques Ellul. In *The Technological Society*, first published in the United States in 1964, Ellul held that the dynamic of technological innovation now sweeps all before its irreversible imperatives. The logic of technological advance, Ellul insisted, requires that all other spheres of collective life, from family to economy to state, come to reflect its utilitarian necessities. Human beings must therefore become as regularized as the machines they now bow before; "there can be no human autonomy in the face of technical autonomy."[13]

Finding the Cartesian account of consciousness incredible, Ellul rejected technological instrumentalism's contention that meaning can only find its origin in the freely willed choices of sovereign individuals. Indeed, on his account, the pitiless march of *la technique* now renders the whole notion of meaning senseless. In a world where neither ends nor means can be fundamentally altered, where human beings can no longer fathom the techniques upon which their lives vitally depend, where the advance of science relentlessly demystifies everything except science itself, where competing ideologies dissolve into so much mush when confronted by the mundane requisites of systematic coordination and large-scale organization, the quest to tease sense from experience is quixotic if not absurd. "In short," Ellul despairs, "we live in a milieu that is totally dead."[14]

In the debate between Cartesian instrumentalists and Ellulian determinists, we hear what appear to be diametrically opposed ways of making sense of things made. Technophiles of Gingrichian bent depict humanity as a body of enlightened subjects whose collective mission is to usher in a utopia of unconstrained control. With the generation of instant virtual communities, made possible by the presence of a microcomputer in every home, the parochialism of the human body's five senses will be finally overcome. With the elimination of centralized control over the mass media, an infinite pluralization of discourses will emerge, bringing an end to the standarized pabulum that passes for culture today. With daily electronic plebiscites conducted via endless interactive cable television programs, democratic citizens will unproblematically direct their will-less servants. And so forth and so on.

Technophobes, by way of contrast, represent our artifactual constructions as a collective subject whose final telos is the envelopment of a mindless humanity within some unhappy synthesis of Max Weber's iron cage, Jeremy Bentham's Panopticon, and Michel Foucault's carceral. Within this dystopia, the lingering remnants of democratic sensibilities are finally crushed. Insinuation of subtle modes of surveillance within the loci of everyday experience, made possible by the presence of a microcomputer in every home, renders superfluous the cruder displays of political power that once ensured popular subjection to order's imperatives. Extension of robotics and other techniques of automation within the capitalist workplace relentlessly segregates employees who possess the cognitive skills necessary to program such machines from those who are their idiot operators. Proliferation of new channels of electronic communication generates not unparalleled educational riches, but ever more trivial pursuits. And so forth and so on.

Is it possible, however, that instrumentalists and determinists are not in fact opposed to one another? Is it possible that, like my parents for too many years, these apparent antagonists are bound together in a state of cheerless wedlock? As I employ it, the term "Cartesianism" designates not merely certain substantive beliefs about the relationship between nature, the conduct of making, and being human, but also certain received *forms* of argumentation. If, as Cartesianism teaches, human beings are fundamentally separate from the world on which they act, then we should not be surprised when debate vacillates effortlessly between, on the one hand, the contention that we are in control of the things we make and, on the other, the contention that those things are our masters. A dualist metaphysic spawns a dualist logic. Does subject rule object, or object subject? Do we control technology, or it us? This is precisely the way we should expect a Cartesian culture to frame the questions it seeks to answer about artisanal artifacts. In both accounts, the metaphysic of use predominates. The first, that of the instrumentalist, fixes the power of agency and the origin of meaning in the creator; doing so, it blinds us to the ways in which artifactual creatures are our creators. The second, that of the determinist, fixes that power and hence the ability to deprive the world of meaning in the creature; doing so, it spawns the sort of resigned fatalism that, in Ellul's case, emerges as Catholic providentialism. Both contentions, however unwittingly, confirm the forms of institutionalized order that rely for their intelligibility and legitimacy on the neutered grammar of use.

The error common to instrumentalist and determinist alike is that which, arguably, defines the Western metaphysical tradition as such: both tease certain conceptual distinctions from the web of everyday experience, reify those categories, and then mistake them for the ontological truth about the relations from which they have been abstracted. Certain of the reality of the detached, self-identical, and autonomous subject, Cartesian instrumentalists "discover" that subject's correlate in the discrete, neatly bounded, and heteronomous object. Because that subject has been antecedently defined as the unadulterated source of all self-movement, of all free agency, the object must be radically passive, an inert thing whose movement is exclusively an external affair of mechanical causation. Cartesian determinists, also taking for granted the ontological adequacy of the distinction between active subject and passive object, do no more than stand this analysis on its head.

Mirroring one another, neither the instrumentalist nor the determinist steps outside the closed circle of a discourse they speak in common. From the mutually transformational arc connecting maker and made, one isolates and then reifies the human capacity to project the powers of Prometheus into the world, while the other isolates and then reifies the capacity of artifacts to bully human agents. Equally one-sided, equally partial, neither does justice to the

sense in which our relationship to things made is one of reciprocal interimplication. Neither, consequently, can furnish much guidance in exploring the ways experience is qualitatively transformed by the artifice weaving in
and out of it, and neither can provide much help in grasping the ways human
beings struggle to fashion sense of that experience.

v. The Hammer and the Reactor (with Apologies to Langdon Winner)

A METAPHOR IS AN ARTIFACT OF LANGUAGE. JUST AS A TOOL EXTENDS THE RANGE OF ACTING,
so does a metaphor push thinking past its accustomed reach. The initial purpose of the spiderweb, as metaphor, is to undercut the plausibility of any claim
taking the form: "I use X in order to achieve Y," where "I" is the Cartesian ego,
"X" is some ethically neutral tool or object essentially separate from "I," and "Y"
is the end "I" consciously entertains prior to initiation of its instrumental action. If that metaphor has accomplished its critical task, it should now be possible to begin to make good on its constructive promise, its capacity to hint at new
ways of thinking about the relations between agents and artifacts.

When students affirm technology's neutrality, and when I ask them to defend that claim, with some regularity I am directed to ordinary tools. In that
spirit, let us consider the familiar claw hammer. If we are to read this artisanal
artifact in a way that sustains its claim to neutrality, we must draw a neat distinction between means and ends. I aim to repair the lower right-hand corner
of a wooden window frame whose pieces, troubled by too many subzero nights,
have finally come unglued. Using my hammer as means, I drive a six-penny
nail into those segments so as to secure them once again. The hammer, so
conceived, is the disinterested instrumentality I employ in order to accomplish an end that I antecedently entertained.

Note how the language of "use" orients attention toward my self and my
intention. But what if the hammer and its conduct were to serve as our focal
point, the pivot on which our sense-making efforts turned? Glancing upward
from that point, might we think of my right arm not as an obedient agent of
my disembodied purpose, but as an animate shaft that amplifies the hammer's power by extending its length? Might it be that my fingers, considered
collectively, are a sort of prehensile tool, a primitive grasping implement, that
now shake hands with a partner who, although silent, is not for that reason
stupid? Has not this hammer, like all good instructors in the practical arts,
taught me certain embodied skills, skills that would be quite different were it
to assume some other shape or heft? Glancing downward, might we think of
this nail as an emissary whose mission is to communicate the hammer's design to the wood of the frame? Might the hammer's blows be so many questions put to materials that partly respond to and partly resist these inquiries?

Is it possible that this exchange, overheard by the being at the hammer's opposite end, dictates the character of *its* replies? In sum, might we think of the
hammer not as an unproblematic tool, but rather as an active participant
within a complex relational transaction that transforms all of its members in
time?

Think of my hammer as a sort of bidirectional conveyor belt. Down one
ramp slides what, for now, we will uncritically call my "purpose." That purpose achieves palpable reality only via its realization as so much labor power,
and that power travels from my arm's tendons through the hammer and into
the nail whose task is to refasten the frame's seam. This journey is an easy one
because the hammer's head so aptly expresses the shape my hand would have
to assume were I without a tool. Its striking surface, called a face by carpenters
worthy of the name, is a fist drawn into a tight knot. Its claw, curving gently
upward and tapering to a thin edge, consists of two fingers spread slightly
apart, poised to undo whatever offenses its face may commit. Joined to a
wooden shaft whose rigidity hyperbolically amplifies the tension in my forearm's musculature, that face endures the pain I would have to suffer in its absence. Just as a spiderweb is a congealed externalization of matters originally
internal, so too is the hammer an objectified articulation of my otherwise invisible capacity to make a dent in the world. That capacity overcomes its
standing as so much potentiality via the metaphor that is my hammer, and
that metaphor's intelligibility is inseparable from its animate counterpart.

As work proceeds, up the other side of this conveyor belt travels so much
vital news. The complex artifact that is this arm-and-hammer responds without reflection, striking tentatively, as it senses the presence of a metal fastener
hidden within the frame. It does so because my grip is a repository of the effects engendered by so much bygone pounding; this hammer has made my
hand the intelligent creature it is today. How its face responds to the distinct
textures of oak or pine, or to a finishing nail as it begins to turn on itself, secures animate articulation in the connective tissues and musculature of my
hand. Yet to talk of connective tissues and musculature is not quite right, for I
never experience these things as such. Perhaps a coroner, in the midst of an
autopsy, does so. But in the midst of hammering, I never will. For me, tissue
and musculature *are* what they *do*, and I only know them as so many engaged
capacities. Accordingly, what is "internal" in the sense that it is hidden beneath the surface of my skin only makes its reality apparent via its vital intercourse with matters external. In this way, my arm is a metaphor whose
intelligibility is inseparable from its inanimate counterpart.

If we were to take the metaphor of the twin-ramped conveyor belt literally,
then we would have to assume that over time matter of diverse sorts passes
between the parties involved in the conduct of hammering and hence that, via
this (misce)genetic exchange, each eventually becomes kin to the other.

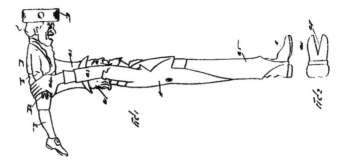

Fig. 1: An anthropomorphic hammer. U.S. Design Patent No. 28,942.
Henry Petroski, *The Evolution of Useful Things*
(New York: Alfred A. Knopf. 1993), 127.

Does U.S Design Patent No. 28,942 offer a critique of alienated labor, of an exploitative economic order in which the species-being of workers is devoured by, swallowed up within, tools they will never own? No doubt. But it is also a graphic representation of a mutually transformational process that, although largely invisible, is not for that reason unreal. What it expresses is what we might call, infelicitously but accurately, the interincorporation of human and tool. But we nonetheless feel pressed to ask: Is this *really* two human beings? Or is it *really* a hammer? A refusal to answer that question is essential to my larger argument; its ultimate undecidability is precisely my point.

Recall that our two-way conveyor belt runs not merely from hammerer to tool, but to window and back again as well. That window's skeleton, once fixed, is what it is only because my labor is now contained within this free-standing thing. When refastened to the north face of my home, like the crafty work of our spider, that window is an enduring testament to my skill. Without it, I cannot keep winter's bite at bay. With it, I am a being who can watch the snow settle without feeling its sting on unprotected skin. As with a hammer, this artifact's service on behalf of my body is inseparable from its metaphorical recapitulation of that same body. Just as hammer mimics arm, so does window ape eye. The gelatinous nucleus of my eye is sheltered by the sockets of my skull, just as the window's glass is protected by its durable casement. Multiple projections of my capacity to see, like the eye of a fly, each pane is a cornea. The drapes regulating the flow of liquid sunshine are so many pupils, while bottles of Windex are lacrimal glands, dispensers of tears rinsing away the dust that accumulates from time to time.

To speak of hammers, windows, and eyes in this fashion is to question our conventional talk of "use," as well as the tidy divisions drawn by Cartesians between user, tool, and artisanal artifact. Is such talk metaphorical? Of course. Is it *merely* metaphorical? Much of the burden of this book is to show why it is not or, better, why the metaphorical relationship between body and artifact expresses the *reality* of that relationship. At this point, though, suffice it to say that, were such talk altogether senseless, we would not laugh at an old Warner Brothers cartoon in which the facade of a home melts into the form of a face, with windows as eyes, door as mouth, television antennae as ears, shingles as hair, and so forth. Such flights of fancy are funny because on some level we grasp the questionability of the rigid partitions we customarily erect between animate and inanimate, human and nonhuman, artisan and artifact.

The incapacities of the Cartesian paradigm of use become still more apparent when we turn from a comparatively simple artisanal artifact to one more arcane. Is a nuclear reactor, for example, well understood as a complex but nonetheless neutral tool? To answer that question, let us begin by asking another: Who stands to the reactor in a relationship comparable to that of a person wielding a hammer? The individual who "uses" the electricity it generates elsewhere does not do so. Purchasing the reactor's product as a commodity, she is a consumer; and consumption, eating its ready-made goods, is quite unlike the activity of one who fabricates something new or repairs some prefabricated but now broken thing. The consequences of my hammer's work are palpably present to my embodied senses; when I rest this repaired frame on an exterior sill, no longer do I feel it wobble precariously beneath the weight of double-pane glass. But the electricity generated by a nuclear plant is an invisible abstraction whose mode of production I understand only via the effects it causes within a 100-watt bulb's vibrating filament. The conceptual as well as physical distance between reactor, its fruits, and the bodies they sustain is infinitely greater than that between a hammer, its work, and my forearm. Only at the risk of being deemed a bit odd will I confess to feeling as fond of the reactors at the Hanford Nuclear Reservation as I do of the hammer in my basement.

If the relationship between reactor and those outside its concrete shell is not analogous to that between hammer and hammerer, then what about those inside this hull? Never, I trust, will I conclude that employment of my hammer requires that I bore a hole and then climb within its wooden handle. But precisely because the reactor does require such conduct, it exacts far more from its workers than the hammer does from me. Should I forget my tool, leaving it to weather the winter unprotected, it will still do its work tolerably well when I stumble across it next spring. The reactor, however, is far less forgiving, and it is so in a way that is inherently paradoxical. As button pushers and monitor observers, reactor operators do work that is no less abstract than is that of a consumer who gains access to its power via the flip of a switch. Yet the risks associated with the inattentiveness bred by such abstraction are far more profound than those incurred when hammer strikes thumb. Should Chernobyl's operators prove as careless as I often am, they will come to know the meaning of negligence at the cost of their lives.

Futhermore, whereas my hammer and I can always part company without doing irreparable harm to either, nuclear plant operators are as dependent on it as it is on them. To illuminate this symbiotic relationship, perhaps we should think of the reactor not as a stupendous tool, but as something akin to a distended uterus. Just as a pregnant woman's blood purifies the sources of nutrition delivered to the unborn thing growing within her, so does the reactor's air filtration system deliver respirable air to those interred within it. Perhaps, therefore, the reactor's chief engineer is not its primary "user," but a very clever fetus invested with the power to move in and out of this manufactured womb at will. Perhaps he is the ghost-in-the-machine, the homunculus, the brain in the bucket, whose existence must be postulated in order to account for the life-giving power of what would otherwise be so much inert concrete and steel. Or perhaps, reversing perspective, that womb is the condition of his existence, for he was able to return to work after suffering a stroke at the age of fifty-six only because a surgeon, whose life-sustaining equipment drew power from this same reactor, inserted into his chest a device whose rhythmic operation now simulates the beating of his once hale heart.

While reactor and hammer are disanalogous in these ways, it would be wrong to deny them all kinship. As with a hammer, the reactor is one thread within a more comprehensive web, a network extending from uranium mines in South Africa, to Malaysian factories where computerized control boards are glued together by women and children paid by the piece, to American factories where workers paid by the hour make lightbulbs, lamps, sockets, wire nuts, Romex cable, wire strippers, and electrical meters, to multinational corporations that transform all these things into marketable commodities, to local power stations whose transformers regularize the flow of electricity, to the rheostat that dims an overbright bulb in a child's bedroom, and so forth and so on. As with a hammer, the reactor is not an isolated tool, but an internally complex node within a maze of transactions relating a multiplicity of artifacts, artisanal as well as human, in determinate ways. Those ways include the capitalist economic arrangements dictating ownership of the plant as well as sale of its power; the state whose regulatory agencies are charged with ensuring its safe operation; the nuclear household where the spread of electrically powered devices has rendered its primary occupants progressively more dependent upon service technicians who, for the most part, are men; and so forth and so on.

Moreover, just as a hammer's work includes its shaping of my hand, so too does the reactor act back upon those implicated in its conduct, and it does so in ways they only partially appreciate. Imagine that the light suffusing this child's bedroom comes not from a vacuum-sealed glass orb but from the dying embers of a red brick fireplace. If there is to be a constant supply of fuel, wood must be chopped, gathered, and carried upstairs. As that child grows older, especially during the coldest months, this will be one of her least-liked chores. It will be a source of constant friction between mother and daughter, as one commands and the other seeks ever more devious ways to foist this responsibility onto her younger sister. This source of conflict evaporates, however, when a slight alteration in the position of a plastic switch suffices to bathe the bedroom in homogeneous light. No doubt, new sources of tension, new battles over the distribution of work within the household, will emerge in time. But providing the means of illumination, because of its thoughtless automaticity, will not be one of them.

The Cartesian paradigm of use ascribes all motive power to the ego, and none to the tool. But all artisanal artifacts, no matter how simple or complex, bear their own internal imperatives. Surely, the sorcerer's apprentice grasped this better than did Descartes. He quickly learned that tools are misunderstood when considered mere compliant servants of the autonomous human will. If only in the minimal sense that each can be deployed for some purposes but not for all, the tool is a recalcitrant thing. Should the apprentice try to use his broom to drive a nail, most likely he will fail. Should he attempt to sweep the floor with his master's hammer, he will make slow progress at best. Hence, by virtue of morphological structure alone, tools stipulate (although they do not specify in detail) the conduct of work, and so "users" cannot help but bend their wills to the peculiar dictates of each.

Artisanal artifacts, again whether as complex as a reactor or as simple as a hammer, remake human relationships as quickly as they produce transformations in nonhuman materials. Prior to fashioning a broom from a sturdy stick, dried twigs, and twine, the sorcerer's apprentice scrubbed the floor each night on hands and knees, using a rag torn from a discarded cotton undershirt. Now, more effectively armed, he does his work upright, stooping only now and then to pick up the debris gathered into an untidy mound. Although still a subordinate, the relationship of neophyte to master has changed in consequence, and that change finds silent but significant expression in the apprentice's slightly more confident gait. Although he cannot say just how, the sorcerer senses that his authority is no longer quite as unequivocal as it was when his subordinate's prostrate body confirmed their inequality at the close of each day.

Entry into the world of any newly invented artisanal artifact signifies more than the mere addition of yet another docile thing to those already in place. Such beings are more like strangers than objects, aliens whose import for present circumstances can never be predicted with complete assurance. Think, for example, of the invention of the stethoscope in 1816. According to what may be an apocryphal tale, because René Laënnec was worried about the moral propriety of resting his head on a woman's chest, he fashioned a listening device from a hollow wooden tube, thereby enabling him to listen to her heart while keeping her breasts at a suitable distance. Widespread adoption of this appliance transformed the practice of medicine in ways anticipated by no one. Whereas traditional methods relied heavily on questioning patients and observing their external symptoms, the stethoscope's more direct access to the body's interior rendered such talk largely superfluous. The stethoscope's diaphragm effectively withdrew authority from the now suspect patient and, via its rubber tubing, funneled the power of knowing into the ears of a professionally detached listener.

Finally, just as artisanal artifacts alter the transactions between human beings, so too do they transform those sustained between their nonhuman relations. Hannah Arendt claims that "(w)ithout being talked about by men and without housing them, the world would not be a human artifice but a heap of unrelated things."[15] Surely this is an anthropomorphic exaggeration. The work of each artisanal artifact presupposes an intricate infrastructure of auxiliary artifacts. My hammer is related to the nail it strikes, to the chain saw that cut down the oak whose timber was fashioned into its tapered handle, to the furnaces in the foundry where its steel head was molded. Should I, along with all other hammerers, switch to compressed-air nail drivers, the chain saw will fall silent, the foundry will require new forging machines, and thousands of extension cords will be fashioned in order to negotiate the network linking these new tools to the electric utilities bringing them to life. As the hammer becomes an endangered species, the patterns of experience in which its work was formerly embedded also fade away. Human hands are remade to accommodate the imperatives of a device whose work is accomplished at the push of a button; service persons skilled in electronic circuitry come to recognize the disorders to which these devices typically fall prey; apprentice carpenters learn new ways of sensing when a nail has gone awry. Granted, we may not be able to trace all of the transmutations occasioned by a new artifact's insertion within the worldwide web. But that incapacity should not be translated into the idealist fantasy that holds that things are unrelated no-things absent our chatter about them. To think otherwise, to think that any given tool can stand alone, is to read into its existence the untenable pretensions of the Cartesian monad.

vi. *The Dialectic of Projection and Reciprocation*

ARTISANAL ARTIFACTS ARE NOT WELL UNDERSTOOD AS THE INSTRUMENTAL MEANS BY which human beings bridge the otherwise empty space between the unsubstantial intentionality of Descartes's mind and the mechanically intersecting inertial objects of Galileo's nature. Like our bodily openings, each such artifact is a conduit enabling us to reach into nature, and its events to worm their way into experience; there is, therefore, nothing unnatural about technology. As one constituent of the more comprehensive arc encompassing the discursive abstractions designated "subject" and "object," the artisanal artifact's significance is neither self-contained nor a mere projection of a self clearly and distinctly separated from that instrument. Calling into being a field of sensible involvements, exploring the relations making the web of experience what it qualitatively is, the artifact mocks the mutually exclusive oppositions erected by the Cartesian paradigm of use.

To furnish a more formal articulation of what was implicit in the previous section, I will now offer a modified exposition of what Elaine Scarry calls the dialectic of projection and reciprocation. In *The Body in Pain*, Scarry writes: "If we cling to objects, we should trust our own clinging impulse; and once we trust that impulse we will acknowledge that such objects are precious; and once we confess that they are precious we will begin to articulate *why* they are precious; and once we articulate why they are precious, it will be self-evident why our desire for them must be regulated and why their benefits must be equitably distributed throughout the world."[16] But why exactly *do* we cling so to objects?

To answer this question, it is helpful to begin by recalling just how fundamental is the link between the condition of being human and our engagement with what Scarry calls "objects." Consider the moment when we finally surrender our grasp on all such things. For now at least, mortality is one of the defining features of the human condition, and the process of aging is a chronic reminder of that inevitability. When aging takes shape as a protracted slide into decrepitude, the world opened up by artisanal artifacts shrivels long before the body dies. As cancer took its toll on my grandmother, only occasionally did my father take her for their once customary Sunday drives through the cheerless suburbs of central New Jersey. In time, these ventures proved too taxing, and so Phoebe retreated within Norman's home, rarely leaving that awful pale green bedroom hidden at the far end of a darkened hallway. Still later, and only for the sake of holiday appearances, she permitted Marjorie, my mother, to lift her body out of bed and into the liver-colored recliner we grandchildren occupied during our mandatory weekly visits. When even that became too much to bear, a rented hospital bed became Phoebe's world, as she was consumed by the imperatives of eating, sleeping, and excreting. Of the many artifacts sustaining her world, this was the last she let go.

To die is to relinquish the artifacts that otherwise incorporate us within a world extending far beyond our arms' reach. To be wracked by acute pain is to find that world closing in on all sides. When unstoppable cries leave ears deaf to anything other than their own sound, when arms can do no more than clutch each other, what was once a human being becomes something not unlike the solipsistic monad Descartes posits as the norm. In the days just before she died, as ever larger doses of morphine accomplished less and less, Phoebe became akin to Prometheus bound. Had we done as I suspect she wished, had we removed the artifacts that kept her body alive for our sake, perhaps she might have withdrawn from the world as a human being. Instead, imprisoned within a diseased cell from which no escape was possible, she was taken from it as a thing.

In *The Drowned and the Saved*, Primo Levy explains that deprivation of ordinary artifacts was essential to the dehumanization of those soon to be inducted into the camps of the Holocaust. His spoon taken from him while en route to Auschwitz, Levy was required to lap up his daily soup "as dogs do."

Stripped of every stitch while standing before the gates of hell, Levy soon realized that clothes do indeed make the man:

> (A) naked and barefoot man feels that all his nerves and tendons are severed: he is helpless prey. Clothes, even the foul clothes distributed, even the crude clogs with their wooden soles, are a tenuous but indispensable defense. Any one who does not have them no longer perceives himself as a human being but rather as a worm: naked, slow, ignoble, prone on the ground. He knows that he can be crushed at any moment.[17]

No matter how threadbare the clothes, Levy reminds us, to be clad is to be protected. But exactly what is thereby protected? Is it one's skin? Or is it one's dignity? For Levy, it seems clear, to ask this question is to fail to understand the interconstitutive relationship between artisanal artifacts and the making of human beings. Only Descartes and his ilk would be foolish enough to think that one can neatly discriminate between satisfaction of the human body's "brute" imperatives and the human being's need to safeguard the conditions of its dignity.

When Adam and Eve find themselves standing naked and ashamed before their pitiless persecutor, they respond by fashioning the world's first artisanal artifacts out of so many fig leaves. In one sense, that deed is a confession of their insignificance. But it is also an act of Promethean defiance, an assertion of their shared capacity to fashion a distinctively human world and so escape wholesale dependence on their maker. Such impertinence, however, cannot be separated from the necessity to labor, and unrelenting labor makes the world a thing of woe: "Cursed is the ground because of you; in toil you shall eat of it all the days of your life; thorns and thistles it shall bring forth to you; and you shall eat the plants of the field" (Gen. 3:17-18). If these protohumans are to manufacture some capacity for self-determination, it would appear that they can do so only by donning another and perhaps still more disagreeable yoke.

And yet matters are not quite so straightforward. Adam can escape this veil of tears if, like Levy's tormentor, he can make Eve his permanent servant. His body can become something other than a mere creature of necessity if she can be compelled to become the surrogate vehicle, the animate tool, through which that necessity is overcome. Relegated to the imperatives of baby making and household maintenance, banished from the garden of distinctively masculine delights, Eve will become a specialist in the prosaic artisanal artifacts that sustain an especially intimate relationship to human bodies and their vulnerabilities—spoons, shoes, blankets, diapers, bedsheets. Yet she is unlikely to recognize just how vital these things are to a distinctively human life because they will be dismissed as trivial, banalities with which no self-respecting intellectual tradition should bother. For much the same reason, nor is she likely to recognize the indispensability of the labors she performs in (re)producing the beings made fully human via their engagement with artisanal artifacts.[18]

With these reminders as context, let me turn to the first moment within the projection/reciprocation dialectic. In its most general sense, "projection" refers to the conduct of fashioning artisanal helpmates for human bodies.[19] That conduct can assume various forms, each of which stands in a different relationship to the bodies involved in it. First, and most obviously, an artifact can stand as a projection of, and so be interpreted in relation to, a specific body part. Think back to the claw of my hammer and its metaphorical recapitulation of the arch of my curved fingers. Or think of a bulletproof vest in relation to your all too easily penetrated skin. Or think of a desktop in relation to my impermanent lap. Or think of the edge of a serrated knife in relation to your teeth. Such a list can be extended indefinitely. To do so, simply identify any given body part—eye, lung, ear, finger, tooth, knee, spine, muscle, kidney—and then look about the world for artisanal artifacts that do that part's work by mimicking its structure and so serving as its prosthetic equivalent. To appreciate how essential such artifacts are to the possibility of living a human life, ask what activities you would have to forgo and what labors you would have to perform if all were suddenly to vanish.

Should you perform this thought experiment, most likely you will consider discrete artifacts rather than the more comprehensive contexts within which they are typically found. But those contexts can be understood in terms of this first form of projection as well. To see the point, consider Scarry's account of the ordinary room:

> In normal contexts, the room, the simplest form of shelter, expresses the most benign potential of human life. It is, on the one hand, an enlargement of the body: it keeps warm and safe the individual it houses in the same way the body encloses and protects the individual within; like the body, its walls put boundaries around the self preventing undifferentiated contact with the world, yet in its windows and doors, crude versions of the senses, it enables the self to move out into the world and allows that world to enter. But while the room is a magnification of the body, it is simultaneously a miniaturization of the world, of civilization. Although its walls, for example, mimic the body's attempt to secure for the individual a stable internal space—stabilizing the temperature so that the body spends less time in this act; stabilizing the nearness of others so that the body can suspend its rigid and watchful postures; acting in these and other ways like the body so that the body can act less like a wall—the walls are also, throughout all this, independent objects, objects which stand apart from and free of the body, objects which realize the human being's impulse to project himself out into a space beyond the boundaries of the body in acts of making, either physical or verbal, that once multiplied, collected, and shared are called civilization.[20]

Because it is too resonant of Cartesianism, I take exception to Scarry's representation of the body as something akin to a fortress whose task is to safeguard the individual within. In addition to its implicit equation of the mind or consciousness with the true self, this representation of the body's "walls" makes too much of the separation of internal from external and too little of the permeability of that border. Her insight, however, is readily abstracted from these errors of misplaced emphasis. Because my office has a ceiling, I need not use my right hand to shelter my scalp from the driving rain. Because it is cooled by a central air conditioner, I need not expend caloric energy by turning my left hand into a fan. Because it has a desk whose drawers can be locked, I need not clutch my grade book at all times. Because it has a computer whose memory is far better than mine, I need not emulate Homer in recalling all I wish to say. Because it has a telephone, I need not position my mouth within earshot of my older child each time I tell him not to abuse his younger sibling. In all these ways, we might say, this room and its artifactual occupants are the agents of my decorporealization. Working effortlessly, they allow me to leave my body behind or, better, to situate my body within a world where its persistent demands need not be of immediate concern. The conditions of my freedom, my deliverance from the realm of necessity, are stitched into the seams of the materialized spaces I inhabit.

Second, some artifacts stand as projections of bodily capacities and/or needs without reference to specifiable bodily parts. Think of the wheels on unicycles, Toyota Celicas, and the chair now supporting my weight as so many projections of the human capacity to locomote, to move from here to there. (Note, incidentally, that something like a snowshoe can be understood as an artifactual projection of a specific body part—in this case, the sole of the human foot—as well as a projection of the human capacity to walk; either will do.) Or think of an abacus as a projection of the otherwise intangible capacity of human beings to count. Or think of our need to remember. Consider alarm clocks, note pads, strings tied around fingers, floppy disks, and calendars, all of which visibly respond to our forgetfulness, all of which incorporate the burden of remembering into the structure of artifacts whose reliability compensates for the ephemerality of recall. Lifting this need out of our bodies, reconfiguring it as so many gears, springs, printed numbers, plastic panels, wire spirals, 3 x 5 cards, these things do work that we, in their absence, would find all-consuming. They prove willing to suffer in our stead precisely because their bodies are not made of flesh and blood, precisely because they rearticulate our needs in the media of plastic, metal, paper, glass, cardboard, cloth, wood. Much quieter than those assigned to the patriarch's dreamworld, these artifacts perform their assigned chores without complaint.

Third, although Scarry does not do so, her logic of artifacts can be taken one step further by noting that the embodied capacity to engage in projection can itself be projected into an artisanal artifact. It is one thing to locate a specific body part's correlate within the structure of an artifact (think of a cornea and the lens of a telescope). It is another thing to discover a general capacity of the human body incorporated within an artifact (think of the capacity to smell and the work of a smoke detector). It is a still different matter, however, to find the abstract ability to do work, without reference to a determinate body part or embodied capacity, embedded within the structure of an artisanal artifact.

In the first volume of *Capital*, Marx performs a conceptual autopsy on the basic industrial machine. All such machines, themselves called into being by labor now ossified, consist of three fundamentally different sorts of parts.[21] The first, the working mechanism, directly alters the material to be transformed via the labor process. Think, for example, of the circular blade of a sawmill, or the drill of an oil rig, or the needle of a sewing machine. If this part were considered alone, or if it were taken to be the essential element, the machine in its entirety could be assimiliated into the category of simple tools. Although they are shaped in diverse ways, there is no difference in kind between the hand-powered crosscut saw and its counterpart in the mill; the teeth on both are so many analogues of my mouth's cutting tools. Its second and third parts must therefore articulate the distinction between a tool and a machine proper.

The second fundamental component of any machine, which Marx labels its transmitting mechanism, joins the working mechanism to the machine's source of energy and, in doing so, gives the otherwise undifferentiated character of that energy specific form and direction. The transmitting mechanism of a sewing machine, for example, consists of various gears, flywheels, pinions, and bands, all of which connect motor to needle and do so in a way that affords the latter its necessary up and down motion.

The third component, the motor mechanism, generates the power that, when routed by the transmitting mechanism, causes the working mechanism to perform its task. A motor mechanism, what Marx calls the machine's "prime mover," can assume several distinct forms. In preindustrial sewing machines, feet generated this artifact's motive power by relentlessly pumping a pedal on the floor. The human body qua motor mechanism can be relieved of its labors, however, when horse, stream, wind, steam, or ox is harnessed as its surrogate. Industrial sewing machines proper appear when the capacity of the human body to do work, its dynamic but undifferentiated potentiality, is projected within a freestanding motor. That motor's task is not to do the work done by the working mechanism proper, not to supplant the transmitting mechanism, but to lift each out of its dormancy, to make each move. Granted, such an automaton is not self-sufficient. Like the human foot, its operation requires some source of fuel if it is to do its work. But so long as it is fed and remains in good health, a motor stands forever poised to unleash its force in the conduct of work.

Any complex machine will unite all three forms of projection outlined here. Think, for example, of that classic complex of complex machines, the automobile assembly line. In shape and function, its robotic arms mimic the work once done by the less steady limbs of manual laborers. The track that conveys cars-in-the-making from one site to another replicates the capacity of human beings to carry things from here to there. Where particular tasks have proven ill suited to mechanization, as in the installation of radios, human energies amplified by various tools still provide the requisite motor power. But where machines have come to serve as freestanding embodiments of that power, as when the assembly line's track hurries along its designated course, a single central motor incorporates the generic capacity of human beings to wield the fires of Prometheus.

These, then, are three forms of artifactual projection. Before moving to reciprocation, I want to note two anti-Cartesian implications of my argument to this point. If you endorse my contention that everyday artisanal artifacts are well understood as so many projections of the organs, needs, capacities, and vulnerabilities of human bodies, and if you accept my contention that what we conventionally call "subject" and "object" are in fact coupled moments abstracted from a more comprehensive web, then it is not altogether clear that we should regard artisanal artifacts, first, as stupid and, second, as inanimate.

First, because Descartes identifies the soul with the mind, and because he confines reason to specifically human beings, he must conclude that artisanal artifacts are necessarily stupid. The most obvious way to contest this hubristic assumption is, of course, to point to the computer. Originally, the term "computer" referered not to a machine but to a profession. Computers were persons employed to make mathematical calculations for firms engaged in surveying, navigation, insurance, and finance; until the late 1920s, it is worth noting, members of this profession were highly trained, well paid, and for the most part men. Around that time, Leslie John Comrie of the British Nautical Almanac Office determined that systematization of the conduct of computing would enable him to replace these workers with young women who, partly because they possessed only rudimentary knowledge of commercial arithmetic and partly because they were women, could be paid considerably less than their male predecessors. Only in the late 1940s did the term "computer" come to refer to the personified machine into which the calculational skills of these women had been projected. To deny that machine the property of intelligence is, I assume, to deny the same to its human counterparts; and that, I would guess, we are reluctant to do.

But is intelligence restricted to such newfangled contraptions? Is there some sense in which it is equally, perhaps even more, apparent in comparatively prosaic artisanal artifacts? To answer this question, consider the NRA's preferred tool, the ordinary revolver. Even from a Cartesian perspective, I assume, it is noncontroversial to claim that a revolver in some sense incorporates specific sorts of knowledge. The structure of its handle, for example, reflects our understanding of the shape assumed by human hands when fingers, clutching something firm, circle back into a palm; its safety catch testifies to our grasp of the human proclivity to act rashly as well as the gravity of the mistakes to which members of this class of artifacts are prone; its steel bullets, each tapering to a tempered point, express what we know about the density of human flesh as well as its susceptibility to penetration.

So long as each of these concessions is situated within the conceptual confines of the Cartesian paradigm of use, none will erode its exclusive ascription of intelligence to the revolver's human designer; to say that a revolver "incorporates" human understanding of this and that is not quite to contend that this artifact is itself intelligent. But what happens if we think of the revolver as something like my hammer? The head of my hammer, on the account offered in the preceding section, is a sort of prosthetic fist, and my forearm is a sort of prosthetic shaft. Each a metaphorical extension of the other, neither is in exclusive charge of the conduct of hammering. To think otherwise is to permit an anxious epistemology, overeager to affirm the sovereign's autocratic control, to deceive us about the meaning of what is more like a democratic exchange between several different but not unrelated sorts of artifacts. In any event, if that hammer is one vehicle by means of which a body projects its transformational capacities into the world, and if that body's good sense is immanent within its skilled habits, and if those habits *are* what they accomplish, then is it not an anthropocentric fiction to locate intelligence exclusively in the "I" of the beholder? Is it not more sensible to ask how intelligence is distributed along various points of the arc defined by the conduct of work, an arc that incorporates "subject" and "object" but whose ultimate fulcrum is the hammer itself? If so, then presumably the same analysis applies when we turn from arm and hammer to arm and revolver.

Imagine a hole produced in a body by the bullet of a .38 caliber pistol. Now imagine a piece of cotton gauze taped over that stitched-up wound, standing in for absent flesh. Safekeeping you when I cannot, that bandage *is* the concrete real-ization, the artifactual articulation, of our intangible but shared appreciation of the inability of severely damaged tissues to repair themselves. To locate that gauze's intelligence, one need only consider the ingenious weaving of its crosshatched threads that ward off harmful bacteria while simultaneously inviting gentle currents of filtered air to do their healing work. Granted, this artifact requires a helpmate if it is to be positioned properly and changed periodically. But in few other cases are we so quick to conclude that the need for assistance signifies wholesale mindlessness. To respond, as the Cartesian no doubt will, by contending that reason is exclusively located within the mind of the agent who "uses" this artifact is to forget that intelligence, realized in the conduct of skillful nursing, is indistinguishable from the artifacts constitutive of that conduct. There is no more reason to isolate that sense in any one of its participants than there is to equate the flavor of a stew with the taste of any one of its ingredients.

Second, on the Cartesian account, part of what distinguishes human subjects from material objects is the fact that the former are sentient, whereas the latter are not. On this account, to think that an artifact is in some sense alive is to fall prey to prescientific animism. To embrace as true any of the familiar stories of artifacts come to life—think, for example, of Pygmalion's Galatea—is to give way to anthropomorphic mythology. This argument is on the mark, of course, inasmuch as the whole point of artifactual projection is to fashion things that can absorb blows without feeling their impact. But perhaps that is not quite the end of the matter.

Scarry questions the Cartesian when she contends that the intimate relationship between human bodies and their artifactual surrogates *"deprive[s] the external world of the privilege of being inanimate*—of, in other words, its privilege of being irresponsible to its sentient inhabitants on the basis that it is itself nonsentient"*:

> A material or verbal artifact is not an alive, sentient, percipient creature, and thus can neither itself experience discomfort nor recognize discomfort in others. But though it cannot be sentiently aware of pain, it is in the essential fact of itself the objectification of *that awareness*; itself incapable of the act of perceiving, its design, its structure, *is* the *structure of a perception*. So, for example, the chair . . . can—if projection is being formulated in terms of body part—be recognized as mimetic of the spine; it can instead—if projection is being formulated in terms of physical attributes—be recognized as mimetic of body weight; it can finally and most accurately, however, be recognized as mimetic of sentient awareness.[22]

Although a salutary corrective, Scarry's formulation here is still not quite right. It is not quite right, I think, because it is still too beholden to the dualistic bent of Cartesian discourse and, more specifically, to its requirement that we choose between the claim that the chair is animate and the claim that it is inanimate.

If it is true that parts, needs, and capacities of living bodies are projected into artisanal artifacts, and if the world called into being by such artifacts is in some sense an essential as well as an immanent condition of our distinctively human lives, then perhaps in an important but difficult to articulate sense that world is itself somehow vital. To see the point, consider once more the spiderweb; or, if we wish to abstract two of the participants from this constellation, consider the relationship between spider and web. True, we suspect, the web cannot feel pain and so in that sense is not sentient. But is the absence of sentiency the defining mark of inanimacy? Certainly, the web is vital in the sense that it is essential to the spider's life. But it is also vital in a sense closer to animacy, and that sense is not merely, to quote Scarry, "mimetic." For that web is the congealed issue of her body's circulating fluids as well as the communicative "means" through which her sensorium stretches into and engages a sensible world. When radial threads tingle with news of prey, when a spider makes, consumes, and then remakes its web using these same partly digested materials, it seems conceptually ham-handed to pronounce that artifact dead on arrival. Not quite alive, not quite dead, the spider's creation eludes our efforts to capture it within a Cartesian net. If the spider's web is an apt metaphor for the artifactual world, the myriad of solidified things spun from the labors of human bodies, then it seems equally artless to define these things in dualistic opposition to those inhabiting the sphere honorifically labeled "animate."

To return to the main story, through participation in artifactual projection, we are lifted beyond the brute immediacies to which we would be confined in their absence. To speak of projection's correlate, reciprocation, is to speak of the fact that artifacts act back upon and so remake their makers. Once more, Scarry:

> (H)uman beings project their bodily powers and frailties into external objects such as telephones, chairs, gods, poems, medicine, institutions, and political forms, and then those objects in turn become the object of perceptions that are taken back into the interior of human consciousness where they now reside as part of the mind or soul, and this revised conception of oneself—as a creature relatively untroubled by the problem of weight (chair), as one able to hear voices coming from the other side of a continent (telephone), as one who has direct access to an unlimited principle of creating (prayer)—is now actually "felt" to be located inside the boundaries of one's own skin where one is in immediate contact with an elaborate constellation of interior cultural fragments that seem to have displaced the dense molecules of physical matter.[23]

For reasons already indicated, I take exception to Scarry's reference to artifacts as "objects," to her epistemological representation of thinking as a matter of having mental "perceptions," and to her failure to explore the qualitative differences between an artifact made of wood (a chair) and one made of words (a prayer). Nevertheless, this quotation nicely gets at the gist of reciprocation: Just as the work performed by human bodies is incorporated within significant artisanal artifacts, so too is the work performed by artisanal artifacts incorporated within significant human bodies. Granted, in my retrograde Cartesian moments, I fancy that my discursively articulated commitments, my conscious convictions, make me who I am. But my body knows better, for it knows that "I" am a being whose lived experience is what it is, first and foremost, because of the unthematized ways of being I have acquired through habitual immersion in an ocean of familiar artifacts.

The capacity of artisanal artifacts to refashion the contexts they enter, as well as those who inhabit those contexts, always surpasses the embodied powers projected within them. (This, I think, is what Marx comprehended when he affirmed that human beings make history, but not under conditions of their own choosing.) Were it necessary for me to expend as much energy in making an artifact as it furnishes in return, it is not clear why I would ever bother to engage in projection; the generation of reciprocational excess is, therefore, essential to the logic of artisanal artifacts. Such excess can take at least two forms. It assumes the form of *spatial* excess when an artifactually mediated action at one site produces a much larger consequence elsewhere. Consider, for example, how the delicate interplay between a backhoe operator's thumb and forefinger is sufficient to engage a cupped steel hand, complete with razor-sharp nails, thereby digging an enormous hole in the ground. Or how a few keystrokes can reformat the entire text of this manuscript, whereas a few others can consign it to oblivion. Or how a small land mine, activated by the lightest of steps, can shred an unsuspecting body. It assumes the form of *temporal* excess when the brevity of artisanal projection is outstripped by years of uncomplaining work. Consider how it took my grandmother but two-weeks' time to knit a canary-yellow scarf, fashioning an unsightly artifact that haunts me to this day. Or how a love letter can preserve a sentiment long after a troubled couple has parted company for good. Or how the foundation of the stucco-covered home in which I now reside, poured sometime in the spring of 1913, remains stable today, even though the laborers who mixed and framed its concrete passed away long ago.

The verbs we most commonly employ when speaking of artisanal artifacts are, for the most part, so many ways of giving articulate form to the fact of reciprocational excess. Recall that projection assumes at least three forms; each finds its corollary in the realm of reciprocation. The head of my hammer *substitutes* for my fist, absorbing more pain than I could bear, and its shaft *amplifies* the power resident within my forearm. As an artifactual projection of the human ability to locomote, a bicycle *extends* that capacity and so permits me to cover more distance in a day than I could in a week on foot. As an artifactual projection of the undifferentiated capacity to work, a single-cell battery *stores* energy and so relieves me of the need to husband my strength through time. In these ways, that which is "external" liberates us from more immediate imperatives, enabling what would otherwise be so many sites of ceaseless suffering to become specifically human. I become the structure of possibilities woven into my thinking flesh via habitual intercourse with my artifactual parents.

We will not do justice to the labors performed by such artifacts, however, if we think of them as so many necessary preconditions, as so many instrumentalities whose work, like that traditionally ascribed to women, establishes the possibility of becoming human but does not participate in its substantive realization. Perhaps the most significant reciprocational work performed by artisanal artifacts involves their constitutive contribution to the creation of an intelligible world. To see how they do so, let us begin by reversing perspective. Rather than ask how artisanal artifacts help human beings make sense, let us first ask how human beings make sense of them.

On Scarry's account, the body parts, capacities, and needs projected within artisanal artifacts stand as the latter's "recoverable referents."[24] The walls of Descartes's one-room shack are a second skin; Richard Nixon's hidden tape recorders are so many electronic ears, giving artifactual form to the human capacity to hear; the iron shackles fashioned by Hephaestus in order to capture Aphrodite and Ares as they make the beast with two backs are a pair of clenched hands, affording enduring artifactual shape to a desire that he, absent their assistance, can never satisfy. Overcoming the opaque "objectivity" of artisanal artifacts is therefore a matter of relating them to, exploring their status as metaphors for, the human body. Because that body's intelligibility is the condition of whatever sense it finds within the "external" world, a disembodied human being, a *cogito sans corpus*, cannot help but be a creature of nonsense, an abstract unthing signifying no-thing.

And yet that body's intelligibility is not a *creatio ex nihilo*, a capacity requiring no account of its origins. To see how that capacity is itself a fruit of the work done by artisanal artifacts, consider Merleau-Ponty's seeing-eye stick:

> The blind man's stick has ceased to be an object for him, and is no longer perceived for itself; its point has become an area of sensitivity, extending the scope and active radius of touch, and providing a parallel to sight. In the exploration of things, the length of the stick does not enter expressly as a middle term: the blind man is rather aware of it through the position of objects than of the position of objects through it. . . . To get used to a hat, a car or a stick is to be transplanted into them, or conversely, to incorporate them into the bulk of our own body.[25]

At first, perhaps, that stick was something akin to a discrete object deliberately employed to locate troublesome impediments. But to see only that is to remain blind to its organic embeddedness in the conduct of making sense. In time, like all well-behaved artifacts, that stick disappeared from view in much the same way my fingers disappear within the situated immediacy of typing on this keyboard. Projecting agency into the world, it reciprocates as a vehicle of insightful exploration, clarifying what is found within the present and escorting conduct into an intelligible future.

As this example suggests, artisanal artifacts are not first and foremost things we struggle to make sense of, but rather resources for making sense. This dimension of their reciprocative work takes at least four forms, and I will deal quickly with each in turn. First, not quite two years ago, a black labrador retriever dubbed Luna(tic) meandered into our home and designated us as her ambivalent caretakers. No matter how bright we are sure she is, I suspect that she will never develop any conscious awareness of her own slightly webbed feet. But what if she were to respond to the discomfort she appears to feel while walking on gravel by fashioning some artifactual surrogate for her too soft pads? If she were to fashion some rough analogue to a pair of Converse high-tops, might she come to "know" her feet and to discriminate them from other body parts, which might in turn set in motion a quest for *their* artifactual help-mates, which might in turn invite her to consider the relationship of such helpmates to one other and so to their embodied correlates as well, which might in turn induce her to think of these correlates as so many interdependent constituents of a single source of artifactual agency, which might finally tempt her to think of herself *as* a self?

That artifactual reciprocation includes as one of its fruits the generation of beings capable of deeming themselves human is, I suspect, what Hegel was getting at with his notion of objectification.[26] Recall that in his *Phenomenology* Hegel argues that human beings, like so many Luna(tic)s, enter the world unable to distinguish subject from object, self from world, human from natural. If such a being is to come to recognize that it is, that it exists as a self differentiated from other beings, it must become aware of something it is not. Creation of that other, Hegel insists, is the task of labor. Through labor, what was hitherto merely a protoself externalizes itself, fashions an object whose objectivity testifies to the reality of the subject called into being via that act. To reappropriate that thing, to acknowledge it as an expression of the human capacity to transform nature's gifts, is to take an indispensable step toward becoming a creature worthy of the name.

Artisanal artifacts enter into the conduct of sense making in a second way as a result of their metaphorical fecundity. The intelligibility of such artifacts, I have suggested, is ultimately rooted in their analogical relationship to human bodies. That sense proves additionally prolific when, abstracted from this ground, it is extrapolated to very different matters. Homer, for example, relies on the art of weaving to explicate the facts of birth and death. The fate of each human being is dictated by three divine female spinners, known collectively as Moirai: Klotho, who spins the thread of life; Lachesis, who measures it out; and Atropos, who determines when it shall be cut. (This association is preserved, incidentally, when we speak of someone's "life span," for the term "span" originally derives from the verb "to spin.") Plato builds on these mythological resonances when, in his *Politicus*, he offers weaving as a metaphor for the distinctive art of the statesman. After disentangling diverse sorts of human beings, much as Penelope each night unweaves the shroud she fashions by day, the statesman draws these threads together once more but now within a body politic whose orderly constitution reveals the rationality of its masculine maker. (Note here, incidentally, how the Homeric metaphor represents humans as creatures whose destiny is ultimately in the hands of female beings, while the Platonic suggests that the city's inhabitants can become truly human only via their subjection to a political art that effectively disparages, even occludes, its metaphorical origins in women's work.)

Much the same sort of artifactual extrapolation is apparent when Descartes employs the simple clock to think about the bumps and bounces of the universe's atomic bits, which in turn informs his representation of the human body as one of the divine mechanic's more sublime projects. The other half of Descartes's bifurcated conception of the self, its capacity to reason, finds its contemporary metaphorical correlate in postmodernity's defining artifact, the computer.[27] Each time I think of my brain as an erratic hard drive, each time I ask my students for feedback, I confirm the power of this artifact to furnish the categories through which I make sense of what it is to be something other than an artifact.

I understand that neo-Kantians may find such metaphorical extrapolations objectionable on the grounds that they misrepresent the ontological distinctiveness of the human spirit and so degrade the essence of being human. It is my suspicion, however, that the Christian god makes sense of himself via his all-too-human creatures, without thereby degrading the essence of his divine being, and so I find this claim unpersuasive. Moreover, even those who contest the ethical propriety of drawing an analogy between a computer's operations and human thinking ironically confirm the former's contribution to sense making. When someone hastily erects an ontological fence in order to prevent contamination of the pure human spirit by this pesky alien, when someone insists that thinking is *not* like the operation of a computer, an understanding of the latter is still constitutive of the conception of human being under defense. If what it is to be a human being only makes sense by contrasting it with what it is not, just as the term "white" only makes sense because some things are not, then a denial of the computer/human analogy simply affirms what it means to deny.

Third, consider how artisanal artifacts participate in the meaningful constitution of things otherwise invisible. Think, for example, of the dilapidated synagogue in my hometown. To represent that temple as a neutral means instrumentally employed by so many individuals to achieve so many subjective ends, which happen to be held in common, is to erect a solipsistic caricature in place of a house of worship. Incorporating a host of lesser artifacts, from menorah to Torah, this edifice is an essential ingredient of the intangible reality of Jewish identity.

To see how this is so, think for a moment of my children, Jacob and Tobin, and their participation in the covenant of Abraham. From a Cartesian perspective, committed to the dualism of mind and body, a circumcised penis is an external and accidental sign of something internal and essentially real. Precisely the same understanding is apparent when that proto-Cartesian, Paul, tells his brethren in Rome that "a person is not a Jew who is one outwardly, nor is true circumcision something external and physical. Rather, a person is a Jew who is one inwardly, and real circumcision is a matter of the heart" (Rom. 2:28-29). Tobin and Jacob, however, know better. They know that circumcision is not an act that, once the scalpel does its work, is over and done, leaving behind merely an epiphenomenal token of something more fundamental. It is better to say that this act, continuously proclaiming itself in their flesh, is constitutive of that identity: "So shall my covenant be in your flesh an everlasting covenant" (Gen. 17:13). Indeed, I would argue that the operatives at Auschwitz understood these words of the Hebraic god far better than did Paul. Knowing that the presence of circumcision combined with the absence of any other indelible marking on the body is, according to Mosaic law, constitutive of the distinction between Jewish and non-Jewish men, they knew perfectly well that to burn a number into the flesh of Primo Levy was to initiate a history that, in 1987, would culminate in a final act of self-negation. "This is the mark," Levy wrote shortly before taking his own life, "with which slaves are branded and cattle sent to the slaughter, and that is what you have become."[28]

The temple is the Jewish body writ large, and the Jewish body is the synagogue writ small. No metaphysic predicated on a categorical distinction between external and internal, between material and immaterial, can begin to appreciate how things visible and invisible conspire to confirm the reality that is Judaism. In part, Jacob and Tobin's sense of their Jewish identity is borne by the prayers they have learned to chant in Hebrew. But of what are those prayers made? Words? In part, no doubt, that is so; but their sense is also incorporated within, and secures dramatic release through, the habits their bodies have come to acquire as a result of so many Friday night services. Soon, if not already, their legs will require no parental prompting to bring them to their feet when it is time to recite the *Kaddish* prayer. Were the words of that prayer spoken in conjunction with different habits, and were those habits articulated in response to the imperatives of differently structured artifacts, their meaning would change as well. It is one thing to recite the Ten Commandments, taken from the Old Testament, as part of a catechism lesson, within a Catholic church. It is something very different to read the Mosaic code, taken from the Torah, as part of a lesson about the Hebraic god's covenant with his chosen people, within a Jewish temple. Meaning, in sum, cannot be unambiguously located in a text, in the psyches (or bodies) of individual believers, or in the artisanal artifact that affords them shelter. Each is a vital participant in a larger intelligible practice, and none can be eliminated without compromising the others. Should the temple be destroyed again, should Judaism be denied the reciprocational work performed by its tangible helpmates, the artifact who insists that he transcends all tangible things will in time become immaterial.

So, artisanal artifacts affirm our standing as self-conscious agents; they provide a host of fertile metaphors for finding intelligible things other than themselves; and they give palpable form to what is otherwise intangible. For my purposes, one more contribution to the conduct of sense making is worth mentioning. Consider, for a moment, the wiretap. As artifactual metaphor, the wiretap is a projection of a specific organ of sense reception, and its most obvious reciprocative work is to extend my capacity to hear. But to note only this is to truncate its biography, to disregard the web of relations it enters and alters. Enabling me to place my ear in many places at once, to eavesdrop without detection, I become akin to the invisible man. Should you come to suspect that this is so, you in turn will become a being who can no longer rest assured that my body's absence signifies that I am indeed gone. The proliferation of wiretaps thereby undermines our confidence in the commonsense capacity of untutored senses to reveal the truth of a situation, and so tears at the fabric of shared sense that sustains an ethos of good faith. (Think, incidentally, of how the same effect is achieved via the placement of surveillance cameras—or their simulacra—in school buses, department stores, backyards, banks, warehouses, and now, I am told, in children's bedrooms.)

The example of the wiretap intimates the capacity of artisanal artifacts to compromise the integrity of a distinctively *collective* world. But if they can unmake that world, then surely they can also participate in making it. How so? As an analogical preface to answering this question, consider the following: There are, I submit, certain fundamental species of artisanal artifacts, species whose members respond to chronic needs of beings with human bodies. One species, akin to the skin and bones that house your internal organs, consists of all those artifacts that contain other made things. Think of desk drawers, broom closets, treasure chests, leather suitcases, shirt pockets, file cabinets, cardboard boxes, and a freight train's container cars. Another fundamental species consists of all artifacts that serve to attach things to one another. Look about the room where you now sit. Now try to identify all the artifacts that fix and so maintain a relationship between two or more made things, things that in their absence would fall asunder. Where I sit, three-inch bolts secure the legs of my desk to its horizontal surface. Thumbtacks affix various long-forgotten reminders to the cork surface of a bulletin board. Paper clips maintain in proper order the pages of student essays, no doubt improving with age. Mortar grips the bricks making up the exterior face of Maxey Hall, and, although unseen, I trust that steel girders secure its second floor to first and third. The metal threads in my lamp socket hold its bulb in place; a wire sustains the connection between computer keyboard and monitor. Various strings lash together the metal pieces of the Calderesque mobile turning above my head, and, although I have yet to put it to the test, I assume that glue holds fast the pages of Elaine Scarry's most recent book.

Imagine what would happen if each and every member of this artifactual species were, without warning, to engage in a sit-down strike, refusing to return to work until the labor they perform is suitably acknowledged and recompensed. The capacity of individual bodies to press things together could never match what was hitherto accomplished by our silent adherents. No matter how Herculean our efforts, we could not do other than languish amidst the rubble of a world gone to pieces.

Especially in a Cartesian world, a world that generally conceives of things as so many self-contained entities, objects related are more readily apparent than are relations themselves. Members of the artifactual species under consideration here are epistemologically suggestive because they stand as so many visible projections, enduring objectifications, of those relationships. But these members do not simply bind this artisanal artifact to that, freeing human artifacts to attend to other matters. They also affirmatively relate persons to one another in particular ways, just as mortar organizes bricks and glue fastens pages. Consider two rectangular dinner tables. Around the first rest six chairs, two to a side and one at each end. At the head of that table stands a patriarch who, as a chivalrous sort, insists that children remain standing until first mother and then he are seated. Once they have done so, all other parties to this ritual must independently engage their chairs in order to pull up to the table. The second table comes equipped not with separate chairs but with two long benches, one placed on each side. Because these benches effectively displace and then relocate father and mother, they challenge the familiar familial hierarchy. Still more troublesome, because it is designed to accommodate several backsides, the very structure of a bench mandates forms of cooperation that compromise the pretense of autonomy encouraged by chairs. It is not altogether clear that father knows best when he can belly up to the dinner table only by enlisting the assistance of his offspring.

Now consider the six dinner forks placed on that table. Each fork is not an ahistorical neutral strip of metal whose meaningfulness is a matter of subjective ascription by so many disembodied Cartesian egos. Far better to understand it in terms of the logic of projection and reciprocation. The fork's metaphorical relationship to the human body is perhaps most readily apparent in its tines, so many surrogate fingers, each equipped with a nail sharpened to a fine point. In part, the fork performs its reciprocative work by enabling human hands to get hold of matters otherwise too hot to handle. Equally fundamental, though, is the work it does in consolidating specific structures of human relatedness; and that cannot be understood apart from consideration of this artifact's history.

Prior to the eighteenth century, regardless of class background, virtually all European peoples ate with their fingers. As a rule, however, commoners grabbed food with all five fingers, while those more refined employed only three, leaving the ring finger and pinkie unengaged. Although dinner (as opposed to cooking) forks appeared in Tuscany as early as the eleventh century, their employment was generally discouraged, especially by the Catholic clergy, on the grounds that flesh and blood fingers were the only tools fit to appropriate the divine gift of food. However, as Europe's feudal nobility began its slow slide into historical irrelevance, it clutched at ever more subtle ways to reaffirm its superiority, and so the four-tined fork came to be deployed as a weapon in class warfare. Although intended by no one, a code of etiquette was soon incorporated within the meaningful structure of this artifact, a code that sneered at those who continued to carve meat with either a hand and a knife or, more awkwardly, a knife in each hand. The capacity of a fork to shame those clumsy in its company was redirected when an ascendant bourgeoisie, ever eager to ape its betters, appropriated this weapon and directed its force against members of the ruder classes. Thus, as patriarch, when I chastise my children for their apparent inability to grasp a fork and its purpose, my words bear the burden of a history I otherwise disdain.[29]

The dinner fork usefully illustrates my earlier claims about the excess of reciprocation over projection. Key to generation of that surfeit is the objectivity of artisanal artifacts, that is, their status as so many enduring and freestanding things. In my introduction, recall, I argued that Prometheus's beneficiaries became specifically human beings only after receipt of his gifts. Before that time, although displaying the form of human beings, these creatures were not in any meaningful sense distinct from animals. Only as they began to build up an artifactual habitat, only as their exchange was given determinate form by made things, did they begin to engage in specifically human relations. Were you and I to encounter one another outside the thick broth of artifacts that make us human, antecedent to any engagement in the dialectic of projection and reciprocation, we would find our unhuman selves nowhere in particular. Our words (should we somehow be capable of speech) would evaporate as soon as spoken; our deeds (should we somehow be capable of something other than instinctive response) would vanish as soon as performed. Only when these tokens are located within an enduring spatiotemporal context, a context whose stability is essential to the intelligibility of what is otherwise evanescent, only then can they come to bear the quality of significance.

To overcome the particularity of what my eyes take in, I can describe what I see to you, and you can do the same for me. Exchanging words, we will come to move in a world of common sense, of things whose significance for the affairs in which we are engaged is mutually understood. When what we speak of is seen through a pair of binoculars, a common world is created in another way. So many artifactual eyeballs, the twin lenses of binoculars are a projection of the capacity to see. That capacity is socialized when our eyeballs, metaphorically plucked from their sockets, are externalized within a freestanding artifact that is now passed between us. I cannot see with your eyes. But the capacity to see, which we share, can be artifactually mediated; and that mediation creates a relational structure that would not be in its absence. When these surrogate organs of vision become something around which our engagement circles, as when we sit in the upper deck to watch the Mets lose another game at Shea, the arc extending from artifactual projection to reciprocational excess takes shape as an intangible but nonetheless real chain linking me to you.

To say that the world becomes common via its artifactual articulation is not to say that the world is composed of so many objects grasped in the same way by all. In *The Human Condition*, Hannah Arendt claims: "Under the conditions of a common world, reality is not guaranteed primarily by the 'common nature' of all men who constitute it, but rather by the fact that, differences of position and the resulting variety of perspectives nothwithstanding, everybody is always concerned with the same object."[30] When Arendt speaks of "the same object," she reveals her unwitting dependence on the Cartesian presupposition that identical ideas, indistinguishable mental pictures, are the conditions of a thing's commonality. But it is not the sameness of the world's objects that guarantees a common world. Rather, the world is common because my conduct is meaningfully related to yours, and that coordination is largely a matter of our patterned negotiation of the significant spaces and times demarcated by artifactually textured things. We need not perceive the "same" temple in order to inhabit a shared world; it is enough that we continue to attend Shabbat services.

Relatedly, to say that the world is shared is not to say that it is harmonious, nor that the work of artifacts is necessarily benign. Yes, the gifts of Prometheus furnish common materials to those engaged in eliciting sense from experience. But materials, unlike determinate objects, do not possess the self-consistent identity Arendt ascribes to objects. As I shall suggest more fully toward the close of part 1, what an artisanal artifact *is* turns on *how* it is situated within the forms of collective practice it helps to articulate. If those practices incorporate relations of domination and subordination, so too will the artifacts implicated within it. As a man, you always get first crack at our binoculars when we go bird-watching. As a woman, I wait without complaint until you hand them over. We have never expressly noted how gender relations enter into our "use" of this familiar artifact. Nevertheless, or perhaps precisely because of our silence, it is an unwitting ally, even a weapon of sorts, in your struggle to retain the unacknowledged prerogatives of masculinity. Should I one day question our accustomed "use" of this artifact, and should you respond by mocking my halting efforts to contest its presumptive neutrality, no doubt you will conclude that my (ac)quiescence signifies endorsement of your Cartesian claptrap.

Before closing this section, intellectual probity requires that I acknowledge the outer limits of the categories of projection and reciprocation. Let me explain. Although my discussion of projection may appear to suggest otherwise, I do not contend that the needs and capacities of human bodies are either uniform or constant or even, as I shall make clear in part 2, that there is such a thing as "the body" standing apart from its cultural construction. If we are to grasp the relationship between human bodies and their fabricated helpmates, we must not reify either; we must not think of their relationship in terms of mechanical or external causation; and we must not forget that both are, and always have been, fundamentally remade as each participates in the dialectic of projection and reciprocation. Thus, with Prometheus and against Haraway, I do not believe that breakdown of the border dividing human beings from nonhuman things is peculiar to postmodernity; that erosion is internal to the very nature of artifactual production.

Although I do assert that human bodies and artisanal artifacts are mutually constitutive, I must also presuppose their analytic distinguishability. If it were impossible to draw any distinction between the two, it would also be impossible to specify the work done by each on the other, and so the categories of projection and reciprocation would make no sense. The distinction I draw between Promethean creators and creatures of Prometheus proves problematic, accordingly, when we turn to what might be considered a fourth form of projection. In this last form, the conduct of projection takes the human body (as opposed to some nonhuman material, whether wood, plastic, earth, ores, or whatever) as its immediate site. In some such cases—scarification, plastic surgery, and haircuts—tools refashion the bodies of which they are projections, and so those bodies are themselves artisanal artifacts (as opposed to the sites where the conduct of projection, returning as reciprocation, does its work). Even so, given that it remains possible to distinguish between two of the agents implicated in this process (e.g., scalpel and human flesh), such conduct does not threaten the coherence of my argument in any fundamental way.

What perhaps does is the cyborg as well as the "human" being (re)produced through genetic cloning. We want to say that the genetically engineered being who assumes human form is indeed human, but we are not quite sure. We want to say that the programmed robot who assumes human form is not in fact, but again we are not quite sure. In these cases, like the snake that swallows itself, the logic of projection and reciprocation collapses into a self-consuming whirlwind, intimating the external boundaries of the categories I employ here. The conceptual tools appropriate to making sense of a creature that/who seamlessly melds the analog technology of chromosomes and the digital technology of computers, a monster Victor Frankenstein never imagined, remain to be fashioned. While those I employ here may not be quite up to this task, it seems clear that those proffered by Descartes are still more inept.

vii. *Weighty Matters*

IF ONLY IMPLICITLY, MUCH OF WHAT I HAVE SAID THUS FAR ABOUT ARTIFACTUAL RECIPROcation casts doubt on the Cartesian affirmation of artifactual neutrality. In this section, as a prelude to asking about the relationship between artisanal artifacts and gender, I want to aggravate that doubt by suggesting that artisanal artifacts are specifically ethicopolitical beings.[31]

For the ancient Greeks, ethical and political questions were held to concern the justice or injustice of relationships between persons. Because the do-main of *technē* was held to involve the relationship between human beings and nonhuman nature, it could not generate such questions. This, I take it, is presupposed in the sharp distinction Aristotle draws between the technical (e.g., shoemaking and pottery) and the practical (e.g., politics and ethics) arts. Antiquity's exclusion of artisanal artifice from the ethicopolitical sphere was reinforced by Christianity, which stipulated that ethics concerns the purity of the will in its relationship to the divine and politics the obedience of the body to sovereign law. One fruit of this tangled history is the National Rifle Associ-ation's Cartesian bromide concerning the relationship between firearms and their users.

Without compromising the premise of artifactual neutrality, a Cartesian may concede that ethicopolitical considerations sometimes dictate the *deci-sion* to produce one artifact as opposed to another. Likewise, without contra-diction, a Cartesian may concede that invention of a given artifact has *consequences* for the organization of political life and the disposition of ethi-cal affairs. But neither of these concessions contests the Cartesian subject-ob-ject dualism, and so neither challenges the status of the former as creator and the latter as creature. So long as choices can be ascribed to the wills of indepen-dent subjects, so long as consequences can be considered external to that which effectuates them, the artifact's status as instrumental means is secure. Should these premises come to appear implausible, the Cartesian may seek to preserve the neutrality of artifacts by conceding their generation of "unintend-ed and unanticipated" consequences. Such a move may indeed safeguard the alleged innocence of artifacts, but it does so at the cost of blaming their "users" for insufficient foresight, and that in turn raises serious questions about whether these autonomous masters are in fact able to keep their artifactual servants in check.

It is my contention, however, that all artisanal artifacts bear ethical and political weight, and that incorporation of that weight within the world is nev-er neutral. To see the point, return for a moment to my binoculars. On the Cartesian account, the ethical import of this artifact is determined by the mor-al disposition of its individual users. You may use a pair of binoculars to locate a nest of spotted owlets and so help preserve an endangered species, or you may use it to peer into my bedroom. Nothing about this artifact dictates one as opposed to the other of these two uses, and so it is by definition neutral.

Put in these terms, this claim is not altogether misguided. However, be-cause it fails to appreciate the more subtle reciprocational work performed by a pair of binoculars, it hides more than it reveals. As a projection of the human capacity to see, a pair of binoculars expands the range of things seen. Insofar as I am a creature of my senses, my body's agency is thereby remade. The effec-tive ratio among the diverse capacities of my five most familiar ways of engag-ing the world, for example, is no longer what it was before. Yesterday, I could neither see nor hear a hummingbird flitting about in Sharon's garden of perennials. Today, artifactually augmented, I can see that creature quite well, although I still can't hear the beating of its wings. By revealing to me that there are things my unaided senses cannot grasp, this artifact causes me to doubt what, till now, I never had cause to doubt. More important, this artifact alters the character of things seen as well as the conduct of seeing by eliminating the foreground as well as the peripheral context that informs unassisted vision. Think about what happens when you press these rubber-lined glass lenses squarely against your eye sockets. Think not of what you now see better but of what you no longer see. Much like a camera lens or a television screen, this artifact enframes things seen, removing them from their accustomed context, severing the stream of sight ordinarily flowing from the viewing body to the things viewed. Doing so, much like the scope of a high-powered rifle, it encourages perception of these things as so many discrete objects disconnected from a now distanced subject. Organizing the capacity to see in this way as opposed to that, my binoculars subtly encourage the Cartesian representation of the knower as an autonomous spectator whose relations to things known, because external, is a matter of mechanical causation. As such, I would venture to guess, this artifact makes it easier to kill.

For another example of artifactual weightedness, consider Don Ihde's telephone. As a projection of the capacity to holler from here to there, the telephone expands the spatial range of human communication, sustaining my intercourse with those I am otherwise likely to forget. But such communication lacks the perceptual richness of face-to-face talk, and invites the sort of dissimulation that comes when the congruence of body language and spoken words is no longer a concern. To note how this artifact thereby refashions communication is not to unequivocally condemn it. I concede that the telephone has made us into beings who are indeed able to make sense of words absent facial cues, and I suppose that is a boon of sorts. However, it is to suggest, quoting Ihde, that every artifact has a "center of gravity which makes it partially selective as to what may be enhanced and what reduced."[32] If the claim to neutrality presupposes the perfect subordination of artisanal artifacts to human wills, then none are neutral. What an artifact is is never simply a matter of its physical structure. No matter how great or slight, its reciprocative work will always open up certain possibilities, while others are foreclosed.

For a final example, think of Karl Marx's power-loom. Marxists too much indebted to Descartes will frame their critique of this machine in terms of the intentions of its inventors (it was designed to dispossess traditional artisans), or in terms of its consequences for the relationship between capital and labor (it is yet another way to squeeze additional profit from exploited wageworkers). These are not unimportant insights. But so long as couched in terms of malicious intentions and pernicious consequences, they will not cast serious doubt on the Cartesian affirmation of this artifact's neutral instrumentality. Marx himself understood that the Cartesian is better answered by pointing to the relationship between the conditions of human embodiment, the internally complex structure of the early power-loom, and the historical circumstances by which both are irreducibly informed.

The power-loom's inventor, John Wyatt, described his creature as a device "to spin without fingers." So long as one attends only to its working mechanism, Marx has no quarrel with this designation. In the power-loom as well as its hand-operated counterpart, the shuttles passing threads back and forth are indeed so many surrogates for human fingers. But to confuse this part with the more comprehensive whole in which it is embedded is to fail to grasp the nature of both. In the preindustrial loom, human hands guide the shuttle's labors. When that shuttle is extricated from those hands, only to be reembedded within a power-loom, its physical structure remains essentially the same. But it is now something other than what Marx calls an "implement," a straightforward amplification of the capacity of two human hands to pass some thing back and forth. What "it" now is is a function of the new relational whole in which it participates, and those relations incorporate a transmitting as well as a nonhuman motor mechanism, neither of which is well understood as a simple projection of human fingers and their capacity to weave. In short, the shuttle is now a motor-powered component whose motions, dictated by the requirements of the loom's transmitting mechanism, demand that this assembly's specifically human parts adapt to its imperatives.

On Marx's account, if we are to undertand why the power-loom's principal product is so much alienated labor, we must understand it as part of a still larger whole, one that includes spatial as well as temporal dimensions: "As a matter of fact, every machine is a combination of these simple aids, or powers, no matter how they may be disguised. From the economic standpoint, however, this explanation is worth nothing, because the historical element is missing from it."[33] Just as it was a mistake to reductively equate the power-loom with its working mechanism, so too is it a mistake to reductively equate the power-loom with its visible assembly. What that assembly is is irreducibly shaped by the larger socioeconomic context that gives specific form to its operation. A capitalist economy, we might say, is a gigantic transmitting mechanism, a complex set of gears, pulleys, pinions, flywheels, and straps, that shapes the work of the power-loom into the concrete form necessary to reproduce the imperatives of capital accumulation. Again, the implication is clear: Although its physical structure may remain the same, once the capitalist transmitting mechanism is overthrown and replaced, the power-loom will no longer serve as its accomplice, perverting the benign logic of projection and reciprocation.

But does this way of putting the matter get things quite right? With this formulation, has a sort of refined Cartesianism found its way back into Marx's analysis? If the power-loom's nature is entirely a function of the economy in which it participates, if the power-loom so obediently surrenders to determination by that context, then must not Marx believe that this artifact is neutral in the sense that its structure and operation bear no internal imperatives apart from that context? To evade that conclusion, without falling prey to technological determinism, it is better to insist on what I call the power-loom's intrinsic weightedness. Granted, we must acknowledge its malleability, its capacity to become different things within different contexts. But to affirm that is not to claim that it is perfectly plastic, altogether a creature of the circumstances in which it finds itself.

Precisely because its motor simultaneously incorporates and amplifies the human body's capacity to project itself into the world, at least in principle, the power-loom dramatically relieves those bodies of the burden of labor. Granted, as Marx would be quick to insist, in a class-based economy that relief is afforded to some bodies only because it is denied to others. But it is not clear that the imperatives of capitalism are sufficient to account for all that troubles us about industrial machinery. Industry advances, Marx insists, as ever more manual competencies are lifted out of human bodies, and as an ever larger class of tools is removed from their hands. The tasks once performed by these hands and tools are then incorporated within and delegated to so many mechanical surrogates: "The tools peculiar to the various specialized workers, such as those of the beaters, combers, shearers, spinners, etc. in the manufacture of wool, are now transformed into the tools of specialized machines, each machine forming a special organ, with a specific function in the combined mechanism."[34] Taken to its logical culmination, it would appear that this process of expropriation and reincorporation must ultimately fulfill itself in the creation of a machine very much like the automaton Descartes imagined the human body to be. In such a machine, the theoretical disjunction between body and soul would be perfectly realized in practice, for all that once defined the body would now be projected within the machine, while the immaterial soul would exclusively define what it is to be a human being.

But, of course, not all human competencies are equally susceptible to artifactual projection. And so, absent realization of Descartes's utopia, human beings are ever more relegated to those dreary tasks that most vigorously resist efforts to lift them out of the body and into the machine. On the automobile assembly line, once again, the most obvious examples include routine maintenance, repair, and replacement of those artifactual surrogates too worn out to continue. Hence the paradox of the motor: It is one of the more sublime manifestations of the Promethean project, the desire to create the artisanal artifacts through which otherwise dumb brutes become human. But to the extent that such artifacts are not self-sufficient, to the extent that they demand service, their most significant reciprocative work may be the transformation of their human helpmates into mindless automatons.

The Cartesian paradigm of use cannot grant the argument implicit in my discussion of binoculars, telephones, and power-looms because it must insist that it is possible, at least in principle, to say what an artisanal artifact is apart from what it does. Here is an object; there are the consequences "it" produces. But on my account, what an artifact is is inseparable from the relations in which "it" is implicated. All artisanal artifacts are in this way akin to the Angolan hoe. Designed for women carrying infants on their backs, this artifact includes a single iron blade but two handles. The work of that blade, standing in for hands too easily cut, cannot be accomplished absent the rocking motions of women laboring in pairs. Its very structure mandates a specific field of ongoing relations, a field from which "subjects" and "objects" may be abstracted at the cost of understanding neither. To label two of the partners to this transaction active, and the third passive, is to fail to see how each is implicated in conduct comprehending all. To call two animate, and the third inanimate, is to fail to see how these handles, linked via a common shaft, join women's hands together, projecting their collective energies into the earth.

To affirm that all artisanal artifacts have a weighted center of gravity is to anticipate the sense in which they are political. The generation of spatial and temporal excess, remember, is essential to the logic of projection and reciprocation, and it is such excess that explains how ostensibly nonpolitical artifacts become political. A quick spin in Leon Kass's automobile will demonstrate. On the most simple level, an automobile amplifies the capacity of human beings to locomote, enabling bodies thus equipped to outrun those confined to bare feet, to animal conveyances (horse, ox), to mechanical contrivances (bicycle, sled). But to leave matters at that is to ignore the automobile's imperious demand for a host of artifactual as well as human kin:

> Consider automobility: by its very nature it entails roads and bridges; the need for fuel and the dependence on oil; the rise of steel mills, auto factories, auto workers, auto dealers, gas stations, garages, body shops, traffic laws, traffic police, parking facilities, and driving instructors; the production of noise, fumes, smog, and auto graveyards; the need for auto mechanics, safety and highway inspectors, insurance agents, claim adjusters, trackers of stolen cars, parking attendants, testing and licensing personnel, and medical personnel to deal with accidents and their human victims, and, thanks also to automobility itself, urban sprawl, homogenization through destruction of regional differences, separated lives for extended families, new modes of courtship behavior, new objects of envy and vanity, and a new battleground between parents and children appear, quite predictably, on the scene[35]

If this is insufficient to persuade you that the automobile is a political thing, consider one of its most significant correlates—the network of highways etched into the body politic of the United States since the 1950s. To the extent that income differentials render it more difficult for some to maintain an automobile, to the extent that those same differentials make it easier for some but not for others to live in the suburbs and commute to the city, to the extent that cities are thereby deprived of the tax base necessary to keep them vital, to the extent that such class-specific migration patterns sap middle-class support for mass transit, to the extent that self-enclosed shopping malls arise in suburbia to satisfy desires they manufacture without respite, the automobile eviscerates the public spaces necessary to what Tocqueville imagined was the American practice of local self-governance. Far more effectively than might any Hobbesian sovereign, automobility has rendered the republican ideal a sham.

Generalizing from examples of this sort, Langdon Winner has argued that what "appear to be merely instrumental choices are better seen as choices about the form of social and political life a society builds, choices about the kinds of people we want to become."[36] This is certainly so. The language of choice will mislead, though, unless we recall that adoption of any given artisanal artifact goes a long way toward rendering the language of voluntarism untenable. Via the location of its walls, a house establishes an ensemble of possibilities for movement, possibilities that are progressively actualized each time I chart a new course through it. While those walls constrain the range of such possibilities, they do not dictate the path I must take on any given day, and so perhaps the language of choice remains appropriate in this context. Comparable opportunities for improvisation are not incorporated, however, within the structure of a nuclear reactor. As a matter of practical necessity, coordination of a reactor's specialized tasks requires the imposition of a centralized and hierarchial chain of command, one that minimizes the likelihood that unpredicted disturbances will occur, one that guarantees rapid communication when they do. The metaphor of the chain is all too apt precisely because it suggests that the links welding human to artifactual energies within a nuclear reactor, like the fetters binding Prometheus, are virtually unbreakable. A reactor is therefore political, first, because its absorption of substantial financial, material, and human resources within a stubborn institutional structure goes a long way toward foreclosing significant debate about and exploration of genuine alternatives; and, second, because its very operation is incompatible with decentralized and/or egalitarian forms of decision making and job allocation. Its very existence, I would argue, effectively compromises efforts to inject democratic sensibilities into the body politic.

These examples should suffice to show why I think it mistaken to ask about the "impact" of politics on technology, or vice versa. The very grammar of that Cartesian question suggests a relationship of mechanical causation between two independent nounlike things. (The same grammar is implicit, note, in the journal title: *Technology and Culture*.) Even as astute a student as Winner misleads when he asks about the relationship between the technical and the political constitution of society. Granted, this way of framing the matter avoids the twin errors of technological instrumentalism and technological determinism. But it does not quite do justice to what I mean to get at via the metaphor of the web. With that metaphor, I mean to call into question any analysis that takes for granted the adequacy of the discursive distinction between the political and the technical. Better, I think, to ask how this very distinction comes to be artifactually materialized than to let it do its work uncontested.

Each artisanal innovation, entering a world already thick with artifacts, is like a bumblebee trapped by the threads of a sticky web. Setting up multiple vibrations, its movements are telegraphed far from their original source. When these waves reach a spider's hideaway, she responds, precipitating additional reverberations in all directions. Traveling across an artifact alive with motion, the spider seeks to fashion sense from what is given in experience. That she can sometimes do so testifies to the mutual embeddedness, the simultaneous implication, of her body and the web teased from its labors. When she calls that sense "political," she testifies to her understanding that the threads she now dances across stretch into a larger world, a world where her lot is not hers alone.

viii. *Calvin (But Not Hobbes) on the Making of Real Men*

IN THIS SECTION, MY AIM IS TO ASK ABOUT THE GENDER OF ARTIFACTS, WHEREAS, IN PART 2, one of my principal aims is to ask about the artifact of gender. Given my contention that human beings and artisanal artifacts are interconstitutively bound up within a more comprehensive web of materialized artifice, it is important to recall that this is an analytic distinction abstracted from that web. As such, the present section can be located here in part 1, which concerns the agency of artifacts, or it could be located in part 2, which concerns the artifact of agency. The distinction is one of emphasis, not of kind.

From the perspective of the Cartesian paradigm of use, it is unintelligible to ask about the gender of artifacts. Predicated on a strict separation of body from mind, the Cartesian presupposes that gender is an effect whose unmediated cause is the form of one's genitalia as well as the desires appropriate to them. The disembodied capacity to reason, by way of contrast, is not in any fundamental way constituted by anatomical equipment and hence by gender identity. To the extent that men and women are like creatures of reason (a premise often negated by representing women as captives of their sexual drives and reproductive capacities), the Cartesian paradigm must conclude that this capacity operates universally and homogeneously in both.

Because the Cartesian mind has no sex, neither does its knowledge; and because technical instrumentalities are the fruits of such knowledge, they too must be genderless beings. Should any trace of gendered subjectivity insinuate itself within the process of inquiry and so threaten to taint the neuter-ality of

knowledge and/or the artifacts to which it gives rise, that danger can be overcome through rigorous application of the prophylactic rules of scientific method. Accordingly, should any given artisanal artifact be found guilty of
participating in the exploitation of one gender by another, that fact must be
explained through reference to the odious wills of human subjects rather than
the intrinsically innocent instrumentalities through which those wills are
made effective.

The Cartesian paradigm of use is implicit in much feminist criticism of
technology, and that is so without regard to party line. To see the point, consider the distinction Iris Young draws between humanist and gynocentric femi-
nisms.[37] The former camp includes liberal feminists who, when turning to
"the problem of technology," typically argue that the question of the relationship between technology and gender is a legitimate one, not because the
former is itself somehow gendered, but because women have been excluded
from access to it. This inequity is to be remedied by ensuring that all human
beings, regardless of gender, have an equal opportunity to participate in determining the uses to which our instrumental means are put.

Many in the camp of gynocentric feminism contend that women—whether because of their experience as daughters or as mothers, the qualities peculiar to female eroticism, their distinctive roles in the sexual division of labor, or
their special connection with the earth—acquire epistemological and ethical
virtues that are absent from men. Schooled in the arts of cooperation rather
than competition, for example, women understand that dependence on and
care for the artisanal helpmates of this world do not necessarily vitiate one's
selfhood. Accordingly, those partial to such feminism argue that women are
especially well equipped to turn toward benign ends instrumentalities that, in
the hands of men, now generate only waste and destruction.

Arguably, the Cartesian paradigm of use informs and infects the arguments of those in both camps. When the liberal feminist argues for inclusion
of women within deliberations aimed at determining the ends of technology,
she presupposes a vision of the subject that, although veiled by its appeal to abstract humanism, is decidedly masculinist. To the extent that her argument
turns on a representation of artisanal artifacts as docile means of human
agents, as objects that do not remake their makers, she presupposes the myth
of the freely willing self whose autonomy is contingent on a radical disavowal
of dependence on anything external to its own ego. That disavowal, I am persuaded, is simply a more specific manifestation of the generalized form of denial that is essential to the coherent constitution of heterosexual masculine
identity; its archetype is the refusal of men to acknowledge emergence from
the bodies of their mothers. (For a familiar example, recall the liberal representation of human beings as fully formed and autonomous egos in the state of
nature.) When the liberal feminist fails to inquire into the artifactual conditions of gender identity, including her own, she proves complicitous with the
order she means to reprove.

I am not persuaded that gynocentric feminists, to stay with Young's categories, do much better. Here, too, technology's ill effects are deemed a function of its misuse when under the control of brutish men. The remedy is to subject these devices to the control of those less prone to think that preservation of the autonomous self requires unidirectional domination over all things external to it. Leaving aside the question of whether this argument simply puts a happy face on the characterological traits women have acquired by virtue of their subordination to men, it should be clear that on this account, as with the liberal feminist, neither the neutrality nor the neutered character of technology is thrown into question. Gender remains located within the confines of human subjectivity, and so its relationship to the gifts of Prometheus is taken to be extrinsic rather than intrinsic, accidental rather than essential, unilateral rather than mutually transformational. The aim of such feminism is to change the subject, not to confuse it with gendered objects.

Unlike both liberal and gynocentric feminists, Calvin is not so sure that artisanal artifacts are either neutral or neutered:

Fig. 2: Calvin and Hobbes comic strip. *Calvin and Hobbes* ©Watterson.
Dist. by Universal Press Syndicate. Reprinted with permission.
All rights reserved.

If nothing else, it seems apparent that Calvin means to affirm an intimate relationship between masculine gender identity, artisanal artifacts, and the work they do in making and unmaking the world. But how exactly are we to make sense of that connection?

If we temporarily confine our attention to this comic strip's first two frames, it is not difficult to argue that Calvin's own understanding of the relationship between self and hammer is broadly congruent with the Cartesian paradigm of use. Such an argument might proceed something like this: Calvin's unthematized conception of his own subjectivity is indicated when he identifies "I" with his capacity to alter the world "at will." That will, he seems to think, is an autonomous faculty, the capacity to choose freely to do this or that. In and of itself, however, Calvin's will can grasp nothing. As an intangible potentiality, a creature as immaterial as is his mind, Calvin's will can secure worldly expression only via his body and, more particularly in this case, via his right hand. But Calvin's body, on this reading, does not participate in any essential way in making his will what it is. It is simply an instrumentality, a passive means of making apparent what is otherwise merely so much abstract intentionality.

The instrumentality of the relationship between abstract will and concrete hand is recapitulated in the relationship between Calvin's hand and hammer. When Calvin states, "I have a hammer," the possessive copula suggests that the sovereign will, actualized via an obedient hand, is essentially distinct from its instrumentality. Correlatively, as with his hand, the intrinsic neutrality of the hammer qua instrumentality is affirmed when Calvin proclaims that it can be used for good or for evil, to "put things together" or to "knock things apart." On this reading, the world consists of so many discrete objects awaiting construction or deconstruction, assembly or disassembly, in accordance with the freely chosen projects of this loud-mouthed microgod.

But how now are we to make sense of this strip's final frame? What are we to make of Calvin's closing assertion, his contention that the relationship between sovereign will and neutral device, between what is internal and what is external, affirms his standing as a specifically gendered being? Calvin does not say, and so we must speculate. From a Cartesian perspective, of course, we must assume that this relationship is merely coincidental. Calvin's hammer is a neutral tool, his gender identity is a function of his immature penis and the heterosexual desires we prospectively ascribe to it, and neither participates in making the other what it essentially is.

It is not difficult to imagine a number of feminist critiques of this Cartesian interpretation of Calvin's concluding remarks. From a sociobiological perspective, one might argue that Calvin's passion for his hammer, most particularly its capacity to "make an incredible din" while demolishing this and that, indicates an excess of testosterone coursing through his prepubescent tissues. From an ecofeminist perspective, one might argue that Calvin's hammer is a sign of his womb envy. Secretly jealous of women and their life-giving powers, Calvin compensates for his reproductive incapacities by bearing a hammer. So armed, he becomes a diminutive mechanical engineer, maniacally bent upon wholesale tranformation of nature into so many compliant artifactual children. From an overlapping psychoanalytic perspective, one might argue that Calvin's hammer is the means by which he establishes an identity apart from his mother. As a boy of five or so, Calvin now understands that he is a being whose body is unlike that of his mother. Moreover, he understands that his identity as a protoman turns on his escape from the world where his mother's body is at home. His hammer, artifactual emblem of the phallus, is the instrumentality that enables Calvin to take his rightful place alongside father in a world defined by its opposition to the private sphere. There, no longer dependent on the woman who would swallow him up, if only she could, Calvin's autonomous "I" participates in making and unmaking a public realm from which women, as a rule, are excluded.

Insofar as these sociobiological, ecofeminist, and psychoanalytic accounts jointly contend that Calvin's hammer is intrinsically related to his gender identity, all depart to some extent from the Cartesian paradigm of use. None, however, breaks entirely free. Note that all are essentially alike in at least three respects. First, all treat Calvin's infatuation with his hammer as an effect produced by the workings of a single, ahistorical, and unilinear cause, whether that be the presence of toxic chemicals in the bodies of boys, the timeless desire of men to secure some surrogate for women's more intimate union with nature, or the universal quest of males to deny any dependence on female bodies. Second, all assume that the directionality of this cause's efficacy runs from Calvin to his tool; all believe, in other words, that Calvin's passion for his hammer is an expression of his antecedently constituted gender identity. And, third, all assume that gender is a distinguishing property of the being called "Calvin" as opposed to a quality of the more comprehensive situation he inhabits. As such, all three accounts share the Cartesian location of gender within the subject as well as its assumption that the distinguishing features of that subject account for the specific ways this artifact is deployed. None, in consequence, is well positioned to make sufficient sense of the interconstitutive relationship between Calvin, hammer, and gender identity, as these are situated within a world of lived experience comprehending all three.

If we are to grasp that relationship, we must refuse to locate gender in the Cartesian subject or, failing that, in the Cartesian object. Recall once more that the reciprocational powers exercised by artisanal artifacts always exceed those projected within it, and recall that such excess refashions the relations between human beings as well as those between things. Gender, I now want to contend, is one of the more enduring creatures generated by the dialectic of projection and reciprocation. Gender is an internally complex materialized artifact, one called into being by and within the relations between artisanal artifacts and persons, artisanal artifacts and other artifacts, persons and other persons. As such, it is not a property found exclusively within women or men; nor is it exclusively a quality of the relations between such beings.

If you remain convinced that gender is so confined, then imagine the following: In this comic strip's first frame, Calvin is holding aloft not a hammer but a rolling pin or perhaps a diaper pin. Do the words of the closing frame still make sense? If not, why not? As with hammers, rolling and diaper pins are artifactual things that participate in fashioning a commonsensical world. Yet neither appears congruent with Calvin's triumphal affirmation of his capacity to make and unmake the world, and so neither seems congruent with a celebration of the virtues of masculinity. But what exactly is the source of the incongruity here? Where does it reside? In the artisanal artifact? In Calvin? Or in the relationship between the two? If the latter is the case, as I believe it is, then does this incongruity prove meaningful *as an incongruity* only because this scene tacitly makes reference to that which is absent from it? That is, if we find that this redrawn comic strip does not make sense, is that nonsense identifiable as nonsense only because it implicitly gestures toward the sort of gendered being whose presence would overcome this incoherence?

To see the same point in slightly different terms, imagine that it is not Calvin but his neighborhood nemesis, Susie, who appears in these three panels. Imagine that Susie clutches a Browning automatic rifle or perhaps a Mattel steam shovel, all the while proclaiming how wonderful it is to be female. Is that not equally incongruous? Can the gendered dimension of that incongruity be located definitively in the rifle or its bearer? Can it be understood as incongruous absent its implicit but conceptually necessary nod toward Calvin and his ilk? Perhaps most revealingly, imagine that in the first frame Susie clutches a sewing needle, the plastic nipple from a baby bottle, or a Teflon-coated frying pan, while in the final frame she shouts: "It's great to be female." What exactly is wrong with the comic strip now? If this too seems somehow odd, does not that tell us much about the way female gender identity and the artisanal artifacts constitutive of that identity are devalued in common? In each of these cases, it seems to me, what puzzles us is located in the difficult to pin down but not for that reason unreal relationship between two different sorts of materialized artifact: the human and the artisanal.

(Incidentally, when you substitute diaper or rolling pin for hammer, are you more or less inclined to contend that this comic concerns the "question of technology"? It is my guess that you are less inclined. If so, how do we explain that? Is it because we uncritically associate the term "technology" with things like hammers, industrial machines, and rockets, but find it strained to apply it to diapers, cooking utensils, blankets, and other artisanal artifacts constitutive of "women's work"? Is it not true that our very conception of what counts as technology has a gendered dimension to it?)

That gender is a relational property of the world rather than a property of human subjects, either individually or in tandem, is intimated by the fact that women and men find it easy to associate particular artisanal artifacts with either the color blue (e.g., electric drills and television remote control devices) or the color pink (e.g., irons and vacuum cleaners).[38] That many artifacts take the bodies of men as their norm is suggested by the fact that Boeing 747 seats are not designed with pregnant persons in mind. That many artifacts incorporate a history of the experiences distinctive to men or to women is indicated by the fact that men, most often responsible for dressing themselves when buttons first became popular among the upper classes in the thirteenth century, button their clothes from right to left, whereas those women who could afford such luxuries were customarily dressed by right-handed female servants who found it more convenient to do so when buttons were placed on the opposite side. But none of these examples is sufficient to sustain the stronger claim I want to make, that is, the claim that gender is itself manufactured by artisanal artifacts.

To see how asymmetrical gender relations are artifactually produced, let us return to that primordial artifact, the room. Better still, since the single room is for the most part an abstraction from a more comprehensive context (leaving aside the peculiar instance of Descartes), let us look at the constellation of rooms that is the home. Does a woman make a house a home, as my great-aunt used to say, or does the home make an otherwise ambiguous creature into the determinate being my great-uncle used to call "his woman"? I contend that my great-uncle was far closer to the mark.

If the term "space" is taken to refer to that which is ill defined, to a locus of shifting boundaries without determinate form, the term "place" can be taken to refer to the artifactual transformation of that void into so many determinate sites. When sufficiently ossified, suggests Kathleen Kirby, place "settles space into objects, working to inscribe the Cartesian monad and the autonomous ego. It perpetuates the fixed parameters of ontological categories, making them coherent containers of essences, in relation to which one must be 'inside' or 'outside,' 'native' or 'foreign,' in the same way that one can, in the Euclidean universe at least, be in only one place at one time."[39] The creatures we think of as Cartesian subjects and objects, in other words, are called into being by the transformation of space into place; neither has an existence antecedent or external to that transformation.

The transformation of space into so many determinate places defined by the artifactually mediated activities constitutive of them (e.g., cooking, eating, defecating, sleeping, entertaining); the assignment of distinct categories of persons to work within and/or care for these places (the laundry room as opposed to the workshop); the normative regulation of movement in and out of those same places; each is facilitated by the walls distinguishing one room from another. But the members of this class of artisanal artifacts do not treat all equally. Granted, their coercions are subtle, so subtle that we may only become aware of the work they perform when one of their number is torn down. Their impassivity, however, should not be confused with impotence. Far more vigorously than many of their artifactual kin do walls participate in the durable construction of specifically masculine and feminine second skins, skins whose gender can be determined in part by noting their relative susceptibility to penetration. The speculative autonomy of my will would mean little in the absence of walls punctuated by doors I can lock; yet those same walls now close around you, sequestering your body in a space where it is susceptible to my intrusions, whether invited or not.

Giving shape to the relations between its human and nonhuman parts, the home is an internally complex domestic machine whose products include the differentiated beings it efficiently engenders: husbands and wives, fathers and mothers, sons and daughters. Like the housing protecting a motor from various pollutants, the external walls of a home define the boundary that separates and, in so doing, constitutes the opposition between inside and outside. Like the transmitting mechanisms of Marx's industrial machine, the internal walls of a home structure the relations between its various working parts. We may be tempted to identify such parts with its specifically human inhabitants, but that is a temptation to be resisted. For the identities of its human components are essentially constituted by their engagement with specific artisanal artifacts, artifacts that tease forth some capacities, while stultifying others.[40]

Think of a Mongolian *ger*. The *ger* is a single-room tent made of a circular frame covered with woolen felt mats. It is divided into separate halves for men and women. The ritually pure male half, to the right of the tent's front flap, contains the possessions of the household's patriarch, including books, guns, saddles, and grain. The impure female half, off to the left, contains milk buckets, a stove, churns, food sacks, cooking utensils, and children's toys. None of these artifacts is a discrete object of use, for each is an intrinsic ingredient of the practices within which it participates. Exactly how each takes part is rule governed, and those rules are gender specific. The content of such rules, fully embedded in the customs relating things to persons, is not to be located in either. When a Mongolian woman grasps the handle of a churn, when she sets to the task mandated by its structure, that small deed is sufficient to establish her membership in the company of women; and in that deed the subordination of all her sisters is simultaneously confirmed. Should she dare to pick up a book or handle a saddle, she will soon learn just how inseparable are artifacts and the relations of domination they engender.

Now think of my mother. Better still, think first of Karl and then of Marjorie. Recall Marx's claim that industry "progresses" as ever more tools and tasks are expropriated from human workers and built into the structure of machines. What was once a hand-held spindle is withdrawn from the domain of manual competence, only to reappear as a vital internal organ of a complex machine. What was once a foot pumping up and down is replaced by a more efficient motor. In time, all that remains for the specifically human parts of industrial machines are those tasks—routine maintenance, repair, and replacement of worn out parts—that are not readily delegated to their mechanical counterparts.

Until she finally left Norman sometime in the early 1980s, Marjorie was something akin to a domestic variant of Marx's industrial maintenance workers. In the postwar years, as the liberal state expanded its functions, as a capitalist economy gobbled up the noncommodified remains of civil society, tasks once located within the household were expropriated and delegated to those more competent. Whereas Marjorie's great-grandmother made clothes for her children at home, my mother ceded that responsibility to Sears. Whereas Marjorie's grandmother educated her offspring in the kitchen, my mother packed us off to public school. Whereas Marjorie's mother nursed sick kids at home, brewing remedies specified in cookbooks and calling for a doctor only in the direst emergencies, my mother routinely summoned the powers of the pediatrician and pharmacist. What remained were those chores that, for one reason or another, were not so readily professionalized and commodified in abstraction from the home. But to refer to the tasks of cooking, cleaning, and child-rearing as so many "chores" is to substitute a homogeneous reification for what was in reality so many cycles of mundane routine given determinate shape by specific clusters of interrelated artisanal artifacts. To call my mother a housewife is to identify her as a being who, although legally married to her husband, was more intimately involved with a wooden-handled broom, a Maytag washer, several dozen dishtowels bearing insipid inspirational sayings, a Hotpoint oven, a cast-iron griddle, an Amana refrigerator, and two flush toilets.[41]

Blessed with five children under the age of eight in 1962, the exterior walls of Norman's home were so many bars marking Marjorie's isolation from a world beyond. Although not conversant with Descartes, on some level, she knew that those walls were not so many neutral instrumentalities, that the obdurate constellation of unhappy relations constitutive of the nuclear family could not be separated from the architecture of suburbia. Reproduction of the class of "women" is literally cast in the foundations of such homes. Their very design, with private washing machines, dishwashers, ovens, and dryers, solidifies in space and perpetuates in time the class of beings necessitated by its structural imperatives. That this class is fundamentally distinct from the class of men was confirmed each time one of these appliances dared to fall ill. Then, my mother's only recourse was to call into my father's home a serviceman, one whose position in the gendered division of labor entailed expertise in forms of knowledge from which she, as a creature of the home, was excluded. Granted, as with a spiderweb's hub, this site was connected to a more extensive world via its telephone and electricity lines, its gas main and sewer pipes, its asphalt roads and concrete sidewalks. But because these axial threads were themselves built to last for generations, they too consolidated the artifactual arrangements that, even now, manufacture beings of her ilk. Granted, her confinement was tempered by daily excursions to the supermarket, to the YMCA, to dance lessons, and whatnot. Yet these exercises, positioning her as a station wagon's vital but replaceable internal organ, simply confirmed her status as a being whose final telos, as near as I can recall, was to fashion nice girls out of the recalcitrant materials furnished by my sisters.

The comparative question to ask of Mongol's ger and Norman's castle is how each transforms space into place, physical as well as psychical. How do these places map out the boundaries that afford space its articulation and, in so doing, tease forth the specifically discursive ingredients of domination? How do "external" differentiations, generated through so many acts of artisanal projection, fashion embodied psyches whose "internal" differentiations are such that some feel "at home" in the world, whereas others do not? How, moreover, do we explain the fact that sometimes a woman, finding her sense-making resources at odds with the artifactual coordinates navigating her body through time and place, will summon the strength to leave? So long as one identifies consciousness with so much neutered subjectivity, so long as one considers artisanal artifacts so much neutral objectivity, this question will remain unanswered. Only when we ask how already gendered bodies effectively disembody themselves through so many acts of artifactual projection, how the world comes to incorporate what has thus been excorporated, how that world reciprocates by refashioning the gendered beings required by its imperatives, only then can we begin to grasp the meaning of the marriage between Calvin and his hammer.

"One is not born, but rather becomes, a woman."[42] I have no quarrel with this claim so long as it is understood that the mode of becoming in question is a sort of making, and that its product is a sort of artifact. To be born anatomically female is to be at best a potential woman, one who has been verbally assigned this status but whose reality is not yet fully manifest. Working their way inside her body, assuming the form of so many gender-specific habits, the reciprocative tasks performed by artifacts will in time afford this creature of Prometheus the normative shape that is recognizable as a real-ized woman. A bundle of indeterminate (but not altogether plastic) potentialities at birth, Susie may become a woman, or she may become a source of gender trouble. She will surely be the latter if, one day, she speaks Calvin's words in the first two frames of this comic, only to proclaim in the third, "Ah, it's great to be female."

But if Iris Young is a reliable guide, Susie is unlikely to surprise us in this way any time soon. Why is it, Young asks, that girls so often throw balls as they do? Why is it that so many throw with such cramped realization of the capacity of human arms to extend forcefully through lateral space? Young argues that girls in "contemporary advanced industrial, urban, and commercial society . . . often do not perceive themselves as capable of lifting and carrying heavy things, pushing, and shoving with significant force, pulling, squeezing, grasping, or twisting with force." This she takes to be an expression of their "inhibited intentionality, which simultaneously reaches toward a projected end with an 'I can' and withholds its full bodily commitment to that end in a self-imposed 'I cannot.'"[43] Such bridled intentionality, she concludes, expresses the concrete circumstances in which growing girls often find themselves. More likely to be discouraged from rough sports, to be deflected from constructing (as opposed to making use of) artisanal artifacts, to be scolded for getting their clothes dirty, to learn that their bodies are delicate objects designed to delight the eyes of others, only rarely will such beings project their embodied capacities without contradiction into the world. Reared so, Susie is unlikely to swing either a baseball bat or a hammer with might tempered by grace, and so perhaps we should not expect much from her in the way of gender trouble.

If Calvin revels in his hammer, it is not because he is male, but because he is becoming a man. The tone of Calvin's utterances in the second frame testifies to the reciprocational powers of an ordinary artisanal artifact. There the artifact demonstrates its animating capacities, its ability to afford Calvin an embodied sense of expansive potentiality, a dynamic sense extending well beyond any specific deed he might do with this particular hammer. Narrowly construed, that hammer is a metaphor for Calvin's arm and fist as well as their joint capacity to reach into the world. But that hammer reaches back into Calvin's body as this originally undifferentiated capacity acquires the form of articulated habit, marrying newly awakened muscles to a feel for what they may yet accomplish. Broadly construed, that hammer is a metaphor not simply for this articulated capacity but for all the artisanal artifacts that, collectively and in ways too complex to be exhaustively mapped, recursively participate in making men out of protomen and so, inasmuch as these are necessarily relational terms, women out of protowomen.

What my argument adds to that advanced by Young is an invitation to return to the things themselves. In support of her argument, Young cites a study in which Eric Erickson asked preadolescent boys and girls to fashion a possible movie set, using miniature replicas of things human and not. Typically, the girls invented indoor scenes, with high walls and enclosures, while the boys went for outdoor action settings. Properly taking exception to Erickson's psychoanalytic explanation, Young writes: "If girls do tend to project an enclosed space and boys to project an open and outwardly directed space, it is far more plausible to regard this as a reflection of the way members of each sex live and move their bodies in space."[44] I agree. But indeterminate references to "space" can never substitute for painstaking explorations of the drab walls, locked doors, narrow hallways, shuttered windows, that transform space into so many claustrophobic places, choking off my mother's vision of what might have been, constricting Susie's muscles whenever she wonders whether she might someday learn how to throw like a boy.[45]

ix. Why Things Fall Apart

CONSIDER MY EYEGLASSES. THE LABOR PERFORMED BY THESE TWO CONCAVE PIECES OF plastic, artificial corneas held in place by twin metal arms, is the condition of my ability to see clearly and distinctly; yet, so long as unscratched and unsmudged, this artifact effectively disappears from view. My ophthalmologist tells me that my spectacles correct my nearsightedness. But, earlier this autumn, I showed Tobin how on a cloudless day its lenses can tease a blaze from a pile of dry leaves. Now, reduced to the indignity of bifocals, I have given my surrogate eyeballs to this flesh and blood Calvin, who has made it clear that they are first and foremost things with which to ignite little brush fires. So, what is this artifact *really*? A pair of corrective lenses, or a thing of incipient terror to our neighbors? It is, I submit, both and so neither.

Recently, I stumbled across a photograph, taken toward the turn of the century, of a one-room tenement flat in Brooklyn. Its Sicilian residents, just recently through customs at Ellis Island, would never think to ask the question put here to my eyeglasses. In the center of their apartment resides a long sheet of rough pine, fitted with legs; at one and the same time, that thing is a writing desk, a platform for a pedal-powered sewing machine, a cutting board, a kitchen table, and a resting place for weary elbows. To a self-respecting Cartesian, this scene must be an epistemological nightmare. To counter its jumble, he might insist that the essence of this apartment's centerpiece is dictated by its true function, which in turn is dictated by the intent of its manufacturer. But such impoverished functionalism only proves plausible so long as we decontextualize this thing by arbitrarily stipulating the exclusive authority of a single context. In response to this contention, our Cartesian might concede that artisanal artifacts are subject to multiple uses, but then go on to insist that this concession confirms what he really meant to say: what any given artifact is is a function of the subjective purposes ascribed to it by its various users. Shall we let him get away with this face-saving maneuver?

In the preceding pages, on several occasions but without elaboration, I criticized Elaine Scarry on the grounds that her rhetoric smells of residual Cartesianism. The radical epistemological potential implicit in her account of the dialectic of projection and reciprocation is sapped to the extent that her language, however unwittingly, suggests a sharper distinction between subject and object than she should prove willing to endorse. Should I uncritically appropriate that language, it will undermine my efforts to suggest that artisanal artifacts, like their "users," are essentially ambiguous creatures of the more or less materialized relations in which they participate, and that whatever meaningfulness they bear is an articulation *of* those relations. To affirm this is not to stand Descartes on his head. It is not to claim that the meaning of an artifact is present within the thing-in-itself (as opposed to within the solipsistic consciousness). To locate meaning in either subject or object is to take for granted the adequacy of this dualism, and then to read this hypostatized bifurcation back into the medium of experience, where it does not belong. By the same token, to affirm the ambiguity of artisanal artifacts is not to disavow my earlier claims about the weightedness of artifacts, their dispositional capacity to open up certain possibilities, while closing down others. It is, however, to refuse to identify such weightiness with the essential nature of these things.

In order to emancipate Scarry's account of the projection/reciprocation dialectic from its partial imprisonment within the confines of an alien epistemology, which in turn will permit a richer appreciation of the nature of artifactual ambiguity, I propose an extension of Friedrich Nietzsche's critique of the Cartesian subject to the Cartesian object. In his *Genealogy of Morals*, Nietzsche insists that "there is no 'being' behind doing, effecting, becoming; 'the doer' is merely a fiction added to the deed—the deed is everything."[46] The ontology informing this claim contends that all existents exist in a condition of perpetual becoming, and that the interconnections each sustains with others are essential to the character of all. Nothing in the world has any intrinsic features, for all existents are thoroughly constituted by their interrelations with, and differences from, everything else. Every existent, in other words, is an event, and every event's distinguishing features are inseparable from the other events that condition and articulate those features. What an existent *is*, in sum, is the confluence of events in which "it" participates.[47]

Because all existents are so constituted, it is only through an act of suspect abstraction that any one "thing" is unambiguously distinguished from the other events to which "it" is now related. What Cartesians call an "object" is, therefore, a fiction invented to stand as a foundation, a ground, for what is then taken to be the essential attributes of this substantial being. Our felt compulsion to manufacture such fictions, Nietzsche proposes, is a product of grammatical structures that, in accordance with the logic of subject and predicate, impel us to speak not simply of effects and their configurations but also of "things" that bear such properties; we are seduced, that is, by "our grammatical custom that adds a doer to every deed." But if the Cartesian object is merely "the sum of its effects," then there is no good reason to posit its separate existence as the antecedent substance that produces those same effects. "The properties of a thing are effects on other 'things': if one removes other 'things,' then a thing has no properties, i.e., there is no thing without other things, i.e., there is no 'thing-in-itself.'"[48]

To illustrate this argument, Nietzsche offers the example of lightning. The Cartesian understanding is implicit in the claim: "Look at the lightning flash." On this account, lightning is taken to be the independent substance that generates the flash qua effect. To oppose this construction, Nietzsche might (but does not) write: "Look at the lightning-flash," where the hyphen signifies not the discrimination of cause from effect, but rather a concurrent configuration of events within which no one substantial thing can be unambiguously discriminated from the other as substance or attribute, cause or effect. We imagine that we can engage in such discrimination only because we abstract from this myriad of events those that happen to concern us at present, and we then treat the sum of those effects as the substantial source of the property that is the flash. But, Nietzsche insists, there is no lightning behind the flash; "it" is that flash, that mobile configuration of effects, nothing more and nothing less. "The popular mind in fact doubles the deed: it posits the same event first as cause and then a second time as its effect. Scientists do no better when they say 'force moves,' 'force causes,' and the like—all its coolness, its freedom from emotion notwithstanding, our entire science still lies under the misleading influence of language and has not disposed of that little changeling, the 'subject' (the atom, for example, is such a changeling, as is the Kantian 'thing-in-itself')."[49]

Nietzsche's argument suggests that there is no good reason to assume the existence of a unified subject who, as determinate substance, somehow grounds the various roles "I" play (father to sons, son to father, teacher to students of politics, student to teacher of cello). Why, then, should we think better of artisanal artifacts? What Descartes calls the "object" is an abstraction torn from a heterogeneous field of human and nonhuman events, events whose dynamic linkages cannot be exhaustively specified in advance of their occurrence. Because the powers embedded within each artifactual knot initiate so many ripples bearing "its" being here and there, we must look beyond its apparently fixed margins in order to determine what it really is. And yet the language of "here and there" will mislead unless we recall that every artifact also speaks the language of "now and then." As beings whose effects are dispersed in space and time, artisanal artifacts happen; and, as such, they are suitable subjects of biographical inquiry. When done poorly, the artifact's appearance of self-sufficient identity will be confused with its complete story. When done well, its tale will prove as problematic as are those of the human artifacts in whose lives "it" is implicated.

After ten years of fighting and an equal number en route back home, the naked body of Odysseus is finally tossed onto the shores of Skhería, home of the Phaiákians. His first deed is to fashion the creature whose work will restore him to some semblance of humanity:

> Here Odysseus
> tunnelled, and raked together with his hands
> a wide bed—for a fall of leaves were there,
> enough to save two men or maybe three
> on a winter night, a night of bitter cold.
> Odysseus' heart laughed when he saw his leaf-bed,
> and down he lay, heaping more leaves above him.[50]

Why exactly does Odysseus laugh? In part, no doubt, he laughs at this artifact's promise to assume a burden his skin cannot. But he also laughs, I suspect, at this leaf-bed's refusal to unambiguously identify itself as either a thing of nature or a thing of artifice; and if that is so, then Odysseus also laughs at Aristotle. In his *Physics*, Aristotle argues that artisanal artifacts are inferior to the natural materials of which they are made. To defend this claim, he argues that in nature the union of form and matter is sufficiently tight such that the telos immanent within any given thing can only generate more of the same. Thus, when an olive tree gives birth to new growth, what is produced is always more olive tree, never a cinnamon-flavored toothpick. In contrast, when something's telos is imposed on it by an external source, as in artisanal artifacts, the union of form and matter is considerably looser, and so manufactured things can become many things and serve many purposes.[51] The artisanal artifact's inherent instability is for Aristotle the mark of its ontological deficiency. Wily Odysseus, however, is unpersuaded. Although unable to articulate these conclusions, he "knows" that ambiguity is a mark of all existents whose being is determined not by essence but by relation; that the hypostatized distinction Aristotle draws between natural and artificial is a philosopher's conceit; and that to fashion a leaf-bed from a bed of leaves is not to violate the latter's nature but to actualize one of the many possibilities it bears as so much latent potential.

Odysseus recovers his specifically human senses when he hears several young women playing with a ball not far away. "He pushed aside the bushes, breaking off / with his great hand a single branch of olive, / whose leaves might shield him in his nakedness" (6:137-39). A moment ago, this "branch" was a thing of nature. As such, it was caught up within a complex of moving events stretching from soil, to root tips, to uppermost leaves, to rays of the sun, a complex in which it was at one and the same time active and acted on. Now, torn from that context, imported within a new web of relations, what is this thing? Although dislocated, it has not altered its appearance, and so, perhaps, we should call it a tree fragment. But to call it that is to neglect the qualitative transformation effected when it became a "shield," an artifact whose work will secure Odysseus against the sort of humiliation felt by Primo Levy when, like Adam, his hands were his only attire.

Whatever we now call it, once Odysseus dons the tunic and cloak given him by the young princess, Nausikaa, he will toss aside his arboreal garb, no doubt forgetting to thank it for the service it performed without complaint. What is it now? Is it now an article of discarded clothing, destined for the Akhaian equivalent of Goodwill? Or is it a thing of nature once more? What might it have become had Odysseus, showing it the gratitude it deserved, planted it in memory of his lost comrades? Once grown, would this be a tree, a monument, or perhaps a clothes-tree? But the heedless Odysseus did not plant it and so, years from now, perhaps a shepherd will fashion this branch into a miniature bow, given to his infant boy as a toy. Still later, infirm with age, perhaps it will become fuel for a roaring fire ignited in sacrifice to Zeus. What will it then be, as its smoke rises to temper the wrath still felt by the divine patriarch toward Prometheus's creatures? Any attempt to answer this question unequivocally, to state definitively what this thing is, will falter on the fact that its biography is as internally complex as that of the man who "wore" it years ago.

If artisanal artifacts are indeed determinate materializations of so much spatial and temporal ambiguity, why is it that we do not live in a world whose "objects" constantly dissolve into the relations by which they are constituted? To answer this question, we must first note that the mutability of artifacts, their capacity to be this or that sort of thing, is not altogether unlimited. The possibilities of artifactual identity are always constrained, to a greater or lesser degree, by the structure of relations in which any given thing is presently implicated. Unlike the god of the *Tanakh*, we never create *ex nihilo*, and so meaning is never fashioned out of a condition of primordial chaos. The world and its things are always already formed, and so meaning making is always a matter of re-formation. Those things may be polysemic (meaning several things at once), or they may be ambiguous (intimating several different meanings without specifying any one clearly), but they are never entirely nonsensical (radically devoid of significance).

How any given artisanal artifact enters the web of intelligibility turns in large measure on how it is interwoven with the materialized artifact that is language. As I shall argue more fully in part 2, out of the heterogeneous array of concrete existents moving through space and time, some things are discriminated while others fall away. The world is mapped out by drawing boundaries around different sorts of things, by discursively severing the connections between this sort of thing and that. Such mapping typically assumes the form of a system of categories, of kinds; and each system is in an important sense arbitrary. Consider, for example, Slavenka Drakulić's account of the fundamental categories to which common artisanal artifacts were assigned by many eastern European women living under communism:

> Collecting principles, so to speak, depend greatly on different kinds of experiences in different communist countries, or—better still—on different *degrees* of poverty. But they basically can be divided into several categories: *general objects* (old cloth, shoes, household appliances and furniture, kitchen pots, baskets, brooms, newspapers); *objects that normal people in normal countries usually throw away* (otherwise known as packaging—bottles, jars, cups, cans, stoppers and corks, rubber bands, plastic bags, gift wrappings, cardboard boxes); *foreign objects* (anything from a foreign country, from a pencil or notebook to a dress, from chewing gum to a candy wrapper); and *objects that might disappear* (a very broad and varying category, from flour, coffee, and eggs to detergent, soap, pantyhose, screws, nails, rope, wire, perfumes, notepaper or books).[52]

Categories, these examples suggest, are never dictated by the putative nature of the things themselves. What those things are is a function of the groups to which they belong, and those groups are themselves so many responses to the imperatives of a more comprehensive web of power relations—in this case, the relations distributing the facts of impoverishment in this way rather than that.

The nouns denoting such general kinds do not, like so many xeroxed duplicates made of words, simply re-present the things to which they refer. Rather, they participate in instituting and sustaining the reality of which they speak. As a rule, categorical nouns exercise this sort of performative power by normatively prescribing the sorts of relations into which an artifact can and cannot legitimately enter. To see this in its most basic form, perhaps for the last time, consider my hammer. The term "hammer" effectively indicates the link between this artisanal artifact and a host of other beings, human and non-human. To call this thing a "hammer" is to situate it, as a member, within the more comprehensive class of tools. As such, like other tools, its generic purpose is to participate in the making and unmaking of other artisanal artifacts. Note, finally, that the naming of this thing effectively specifies the sort of relationship it is to sustain with the human body. It is to be picked up with one's hands rather than one's teeth, at this end rather than that, and it is to be swung in an arc rather than, say, jabbed straight ahead.

The relational reality called into play by the term "hammer" is quite unlike that invoked were I to call this "same" thing a "club." Although its physical structure changes not a whit, such recategorization is sufficient to alter its nature. This latter designation, establishing this thing's membership in the more comprehensive class of "weapons," specifies that its nonhuman kin(d) include things like sawed-off shotguns and bayonets, and it suggests that the conduct "it" facilitates are so many "assaults." Granted, this alternative designation does not in and of itself dictate a different relationship to my body; most likely, I will swing a club just as I do a hammer. But it certainly implies a different relationship to other human bodies, who, with good reason, will prove more circumspect in the company of a club than a hammer. To call this thing a club is, in sum, to state our reasonable expectation that it will acquire a biography distinctly unlike that befitting a hammer.

For a less straightforward example of the performative character of categorical nouns, think of the pocket watch my father gave me on the day I graduated from Oberlin College. Originally purchased by those who built Atlantic City's Traymore Hotel, given to the supervisor of that construction on the day its doors first opened, the watch has on the inside surface of its back cover, etched by some unknown artisan, an exquisitely detailed depiction of the Traymore's exterior, along with an inscription reading: "From the boys, March 15, 1915." But what exactly is this thing? Since it was purchased, shall I call it a "commodity"? If I do so, I will thereby stipulate certain of its properties as well as designate the sorts of connections into which it can enter with other human and nonhuman artifacts. If it is in fact a commodity, its identity is not in any constitutive sense bound up with that of its maker; it is alienable in the sense that it may be freely exchanged between persons; and, as a participant in a market economy, it is homogeneous with all other commodities in the sense that its value is determined by its price. But if I am to be true to those who purchased it, should I not call this thing a "gift"? And if it is that sort of thing, then does it not possess properties quite unlike those definitive of a commodity? A gift is inalienable in the sense that, at least in principle, it is removed from the circulations of a market economy, and its qualitative value cannot be pried loose from the relationship it served to cement between givers and receiver. This gift's fertility, its capacity to breed human relations, was dramatically demonstrated when it was given to me not as a generic gift but as the particular sort of gift that is an heirloom, thereby consolidating my indebtedness to my father. Were I someday to repudiate this debt, were I to retransform this gift into a commodity, it would thereby become an accomplice to a violation. But that I will not do. Well aware of its power to fashion a complex of dependencies, I will in time tie this intergenerational knot round the heart of my elder son.

The categorical indeterminacy displayed by hammer and watch can, incidentally, be a property of human artifacts as well. An obvious example is the traffic in women. Seized from the Trojans, Briseis is now a part of Achilles' booty. As such, and much like the female calculators whose intelligent skills were expropriated and then relocated within much brighter computers, Briseis has inched considerably closer to the uncertain line separating human from nonhuman artifacts. We want to say that Briseis is still really a person, and we want to claim that we should not do to her things we find morally unproblematic when done to artifacts (e.g., discard them when they outlive their utility). To shore up this contention, no doubt, the humanists among us will affirm the essential or natural character of the distinction between human and nonhuman. But I cannot make that move. Fabrication of the category of human being is an operation that can never wholly hide either the conventionality of its construction or the permeability of the boundaries it posits. In addition to the categories "human" and "nonhuman," we must add those of "more or less human" as well as "more or less nonhuman." And we must admit that what today we label a person or a thing can slide back and forth between these poles tomorrow. Just as artisanal artifacts can sometimes appear as automatons in the literal sense of the term, as beings capable of spontaneous motion, so too can persons sometimes appear as automatons in another sense of the term, as things capable of nothing other than mechanistic motion.

First owned by her father, later confiscated by Achilles, finally appropriated by Agamemnon, Briseis is now a slave. Is a slave *really* a human being? Or is a slave *really* just one of Aristotle's animate tools? Or is the slave an ambiguous artifact whose identity is the subject of a contest between those who would define it in very different ways? What, correlatively, is Briseis's womb? Is it an essential part of her being as a woman, and is that essence violated when it is appropriated for another's use? Or is her womb a tool available for efficient use as she sees fit? Or is her womb an ambiguous artifact whose identity may become the subject of conflict between those who would define her exclusively in terms of her child-bearing capacities and those who would emancipate her from that designation? What, correlatively, is Briseis's fetus just prior to its abortion? Is it a thing to be disposed of as one would an unwanted toy? Or is it a person, potential or otherwise, who is entitled to the burial rituals we ordinarily reserve for those already born? Or is her fetus an ambiguous artifact whose final disposition will say much about the current balance of power between those who would constrict and those who would expand the freedom of Briseis and her ilk?

Language, to recapitulate, is constitutive of reality in the sense that to name some thing is to specify the sorts of relations into which it can enter as well as the sort of life it can be expected to live. But to say that language is performative in this way is not to say that language is the exclusive *cause* of its capacity to enter into such relations. We must always remember that artisanal artifacts are not merely so many solidified chunks of discourse. I will come back to this point in part 2. For now, it will suffice to note that to designate an artisanal artifact an instance of some broader class is to make a general statement about what this thing can be expected to *do*. Granted, to call something a hammer is not to indicate the particular ends for which it must be employed; but it is to specify the kind of conduct appropriate to a thing of this sort. If you use the heel of your shoe to bang in a nail, then I suppose for the time being your shoe is a hammer. But if you use a feather or a Waterford crystal goblet for the same task, things will not go well. Linguistic specification of some thing, in other words, attributes to it characteristic capacities, and these capacities in turn constrain what can and cannot be called this sort of thing. A stick of butter carved in the likeness of a hammer may no longer be a stick of butter, but neither is it a hammer, and no amount of talk will make it so.

As a rule, we do not happen upon human or nonhuman artifacts wavering uncertainly between distinctly different categories. For the most part, artisanal artifacts are married to human artifacts within familiar situations, situations whose imperatives dictate what the former are to be called and how they are to relate to the latter. As such, artisanal artifacts customarily acquire a taken-for-granted status analogous to the "things" of nature, and so appear to invite their own construction in the terms furnished by the Cartesian paradigm of use. That construction, however, says little about the true nature of these things, but much about their stabilization within so many streams of routinized conduct. To be taken in by that appearance of facticity, to borrow a neat metaphor from Nicholas Thomas, is to fall prey to a sort of optical illusion; it is, he explains, to "take the 'concrete and palpable' presence of a thing to attest to the reality of that which we have made it signify."[53]

Every once in a while, however, artisanal artifacts proclaim their fictionality, their status as so many made-up things. Sometimes, like Cartesian egos no longer able to sustain their clear and distinct identities, they do so by falling apart. When the stem of the toothbrush I have been using for months snaps in half, it announces its status as a made thing and so poses questions concerning the circumstances of its creation. To try to reattach one end to the other, using tape or glue, is to come to understand more than I care to know about the distinctive properties of hardened plastic. By violating my familiar routine, it has told me more about itself than I knew when it habitually disappeared within experience.

Another way to fashion a question from an artifact is to subject it to the intellectual equivalent of artisanal breakdown. Such, I think, is an apt way to characterize the project of genealogical inquiry. Consider the biography of the obstetric forceps. This artifact was perhaps the most diabolically clever of the weapons deployed by early modern physicians in France and England in their ongoing struggle to disempower the company of midwives. By custom, midwives were not permitted to use nonhuman instruments as part of their practice. Artifactually mimicking the shape assumed by a midwife's extended arms and slightly cupped hands, each newly fashioned pair of forceps served as a surrogate not for the hands of male surgeons but for the skills they lacked. In 1634, sensing that their days were numbered, English midwives petitioned the bishop of London: The work of a physician "and the work belonging to midwives are contrary one to the other, for he delivers none without the use of instruments by extraordinary violence in desperate occasions, which women never practiced nor desired, for they have neither parts nor hands for that art."[54] This conflict came to an end only when this artifact was securely established as a specialized tool monopolized by members of the healing profession rather than as a ploy designed to disqualify a community of lay experts. Only when this thing became fact rather than fiction could attention shift from its expropriative work to that of its "technical" service as a Cartesian means. Only then could the operative question in any delivery gone awry be whether the obstetrician at its far end was competent in his use of an artifact itself deemed innocent.

To see how the workings of power cover their tracks by dictating what is to be taken as fact and what is to be dismissed as fiction is to recover some sense of an artifact's specifically political qualities. Consider the boilers that powered steamboats up and down the Mississippi River during the first half of the nineteenth century.[55] Between 1816 and 1852, over five thousand persons were either killed or injured in steamboat explosions. Under pressure, the federal government began to ask whether these complex artifacts should be subjected to safety regulations. Steamboat owners, not surprisingly, resisted this encroachment on their commercial autonomy. The outcome of this struggle was etched into the structure of this artifact when, after consulting with steamboat manufacturers and government representatives, the American Society of Mechanical Engineers codified uniform standards. Henceforth, to be a boiler worthy of the name, an artifact of this ilk had to be made of materials tempered this way rather than that, incorporate walls of a certain thickness, be equipped with release valves at specified locations and so on. So constructed, this artifact effectively articulated the balance of forces between political opponents. In time, successfully masking its reality as the artifactual embodiment of a negotiated truce, it disappeared within the domain of the taken for granted.

If it is true that at least some artisanal artifacts give expression to the configuration of relations affording them determinate shape, then in an important sense they must be immanently political; and, at least in principle, it should be possible to "read" them in a way that discloses that political content. That, in any event, is one of the premises of part 3's inquiry into three specific artifacts. Genealogical inquiry aimed at making visible the conflict contained within apparently self-contained and self-evident artifacts is well-advised, I would argue, to take the words of that closet Nietzschean, William James, as its motto:

> What really *exists* is not things made but things in the making. Once made, they are dead, and an infinite number of alternative conceptual decompositions can be used in defining them. But put yourself *in the making* by a stroke of intuitive sympathy with the thing and, the whole range of possible decompositions coming at once into your possession, you are no longer troubled with the question which of them is the more absolutely real. Reality *falls* in passing into conceptual analysis; it *mounts* in living its own undivided life—it buds and bourgeons, changes and creates. . . . Philosophy should seek this kind of living understanding of the movement of reality, not follow science in vainly patching together fragments of its dead results.[56]

Perhaps the simplest but in some ways the most profound way to be true to James, to reveal the art in artifact, is to ask: What *is* this thing? Nietzsche once wrote: "The lordly right of bestowing names is such that one would almost be justified in seeing the origin of language itself as an expression of the ruler's power. They say 'This is this or that'; they seal off each thing or action with a sound and thereby take symbolic possession of it."[57] If the birth of a new artifact is accompanied by labor pains stemming, at least in part, from the struggle to name it, then to turn that name into a question is to take the first step toward transforming a Cartesian object into a political subject.

x. *Becoming Clytaemestra*

To round off part 1's discussion of artisanal artifacts, and to do so in a way that gestures toward part 2's more detailed discussion of the artifact of gender, let me return to my starting point: the web. On Aeschylus's telling, in order to propitiate Artemis, Agamemnon must sacrifice his daughter, Iphigeneia. Only then will the winds stir, bringing to life the ships becalmed in the harbor at Aulis. Only then can Agamemnon begin his expedition to Troy, and so make good on his vow to restore Helen to his brother, Menelaus.

When the triumphant Agamemnon finally returns to his home at Argos, he is met by Iphigeneia's mother, Clytaemestra. For more than ten years, the horror of her daughter's blood washing over the altar at Aulis has eaten away at her soul. Luring her husband into the bath, Clytaemestra entangles the naked Agamemnon in a robe and stabs him three times. "Caught in this spider's web,"[58] he dies. To the bewildered chorus, Clytaemestra offers this account of her deed:

> That he might not escape nor beat aside his death,
> as fishermen cast their huge circling nets, I spread
> deadly abundance of rich robes, and caught him fast.
> I struck him twice. In two great cries of agony
> he buckled at the knees and fell. When he was down
> I struck him the third blow, in thanks and reverence
> to Zeus the lord of dead men underneath the ground.
> Thus he went down, and the life struggled out of him;
> and as he died he spattered me with the dark red
> and violent driven rain of bitter savored blood
> to make me glad, as gardens stand among the showers
> of God in glory at the birthtime of the buds. (*Agamemnon*: 1381-92)

Draining the vital fluids from her prey, bathing in Agamemnon's polluted blood, Clytaemestra recovers the life that was snatched from her on the day Iphigeneia became a corpse.

Years later, caught up within the spiral of violence consuming his kin, Agamemnon's son, Orestes, slays Clytaemestra. To defend what he has done, Orestes reminds the chorus of his father's death at the hands of his mother. Sensing that words are inadequate to do justice to his cause, Orestes holds high above his head the blood-stained robe, the web, with which Clytaemestra entrapped her husband:

> And this thing: what shall I call it and be right, in all
> eloquence? Trap for an animal or winding sheet
> for dead man? Or bath curtain? Since it is a net,
> robe you could call it, to entangle a man's feet.
> Some highwayman might own a thing like this, to catch
> the wayfarer and rob him of his money and
> so make a living. With a treacherous thing like this
> he could take many victims and go warm within.
> (*The Libation Bearers*: 997-1004)

This quotation is a puzzle. On the face of it, we would expect Orestes to exhibit this damning piece of physical evidence, secure in the knowledge that his audience will find its self-contained significance incontestable. What he sets before these terrified old men is, after all, simply a robe caked with dried blood. Regardless of how it is employed, we Cartesians are inclined to say, it remains the same object. If it changes over time, that is only because the subjective intentions of its users differ. Yet if matters are indeed quite so simple, then what are to we to make of Orestes' question: "And this thing: what shall I call it and be right, in all eloquence?"

What Orestes grasps, I think, is that there is no such thing as the thing-in-itself. To ask what this thing is is not to ask the epistemologist's question concerning the adequacy of idea to object, of name to thing, of definition to inherent properties. Rather, it is to ask how this thing, antecedent to any discrimination of subject from object, is caught up within a web of relations forever in the midst of being rewoven. This thing, Orestes seems to contend, is what it does in the affairs in which it is implicated. That, though, is not to say that it is what it is used for. Such a Cartesian formulation, encouraging us to believe that this thing remains self-identical through time, fails to accommodate Orestes' apparent conviction that "it" really becomes one thing after another as it moves from one context to another. This thing was once used to ward off the chill of night, but that does not make it a coat. This thing might have been used to cover Clytaemestra's nakedness when her body was lowered into the ground, but that would not make it a shroud. This thing was in fact used to entangle the feet of an unsuspecting Agamemnon, but that does not make it a weapon.

It is Cassandra, not surprisingly, who most dramatically recognizes the sense of Orestes' question. Torn from her home in Troy, forcibly removed to Argos, she prophetically envisions Agamemnon's death. As a specter of Clytaemestra appears before her, she cries out:

What is that thing that shows?
Is it some net of death?
Or is the trap the woman there, the murderess?
(*Agamemnon*: 1114-16)

Here, Orestes' uncertainty concerning the nature of the murderous artifact finds its correlate in Cassandra's uncertainty concerning the identity of the murderous agent. Just what is the trap of which Cassandra speaks? Is it the robe, or is it Clytaemestra? To select one as opposed to the other is to distinguish discursively what, within the thick of experience, is altogether tangled; the trap is a relational whole whose parts can be distinguished for analytic purposes, but that never exist *as* so many discrete entities. To feel obliged to answer Cassandra's question is, in short, to fall prey to an ailment for which Nietzsche is the appropriate physician.

There is still more sense to Cassandra's vision. When Cassandra finds it impossible to solve this conundrum, she unwittingly acknowledges one of the more disconcerting implications of the projection/reciprocation dialectic. That dialectic suggests that the world of artisanal artifacts is in an important sense human bodies writ large, and that bodies in turn are so many worlds of artifice writ small. To the extent that this is so, as I suggested earlier, all efforts to draw unambiguous lines of demarcation between animate and inanimate, inside and outside, human and nonhuman, must prove suspect. A sort of kinship thus joins matters a Cartesian must consider mutually exclusive if he is to remain assured of his own autonomy vis à vis the world of objects. If, however, what the Cartesian considers acting *on* the world is in fact a matter of acting *in* the world, and if the fruits of such action are reincorporated with*in* the agent, then the miscegenation of subject and object is unavoidable. Like that between races, such crossbreeding provokes anxiety, and that anxiety typically generates efforts to shore up the crumbling wall separating this from that. Yet when Cassandra stares wildly at the ghost of Clytaemestra, when she asks "What can I call her and be right?" (*Agamemnon*: 1232), she is compelled to admit that this wall cannot be repaired.

The curse of Cassandra, imposed by Apollo after she spurned his sexual offensive, is to speak the truth but never to be believed. Seeing things ordinarily rendered invisible by the world's taken-for-grantedness, Cassandra watches as the lines separating maker from made, person from thing, dissolve into so many now intersecting, now diverging, relational waves. The uncertain shapes she spies within these mobile complexes are properly labeled *daemons*, marginal creatures, shadowy beings, suspended somewhere between order and chaos, sanity and madness. Those who, like Apollo, have a vested interest in maintaining the current regime of power must check these unsettling creatures; for their appearance reveals the fictionality of the factual, and that is a truth that cannot help but derange the body politic.

Let us leave Cassandra's perplexity for a moment and return to that of Orestes. In an age given to indiscriminate extension of the metaphor of the text, at least within the academy, perhaps it is important to recall that Orestes' struggle to find a linguistic artifact suitable to the thing he holds aloft is not identical to the struggle of Clytaemestra when she casts about for an artisanal artifact suitable for skewering her husband. Although the "robe" may be called a garment, a weapon, a burial shroud, or whatever, the fact of its tangibility means that its participation in human affairs is constrained in ways words are not. The distinguishing physical properties of any given artisanal artifact, remember, open up certain relational possibilities while closing down others. No matter how hard she might try, Clytaemestra will be hard pressed to slit Agamemnon's throat with this robe. As she sensibly recognizes, some other sort of artifact—preferably one made of metal—is required for that end. The words constitutive of any given language, by way of contrast, are far more malleable. So long as I can persuade you to come along, at least in principle, I can associate any meaning with the sound made by my vocal apparatus when I say "robe." Granted, this thing may resist its relocation from one discursive category to another by virtue of the conventional sense-making web in which it is caught; but such resistance is not of the same sort the robe displays when, for example, Orestes tries to persuade it to stand up on its own. When different kinds of materialized artifacts combine in different ways, different sorts of meaning are intimated. One of the qualities distinguishing the artisanal artifact Orestes brandishes from the linguistic artifacts he speaks is the way each appeals to the senses.[59] Although tangible robe and intangible words are indissolubly confused within this web of circumstance, for analytic purposes we can unravel its strands in order to show how each artifact appeals, first and foremost, to a different embodied sense. To state the obvious, the robe addresses itself to our eyes, while Orestes' words appeal to our ears. To see why this is a difference that makes a difference, consider the relation of each to temporality. The meaningfulness of the words Orestes speaks is a synthetic reality unfolding over time. Their intelligibility, like that of a melody, is inseparable from the duration separating first from last; each word must effectively disappear, even though it is at one and the same time retained in memory, in order to make room for its successor. Were Orestes to speak all of his words simultaneously, the chorus would hear only mush. The robe, however, need not make way for some other artisanal artifact in order to be significantly apprehended. It is seen in a flash, just as are all other things occupying the foreground of this field of vision. Whereas all other senses construct their syntheses out of things in the making, the eyes immediately grasp many things as coexistent parts of a single whole. Granted, the seeing of some thing may extend through time; but that duration is not intrinsic to the intelligibility of what is seen. As such, the sense of sight is the phenomenological condition of the significant reality we call the present.

The robe's participation in the making of sense cannot be exhausted in words because, to introduce a term I will make much of in part 2, it is a matter of "feeling," and that is so in at least two senses of the term. First, as a thing of texture, of color, of weight, of smell, it bears meanings irreducible to the propositional; or, perhaps better, it opens up possibilities of perceptual discrimination that remain beyond the range of available linguistic articulation. If our senses are sufficiently acute, we may be able to sniff out the odor of Agamemnon's body lingering within the folds of this robe, and that smell will be inseparable from how this thing is significant. If asked, we will be hard pressed to provide an adequate description of just what that odor is. No doubt, we will resort to clumsy analogies (the robe smells like Agamemnon's sun-baked skin, which in turn smells like a musty leather boot), knowing full well that no verbal account will quite do justice to how this artifact is sensibly incorporated by and within the sense-making apparati of our bodies.

The robe is a matter of feeling in a second sense as well. Were Orestes hidden behind a screen while addressing us, the robe would become meaningful via his words alone. But he is not hidden, and so we see the encrusted blood saturating its sleeves. It is far too intellectualized to say that those stains make sense to us because they stand as meaningful symbols, or even visible reminders, of Agamemnon's death. It is closer to the mark to say that they themselves are profoundly horrible. "Dip it and dip it again, the smear of blood conspires / with time to spoil the beauty of this precious thing" (*The Libation Bearers*: 1012-13). The feeling of horror, our visceral response to what we see right now, is evoked by the constellation of parts making up this lived whole. That feeling is neither an objective trait of the robe nor a subjective emotion adventitiously added to it by human witnesses. It is a quality *of* this situation, not of one of its parts isolated from the others. When those qualities are afforded discursive articulation, granted, they acquire a measure of definition otherwise lacking. But to think that such articulation is the condition of their existence is to reductively identify the body's complex of sense-making capacities with its organ of conception.

To say that the feeling of horror is evoked by, and is an integral part of, this situation is not to say that all assembled grasp it in the same way. To anticipate another argument of part 2, consider how the artifact of gender enters into the sense of this scene. Should we conclude that because the women of Argos say not a thing at this moment, because they only weep, the robe is meaningless to them? Should we conclude that because the chorus of elderly men chatters on incessantly in the face of this thing, it is the collective monopolist of meaning? Or should we conclude that the wordlessness of these women articulates their recognition that the awfulness of this spectacle must remain in the realm of the inexpressible if it is to be what it truly is? Correlatively, should we not take the men's prattle as the mark of their inability to grasp the dilemma that puzzles Cassandra and Orestes alike, of their desperate desire to name this thing and so vanquish its terror?

Part of the horror occasioned by the evidence Orestes exhibits can be understood in terms of its relationship to the body's diverse organs of sense making. Another part can be understood in terms of its violation of the projection/ reciprocation dialectic, as that dialectic pertains to this sort of thing. In his hands, Orestes now clutches something akin to a category mistake. This thing we call a "robe." So named, it is the sort of artifact that is to protect a body from cold; the organization of its parts responds and testifies to the vulnerability of the thin membrane separating what is within a human body from what is without. As a member of the larger class of things so designed, it participates in a moral economy, an economy of things concerned with caring for embodied human beings. But the thing Orestes displays is a thing that has refused to abide by its name, to live the sort of biography we have come to expect of this kind of thing. Violating the solicitude stitched into its seams, serving as an accomplice to a crime, it has become a weapon. So labeled, defined by its membership within a very different company of artifacts, it is now associated, not with the knife used by a surgeon to remove a painful lesion, but with the knife used to pierce an enemy's heart. Clytaemestra's dramatic revelation of this thing's referential instability does more than merely unsettle our sense of what it is. Recall that the identity of an artisanal artifact is never self-contained; what it is can only be understood through reference to the comprehensive network in which it participates. Accordingly, when this thing's identity is destabilized, the reverberations thereby set in motion ripple far beyond the crime scene. The panic felt by Orestes' audience indicates just how profoundly this thing now threatens the conventionality of a world in which women serve men without question. Were Clytaemestra, after Agamemnon's bath, to hold this artifact behind him so that he might more easily slip his arms into its sleeves, it would affirm its status as a contributor to a patriarchal world they inhabit in common. For it to do so, they need not see this thing in exactly the same way; no doubt, Clytaemestra appreciates the nuances of its textures and colors far better than does Agamemnon. Habitual coordination of their complementary movements is more than enough to ground this artifact in the unquestioned reality of ongoing domestic bliss.

But it is just this world that Clytaemestra has transgressed. Terrible in her "male strength of heart" (*Agamemnon*: 11), Clytaemestra has taken an ordinary artifact, and with this thing she has upended the regime of the patriarch. Doing so, she has refused to abide by the name "woman," and so by the biography rightfully anticipated of an artifact so named. That deed, Aeschylus tell us, is the culminating act in a series of refusals initiated long before. While Agamemnon was still fighting at Troy, Clytaemestra had already taken the first steps toward becoming an embodiment of gender trouble, a monster of sorts. What made her so was her ever more complete abandonment of the artisanal artifacts that make women women and, still more disturbing, her acquisition of the artisanal skills that make men men. Prometheus, recall, violated the order of things when he stole fire from the divine patriarch; and Zeus, you will recall, punished Prometheus's beneficiaries by creating the "damnable race of women." It is a violation of god and man, therefore, when a member of that race dares to appropriate the power of flame; and yet that is exactly what Clytaemestra has done. Learning that the signal announcing the fall of Troy has been spotted at last, she triumphantly explains that it was she who fashioned the relay of flame-bearing messengers running from Troy to Argos, a chain whose ultimate origins can be traced clear back to "Hephaestus, who cast forth the shining blaze from Ida" (*Agamemnon*: 281). If Clytaemestra is now a man trapped in a woman's body, it is because she commands a technology hitherto reserved to her superiors, and it is that mastery that dares her to speak in a domain previously reserved to real men: "Grave gentlemen of Argos assembled here, / I take no shame to speak aloud before you all" (*Agamemnon*: 855-56).

To restore the regime of the patriarch, Clytaemestra must be condemned for murdering her husband, and Orestes must be found blameless in the killing of his mother. But if that is to happen, yet another layer of artifice, yet another sort of materialized artifact, must be woven into the fabric of the world. Enter the parthenogenetic lawgiver, Athena:

> Then, since
> the burden of the case is here, and rests on me,
> I shall select judges of manslaughter, and swear
> them in, establish a court into all time.
> Litigants, call your witnesses, have ready your proofs
> as evidence under bond to keep this case secure.
> I will pick the finest of my citizens, and come
> back. They shall swear to make no judgment that is not
> just, and make clear where in this action truth lies.
> (*The Eumenides*: 481-89)

Were the old order still secure, in order for Orestes to secure absolution, it might be enough for him to wash his hands in the blood of a sacrificial pig. Were he to do so, his immaterial guilt would effectively materialize in his hands; and those hands, surrogates for his polluted soul, would be purified once bathed in the blood of a being who dies so that Orestes need not. But these traditional ways are insufficient to salvage a fundamentally diseased order. Hence, equipped with words alone, Athena fashions the internally complex institution we designate by the term "court," and with these words she invests that court with the authority to state judgments that will be accepted as final by all. That the fictionality of the court will remain hidden from all, that it will become a fact whose legitimacy is beyond question, is assured by ascribing its origins to a warrior-goddess of indeterminate gender, perhaps the most sublimely self-confirming artifact ever fashioned within the city of Athens.

"Did she do it or did she not?" asks Orestes. "My witness is this great robe" (*The Libation Bearers*: 1010-11). Now speaking not before the elders of Argos but before a jury of his peers, Orestes demands that this artifact testify in his defense. Removed from its familiar domestic context, thrust into the relational nexus that is the courtroom, this thing is now an instance of the sort called "evidence." Its previous identity, however, is not erased. Indeed, its intrinsic ambiguity, its status as a thing wavering uncertainly between the categories of weapon and garment, is the condition of its standing as evidence, as a thing whose meaning is to be contested according to the rules of courtroom procedure. The task of the trial, accordingly, is to overcome the equivocality of this thing by determining just what it shall be compelled to signify.

The purpose of this trial is to check the anarchy engendered by Clytaemestra. If that end is to be achieved, the jury must be persuaded that it is worse for a wife (Clytaemestra) to kill her husband (Agamemnon) than for a son (Orestes) to murder his mother (Clytaemestra). If that is to happen, Clytaemestra must be divested of her status as parent (which, at least in principle, will sap much of the sense from her grief for Iphigeneia). Apollo, the patron saint of attorneys everywhere, explains how this trick is to be pulled off:

> The mother is no parent of that which is called
> her child, but only nurse of the new-planted seed
> that grows. The parent is he who mounts. A stranger she
> preserves a stranger's seed, if no god interfere.
> (*The Eumenides*: 658-61)

Affirmation of the identity-conferring right of the father in the matter of reproduction successfully restores a world in which robes unproblematically respond to the vulnerabilities of naked bodies, and it does so by fashioning Clytaemestra into something akin to an artisanal artifact. When Clytaemestra demonstrated that she is a being capable of murder, she also showed that she is capable of being a man. But if she is a man, then by definition she must be fully human (in contradistinction to all things, including women, that are not). But if Clytaemestra is a man, then Orestes must be guilty of homicide, the deliberate killing of another human being. To nip this chain of reasoning in the bud, Clytaemestra must be objectified or, rather, depersonified. To do that, she must be defined not in terms of the deeds she already has or may yet perform, but rather in terms of her anatomy—more specifically, *as* her womb; and that womb must be construed not as a source of active agency but rather as a passive milieu, a Cartesian object, whose task is confined to housing what is truly active, the male seed. In sum, Clytaemestra must become what Euripides, in his *Orestes*, calls an *oikurema*, a being whose participation in the projection/reciprocation dialectic is restricted to the necessary work she does within the home, which in a way is her womb externalized.

Breaking the jurors' stalemate, Athena proclaims: "This is the ballot for Orestes I shall cast" (*The Eumenides*: 735). Acting not as a goddess but as a juror, not as the court's creator but as its creature, Athena now speaks *in the name of* the law. She votes, that is, as one installed in the midst of a chain of antecedently constituted conventions whose authority issues from the court's status as arti-fact rather than arti-fiction. Were this complex materialized artifact to call attention to itself as a made-up thing, were Cassandra to be permitted to tell what she knows, the law's authority could be no more than so much power propped up by terror. But because Cassandra has been silenced, the words Athena speaks in exonerating Orestes are sufficient to recreate a world in which wives respect rather than abuse the artifactual conditions of their husbands' well-being. The practices constitutive of patriarchy, transformed as a result of the collaborative efforts of Apollo and Athena, are thereby restitched into the seams of a culture that will now ask law to do the work once done by custom. The blood-stained robe, a vivid reminder of the pollution engendered when the natural order of things is treated as if it were merely conventional, can at last be banished from the everyday intercourse of men.

Notes

1. It appears that for many years professional students of spiders characterized the relationship between webs and their makers more or less in accordance with the Cartesian paradigm of use. In recent years, the limitations of this interpretation have become increasingly apparent. See "Crafty Signs Spun in Web Say to Prey, 'Open Sky,'" *New York Times*, 19 April 1994, 5(B).

2. Daniel Miller, *Material Culture and Mass Consumption* (Oxford: Basil Blackwell, 1987), 106.

3. Miller, *Material Culture*, 130. For a similar claim, see Elaine Scarry, *The Body in Pain* (New York: Oxford University Press, 1985): "Knowledge about the character of creating and created objects is at present in a state of conceptual infancy. Its illumination will require a richness of work far beyond the frame of any single study: like the activity of 'making,' the activity of 'understanding making' will be a collective rather than a solitary labor" (280).

4. Obviously, I do not mean to assert that the academy has produced no helpful analyses of the artisanal artifact. My work here would not be possible in the absence of that done by Daniel Miller, Don Ihde, Langdon Winner, Albert Borgmann, and others cited here and there throughout this text.

5. For my attempt to trace the undoing of the Thomistic synthesis, see *Politics/Sense/Experience: A Pragmatic Inquiry into the Promise of Democracy* (Ithaca, N.Y.: Cornell University Press, 1991), 68-86.

6. Although I will not argue the point here, it should be noted that I use the masculine pronoun to indicate what I hinted at in my preface. The Cartesian paradigm of use is, I believe, a specifically gendered discourse. For an argument to this effect, see Carolyn Merchant, *The Death of Nature* (San Francisco: Harper, 1990), *passim*.

7. René Descartes, *Discourse on Method*, trans. Donald Cress (Indianapolis: Hackett, 1980), 32.

8. For a wonderful account of the historical and conceptual interdependence between the Cartesian account of the self and contemporaneous technological innovations, especially the telescope and microscope, see Robert Romanyshyn, *Technology as Symptom and Dream* (New York: Routledge, 1989), 39-48.

9. Joseph Pitt, "The Autonomy of Technology," in *From Artifact to Habitat*, ed. Gayle Ormiston (Bethlehem: Lehigh University Press, 1990), 130. Claims of this sort have a long history. In 1556, in his *De Re Metallica*, the al-

chemist Agricola wrote: "It is not the metals which are to be blamed, but the evil passions of men which become inflamed and ignited; or it is due to the blind and impetuous desires of their minds." Quoted in Merchant, *The Death of Nature*, 38.

10. Quoted in Janine Morgall, *Technology Assessment: A Feminist Perspective* (Philadelphia: Temple University Press, 1993), 15.

11. As a rule, I avoid the term "technology" in this work. When it is employed, as in my subtitle, the term should be read in light of this paragraph's argument and hence ironically.

12. Emerson, quoted in Albert Borgmann, *Technology and the Character of Contemporary Life* (Chicago: University of Chicago Press, 1984), 58.

13. Jacques Ellul, *The Technological Society*, trans. John Wilkinson (New York: Knopf, 1976), 138.

14. Ellul, quoted in *Technology as a Human Affair*, ed. Larry Hickman (New York: McGraw-Hill, 1990), 343. With respect to the question of meaning, note in this same essay Ellul's intriguing but undeveloped claim to the following effect: "I feel that women are now far more capable than men of restoring a meaning to the world we live in, of restoring goals for living and possibilities for surviving in the technological world. Hence, the women's movements strike me as extraordinarily positive" (352). I suppose my efforts in this book might be read as an attempt to put some flesh on this statement's bare bones.

15. Hannah Arendt, *The Human Condition* (Chicago: University of Chicago Press, 1958), 204.

16. Scarry, *Body in Pain*, 306.

17. Primo Levy, *The Drowned and the Saved*, trans. Raymond Rosenthal (New York: Vintage, 1989), 114.

18. Leaving aside his untenable determinism and reductionism, Friedrich Engels gets something undeniably right when, in *The Origin of the Family, Private Property, and the State* (New York: International Publishers, 1942), he states: "According to the materialistic conception, the determining factor in history is, in the final instance, the production and reproduction of the immediate essentials of life. This, again, is of a twofold character. On the one side, the production of the means of existence, of articles of food and clothing, dwellings, and of the tools necessary for that production; on the other side, the production of human beings themselves, the propagation of the species" (5).

19. I acknowledge that not *all* things manufactured by human beings are equally well understood in these terms. The term "projection" is helpful in making sense of a general class of artifacts, a class I am tempted to call "useful," but which I will not because it is too resonant of Cartesianism. Rather than offer some formal specification of the conditions of membership in this class, I will instead indicate its domain by citing various examples, hoping that their family resemblances will suffice to indicate its general character. Be that

as it may, not particularly well understood in terms of projection are the artifacts we associate with play (e.g., a chess board and a jump rope). Likewise,
and although I find problematic the distinction drawn between "useful" and
"fine" arts, I also concede that artifacts conventionally associated with the latter (e.g., Leonardo da Vinci's *Mona Lisa* and Duke Ellington's *Harlem*) are not
terribly well understood as metaphorical projections of human body parts and
capacities. Incidentally, I also concede that as a rule the logic of projection will
not explain the empirical origins, or the actual intentions at work, in the creation of any given artifact. Alexander Graham Bell may well have been motivated to invent the telephone by an insatiable lust for fame, by a wish to secure
the praise of his mother, by an aimless penchant for technological bricolage.
Whatever the content of his desire, in functional and structural terms, the
telephone receiver is well understood by pointing to the analogy between the
transmitter in its mouthpiece and the voice box in my throat as well as that
between the speaker in its earpiece and the drum in my ear (note the reverse
metaphorical application). The categories employed here offer a way of fashioning sense from artifacts and the work they do; whether they also explain
the origins of some thing is a matter for investigation, not presupposition.

20. Scarry, *Body in Pain*, 38-39.

21. Karl Marx, *Capital*, vol. 1, trans. Ben Fowkes (New York: Vintage,
1977), 492-508.

22. Scarry, *Body in Pain*, 285, 289.

23. Scarry, *Body in Pain*, 256.

24. Scarry, *Body in Pain*, 284.

25. Maurice Merleau-Ponty, *Phenomenology of Perception*, trans. Colin
Smith (London: Routledge & Kegan Paul, 1962), 143. In her "Sexual Ideology
and Phenomenological Description," in *The Thinking Muse*, ed. Jeffner Allen
and Iris Marion Young (Bloomington: Indiana University Press, 1989), Judith
Butler argues that Merleau-Ponty's phenomenology is ideological in the sense
that it represents as universal and natural distinctively masculine conceptions
of subjectivity and sexuality. While I find Butler's argument persuasive, there
is no reason in principle why one cannot fold an account of gender specificity
into Merleau-Ponty's phenomenological account of embodied experience.

26. Perhaps this is the place to note the obvious: In many respects, Scarry's account of the projection/reciprocation dialectic closely parallels, and is in
large measure derivative of, Marx's account of dialectical materialism. To see
the connection, consider the opening sentences in the first of Marx's "Theses
on Feuerbach," in *The Marx-Engels Reader*, ed. Robert Tucker (New York:
Norton, 1978): "The chief aspect of all hitherto existing materialism—that of
Feuerbach included—is that the thing, reality, sensuousness, is conceived only
in the form of the object or of *contemplation*, but not as *human sensuous activity*, practice, not subjectively. Hence it happened that the *active* side, in contradistinction to materialism, was developed by idealism—but only abstractly,

since, of course, idealism does not know real, sensuous activity as such. Feuerbach wants sensuous objects, really distinct from the thought objects, but he does not conceive human activity itself as *objective* activity" (143).

27. For a fascinating argument to the effect that Descartes's notion of consciousness expresses his metaphorical appropriation of the camera obscura, and more particularly the sort of inverted visual representations made possible by this black box, see Lee Bailey, "Skull's Darkroom: The Camera Obscura and Subjectivity," in *Philosophy of Technology*, ed. Paul Durbin (Dordrecht: Kluwer Academic Publishers, 1989), 63-79.

28. Levy, *Drowned*, 119.

29. For a wonderful example of the social transformations effected by a technological invention, see Albert Borgmann's discussion of the displacement of the kitchen stove by central heating in his *Technology*, 41-42.

30. Arendt, *Human Condition*, 57-58. Arendt is on stronger ground when she writes:

> The term "public" signifies the world itself, in so far as it is common to all of us and distinguished from our privately owned place in it. This world, however, is not identical with the earth or with nature, as the limited space for the movement of men and the general condition of organic life. It is related, rather, to the human artifact, the fabrication of human hands, as well as to affairs which go on among those who inhabit the man-made world together. To live together in the world means essentially that a world of things is between those who have it in common, as a table is located between those who sit around it; the world, like every in-between, relates and separates men at the same time. (52)

31. For my purposes, it is not necessary to distinguish between ethical and political questions. My aim is to contest the claim that artisanal artifacts are inherently neutral, and for that purpose I need not work through this distinction. Recognition of the political and ethical standing of artisanal artifacts was implicit in the Greek homicide laws, fashioned by Draco, which included provision for the trial and expulsion of any artifact that unwittingly harmed those who live in its company. See Robert Bonner and Gertrude Smith, *The Administration of Justice from Homer to Aristotle*, vol. 1 (Chicago: University of Chicago Press, 1930), 63, n5. See Hans Jonas, *The Imperative of Responsibility* (Chicago: University of Chicago Press, 1984), for a careful exploration of the ethical and political dilemmas posed by various contemporary technologies. My analysis differs from that of Jonas in at least one significant way. He seems to believe that the segregation of technical from ethical issues, and hence the confinement of the latter to interhuman affairs, was tenable so long as the human capacity to engender artifactual interventions in the world was quite limited. On his account, accordingly, it is only within modernity that it becomes necessary to figure out how to incorporate material artifacts within ethical dis-

course. Given my account of the projection/reciprocation dialectic, I must contend that ethical and technical issues have always been essentially linked.

32. Don Ihde, *Existential Technics* (Albany: State University of New York Press, 1983), 56.

33. Marx, *Capital*, vol. 1, 492-93.

34. Marx, *Capital*, vol. 1, 501.

35. Leon Kass, "The Problem of Technology," in *Technology in the Western Political Tradition*, ed. Arthur Melzer, Jerry Weinberger, and Richard Zinman (Ithaca, N.Y.: Cornell University Press, 1993), 12-13.

36. Langdon Winner, *The Whale and the Reactor* (Chicago: University of Chicago Press, 1986), 52.

37. Iris Marion Young, "Humanism, Gynocentrism, and Feminist Politics," in *Throwing Like a Girl* (Bloomington: Indiana, 1990), 73-91.

38. See Judy Wajcman, *Feminism Confronts Technology* (University Park, Penn: Pennsylvania State University, 1991), 90.

39. Kathleen Kirby, *Indifferent Boundaries* (New York: Guilford, 1996), 19.

40. Ivan Illich begins to get at a similar notion when, in his *Gender* (New York: Pantheon, 1982), he writes: "The *domus*, not people, seems to be the subject of history, the basic social unit. The house, at once building and family, links men and women to their possessions, which relate them to each other. . . . Material life is created by the home, the main acting subject, through its men and women. . . . Therefore, *to be at home* must mean something different for the two of them" (117, 121).

41. Here I do not mean to suggest that expropriation and commodification of tasks once conducted within the household, as well as the mechanization of the tasks that remained behind, lightened the burden on housewives. For a nice analysis of this issue, see Ruth Schwartz Cowan, *More Work for Mother* (New York: Basic Books, 1983). Her basic argument suggests that although industrialization reorganized the form and content of housework, it did not reduce the amount of work required to maintain a household:

> Some of the work that was eliminated by modernization was work that men and children—not women—had previously done: carrying coal, carrying water, chopping wood, removing ashes, stoking furnaces, cleaning lamps, beating rugs. Some of the work was made easier, but its volume increased: sheets and underwear were changed more frequently, so there was more laundry to be done; diets became more varied, so cooking was more complex; houses grew larger, so there were more surfaces to be cleaned. Additionally, some of the work that, when done by hand had been done by servants, came to be done by the housewife herself when done by machine; indeed, many people purchased appliances precisely so that they could dispense with servants. (98-99)

42. Simone de Beauvoir, *The Second Sex*, trans. H. M. Parshley (New York: Vintage, 1989), 267. In affirming de Beauvoir's claim here, I do not

mean to deny that differents sorts of gender identities are fashioned via intercourse with different sorts of artisanal artifacts; think, for example, of the difference between the code of masculinity informing manual laborers in the
United States and that of computer hackers. Nor do I mean to deny that we
need to distinguish between hegemonic and subordinate codes of masculinity
and femininity within any given culture; think, for example, of the difference
between the norms of femininity operative amongst urban African-American
young women as opposed to those of their suburban Caucasian kin.

43. Iris Marion Young, "Throwing Like a Girl," in *Throwing Like a Girl*,
143, 145, 148.

44. Young, "Throwing Like a Girl," 151.

45. I trust it is clear that I'm not arguing for a unilinear causal relationship, or a one-to-one correspondence, between the "external" artifacts of the
world and the "internal" effects they produce in the psyche; I am not arguing
that to give your baby boy a toy gun is to make him a serial killer. Nor am I arguing for a sort of gussied-up technological determinism. Were I doing that, I
would have to believe that any significant alteration in the artisanal artifacts
constitutive of gender must in time produce a corresponding alteration in the
structure of gender relations. But gender relations, it seems clear, can become
so ossified that they successfully resist whatever pressures are brought to bear
on them by technological innovation; think, for example, of the microwave
oven. I am not persuaded that incorporation of this artifact within American
households, although it has had a fairly dramatic effect on the character of domestic food preparation, has substantially altered the gendered division of labor. Nor, finally, do I mean to dismiss out of hand biological, ecofeminist,
psychoanalytic, and other accounts of the formation of gender identity. Instead, I want to argue that the part played by artisanal artifacts in the formation of gender identity has not been sufficiently explored, and I want to suggest
that the work done by such artifacts is well understood in terms of the dialectic
of projection and reciprocation. Whether such an account can be supplement-
ed by alternative theoretical traditions without contradiction remains to be
seen.

46. Friedrich Nietzsche, *On the Genealogy of Morals*, trans. Walter Kaufmann (New York: Vintage, 1967), 45.

47. To explain this point, in his *Nietzsche: Life as Literature* (Cambridge:
Harvard University Press, 1985), Alexander Nehemas draws a helpful parallel
with Ferdinand Saussure's contention that linguistic terms draw their meaning not from their reference to something outside language, but to the relations of difference sustained between one term and another. In part 2, when I
take up the question of the discursive constitution of the subject, I will develop
this parallel in some detail.

48. Friedrich Nietzsche, *The Will to Power*, trans. Walter Kaufmann and
R. J. Hollingdale (New York: Random, 1967), 268, 296, 302.

49. Nietzsche, *Genealogy of Morals*, 45.

50. Homer, *The Odyssey*, trans. Robert Fitzgerald (New York: Vintage, 1990), 5:506-12.

51. Aristotle, *Physics*, trans. Hippocrates Apostle (Bloomington: Indiana University, 1969): 193b.

52. Slavenka Drakulić, *How We Survived Communism and Even Laughed* (New York: W. W. Norton, 1992), 181-82.

53. Nicholas Thomas, *Entangled Objects* (Cambridge: Harvard University Press, 1991), 176.

54. Quoted in Merchant, *Death of Nature*, 153.

55. I owe this example to Andrew Feenberg, "Subversive Rationalization: Technology, Power, and Democracy," in *Technology and the Politics of Knowledge*, ed. Andrew Feenberg and Alastair Hannay (Bloomington: Indiana University Press, 1995), 14-16.

56. William James, *A Pluralistic Universe* (Cambridge: Harvard University Press, 1977), 117-18.

57. Nietzsche, quoted in Kathy Ferguson, *The Man Question* (Berkeley: University of California Press, 1993), 64.

58. Aeschylus, "Agamemnon," in *Oresteia*, trans. Richard Lattimore (Chicago: University of Chicago Press, 1953), 1492. All succeeding quotations from the *Oresteia* trilogy are taken from this edition, and will be referenced by title and line number only.

59. In the remainder of this paragraph, I draw heavily from the argument advanced by Hans Jonas in his "The Nobility of Sight: A Study in the Phenomenology of the Senses," *The Phenomenon of Life* (New York: Harper & Row, 1966), 135-56.

2

AGENTS AS ARTIFACTS

i. *SpiderWoman*

A THENS'S ARTISANS, SOLON ONCE CLAIMED, ARE THE CHILDREN OF HEPHAESTUS AND Athena. The sons of Hephaestus, working at their forges, can turn ore to molten metal only because they are accessories to the crime of Prometheus. Taming Zeus's thunderbolt, they confine its power within the walls of their blackened furnaces, and there it no longer provokes preternatural terror. The daughters of Athena, working at their spinning wheels and looms, are equally adept at folding nature's gifts into durable artisanal artifacts that temper the harshness of the human condition. Yet the fruits of their labors are routinely overlooked, perhaps because a woman engaged with an embroidery needle or a twisting spindle is seldom heard above the clang of hammer on anvil.

Although muffled, a spinner's occupation is by no means powerless; no less than the smith's is her craft capable of fashioning things that rival the gods. Consider Athena's most famous child. Surpassing all mortals in her accomplishments as a weaver, Ovid tells us, Arachne dared to challenge her patron to a contest of skill. At the heart of her tapestry, amidst the pantheon of Olympian gods and goddesses, Athena placed a self-representation: "To herself the goddess gives a shield and a sharp-pointed spear, and a helmet for her head; the aegis guards her breast; and from the earth smitten by her spear's point upsprings a pale-green olive-tree hanging thick with fruit; and the gods look on in wonder."[1] Thus does Athena announce who she is: she is the warrior-goddess whose metal arms harbor the capacity to call life from the ground, whose greatness must be acknowledged by all who would call themselves Athenians.

With completion of this tapestry, however unwittingly, Athena concedes her defeat at the hands of Arachne. To project her artisanal powers within the world of mortals is to become enmeshed within the mundane logic of artifactual reciprocation. When Athena concludes that all will sing her praises only when evidence of her skill is sewn into the seams of this palpable thing, her identity becomes bound up with its biography. Because the conduct of craft engenders so many freestanding things that in time become entangled with things made by many others, to insert some new artifact into the world is to become party to its comedies as well as its tragedies, its happy coincidences as well as its histories run amok. Even should Athena return to Olympus, vowing never to descend again, this thing will remain behind, mocking her struggle to escape implication in the contingencies of human affairs. Compromising the distance it is intended to affirm, Athena's tapestry is a sticky web whose first catch is the warrior-goddess.

Athena is furious when she discovers that Arachne's tapestry is in no way inferior to her own. Deriding the Olympians so nobly portrayed in Athena's tapestry, Arachne has incorporated within her net tale upon tale of the rape of mortal women and girls by so many deceiving gods. Athena's response to this unbearable taunt is so much wordless violence. Demolishing her rival's "embroidered web with its heavenly crimes," Athena sprinkles the herb of Hecate over Arachne's body; "and forthwith her hair, touched by the poison, fell off, and with it both nose and ears; and the head shrank up; her whole body also was small; the slender fingers clung to her side as legs; the rest was belly. Still from this she ever spins a thread; and now as a spider, she exercises her old-time weaver-art."[2] Now mute, Arachne can tell no one of Athena's humiliation; but neither, of course, can she warn anyone of Athena's awesome power. Athena's victory is pyrrhic at best, for it comes at the cost of silencing the only mortal who could fully appreciate and so truly testify to the glory of her skill.

Once banished from the company of humans, what is Arachne? Does she remain a woman? Or is she now really a spider? Or is she now some sort of daemon, a spiderwoman, a being who falls through the cracks demarcated by our familiar categories of identity? Thrust into a dusty corner, where the light of the public world rarely shines, she is not wholly excluded from participation in the dialectic of projection and reciprocation. Her making, however, does not fashion the sorts of things deemed truly important by the noisy sons of Hephaestus. Labeled a creature of mere instinct, defined by her distended belly, denied the dignity of a fully human being, her intercourse with artifacts is confined to those most immediately associated with reproduction of the conditions of biological existence. Just as a woman brings forth babies from a place unseen, so too does Arachne tease threads as if from nowhere. Just as a woman's work involves care for so many perishable things, nonhuman as well as human, so too does Arachne fashion so many ephemeral webs, each of which is consumed at sundown. Just as a silenced woman cannot trace the significance-bearing threads linking her life to others similarly situated, so too does the speechless Arachne spin her way through days stripped of their capacity to engender shared meaning.

ii. Relocating the Thread

THE ANCIENT GREEK TERM *TECHNĒ* CAN BE TRACED TO THE INDO-EUROPEAN ROOT *TEKS,* which means "to weave." Following the path suggested by this etymological clue, in part 1, I asked how artisanal artifacts are woven into a world of intelligible things. The Cartesian paradigm of use, I argued, is ill equipped to address this issue. The dialectic of projection and reciprocation is better suited, in large part because it questions the mutually exclusive opposition we Cartesians conventionally draw between human beings and artisanal things. When we embrace that opposition, we refuse to acknowledge any kinship between its terms, and so push artifacts into the homogeneous category of the subordinated other. In opposing this paradigm, I have argued that the borders between these two sorts of materialized artifacts are more permeable than we ordinarily admit. The distinction between persons and artisanal things, on the account offered above, is not a distinction between two ontologically distinct and hierarchically ordered kinds of beings, each of which is defined by its members' possession of fixed substantive attributes. Rather, it is a relational distinction whose continuous rearticulation transforms both in time.

If part 1 asked in what sense it is appropriate to affirm the agency of artisanal artifacts, part 2 asks in what sense it is appropriate to affirm the artifactuality of human agents. Recall my extrapolation of Nietzsche's deconstruction of the self-identical subject to the Cartesian object as well as my contention that language helps to overcome the inherent ambiguity of artisanal artifacts by transforming these made-up things into facts, that is, objects that appear given in the nature of things and so self-evidently real. I now want to point this argument back toward its original target, the human agent. The Cartesian paradigm of use conceives of the human agent as an instrumental actor standing astride a world of discrete external objects awaiting manipulation in accordance with the dictates of the subjective will. Assurance of this being's autonomy can only be sustained by refusing to inquire into the conditions of its artifacticity, its generation as a distinctive sort of materialized artifact. To check that refusal, part 1 explored the sense in which the agent is a creature of the materialized artifacts I call artisanal. With much the same end in mind, part 2 explores the sense in which the agent is a creature of the materialized artifacts I call linguistic.

My argument in part 2 is broadly congruent with those currents of postmodern theorizing that affirm the "discursive constitution of the self." But it is not entirely congruent. To explicate the critical dimension of my affirmation, in sections iii-v of part 2, I explore arguments advanced by Hannah Arendt, Richard Rorty, and Judith Butler concerning the relationship between language and human being. Doing so, I explain why I am unwilling to afford privileged status to language in the fashioning of human artifacts. Artifactual reciprocation assumes many forms, and so human agents are internally complex creatures of Prometheus. They are not well understood reductively, no matter what the terms of that reduction.

In part 1, I suggested that artisanal artifacts can be rendered intelligible by exploring their metaphorical relationship to human bodies; the term "projection" is in effect a shorthand way of gesturing toward the analogical relationship between artisanal artifacts and their correlates in various body parts and capacities. As I will suggest in sections vi-vii, a related argument can be made about language. Absent the body's extradiscursive contribution, language cannot participate in the generation of sense. The linguistic turn in philosophy, in other words, now needs to be tempered and complemented by a corporeal turn. Accordingly, through a rehabilitation of the category of embodied feeling, I suggest that the linguistic articulation of significant things grows out of the extradiscursive but not for that reason senseless ways matters are drawn within the web of experience.

In the closing sections of part 2 (viii-x), I return to the relational artifact of gender. To do so in a way that incorporates part 2's argument to that point, I begin with the thorny debate within feminism concerning the category of "experience." After elaborating the criticisms conventionally directed against this category, I argue on behalf of its chastened rehabilitation. More modest than most, my conception is defined by its refusal of the epistemological pretensions implicit within most affirmations of experience, most notably those advanced by proponents of what has come to be known as feminist "standpoint theory." To illustrate why I believe this revised conception of experience is vital to any feminism worthy of the name, I show how its deployment contributes to making sense of the "disease" endured by Adrienne Rich during her first pregnancy. Finally, picking up where I left off in my discussion of Calvin and Susie, but now turning to Vulcan and Venus, I amplify my claims concerning the rootedness of gender in a division of labor whose rules regulate access to and deployment of the artisanal artifacts that make beings human. Together, the arguments of parts 1 and 2 inform my reading of the three exemplary artifacts examined in part 3.

iii. *Father to Himself*

POINTING BACK TOWARD MY DISCUSSION OF ARTISANAL ARTIFACTS AND AHEAD TOWARD my consideration of linguistic artifacts, Hannah Arendt's *The Human Condi-*

tion serves as a useful bridge between the first and second parts of this work. Toward the beginning of this remarkable book, Arendt states that her aim is to explore the *vita activa*. That exploration entails a categorization of "the most elementary articulations of the human condition, with those activities that traditionally, as well as according to current opinion, are within the range of every human being." Her concern, she explains, is with "those general human capacities which grow out of the human condition and are permanent, that is, which cannot be irretrievably lost so long as the human condition itself is not changed."[3]

There are three such articulations: labor, work, and action. Labor, the least worthy of the three, involves the recurrent activities we cannot help but undertake if we are to satisfy basic biological imperatives. The cycles of sleeping and waking, eating and defecating, ovulating and menstruating, are obvious examples. Common to animals as well as human beings, labor is intrinsically meaningless because it cannot take us beyond the futile sphere of necessity:

> The most powerful necessity of which we are aware in self-introspection is the life process which permeates our bodies and keeps them in a constant state of a change whose movements are automatic, independent of our own activities, and irresistible—i.e., of an overwhelming urgency. The less we are doing ourselves, the less active we are, the more forcefully will this biological process assert itself, impose its inherent necessity upon us, and overawe us with the fateful automatism of sheer happening that underlies all human history.[4]

Sounding suspiciously like Descartes, Arendt contends that the body is essentially an organic machine, an automaton. Because the labor of this body contributes only to the cause of self-preservation, because labor is an "activity in which man is neither together with the world nor with other people, but alone with his body, facing the naked necessity to keep himself alive,"[5] it is unpolitical, even antipolitical. Like Arachne punished, the laboring body is merely a creature of the instincts that keep it alive but also unfree and so unhuman.

Work, by way of contrast, lifts beings out the arena of animal instinct and into a distinctively human world of artifacts. Defined as instrumental activity aimed at production of things for use, work fashions a constellation of durable artifacts; houses, chairs, and the tools employed to make them are obvious examples. It is within the enduring context called into being by such things that labor's monotonous cycle of production oriented to immediate consumption is situated:

> Viewed as parts of the world, the products of work—and not the products of labor—guarantee the permanence and durability without which a world would not be possible at all. It is within this world of durable things that we find the consumer goods through which life assures the means of its own sur-

vival. Needed by our bodies and produced by its laboring, but without stability of their own, these things for incessant consumption appear and disappear in an environment of things that are not consumed but used, and to which, as we use them, we become used and accustomed.[6]

While the body's labor power is preoccupied with nothing but reproduction of itself, the fruits of work locate us within a world we share with others. "To live together in the world means essentially that a world of things is between those who have it in common, as a table is located between those who sit around it; the world, like every in-between, relates and separates men at the same time."[7]

It is within the artifactually constituted space Arendt calls "the world" that the most fully human form of activity, action, transpires. The speaking of great words and the performing of great deeds, action's principal forms, are distinguished from labor and work insofar as they alone are ends unto themselves; action's end is nothing more and nothing less than its own impermanent appearance within the world. Such transitoriness does not, however, signify action's meaninglessness. In fact, on Arendt's account, it is only with action that meaning enters into the world. Because labor does not lift us above the dumb animal, because all things fashioned by work are so many means to other ends, and because meaning can only concern that which is neither animal nor utilitarian but human and intrinsic, "*homo faber* is just as incapable of understanding meaning as the *animal laborans* is incapable of understanding instrumentality."[8]

Considered individually, exemplary actions engender meaning by disclosing the singularity, the identity, of the doer: "In acting and speaking, men show who they are, reveal actively their unique personalities and thus make their appearance in the human world, while their physical identities appear without any activity of their own in the unique shape of the body and sound of the voice."[9] Considered cumulatively, such self-revelatory actions collide in unpredictable ways, creating what Arendt calls the "web of human relationships":

> The realm of human affairs, strictly speaking, consists of the web of human relationships which exists wherever men live together. The disclosure of the "who" through speech, and the setting of a new beginning through action, always fall into an already existing web where their immediate consequences can be felt. Together they start a new processs which eventually emerges as the unique life story of the newcomer, affecting uniquely the life stories of all those with whom he comes into contact. It is because of this already existing web of human relationships, with its innumerable, conflicting wills and intentions, that action almost never achieves its purpose; but it is also because of this medium, in which action alone is real, that it "produces" stories with or without intention as naturally as fabrication produces tangible things.[10]

All genuine action is boundless, for it reverberates throughout the web of human relationships, prompting so many unanticipated responses, each provok-
ing its own cascade of oscillations in turn. "(T)he smallest act in the most
limited circumstances bears the seed of the same boundlessness, because one
deed, and sometimes one word, suffices to change every constellation."[11] To
extract a promise from a being capable of genuine action is to seek to contain
its limitlessness, to curb its unpredictability, to secure a hedge against the future. To exercise the virtue of forgiveness is to concede that no promise is
strong enough to check action's inherent tendency to punch its way through
all barriers.

I am alternately enticed and repelled by Arendt's arguments.[12] On the one
hand, her deployment of the metaphor of the web challenges pretensions to
Cartesian autonomy. She understands that artisanal artifacts, by virtue of
their capacity to locate us in a shared world, are something other than so many
inert objects apprehended by so many discrete individuals. And she knows
that the capacity of artifacts to satisfy needs that would otherwise consume
the body's energies enables it to become human. On the other hand, her con-
signment of reproduction to the category of labor, when joined to her claim
that labor's ontological inferiority renders it unfit for entry into the public
realm, appears to relegate women to permanent residence within the unworld
of Arachne. Her very distinction between labor and work occludes the ways
the former is always given its distinctive shape by the latter; think, for example, of the durable artifacts constitutive of the practices of child rearing. And
her categorical identification of embodied needs with the antipolitical sphere
of necessity fails to grasp how and why such needs sometimes and with good
reason become subject to specifically political articulation.

But these are not my principal concerns in this context. For present purposes, what I want to call attention to is the way Arendt represents the relationship between two of the three articulations that, on her account, define
the *vita activa*. As I read her, Arendt vacillates between two distinct characterizations of the relationship between work and action, and hence between the
"world" of artisanal artifacts and the "web" of human relationships. One representation is very much at odds with my account of the dialectic of projection
and reciprocation, while the other offers a helpful complement.

At times, driven by the imperatives of her anti-Marxist polemic, Arendt
insists on a radical dissociation of action and work. In the modern world,
which she likens to a beehive whose occupants are relentlessly devoted to the
production and consumption of perishable goods, the possibility for signifi-
cance-creating action has all but disappeared. This has occurred because of
two reversals within the hierarchy of the *vita activa*. The more recent, which
concerns the elevation of laboring over making, need not occupy us now. The
earlier reversal, whose archetype can be found in Plato's representation of the
republic as a fabricated object, involves the elevation of work to the place occu-

pied by action in nobler times. The larger consequences of action's displacement by work are apparent in the contemporary hegemony of "the typical attitudes of *homo faber*":

> his instrumentalization of the world, his confidence in tools and in the pro-
> ductivity of the maker of artificial objects; his trust in the all-comprehensive
> range of the means-ends category, his conviction that every issue can be
> solved and every motivation reduced to the principle of utility; his sovereign-
> ty, which regards everything given as material and thinks of the whole of na-
> ture as of "an immense fabric from which we can cut out whatever we want to
> resew it however we like"; his equation of intelligence with ingenuity, that is,
> his contempt for thought which cannot be considered to be "the first step . . .
> for the fabrication of artificial objects, particularly of tools to make tools, and
> to vary their fabrication indefinitely"; finally, his matter-of-course identifica-
> tion of fabrication with action.[13]

In the modern world, Arendt insists, we have virtually forgotten that fabrication of a world of durable things is merely a means, vital but subordinate, to
that which is an end in itself; in consequence, the space for action has almost
entirely vanished. Desperate to rescue the possibility of genuine meaning from
such conflation, Arendt insists on a strict segregation of work from action,
world from web. Only if each is meticulously isolated from the other will we
prove able to withstand the temptation to eliminate the contingencies of action "by introducing into the web of human relationships the much more reliable and solid categories inherent in activities with which we confront nature
and build the world of the human artifice." Action, she concludes, is "the only
activity that goes on directly between men without the intermediary of things
or matter."[14]

   In defense of this strict bifurcation, Arendt cites Aristotle's representation
of the *bios politikos* as a sphere of action (*praxis*) and speech (*lexis*), "from
which everything merely necessary or useful is strictly excluded." This characterization of political life does not imply that (male) citizens are forbidden
from speaking about the durable goods that comprise the world. Arendt grants
that political speech is often, and legitimately, "concerned with the matters of
the world of things in which men move, which physically lies between them
and out of which arise their specific, objective, worldly interests." But it does
imply that genuine action, no matter what its subject matter, calls into being
"an altogether different in-between which consists of deeds and words and
owes its origin exclusively to men's acting and speaking directly *to* one another." What makes action's "in-between" so unlike that called into being by our
artisanal artifacts is its essential intangibility: "(A)ction, speech, and thought
have much more in common than any one of them has with work or labor.
They themselves do not 'produce,' bring forth anything, they are as futile as
life itself."[15]

At other times, perhaps indicating that she has absorbed more Marx than she cares to admit, Arendt insists on the inseparability of action and work. There are, she concedes, at least three connections between world and web. First, because action creates nothing that lasts, it can endure through time only insofar as its immaterial appearance is preserved through work. "If the *animal laborans* needs the help of *homo faber* to ease his labor and remove his pain, and if mortals need his help to create a home on earth, acting and speaking men need the help of *homo faber* in his highest capacity, that is, the help of the artist, of poets and historiographers, of monument-builders or writers, because without them the only product of their activity, the story they enact and tell, would not survive at all."[16] Achilles' prowess at Troy will win him immortality only if his pitiless slaughter of Hector becomes the subject of an epic poem. Arachne's renown as a weaver will be assured only so long as Athena does not savage the tapestry that is her skill's palpable incarnation. The tangible artifact thus stands as a palpable expression of our desire to remember the remarkable.

Second, because action is so ethereal, because it produces nothing akin to work's stable products, it requires a lasting place, a defined space, within which it may appear. If the exceptional character of action is to be appreciated as such, it must take place against a backdrop that is more prosaic than is action itself. If the world of artisanal artifacts were as ephemeral as is the web of action, each would disappear within the other; and so meaning, which requires the contrast between the ordinary and the extraordinary, could not be. Arendt illustrates the specifically political import of this claim by explicating the relationship between political action and the fabricated artifact that is a city's legal code. To the Greeks, Arendt argues,

> the laws, like the wall around the city, were not results of action but products of making. Before men began to act, a definite space had to be secured and a structure built where all subsequent action could take place, the space being the public realm of the polis and its structure the law. . . . [T]he wall around the polis and the boundaries of the law were drawn around an already existing public space which, however, without such stabilizing projection could not endure, could not survive the moment of action and speech itself.[17]

Unlike labor, the conduct of work is unpolitical but not antipolitical. While lawmaking, for example, is not itself a form of political action, it is an indispensable condition of politics. Absent the walls that inhibit its explosiveness, each incident of action can be nothing other than a senseless thunderbolt in a vacuum.

Third, Arendt seems to contend that the world of work exercises some sort of efficacy independent of the wills of its makers. It is one thing to say, as Arendt sometimes does, that the *vita activa* is "rooted in a world of men and of man-made things which it never leaves or altogether transcends." To say this is to say that absent the objectivity of artisanal things, their ability to answer human needs without constant supervision, human beings could never escape the elementary imperatives to which labor responds. It is a rather different matter, however, to state that "because human existence is conditioned existence, it would be impossible without things, and things would be a heap of unrelated articles, a non-world, if they were not the conditioners of human existence."[18]

Perhaps the first point of contact between work and action, web and world, does not compromise Arendt's affirmation of their essential difference. To note action's dependence on work for its memorialization is not in and of itself to concede their essential interconnection. It is less clear that she can acknowledge the second link and yet still maintain that deeds, "in their living reality, are of an altogether different nature than these reifications." For if action can only appear as such by virtue of its juxtaposition to a context that is not itself the product of action, then its very possibility is inseparable from that which it is not. Lastly, I do not see how Arendt can contend that the artifacts human beings make "constantly condition their human makers,"[19] and yet still affirm the autonomy of a radically immaterial sphere of action. While a condition of human existence is something we cannot do without, a conditioner of human existence is something that actively participates in its transformation. Arendt never explains exactly what mode of causality is involved in such conditioning, and I suppose she might try to save her argument by distinguishing this mode from that involved in fabrication. But even if she were to do that, the fact remains that she has conceded that artisanal artifacts possess some sort of efficacy; that this efficacy participates in making actors who they are; and, given that action is a form of self-disclosure, that what is disclosed will therefore be what those actors have become, at least in part as a result of their engagement with artisanal artifacts.

So, which is it? Are world and web radically separate, or are they necessarily interrelated? Because this tension remains unresolved in *The Human Condition*, this question cannot be definitively answered. Be that as it may, I want to say two things about the significance of this irresolution; and, in doing so, I will initiate an argument that will unfold more fully over the course of the following two sections.

First, to hark back to a point made in my preface, I am persuaded that when Arendt insists on the essential disjunction of world and web, she confuses an analytic distinction with the experience from which it has been teased. Ascribing ontological status to a distinction that is itself a product of work, the work of thinking, she forgets the priority of lived experience to theory's refined fruits. To hypostatize these fruits, to think that their neat boundaries are replicated within the web of the world (to deliberately mix Arendt's metaphors), is to fall prey to the view that the peculiar form of activity called thinking gives exclusive access to what is real; and that, in turn, is to forget that the world of weal and woe, matters suffered and things enjoyed, furnishes the praxical ground from which thinking teases its issues.

When Arendt's hypostatized distinction between work and action, world and web, is translated into a call to action, it mandates an aristocratic (not to mention patriarchal) politics. Elevating action above work, and work above labor, Arendt's hierarchy echoes Aristotle's philosophical rationalization of classical Greece's class stratifications. That echo's import for present conduct becomes apparent when Arendt suggests that recovery of the possibility of pure political action requires wholesale exclusion from the public sphere of *animal laborans*, that caricature of the voracious stomach, as well as this creature's slightly less crass companion, *homo faber*, that personification of the hands' restless desire to build. If citizens are to engage in action, which again "goes on directly between men without the intermediary of things or matter," the body's necessities as well as its instrumental concerns must be expelled from the political scene. If immaterial action is to remain untainted by the grubby materialism of those unheroic souls who cannot help but think with their bodies, the web of political action must stand as a self-enclosed end-in-itself. Granted, as I noted above, Arendt concedes that "most words and deeds are *about* some worldly objective reality in addition to being a disclosure of the acting and speaking agent." But that concession can temper the procrustean terms of this divorce only if web is to world what she says it is not: "an essentially superflous superstructure affixed to the useful structure of the building itself."[20] Only if this relationship is indeed one of structure to superstructure can the persons who inhabit it remain confident that the selves they disclose in public are something other than the artifacts they have become.

Within experience, we shall never discover the web Arendt speaks of. Within experience, we shall never stumble across a realm in which our relations with other human beings are neatly segregated from our relations to artisanal things. That Arendt cannot escape this conclusion is indicated not merely by her express affirmation of the interconnectedness of action and work, but by the very metaphor she employs to speak of action's intangible "product." Arachne's web is not some intangible unthing; were that the case, no vibrations could ever travel up and down its strands, no news of action occurring here could ever travel there. Arendt's own metaphor, in other words, is ill suited to intimate the defining features of a sphere neatly distinguished from the artifactual. Should a community of arachnids endeavor to live out their days on Hannah's web, they would soon fall into nothingness.

I am persuaded that Arendt's difficulties here stem from what might best be called residual Cartesianism (which in turn stems from so much residual Aristotelianism in Cartesianism). Recall that Descartes radically segregates subject from object in order to affirm the autonomy and hence the mastery of the former over the latter. Does not Arendt do something analogous by other means? Arendt's metaphor of the beehive makes clear her fear that human beings are now being devoured by the things they make—indeed, that most are now mere laborers who can no longer recognize their own productive activity within the artifact that is the beehive, let alone participate in something as distinctively human as politics. Arendt's response to this diagnosis, as we have seen, is her threefold categorization of the human condition. That scheme, following Aristotle's *Ethics*, holds that action is more noble than work and hence, by implication, that web is more excellent than world. This construction installs a relationship of superiority and inferiority, domination and subordination, at the core of Arendt's ontology; and that in turn enables her to reaffirm the mastery of persons over products, the autonomy of makers over things made. Through the legerdemain of conceptual trifurcation, Arendt assures us that we, as agents, may yet escape wholesale engulfment within the world of things if only we can reconstruct (an unfortunate verb, yes?) and then police the clear and distinct partition between us and it.

As with Descartes, the logic of Arendt's argument presses her toward representation of artisanal artifacts as so many heteronomous servants. Only if they resume that status can we be confident that these less than human things, like women confined to the household, will recall their status as so many mere means and so concede their inability to participate in the exclusively intrahuman generation of real meaning. Correlatively, as with Descartes, Arendt must deny artisanal artifacts any political standing. Were she, following Winner, to contend that the introduction of a new artisanal artifact into the world is a political act (think of the forceps); were she to grant that some artisanal artifacts are themselves political inasmuch as they mandate that human relationships be structured in this way rather than that (think of a nuclear reactor); were she to acknowledge the artifacticity of the line she draws between world and web, she could no longer contend that the web of political relationships is a thing unmade. Conceding that, she might also find it necessary to ask whether artisanal artifacts should be granted citizenship of a sort, which in turn might impel her to ask whether the claims of justice should be extended to the artifactual creatures whose parents and children we are.

The second point I want to make about Arendt's ambiguous representation of the relationship between work and action, world and web, is a corollary of the first. Her representation of the object as a heteronomous means finds its counterpart in her characterization of the subject as something oddly reminiscent of the Cartesian ego. Recall that the paradigmatic form of action, speech, derives its existential significance from its capacity to reveal the unique identity of the individual agent: "Action and speech are so closely related because the primordial and specifically human act must at the same time contain the answer to the question asked of every newcomer: 'Who are you?' . . . In acting and speaking, men show who they are, reveal actively their unique personal identities and thus make their appearance in the human world."[21] This is not to say that the interior reality of some antecedent "who" is afforded unmediated expression through the words it speaks in public. Arendt insists that the self one discloses in speech is never fully determined by that self. The embeddedness of action in togetherness, what Arendt calls "plurality," is an inescapable dimension of the human condition. Because the self cannot be unambiguously isolated from the more comprehensive web called into play by the intersecting actions of many others, because that web is never subject to the intentional control of any individual or collective agent, the identity of the self disclosed in action can never be specified in advance of action itself. For this reason, and unlike the Cartesian ego, the Arendtian agent can never dream of becoming exclusive author of his own biography.

However, in another sense, the Cartesian and Arendtian pretensions to autonomy are akin. According to Arendt, the individual's insertion into the world via speech "may be stimulated by the presence of others whose company we may wish to join, but it is never conditioned by them; its impulse springs from the beginning which came into the world when we were born and to which we respond by beginning something new on our own initiative." Asked to explain the human capacity for action, the distinctive capacity of human beings to reshape existing cultural forms and sometimes even invent new ones, Arendt appeals to the "miracle" of "natality," which she defines tautologically as "the capacity of beginning something anew, that is, of acting." But this appeal to something like an uncaused cause, to a secular analogue of the Hebraic god's *creatio ex nihilo*, is no explanation at all. Arendt cannot do any better, however, because her basic conceptual scheme requires that she eschew inquiry into the conditions of agency. Such inquiry, which would entail regarding the agent as some sort of artifact, would necessarily cast doubt on action's radically unconditioned and so its heroic quality. Thus, when she compares action to a "second birth," she must also hold that this birth is categorically unlike the first. If action is to retain its status as a radically new beginning, something altogether unexpected, it can acknowledge the role of no (m)other in its generation: "With respect to this somebody who is unique it can be truly said that nobody was there before."[22] When it comes to action, the agent must ultimately father himself.

iv. *Mother to Herself*

HANNAH ARENDT'S *THE HUMAN CONDITION* VACILLATES BETWEEN THE NOSTALGIC AND the postmodern. Seeking to preserve the fleeting form of political being called into existence by the verbal deeds of glory-seeking citizens, Arendt harks back to the assembly of ancient Athens. Insisting that meaning cannot be in the absence of such utterances, she prefigures that strain of postmodern philosophy that affirms language's primacy in the constitution of significant reality. Yet, even when Arendt most vigorously insists on the essential difference between the "web" of immaterial actions and the "world" of tangible artifacts, she never forgets that any adequate account of the human condition requires consideration of both. That recollection is more or less absent from those more recent thinkers who treat language as an autonomous reality, a reality disconnected from the stubborn world of artisanal things. Doing so, such accounts effectively recapitulate the error Arendt commits when she conflates analytic distinctions teased from experience with experience itself. In advancing this charge, I do not mean to repeat the silly claim that postmodern philosophy is a sort of idealism that effectively obliterates the distinction between texts and social reality; that charge does not do justice to the more subtle versions of the argument on behalf of the discursive constitution of all reality. I do, however, want to claim that when inquiry into language is dissociated from inquiry into the tangible artifactual things that locate our words within the world, our conception of social reality is truncated; and I want to claim that until we come to a more adequate appreciation of the relationship between web and world, words and things, meanings and bodies, our demonstration of the contingency of what is real will prove incomplete. That failure, I think, is exemplified by Richard Rorty's neopragmatism.

For two reasons, Rorty is an ideal foil for my reconceptualization of what is involved in affirming the discursive constitution of reality. First, because Rorty affirms primary allegiance to pragmatism, his work affords an opportunity to distinguish my appropriation of that tradition from his, especially with respect to the category of experience. Second, because the specifically political implications of Rorty's pragmatism are well disclosed in his remarks on feminism, a consideration of those remarks offers an opportunity to anticipate my rather different account of the materialized artifact that is gender.

Rorty's account of pragmatism's contribution to the cause of feminism takes shape as a brief against those who would justify its political claims through reference to women's experience, where the term "experience" denotes some extralinguistic reality awaiting emancipation from its present patriarchal fetters. "All awareness," Rorty insists, "is a linguistic affair," and hence "what you experience yourself to be is largely a function of what it makes sense to describe yourself as in the languages you are able to use."[23] (The rest of part 2, if you wish, may be read as an attempt to specify what remains after Rorty's "largely" is subtracted from the "entirely" to which it tacitly refers.) Because we "never encounter reality *except under a chosen description*,"[24] feminists ought to find talk of women's experience no more credible than that of women's nature. Both terms should now be consigned to the dustbin of ontotheological speculation.

Because the term "experience" denotes a natural kind characterized by a fixed set of intrinsic features, should we foolishly persist in its invocation, the unhappy result will be the generation of so many interminable disputes concerning the relative accuracy of various linguistic representations to its real content. Accordingly, if feminists want to circumvent "hard-to-discuss (I am tempted to say 'metaphysical') questions about whether women have a different *experience* than men, or Africans a different experience than Europeans, or about whether the experience of upper-class African women is more like that of lower-class European men than that of upper-class European women," they should agree to ask only "easier-to-discuss (more evidently empirical) questions about what *language* these various groups of people use to justify their actions, exhibit their deepest hopes and fears, etc." The task for feminists, therefore, is not to seek the truth of gender-specific experience but to propose "creative misuses of language," which, when put into public play, may induce women to feel "revulsion and rage where once they felt indifference or resignation."[25] If there is a "method" of feminist political transformation, its first rule must be the injunction to "redescribe lots and lots of things in new ways, until you have created a pattern of linguistic behavior, which will tempt the rising generation to adopt it, thereby causing them to look for appropriate new forms of nonlinguistic behavior, for example, the adoption of new scientific equipment or new social institutions."[26]

To illustrate Rorty's point, recall the argument I offered in my introduction concerning the realization, the making real, of sexual harassment. On Rorty's account, how and whether a woman in a sexist workplace will "experience" such harassment is a function of the language she now speaks. In the absence of a specifically feminist vocabulary, she can secure no distance from received discursive constructions of what is happening to her, and so sexual advances will take shape as so much harmless, perhaps even flattering, flirtation. Under these circumstances, her emancipation is first and foremost a matter of metaphorical redescription. Should she learn the discourse of sexual harassment, for example, she may in time come to think of herself as a political being whose legally enforceable rights are violated by such unwelcome advances. Her previous identity as a creature whose job entailed putting up with the salacious intimations of her male coworkers will be rendered questionable, and the cause of her liberation will be advanced in consequence.

Rorty's recommendations concerning feminist strategy, it should be evident, follow from his more general endorsement of philosophy's linguistic turn. That turn was initially prompted by an acknowledgment of certain difficulties within the Enlightenment's depiction of language as a transparent vehicle that, when suitably purified by scientific method, truly expresses a speaker's antecedent ideas or accurately represents objects in nature. Belief in the possibility of such expression and/or representation presupposes the epistemological availability of a reality that, because it is knowable apart from language's filter, can be employed as a criterion in adjudicating competing descriptions of it. But this article of faith is effectively undone when language's irreducible role in shaping all human experience, including that of cognition, is admitted. To concede this role is not to deny the stubborn reality of things other than words, but it is to say that we can have no access to such things independent of the categories of a given language. Ernesto Laclau and Chantal Mouffe offer a helpful account of this general point:

> The fact that every object is constituted as an object of discourse has *nothing to do* with whether there is a world external to thought, or with the realism/ idealism opposition. An earthquake or the falling of a brick is an event that certainly exists, in the sense that it occurs here and now, independently of my will. But whether their specificity as objects is constructed in terms of "natural phenomena" or "expressions of the wrath of God," depends on the structuring of a discursive field. What is denied is not that such objects exist externally to thought, but the rather different assertion that they could constitute themselves as objects outside any discursive condition of emergence.[27]

In sum, because reality cannot be ascertained apart from its discursive constitution, neither the empiricist account of language as a system of meanings drawing sense from its representation of a world of objective referents, nor the phenomenological account of language as a system of meanings drawing sense from its expression of so many subjective intentions, now appears credible.

If the adequacy of word to thing is not the source or condition of its meaningfulness, then what is? To answer that question, as Rorty would have us do, a brief turn to Ferdinand Saussure is in order. On Saussure's semiological account, which is anticipated in Nietzsche's critique of the Cartesian subject and recapitulated in Derrida's notion of *différance*, language is a conventional system of signs whose meaningfulness is exclusively a function of the play of its internal differences. "All of which simply means," Saussure writes, "that *in language there are only differences*. More than that: a difference normally presupposes some positive terms between which it is established; but in language there are only differences *without positive terms*."[28] All language, therefore, is ultimately arbitrary in the sense that the meaningfulness of its phonemes is determined entirely by their internal relations to one another. Since any linguistic element depends for its individuation on its differential relations to others, it follows that the meaning of any single element is necessarily a function of what it is not. The term "black," to cite an obvious example, draws its sense from its relationship to the term "white," not from its accurate representation of some extradiscursively ascertained color. The lines linking meaning to meaning, in sum, are lateral; they move from one another rather than from word to idea, thing, or event.

No doubt in anticipation of my needs, Rorty's endorsement of the Saussurian account of language assumes the form of yet another deployment of the web metaphor. In an essay titled "Inquiry as Recontextualization," Rorty suggests that we should think of "human minds as webs of beliefs . . . which continually reweave themselves so as to accommodate new sentential attitudes."

We engage in such reweaving when we wish to overcome the strain, the dissonance, that crops up when we find that our beliefs are no longer congruent with one another. But such beliefs, which again have no existence apart from the language by which they are constituted, are never *about* something outside or beyond that discursive web. "For a belief is what it is only by virtue of its position in a web. . . . [W]e use the term 'about' as a way of directing attention to the beliefs which are relevant to the justification of other beliefs, not as a way of directing attention to nonbeliefs."[29]

To contend that the web of belief is self-contained in this way is not, Rorty insists, to deny the efficacy of *causal* relationships between what we believe and occurrences within and without our bodies. In fact, Rorty is happy to acknowledge that immaterial beliefs can "produce movements in the organism's muscles—movements which kick the organism itself into action. These actions, by shoving items in the environment around, produce new beliefs to be woven in, which in turn produce new actions, and so on for as long as the organism survives." Accordingly, Rorty is quite willing to speak of language's "objects," so long as this signifies nothing other than "what we find it useful to talk about in order to cope with the stimulations to which our bodies are subjected."[30] What Rorty will never say is that language is capable of stating a truthful account of what those causal forces are in themselves; for truth is a property of the relations between sentences, never of the adequacy of sentences to brute facts.

What does this line of reasoning imply for the way we think about human identity? Acknowledgment of the discursive constitution of reality draws us away from Descartes's autonomous monad, that atom of self-consciousness trapped within an alien body, and toward the contextualized agent, caught up within linguistic structures that antecedently establish the possibility of selfhood. If indeed all meaning is a function of the differential signs that comprise any given language, then the same must be true of all personal identity insofar as it too is meaningful. "(T)here is no self distinct from this self-weaving web. All there is to the human self is just that web."[31] Language's grammar, the impersonal system of rules prescribing what can and cannot be said intelligibly, effectively dictates the parameters of meaning within which persons are constituted as identifiable agents; and these parameters establish the possibility of meaning through processes of differential semantic articulation. When I claim that "I am white," that affirmation is meaningful because of its unstated reference to other discursive claims (e.g., "I am not black"), not because it accurately represents some color ascertainable apart from language's categories.

Correlatively, because "human beings are simply incarnated vocabularies," we can no longer find credible any claims concerning the "natural" or "authentic" self. To believe that the self one now is is one's true self, where the term "true" means something like corresponding to an antecedently existent or necessary reality, is to forget that "the human self is created by the use of a vocabulary rather than being adequately or inadequately expressed in a vocabulary."[32] Just as there can be no correspondence between words and the things to which they refer, so too there can be no correspondence between human identity and some extradiscursive reality. To expend one's life in pursuit of such a phantasm is to retreat into the comforting arms of a metaphysical tradition that perished on the day our last god died.

At first blush, it would appear that Rorty's constructivist account of the relationship between selfhood and language is very much at odds with that advanced by Arendt. Arendt, recall, invokes the miracle of natality to explain the radically unconditioned character of speech or, more accurately, speech when it assumes the form of heroic action. Arendt will be hard pressed to maintain this honorific representation of action if the revelation of individual identity in speech is merely a fruit of what language permits one to say. Yet that is precisely what Rorty affirms when he contends that men and women are "nothing more than the presence or absence of dispositions toward the use of sentences phrased in some historically conditioned vocabulary."[33] Arendt's representation of action as the eruption of the extraordinary, along with her categorical rejection of all terminology drawn from the sphere of fabrication in speaking of the actor, is not easily reconciled with Rorty's representation of the agent as an artifact exhaustively constituted by the linguistic conditions of its appearance as such.

Yet in another way their readings of agency are surprisingly congruent. Were Arendt to ask Rorty to explain the capacity of human beings to bring something new into the world, he would respond by invoking the category of "genius." How, Rorty asks, are we to explain the capacity of the uncommon individual to "get out from under an old final vocabulary and fashion one which will be all his own"? His answer consists of his citation of the capacity of exceptional persons, by their "own sheer strength," to engage in "self-creation," where "self-creation" is tautologically defined as "the capacity to create one's own language, rather than to let the length of one's mind be set by the language other human beings have left behind." If such self-creation is indeed a matter of "giving birth to oneself,"[34] as Rorty maintains, then it would appear once again that success in this enterprise is contingent on denying the role of any (m)other in that accomplishment. Rorty's category of "genius," in short, is as empty of explanatory power as is Arendt's category of "natality."

If they are to preserve their shared elitist pretensions, neither Rorty nor Arendt can afford to inquire into the conditions of what they respectively call genius and heroism. Neither, in consequence, can explain how the artifact that is the human being comes to assume the meaningful shape it does, nor how that artifact sometimes manages to refashion the agencies that afford it form. Whereas Arendt fails to show how the materialized artifact of language constrains and conditions the speaking subject, Rorty fails to show how the discursively constituted subject ever proves able to say something genuinely new. Defining meaning making as the privilege of an aristocratic few, together, they relegate the vast majority of human beings to the status of bees humming a tune composed by others.

In the preceding section, I criticized Arendt on the grounds that she confuses the analytic categories of web and world with the experience from which those categories have been teased, and I argued that Arendt thereby betrays a sort of residual Cartesianism. I now want to argue that Rorty does much the same when he categorically rejects "the idea that there are nonlinguistic things called 'meanings' which it is the task of language to express."[35] My more general purpose in doing so is to contest any argument that abstracts discursive meaning from its more comprehensive context by collapsing the category of experience into that of language. As such, my criticism can also be applied to Murray Edelman, who writes: "It is language about political events, not the events in any other sense, that people experience; even developments that are close by take their meaning from the language that depicts them. So political language *is* political reality; there is no other so far as the meaning of events to actors and spectators is concerned."[36] It can also be applied to Gayatri Spivak, who writes: "We know no world that is not organized as a language, we operate with no other consciousness but one structured as language—languages that we cannot possess, for we are operated by those languages as well. The category of language, then, embraces the categories of world and consciousness even as it is determined by them."[37] And, finally, it can be applied to Joan Scott, who "refuse(s) a separation between 'experience' and language" on the grounds that "experience is a linguistic event (it doesn't happen outside established meanings)."[38]

To set a context for my criticism, return to Saussure for a moment. Recall his contention that all meaning is lateral rather than frontal, that it moves from one sign to another rather than from sign to referent. Because each sign is meaningful by virtue of its relationhip to some other sign that in turn is meaningful by virtue of its relationship to some other sign, and so forth and so on, Saussure concludes that the meaning of any given sign presupposes and tacitly invokes the linguistic totality, the unified system, of which it is a member. My concern about this conclusion, which Rorty's web metaphor recapitulates, can be stated in the form of a question: If the noun "language" is to invoke an identifiable subject of inquiry, what violence must first be done to it and the world it inhabits? If language is to stand as such a subject, I would respond, it must first be abstracted from the materialized realities in which it is concretely embedded and embodied. The complex of linguistic artifacts, that is, must be pried loose from the praxical context of mobile everyday engagements in which we are vitally immersed not merely as speakers and listeners but as doers and sufferers, creatures of Prometheus in both senses of the phrase. Only then can this particular participant in the constitution of materialized reality be fashioned into a conceptual whole available for analysis apart from its more inclusive artifactual situation.

Such abstraction, I happily grant, is a necessary moment of all thinking. If experience is to be something other than a "buzzing and blooming confusion," to quote William James, we must discursively distinguish one thing from another. This move becomes problematic, however, when we effectively "forget" that language is always relationally implicated in a palpable web of experience whose strands trail off indeterminately to ambiguous places that, although not known as so many determinate sites, are not for that reason entirely without sense. Thinking's abstractive enterprise turns pernicious when the web of which Rorty speaks comes to be treated as an existentially distinct and self-subsistent totality whose discriminations can be understood without reference to anything beyond itself.

Rorty, in other words, is guilty of a peculiarly postmodern version of what John Dewey called the "intellectual fallacy" and William James called "vicious intellectualism." Dewey explains:

> Philosophy, like all forms of reflective analysis, takes us away, for the time being, from the things had in primary experience as they directly act and are acted upon, used and enjoyed. Now the standing temptation of philosophy, as its course abundantly demonstrates, is to regard the results of reflection as having, in and of themselves, a reality superior to that of the material of any other mode of experience. The commonest assumption of philosophies, common even to philosophies very different from one another, is the assumption of the identity of objects of knowledge and ultimately real objects. The assumption is so deep that it is usually not expressed; it is taken for granted as something so fundamental that it does not need to be stated.[39]

Rorty's insistence upon the discursive constitution of reality is salutary to the extent that it reminds us, first, that anything we identify as a determinate thing is always framed in language; and, second, that because no meanings are given in the nature of things, all are contingent and so contestable artifacts. As such, the concept of the discursive has proven a serviceable political weapon. But this category threatens to become a fetter when it shows signs of becoming an all-consuming concept from which nothing, by definition, can escape. "Philosophers," warns James in *A Pluralistic Universe*, "have always aimed at clearing up the litter with which the world is apparently filled. They have substituted economical and orderly conceptions for the first sensible tangle."[40] Such substitution is a form of distortion, not because our intellectual productions misrepresent what is really out there, but because we are so often fooled into thinking that experience is exhausted by them.

When Rorty collapses experience into the intralinguistic world of discourse, when such logocentric thinking denies the reality of extradiscursive but sensible experience, he reveals his infection by the metaphysical tradition he claims to overcome. Rejecting the essentialist conviction that the god of the Judeo-Christian tradition gave the things of this world names revealing their true nature, Rorty embraces this error's mirror image. Ascribing to language the role once played by that divinity, what might otherwise be a form of life-affirming atheism undercuts its own emancipatory thrust when that god reappears as Discourse, Author of All Things.

Recall part 1's argument to the effect that the grip of Cartesianism remains apparent in the dualistic debate between instrumentalist and determinist accounts of technology. Something similar, I think, is at work here. Whereas the objectivism of the metaphysical tradition suggested that the right words will somehow disclose the reality of things, the collective subjectivism of logocentric philosophy implies that things are no-things, mere senseless matter, in the absence of the words making them what they are. Whereas Descartes insisted that all nonhuman things are valueless until taken up as means within the projects of human subjects, Rorty implies that all nonhuman things are quite senseless until appropriated by the categories of human discourse; to me, both contentions smell of so much anthropocentrism.

When matters are framed thus, have we escaped the terms of Cartesianism, or are we simply dishing up more of the same, albeit now in the form of an upside-down cake? That the latter is closer to the mark is suggested when Rorty contends that "the world is out there, but descriptions of the world are not." What are we to make of his use of the term "world" here? Given his unequivocal rejection of any sort of linguistic representationalism, given his view that the meaning of all terms is exclusively a function of their differential relations to others, this word cannot refer to, be about, draw its sense from, anything outside the self-contained web of language, anything in "the world." But if that is so, then what are we to make of Rorty's contention that "our relation to the world . . . is not the sort of relation we have to persons"?[41] When Rorty sharply distinguishes intrahuman from human/world relations, is he surreptitiously smuggling in some unacknowledged but substantive conception of the reality that lies outside language, beyond the realm of discursive intelligibility? In this context, I do not intend to provide all the evidence necessary to sustain the claim that Rorty does in fact do so. Suffice it to say that he gives some hint of that conception when he affirms the world's indifference to human designs, when he argues that the relationship between events in the world and beliefs is one of mechanical stimulation, and when he endorses Wittgenstein's representation of vocabularies as so many more or less efficient "tools" for realizing our ends in the world.[42] What should be readily apparent is the Cartesian tenor of each of these claims. For Descartes, recall, the world consists of so many indifferent Galilean objects in mechanical motion, and one of the virtues of modern science is its capacity to facilitate invention of the tools that subordinate these neutered objects to human purposes. In much the same manner, I think, does Rorty conceive of the relationship between what he calls "the world" and language. This ontology is all the more insidious precisely because it goes unacknowledged, precisely because Rorty insists that we can never speak of that which is beyond language. We are hardly likely to go looking amidst Rorty's words for that which, on his account, can never be spoken.

Perhaps, in opposition to Descartes, the words we speak are neither so many mirrors of nature nor, in opposition to Rorty, so many free-floating signifiers. Perhaps neither of these metaphors adequately indicates the way in which meaning is fashioned from the qualitatively rich material brought into play by the dialectic between human beings and a world of experience that is as much in them as they are in it. Perhaps, to use the terms of part 1, language is deeply embedded within the mutually transformational logic of projection and reciprocation. And perhaps such embeddedness implies a reading of the relationship between language, experience, and embodied agency that is considerably more complex than that offered by either Arendt or Rorty.

v. *Sugar and Spice, Snips and Snails*

SEVERAL FIGURES (CARICATURES?) NOW STALK THE PAGES OF THIS TEXT. PERMIT ME TO RE-call two. The first, making his debut in part 1, is the Cartesian self who treats all things as so many neutered objects available for exploitation on behalf of his value-creating ends, the autonomous ego who is persuaded that the relationship of language to world, once purified by scientific method, is one of unproblematic representation. Although the second figure delayed her official appearance until part 2, she was prefigured in part 1's discussion of the Cartesian monad's alter ego, the self who is a heteronomous creature of technological determinism. That figure's postmodern incarnation takes shape as the self who acknowledges that all meaning is arbitrarily imposed on an intrinsically senseless world, who understands that her status as a subject is wholly a discursive artifact engendered by the linguistic categories speaking through her.

Our first figure, it seems to me, looks suspiciously like the omnipotent creator of the Judeo-Christian tradition, while the second looks suspiciously like that god's impotent creature. Neither relates the conduct of creation to the dialectic of projection and reciprocation, a dialectic whose logic stipulates that neither of these two moments is ontologically prior to the other. Equally important, neither of these two figures inhabits a body capable of significant participation in the project of making sense. The Cartesian self is without that capacity because its body is merely a stupid machine, while the postmodern body is itself a creature of sense only because of its antecedent constitution by the discursive categories that render it meaningful.

I find neither of these children of philosophical speculation appealing candidates for adoption. As a first step toward an alternative account of the relationship between embodied agency, language, and the world, I want to offer an extended discussion of Judith Butler's reflections on these same questions. In the self-critical moves she has made between publication of *Gender Trouble*

(1990) and her more recent *Bodies That Matter* (1993), Butler indicates how we might pass beyond these inverted twins. Doing so, she helps us get a handle on the governing question of part 2: In what sense is it appropriate to think of human beings as artifacts, as things made, rather than as autonomous sources of unfettered agency?

As in my discussion of Arendt and Rorty, the aim of this section's first half is to ferret out the residual Cartesianism in Butler. Its second half, which elaborates Butler's halting efforts to shed this residue, offers a more adequate account of the concept of materialization that I invoked but did not specify with any care in the introduction to this work. Recall that the Cartesian paradigm of use is undergirded by a particular ontology, one that depicts the universe not as an organism but as a mechanism composed of so many discrete corpuscles whose movements can be explained exclusively through reference to the workings of efficient causation. Inasmuch as the term "materialization" addresses the complex processes through which things come to be real, it too must implicate specific ontological commitments. Accordingly, and again following Butler's lead, the second half of this section seeks to show how a critical rehabilitation of the Aristotelian categories of form and matter might furnish the speculative ground for such a non-Cartesian ontology. The following two sections, which give the ontology of materialization a specifically pragmatist twist, explore its implications for our understanding of the relationship between experience, language, and human bodies in the project of engendering the artifact that is sense. How this ontology informs the dialectic of projection and reciprocation, especially with respect to questions of gender, is the subject of part 2's final three sections.

Butler's *Gender Trouble* opens with the following question: "What happens to the subject and to the stability of gender categories when the epistemic regime of presumptive heterosexuality is unmasked as that which produces and reifies these ostensible categories of ontology?"[43] Very much in the spirit of Rorty, Butler's aim is to criticize all arguments that suggest that representations of gender identity can be deemed true or authentic by virtue of their accurate correspondence to, or expression of, some extradiscursive reality. In part, she directs this criticism against those who assume the naturalness of binary heterosexual identities and so the unproblematic congruity of anatomy, gender identification, and sexual desire. However, a still more substantial portion of Butler's argument is directed against those who would ground critiques of, as well as resistance to, compulsory heterosexuality in appeals to the repressed reality of extradiscursive sexuality and its subterranean promptings.

Butler's quarrel with arguments of this latter stripe can be illustrated by considering her criticism of Julia Kristeva. Kristeva's appeal to the "semiotic" is an appeal to the primacy of heterogeneous libidinal drives allegedly rooted in the extradiscursive reality of the maternal body. To say that such drives are extradiscursive is to say that their ontological standing is not derivative or contingent on their linguistic formulation. But that, Kristeva insists, is not to say that these drives must remain mute. Rather, it is to say that they cannot be given adequate expression via the reified forms of language that she, following Lacan, calls "the Symbolic." Recovery of these drives from the Symbolic is possible only via the polysemic language of poetry. Subversion of the law of the father, in other words, can occur only via appropriation of linguistic forms that cannot help but prove hopelessly ambiguous, even unintelligible, to those ill-conceived phallic subjects who only speak prose.

To Kristeva's argument, Butler offers a deceptively simple counter: "(I)f we can attribute meaning only to that which is representable in language, then to attribute meanings to drives prior to their emergence in language is impossible."[44] Any account of "extradiscursive" reality, however imagined, must itself be elaborated in the terms of an existing language game; only within language can we articulate the significant reality of that which is said to stand behind, before, or beyond language. But if that is so, then language can never be true to its subject, and this is so in two different ways. First, as Rorty also insists, because the extradiscursive can never be isolated from our discursive practices so as to function as a standard for determining the accurate correspondence of the latter with the former, we can never be sure that language truly represents that about which it allegedly speaks. Second, even should such a reality exist, we can never truly speak of it, for the mere act of doing so will transform "it" into something other than what it extradiscursively is.

To this point, Butler's argument is conceptual in character. Its aim is to demonstrate the logical fallacy involved in affirming the reality of the unrepresentable via the representations of language. But that does not exhaust Butler's ambition. Her larger aim is to show that the drives to which Kristeva appeals are actually *creatures* of their linguistic formulation. In other words, Butler supplements her conceptual criticism with a claim concerning the power of discourse to produce effects that, in time, are taken to be independent causes. To make this argument, she draws on Foucault. In his introductory volume to *The History of Sexuality*, Foucault criticizes those who appeal to the power of primordial sexuality, however construed, as an antidote to the "unnatural" agencies of bourgeois repression. That we have come to believe in such a power, as when we assert that emancipatory politics should free us from the "artificial" constraints now imposed upon our sexuality, says nothing about the "nature" of sexuality but everything about the power of discourse to fashion a world in its own image. Understood genealogically, "sex" is a fictitious unity, an hypostatized noun, that secures its apparent reality only via its chronic discursive iteration.

Kristeva, Butler insists, is taken in by a similar trick of grammar when she contends that the archaic desire to give birth is the paradigmatic drive resident within the maternal body: "Insofar as Kristeva conceptualizes this maternal instinct as having an ontological status prior to the paternal law, she fails to consider the way in which that very law might well be the *cause* of the very desire it is said to *repress*. . . . [W]hat Kristeva claims to discover in the prediscursive maternal body is itself a production of a given historical discourse, an *effect* of culture rather than its secret and primary cause."[45] Standing Kristeva on her head, Butler argues that when maternality is regarded as the essence of being woman, and when that essence is located in the extradiscursive reality of the female body, the result is to occlude those sociopolitical forces that conspire to oppress women by representing them as beings whose destiny is to make babies. However unwittingly, Kristeva thereby plays into the hands of those who affirm the exclusive legitimacy of heterosexual desire and procreative sex.

The route delineated by Butler's critique of Kristeva dictates the path of her counterargument. If the maternal instinct Kristeva discovers in the body of the "natural" woman is in fact a cultural artifact, then the appropriate remedy is to "reverse the very order of this causality." To think genealogically is to come to see that Kristeva's maternal instinct, masquerading as an uncaused cause, is in fact a heteronomous effect. Applied to gender more generally, what genealogy must reverse is the conviction that the brute fact of anatomical structure, one's sex, is somehow the cause of one's "true" gender identity as well as the disposition of erotic energies along heterosexual lines; here, critical inquiry will demonstrate that the "production of sex *as* the prediscursive ought to be understood as the effect of the apparatus of cultural construction designated by *gender*." Applied to questions of identity still more generally, what genealogy must reverse is our confident assurance that the Cartesian ego is the rational creator of the cultural forms it inhabits; here, genealogical inquiry will investigate "the political stakes in designating as an *origin* and *cause* those identity categories that are in fact the *effects* of institutions, practices, discourses with multiple and diffuse points of origin."[46]

So, Butler's aim is to turn round the arrow of causation such that what was once labeled "effect" comes to be labeled "cause," and vice versa. But to redirect that sign is not in and of itself to explain what sort of causal work this arrow specifies. To compress a complex argument into a formula, Butler answers this question by appealing to the overlapping concepts of "reiteration" and "performativity." With these terms, she designates the principal causal mechanisms that account for the fabrication of the "regulatory fictions" that are "intelligible genders," in other words, those that "institute and maintain relations of coherence and continuity among sex, gender, sexual practice, and desire."[47]

By "reiteration," Butler refers to incessant repetition of those grammatical forms that in time generate the stable appearance of the allegedly autonomous agent: "(T)o understand identity as a *practice*, and as a signifying practice, is to understand culturally intelligible subjects as the resulting effects of a rule-bound discourse that inserts itself in the pervasive and mundane signifying acts of linguistic life."[48] These rules—think, for example, of those that regulate coherent employment of the personal pronoun "I"—are constitutive of, but also invisible to, the subject. They are constitutive insofar as the very possibility of being an intelligible self, which includes the imperative that one be a determinate gender, presupposes their invocation. They are simultaneously invisible insofar as, like your eyes, they define the place from which you see but are never themselves seen.

Reiteration's self-fashioning work is complemented by that of performativity. To understand this second causal agency, it is important to note that Butler, again following Foucault, means the term "discourse" to be more inclusive than the term "language," narrowly construed. The "discourse of gender," for example, refers to all of the institutions and norms that reproduce, enforce, and legitimate the ritualized forms of intelligible conduct constitutive of compulsory heterosexuality. So construed, this discourse includes conventions of sex-specific dress, relations of rule within the traditional nuclear family, the spatial segregation of work into private and public spheres, the commodification of heterosexual desire, partitioning of the body into erogenous and nonerogenous zones, the sentimentalization of adolescent heterosexual love. All of this and more enters into the network of powers whose efficacy compels the embodied performances that, in conjunction with the grammatical forms whose reiteration fashions the illusion of the self-subsistent "I," come to be normalized as the effect we mistakenly designate as the extradiscursive cause called "sex."

With *Gender Trouble*'s basic argument in place, I now want to pose three interrelated questions about Butler's argument. The first concerns the ambiguous metaphorics embedded within her account of causal efficacy; the second her representation of genealogical inquiry as a sort of "reversal"; and the third her account of the relationship between fashionable human bodies and the agencies of their discursive constitution. My purpose in doing so, again, is to indicate how Butler, perhaps our most subtle contemporary critic of Cartesian metaphysics, remains embedded within the discursive order she means to disrupt.

Beneath the abstract rubric of causality, Butler subsumes several rather different accounts of discursive constitution. Their dissimilarities are implicit in the various verbs she employs to articulate the relationship between the agencies of discursive causation and that which they bring into being. Consider, for example, the following: "(T)he subjects regulated by such structures [reiteration and performativity] are, by virtue of being subjected to them, formed, defined, and reproduced in accordance with the requirements of those structures." Elsewhere, muddying the waters still more, she uses the terms "produce," "establish," "constitute," and "construct" to specify how subjects are made. That Butler is inattentive to the differential import of these verbs is apparent when she treats them, or at least some of them, as synonyms for one another: "Paradoxically, the reconceptualization of identity as an *effect*, that is, as *produced* or *generated*, opens up possibilities of 'agency' that are insidiously foreclosed by positions that take identity categories as foundational and fixed."[49]

But are such terms indeed synonymous? Butler's verbs, I would suggest, mix up several idioms of causality, each of which implies a different relationship between cause and effect. For example, when drawn from the domain of biological beings, the term "reproduce" typically implies causality in an agrarian and/or procreative guise. By way of contrast, when teased out of the sphere of fabrication, the verb "construct" typically implies causality in the guise of artisanal manufacture. Whereas the former suggests that the workings of causal forces are in some sense internal to the being undergoing their efficacy (as in the case of a pregnant woman), the latter suggests that those workings are externally impressed upon that being (as in the case of a metalworker shaping silver into a goblet). Whereas the former assumes that reproducer and re-produced are of the same species of being (as in mother and child), the latter assumes that maker and made are of different kind (as in the case of metalworker and silver ore). Whereas the former implies that the intelligibility of that which is created is immanently but not consciously present as the unfolding power of maturation (as in the child who grows to adulthood), the latter implies that the creature's intelligibility is contingent upon the antecedent design that informs the creator's fabrication (as in the artisan who envisions the finished form of an artifact prior to the onset of work). Because Butler's verbs gesture toward such divergent conceptions of projective agency, her terminology raises at least as many questions about the conduct of discursive constitution as it answers.

My second question concerns Butler's call to "reverse" the causal arrow conventionally drawn between sex and gender or, more generally, between identity and discourse: Is a simple reversal of received terms, an inversion of accustomed polarities, adequate to her (or our) purposes? This question cannot be answered definitively until the ambiguities resident within Butler's metaphorics of causality are cleared up. Be that as it may, in the absence of such clarification, I wish to suggest that on balance the argument of *Gender Trouble* inclines Butler toward a Cartesian conception of causality, and hence toward a conception that presupposes the externality of cause and effect as well as the mechanical character of their conjunction.

For an example of such a Cartesian conception, consider the causal line drawn in orthodox discourse between anatomy and sexual orientation. As conventionally understood, the former is taken to dictate the latter in an altogether unmediated manner. The fact that my body is equipped with a penis is taken to be the antecedent and discrete cause of my brute desire to have intercourse with women, which in turn is taken to be the unambiguous mark of my clear and distinct identity as a heterosexual. This account is crucial to the maintenance and legitimation of compulsory heterosexuality insofar as it roots sexual identity qua determinate effect in the apparently unquestionable reality of a biological attribute qua linear cause.

In and of itself, Butler's call to reverse the direction of the causal arrow pointing from my member to my membership in the company of heterosexuals does not question the character of the causal linkage signified by that arrow; it only places what we now take to be an effect in the spot presently occupied by what we now take to be a cause, and vice versa. Why such a project of simple reversal is problematic can be indicated by returning to the father of genealogical inquiry. Recall that in part 1 I appropriated Nietzsche's critique of the Cartesian subject in order to question the self-subsistent Cartesian object. Rather than repeat that argument in its entirety, let me simply remind you that Nietzsche offers the example of lightning in order to suggest that all things, as so many dynamic existents, are what they are by virtue of the relations they sustain with other equally mobile things. Also, recall that Nietzsche employs this example to show that the apparently self-subsistent thing is merely "the sum of its effects"; that there is no good reason to posit its separate existence as the antecedent substance that produces those same effects; and, finally, that to consider such a thing as the isolable cause of some other discrete thing is to layer fiction on fiction.

If Nietzsche is right in this regard, then the problem with *Gender Trouble* is not, as some have contended, that it dissolves the material world into so many immaterial creatures of discourse. Rather, the problem with *Gender Trouble* is that its uncritical call to "reverse" the poles of received causal explanations entails postulation of an independent subject that, no matter how resolutely material, must stand apart from the effects it is said to cause; only then, after all, can the former's efficacy with respect to the latter be identified as such. That Butler does indeed think in these terms is indicated when she contends that "sanctioned heterosexuality and transgressive homosexuality . . . are indeed effects, temporally and ontologically later than the law itself, and the illusion of a sexuality before the law is itself the creation of that law." The sense of this claim requires, first, that Butler abstract something called "discourse" (or, in this case, "the law") from the heterogeneous web in which it is constitutively implicated; second, that she ascribe unilinear efficacy to this hypostatized entity; and, third, that she treat this self-subsistent entity as the external cause of identity, now relegated to the domain of dependent effects. Butler, in sum, retains a conception of causality that is at odds with her effort to apply Nietzsche's contention that "there is no doer behind the deed" to the specifically gendered agent. Her salutary insistence that "gender is always a doing, though not a doing by a subject who might be said to preexist the deed,"[50] is vitiated to the extent that something akin to that suspect subject reappears within the realm of causality.

If the preceding argument has merit, then might we suggest that *Gender*

Trouble is predicated on an unusually refined version of the subject/object dualism, but with the twist that the mechanisms of discursive constitution now occupy the place once held by the Cartesian subject? Moreover, if I am right to contend that Butler's construction of the relationship between cause and effect secures expression via Cartesian grammatical forms, then am I wrong to ask whether her argument harbors some of the gendered traces secreted within Descartes's reading of the instrumentalized relationship between human beings and the world? If the little god we call the Cartesian ego is a masculine subject whose relationship to a passive, senseless, and typically female nature is one of unilateral imposition, should it not give us pause to find something very much like this ego's construction of causality reappearing within the domain of feminist theory?[51]

My third question concerns Butler's representation of the body in *Gender Trouble*. If gender identity is a creature of the work done by the agencies of discursive constitution, what exactly is the character of that work and how are we to conceive of that on which those agencies operate? Metaphorically put, given the argument of the preceding paragraph, we should expect the conduct of such causation to appear more akin to a hammer beating silver than to a seed sprouting from moist soil. That *Gender Trouble* does in fact presuppose some such representation is intimated by Butler's account of performativity and reiteration. Each appears to do its work through so many acts of blunt repetition; "all signification takes place within the orbit of the compulsion to repeat."[52] Dress me in petticoats every day, and my body will become a curtseying machine. Call me a "girl" often enough, and "I" will come to think of myself as one who belongs by nature to the company of little women.

As to the question of the *what* on which discursive constitution works, let me begin by indicating three answers that will not do. First, and against Kristeva, no longer can we entertain the illusion of a true body beyond the "law"; we cannot turn to some teleological figure whose essential nature, once released from the crust of convention, will march us down the path to perfect freedom. Second, and against Descartes, no longer can we think of the body as that sometimes churlish but always mindless servant to an immaterial "I" whose relationship to its embodiment is purely contingent; Descartes's self-contained "sum," we now understand, is itself an appearance created and sustained by the body's discursive constitution. Third, and finally, no longer can we make do with Foucault's body. Sometimes, as Butler rightly notes, the body of Foucault looks not unlike that of Kristeva. This is the disciplined body, and what discipline has straitened is a prediscursive riot of erotically charged energies blessed with latent emancipatory import. On other occasions, more akin to Descartes, Foucault's body appears as the necessary material presupposition of its acquisition of discursive intelligibility. Each of Foucault's two bodies, however, smuggles in a fictional entity under the cover of extradiscursive reality, and so each ultimately falls prey to the fallacy of Kristeva.

If "the body" must always appear in quotation marks, if "it" is an unspeakable thing until discursively constituted, then "it" cannot be said to have any reality absent such constitution. To contend otherwise, Butler insists, is to engage in a sort of ontological legerdemain and so to render the always historically specific body immune to genealogical inquiry. Pressed to its logical conclusion, accordingly, Butler's exhortation to deconstruct "the body" into its constitutive acts, as these are performed in accordance with the demands of compulsory heterosexuality, cannot help but make the body disappear as a possible object of inquiry—except, of course, insofar as that inquiry is inquiry into these same acts and nothing else: "That the gendered body is performative suggests that it has no ontological status apart from the various acts which constitute its reality."[53]

But this conclusion proves vexing when juxtaposed to the answer I provided to my second question. Butler's contention that the body has no reality independent of the acts by which it is constituted coexists uneasily with her call to reverse the causal lines conventionally drawn between the body and its gendered identity. If the body cannot be said to antecede its discursive constitution, then what is it on which the agencies of discursive constitution do their work? The answer, I presume, can only be nothing. But if that is the case, then operation of the mechanisms of discursive constitution must bring into being that which they were earlier said to affect; and, strictly speaking, that operation, like the divine performatives uttered in the beginning, must be a *creatio ex nihilo*. But if that is the case, if the effects of discursive constitution are indistinguishable from its causes, then it is not clear how one can employ a linear conception of causality, let alone call for a reversal of the lines conventionally drawn between cause and effect. Absent the prior existence of some thing susceptible to causal efficacy, there can exist only so many causes (or, alternatively, so many effects). But if the world is populated exclusively by causes that, at one and the same time, are so many effects, then either the category of causality is superfluous, or it must be rethought in a way Butler does not attempt. At the end of the road paved with Butler's reflections on the body, we might say, stands the incorrigible author of the gay science.[54]

Although portions of Butler's argument appear to mandate this conclusion, "the body" does not quite vanish from *Gender Trouble. How* it makes its appearance is, I think, what enables Butler to move toward recognition and removal (for the most part) of her residual Cartesianism. In *Gender Trouble*, the question of the body is formulated as follows: "How do we reconceive the body no longer as a passive medium or instrument awaiting the enlivening capacity of a distinctly immaterial will?" To the extent that she offers one in this text, Butler's answer is to claim that to be a body is to be a thing whose intelligible reality is a creature of the differentiation of various parts via so many acts of boundary definition and functional specification. The precise character of those acts, the location of particular borders and the purposes ascribed to particular parts, is culturally variable. In contemporary Western cultures, that character is first and foremost a creature of the imperatives internal to compulsory heterosexuality: "Pleasures are said to reside in the penis, the vagina, and the breasts or to emanate from them, but such descriptions corre-spond to a body which has already been constructed or naturalized as gender-specific. In other words, some parts of the body become conceivable foci of pleasure precisely because they correspond to a normative ideal of a gender-specific body."[55]

For my purposes, what is noteworthy about this account of the body is the way it inclines Butler toward an account of discursive constitution, not in the Cartesian terms mandated by *Gender Trouble*'s project of reversal, but rather in terms of matter's acquisition of intelligible form. Butler's turn away from the idiom of cause and effect and toward that of form and matter is, I would argue, what chiefly distinguishes *Bodies That Matter* from its predecessor; and, although I suspect that she would be quick to reject this contention, this is a turn that directs her away from the all-consuming discursivism Richard Rorty peddles as pragmatism and toward the meatier fare served up by William James and John Dewey. So oriented, the idiom of form and matter opens up new ways of thinking about the sense in which human beings are distinctive sorts of materialized artifacts as well as how those artifacts participate in the conduct of making sense.

At least in part, *Bodies That Matter* is an exercise in autocritique. That this is so becomes apparent when Butler, recapitulating the second of my three questions about *Gender Trouble*, wonders whether most extant accounts of discursive constitution presuppose the existence of a determinate matrix that "acts in a singular and deterministic way to produce a subject as its effect. That is to install the 'matrix' in the subject-position with a grammatical for-mulation which itself needs to be rethought. Indeed, the propositional form 'Discourse constructs the subject' retains the subject-position of the grammat-ical formulation even as it reverses the place of subject and discourse. *Con-struction must mean more than such a simple reversal of terms.*" So long as our talk is governed by such Cartesian grammar, debate will shuffle back and forth between all too familiar poles. At one end stand those for whom the no-tion of discursive "construction has taken the place of a godlike agency which not only causes but composes everything which is its object."[56] At the other end stand those who insist that construction presupposes a constructing agent, a voluntarist subject who is not himself a creature of discourse. As with the argument between those who affirm that technology is our creature and those who affirm that we are its creatures, confined to this opposition, argu-ment stalls at a comfortable but quite dead end.

In *Bodies That Matter*, Butler seeks to step beyond the terms of this im-passe. Just how to do so is a tricky matter, indeed. In order to escape the insa-tiable maw of monistic idealism, she must reject—or at least qualify—the claim that language "goes all the way down." But she cannot mark the limits of language by positing some extradiscursive reality, for any such postulation will itself be articulated in terms of this or that language. To further complicate matters, Butler wants to retain her contention that "discourse" exercises some sort of efficacy in its relationship to "the body." Yet she now appears to recognize that *Gender Trouble*'s call to reverse conventional causal polarities will not do.

To maneuver through these straits, Butler tentatively proposes a reworking of the Aristotelian vocabulary of form and matter. Such efforts at conceptual reconfiguration are unavoidable, since thinking can never begin de novo, but they are also treacherous. Because the form/matter distinction is part and parcel of a conceptual tradition whose intelligibility turns on affirmation of an extradiscursive reality, of a realm of nature independent of culture, of a domain where women (but not men) are peculiarly at home, no matter how nuanced, its contemporary reappropriation may simply bolster the cause of those who would render patriarchal and heterosexist practices immune from critical inquiry.

To appreciate the exact cause for concern here, recall the etymological link between *matter* and *mater*, which in turn recalls the conceptual relationship between materiality and femininity. Although Butler explores this connection via a consideration of Irigaray's reading of Plato's *Timaeus*, of more obvious relevance is Aristotle's account of reproduction. Deploying mechanical metaphors to disparage female procreative power, that account holds that women contribute the passive matter of generation, whereas men bestow the immaterial but active principle that shapes matter to intelligible form, and so actualizes what otherwise remains so much potentiality:

> The female always provides the material, the male provides that which fashions the material into shape; this, in our view, is the specific characteristic of each of the sexes: that is what it means to be male or to be female. Hence, necessity requires that the female should provide the physical part, i.e., a quantity of material, but not that the male should do so, since necessity does not require that the tools should reside in the product that is being made, nor that the agent which uses them should do so. Thus the physical part, the body, comes from the female, and the Soul from the male, since the Soul is the essence of a particular body.[57]

Just as the master of the household brings its otherwise inchoate materials to rational form, so does his soulful tool cause matter's transition from undifferentiated stuff to the shaped entity that is an embryo. Reason thus confirms Apollo's declaration that the true parent, the source of a child's legitimate identity, is he who mounts.

Whether the prophylaxis of genealogical inquiry is sufficient to overcome this unsavory baggage cannot be answered a priori. Why, then, does Butler decide that this is a gamble worth taking? Much of the answer concerns a nagging philosophical itch. "The linguistic categories that are understood to 'denote' the materiality of the body are themselves troubled by a referent that is never fully or permanently resolved or contained by any given signified." The concept of matter matters because it responds to our persistent desire to acknowledge the palpable reality of that which is shaped to significant form *in* (as opposed to *by*) discourse. To confess to this desire is not to claim that this referent can be accurately captured in representationalist discourse. "To posit by way of language a materiality outside of language is still to posit that materiality, and the materiality so posited will retain that positing as its constitutive condition."[58] But it is to affirm that discourse, however conceived, does not exhaust all being and, hence, to overcome the monistic conclusion that discourse's work is a *creatio ex nihilo* from which no exit is possible.

But why ask Aristotle, of all people, to scratch this itch? Butler's rehabilitation of Aristotle is extremely attenuated, and so much of what I say here is speculative extrapolation. Be that as it may, for Butler, the principal virtue of the Aristotelian concept of matter, the stuff of which discursively articulated realities are made, appears to be that it is not Cartesian. Granted, at first blush, it might appear that the passivity of Aristotelian matter renders it indistinguishable from its Cartesian counterpart. But that is not quite right. The inquiry of modern science is predicated on affirmation of the existence of so many inert and homogeneous atoms whose interactions are altogether exoteric and mechanical, whereas Aristotelian inquiry ascribes to matter the distinctly un-Cartesian properties of temporality and potentiality:

> In both the Latin and the Greek, matter (*materia* and *hyle*) is neither a simple, brute positivity or referent nor a blank surface or slate awaiting an external signification, but is always in some sense temporalized. This is true for Marx as well, when "matter" is understood as a principle of *transformation*, presuming and inducing a future. . . . Insofar as matter appears in these cases to be invested with a certain capacity to originate and to compose that for which it also supplies the principle of intelligibility, then matter is clearly defined by a certain power of creation and rationality that is for the most part divested from the more modern empirical deployment of the term.[59]

To ensure the father's singular claim to determine the identity of his child, Aristotle construes the female as a principle that, although animate, is nonetheless unreal in the sense that it does not substantively participate in constituting the essence of that which form teases from it. To ensure the omnipotence of that father, now posturing as the autonomous subject, Descartes drains the life force from Aristotle's matter. Refusing ancient and modern patriarch alike, Butler injects into Descartes's dead matter a fix of revivifying blood, and assigns to Aristotle's passive matter the capacity to "presume and induce" its own assumption of intelligible form. Doing so, we might say, Butler emerges as the Victor Frankenstein of postmodernity.

The temporality Butler ascribes to matter is more akin to that of a seed than that of a stone. For Descartes, time is a matter of moving from one discrete moment to another through so many equidistant points in so much undifferentiated space. For Butler, following Aristotle, matter's temporal articulation entails what I will call its qualitative conservation. What I mean by this can be understood by considering any thing—an oak tree, an adult woman—in which one can intelligibly affirm that its differentiated histories remain incarnate within, indeed constitutive of, this later formation. "Hence, it is important to underscore the effect of sedimentation that the temporality of construction implies. Here what are called 'moments' are not distinct and equivalent units of time, for the 'past' will be the accumulation and congealing of such 'moments' to the point of their indistinguishability."[60] Because they *are* so many temporal articulations, discursively constituted realities can never escape the burden of the past (and so they will never achieve the sovereign autonomy guaranteed by Cartesian rationalism). But precisely because the passage of time continually reshapes that into which its events are organically incorporated, these beings are capable of transformations that are something other than mere mechanical repetitions of what has already transpired.

It is when Butler's account of matter's temporality is folded into an account of its potentiality that the resuscitation of Aristotle becomes a dicier affair. Aristotle typically represents matter as a sort of neutral (but not lifeless) substratum. "For my definition of matter is just this—the primary substratum of each thing, from which it comes to be without qualification and which persists in the result."[61] An essential property of matter, on this account, is its potentiality, where potentiality is taken to be a more or less indeterminate capacity for assuming various actualizations in time. But how exactly are we to conceive of the relationship between potential and actual? We know that Butler cannot adopt the Cartesian contention that matter's ends are exclusively imposed by unconstrained human egos; to do that is to rehabilitate the gendered notion of subjectivity she means to contest. But neither can she endorse the Aristotelian conviction that matter's ends are somehow located in and dictated by nature; to do that is to abandon her insistence that there is no reality that is not a creature of its discursive constitution.

Butler's response to this conundrum must turn on how she articulates the relationship of matter to form. In this regard, although she herself does not do so, it is helpful to recall that the Latin *forma* replaced two Greek words: *morphē* and *eidos*. Typically, the former was employed in reference to the palpable appearance or shape of some thing, the arrangement of its visible parts, functionally defined, in this way rather than that. The latter, in its distinctively Aristotelian sense, designates the teleological essence of some thing, the invisible purpose common to it and all other members of the same species. When these two notions are categorically opposed to one another, as in much post-Platonic philosophy, they all too readily spawn the facile disjunctions between idealism and materialism, reality and appearance, intelligibility and perceptibility. To forestall such antinomies, Butler urges us to recall the sense of the Aristotelian term "schema": "*Schema* means form, shape, figure, appearance, dress, gesture, figure of a syllogism, and grammatical form. If matter never appears without its *schema*, that means that it only appears under a certain grammatical form and the principle of its recognizability, its characteristic gesture and usual dress, is indissoluble from what constitutes its matter."[62] Note how this quotation productively muddies the distinction between the arrangement of some thing's parts into a palpable shape (its material morphology) and its intangible principle of intelligibility (its eidetic form). No more, the term "schema" intimates, can matter be discovered apart from some realized actuality than can form be discovered apart from its embodiment in matter. To think otherwise, to think that form and matter are ontologically distinct realities, is to fall prey once again to those grammatical tropes that induce us to believe in the hypostatized reality of concepts abstracted from that which, absent either the matter of which it is formed or the form of which it is the matter, cannot be.

With this argument in place, Butler can now respond to one of *Gender Trouble*'s worries. If neither form nor matter can be labeled the antecedent cause of the other, while that other is relegated to the status of mere "effect," then Butler need not, indeed cannot, simply "reverse" the representationalist account of discourse's relationship to materiality by affirming an equally one-sided logocentric account:

> (T)he process of signification is always material; signs work *by appearing* (visibly, aurally), and appearing through material means, although what appears only signifies by virtue of those non-phenomenal relations, i.e., relations of differentiation, that tacitly structure and propel signification itself. . . . Hence, it is not that one cannot get outside of language in order to grasp materiality in and of itself; rather, every effort to refer to materiality takes place though a signifying process which, in its phenomenality, is always already material.[63]

To acknowledge that "(l)anguage and materiality are fully embedded in each other, chiasmic in their interdependency, but never fully collapsed into one another"[64] is to find it unnecessary to presuppose matter as discourse's extradiscursive "outside" or, alternatively, to abjure its existence altogether. Denying that there exists a body knowable apart from discourse, while at the same time affirming that the body is not merely a creature *of* discourse, Butler can now say what she could not in *Gender Trouble*.

But is this declaration of the interconstitutive relationship between form and matter, effected via the term "schema," sufficient to satisfy Butler's theoretical ambitions? The answer, I think, must be no. To affirm that form and matter are dynamically interwoven in the constitution of things that matter, where the term "matter" refers to a thing's intelligibility as well as its assumption of a determinate palpable shape, is not to show *how* they come to be so connected. Hence this solution fails to do what was accomplished in *Gender Trouble* via Butler's call for a reversal of our conventional understanding of cause and effect. Unless she is willing to forgo all claims concerning efficacy, in other words, she must inquire into the notion of causality implied by a critical reappropriation of the Aristotelian vocabulary of form and matter; and that requires a rethinking of Aristotle's organicist contention that the ends of things are not imposed from without, but arise from within.

From Aristotle's essentialist teleology, Butler seeks to extract the claim that what is transformed is what in some sense already possesses the capacity to be so transformed. This, I believe, is what Butler is getting at when she speaks of matter's capacity to "presume and induce" its future incorporations. Folding the past into its present, this ambiguous but never formless stuff serves as a vital ingredient, indeed an essential condition, of the transformational conduct through which it comes to be something other than what it was. Think, by way of illustration, of a meticulously sculpted bonsai tree. Is its present shape the fruit of nature or of artifice, of internal drives or of external coercion? Predicated on a misguided opposition, this question should itself be rejected. Clearly, this tree's palpable form embodies the labor of the hands that twisted its roots and branches this way rather than that. Yet, just as clearly, that shape would be impossible absent the capacity of its woody tissues to be so shaped, absent the pulsing energies obscured by time's organic sedimentation within this obdurate reality.

Actualization of matter's latent *potentialities* is, on this account, at one and the same time an actualization of *potencies* immanent but, till now, unrealized. The powers made real at any given moment, however, are never exhaustive of matter's residual possibilities. To make this point, Butler gives the term "schema" one last twist: "We might historicize the Aristotelian notion of the *schema* in terms of culturally variable principles of formativity and intelligibility." The fashioning of real things is a matter of their "materialization," where this term refers to the contingent processes through which always-already-formed matter is reformed via its incorporation of specific configurations of discursive power that constitute it as an intelligible exemplar of this or that sort of thing. To illustrate, Butler cites Foucault's account of the relationship between body and soul in *Discipline and Punish*. In her neo-Aristotelian vocabulary, the "normative and normalizing ideal" that is the humanist soul, given its most perfect articulation in the routines, ritual, and rules of the modern penitentiary, is the schema that "forms and frames the body, stamps it, and in stamping it, brings it into being."⁶⁵ As with the bonsai tree, the body thus fashioned is not well understood as an inert effect of causes operating externally and mechanically. Rather, that body is simultaneously a creature of the power relations it incorporates as well as an essential participant in their realization.

But what exactly does Butler mean when she affirms that the schema of the penitent soul "brings into being" the body thought to house it? Does she thereby recapitulate *Gender Trouble*'s problematic representation of discursive construction as a *creatio ex nihilo*, a move that would appear to contradict the very point of her rehabilitation of Aristotle's vocabulary of form and matter? A response is implicit, I think, in her contention that the term "being" must always be placed "in quotation marks, for ontological weight is not presumed, but always conferred." The term "weight" hints that "being" and "not-being" are not exhaustive of our ontological possibilities. Significant realities can "weigh" more or less, depending on the degree of their materialization, the extent of their incorporation of the power-laden schema within which intelligible things are fashioned. What weighs most, ontologically speaking, are those beings that display the most perfect (and so the least remarkable) union of eidetic form and material morphology. Those that are "heaviest," in other words, are those matter-of-fact things that are most resistant to (but also most in need of) genealogical scrutiny: "Insofar as power operates successfully by constituting an object domain, a field of intelligibility, as a taken-for-granted ontology, its material effects are taken as material data or primary givens. These material positivities appear *outside* discourse and power, as its incontestable referents, its transcendental signifieds. But this appearance is precisely the moment in which the power/discourse regime is most fully dissimulated and most insidiously effective."⁶⁶

As this quotation intimates, in order to complete the vocabulary spun out of a postmodernized Aristotle, to the terms "schema" and "materialization," we must now add "materiality." If this vocabulary's concern is the *"process of materialization that stabilizes over time to produce the effect of boundary, fixity, and surface we call matter,"*⁶⁷ then the term "materiality" designates materialization's capacity to cover its tracks by representing the realized fruits of its transformative work as so many unquestionable realities. (To see the point, one need only recall part 1's discussion of the processes by which artisanal artifacts come to be mistaken for Cartesian neutral means as a result of their incorporation within stabilized webs of power relations.) To take such ponderous beings as so many incontestable facts akin to those "found" in nature, as positivist social science would have us do, is simply to cede the field of critical inquiry as well as the terrain of political conflict to the powers that be.

On this account, whether applied to human or artisanal artifacts, genealogical inquiry emerges as a more modest enterprise than we, in the best of all possible worlds, might want it to be. While such inquiry's aim is still to show

how things come to be real, no longer can it advance the sort of strong causal claims encouraged by *Gender Trouble*'s Cartesian residues. "The production of material effects is the formative or constitutive workings of power, a production that cannot be construed as a unilateral movement from cause to effect."[68] Materialization cannot be so construed because the terms "form" and "matter" must now be read not as discrete nouns but as co-constitutive verbs. While our grammar tempts us to say that form shapes matter, or that matter acquires form, we should say neither. For form *is* the patterned concurrence of materializing events happening within boundaries specified with more or less fixity and always subject to rearticulation, while matter *is* so much temporalized trans-form-ative activity. Moreover, as Nietzsche's critique of fetishistic understanding of causality reminds us, the sense of the terms "form" and "matter" is derivative on their semantic differential, not upon either's representation of some antecedent reality. This distinction is, therefore, functional rather than ontological, and so what we now identify as form may for other purposes be identified as matter, and vice versa. In sum, the distinction between form and matter is neither one of substance nor one of temporal priority. Rather, it is an analytic distinction between two interrelated moments within the comprehensive processes that eventuate in appearance of the materialized things that we all too often abstract from this mobile configuration in order to satisfy our desire to locate discrete agencies that/who may be held responsible for causing this or that effect.

The neo-Aristotelian terminology proposed here, especially when tempered by a dose of Nietzschean pragmatism, suggests a sort of causal efficacy that is quite unlike that imagined when metaphors drawn from mechanical *technai* are wedded either to a Platonic theology, which regards creation as the demiurgic imposition of ideal form on recalcitrant matter, or to a Cartesian theology, which, in order to remain assured of the Judeo-Christian god's omnipotence, ascribes to that divinity not merely the capacity to shape but to create matter as well. Each of these more confident understandings is informed by the metaphysics of a subject who remains persuaded that he is not a creature of power's transformative work. When that creature's pretension to autonomy is displaced, then so goes that creature's capacity to discover analogues to such autonomy in the domain of causality. To paraphrase Foucault, now that we have cut off the head of the monarch, we must decapitate his counterpart in the domain of causality as well.

To bring this section of my argument to a close, let me indicate what the terminology I have teased from Butler might accomplish by returning briefly to the sex/gender relationship. No longer, on this account, should we ask whether the cultural construction of gender identity is an accurate reflection of the nondiscursive reality of sex. Nor should we ask whether "sex" is an illusion whose appearance of reality will disappear once we recognize that "it" has no existence apart from its extrinsic cause, the discursive construction of gender identity. Instead, we should ask: "What are the constraints by which bodies are materialized as 'sexed,' and how are we to understand the 'matter' of sex, and of bodies more generally?"[69] The sexed body, we can now reply, is a creature of the differentiation and organization of its various parts via so many acts of functional specification and boundary definition. Within the historically contingent schema of Enlightenment modernism, the character of these acts is largely dictated by the imperatives of compulsory heterosexuality, and their product is a body whose sexual organs are these but not those, a subject who can imagine erotic pleasures deriving from this place but not that, an agent who knows that this part is to be inserted here but not there. So fashioned, the body *is* an ongoing border project, and its politics consists of so many efforts to police the boundaries that designate the transgressions in terms of which its heterosexual integrity is defined. When the power relations invested within that body successfully hide themselves beneath the veneer of its facticity, when the norms and roles constitutive of gender identity are deemed inviolable because mandated by the "nature" of the sexed body, we can say that the materiality of sex, the unity of eidetic form and material morphology, has been accomplished. But, once again, the "sex" so materialized is neither an extradiscursive given, nor a lie we should unmask. True, it is a fiction in the sense that it is a thing contingently generated rather than given in the nature of things. But it is a necessary fiction, and this for two reasons. First, "sex" is the discursive means with which we acknowledge the obdurate ontological weight of the materialized body. Second, and perhaps paradoxically, when linked with the co-constitutive category of "gender," this conceptual pairing effectively reminds us that the significant possibilities of materialized bodies always outstrip their appearance of stubborn self-evidence.

To illustrate the possibilities implicit in this vocabulary, let us return once more to Clytaemestra. Recall that toward the end of *Agamemnon*, as the specter of Clytaemestra appears before her, a terrified Cassandra asks: "What can I call her and be right?" Doing so, she anticipates Orestes' later question concerning Agamemnon's "robe": "What shall I call it and be right, in all eloquence?" The logic of materialization helps us understand why these questions echo each other.

Clytaemestra and the robe with which she murders her husband are both materialized artifacts. The wool given to Clytaemestra by a servant girl was shaped to form as she, implicated in the dialectic of projection and reciprocation, wove its fibers into this determinate thing. The ambiguous being of that wool included this robe as one of its possibilities, whereas others remained beyond its range; never, for example, would it materialize as a knife. This robe's constitution as a thing that matters is a matter of its materialization as this sort of thing rather than that in accordance with familiar discursive categories. But the robe's sense cannot be fully grasped absent reference to the imperatives of human embodiment. The robe is not what it is simply by virtue of its name; that name is a way of articulating its sympathetic relationship to the need of warm-blooded creatures to secure protection against the elements. Were this not so, were the robe not an excorporated surrogate for the skin it ought to safeguard, it would occasion far less horror when it turns against its "nature" by holding Agamemnon fast as Clytaemestra spills his lifeblood.

Although perhaps more difficult to grasp than an artisanal artifact, and although its specific modalities of materialization are different, Clytaemestra is also an artifact, so much formed matter. At the moment of her birth, I see little reason to doubt that the first words uttered by her disappointed father, Tyndareus, were: "It's a girl." That statement was not so much a declaration of fact, but rather the first moment in her progressive materialization as what in time would become a "woman." These words are performative in the sense that they do some-thing, help to fashion this body of ambiguous import into a determinate thing. These words serve not to prescribe an identity for what is otherwise radically inchoate, not to create a something out of nothing, but rather to embed this already formed matter within a complex of customary relations to other human bodies and the durable world of artifactual projections. Activation of those relations, the work of so much artifactual reciprocation, will in time invest the appellation spoken by Tyndareus with the substantial weight borne by any materialized artifact. We will be assured of the success of that work when Clytaemestra's "sex organs," effectively identified and demarcated through her father's invocation of the term "girl," come to be regarded as the clear and distinct evidence of her essential identity as a woman. So long as that trick works, so long as there is no disjunction between the materialized artifact that is her sexed body and the identity ascribed to her, Clytaemestra's easy intelligibility to herself as well as to others will be the token of her materiality.

Clytaemestra usurps Agamemnon's authority while he is in Troy, and kills him when he returns. First a "tyrant," now a "murderer," she can no longer be a "woman." A woman, after all, is not the sort of being who could do *that*. What was once so much unquestioned materiality has now disclosed its contingency. In consequence, Clytaemestra becomes neither a man nor a woman, but something unthinkable: "To such end a lady's / male strength of heart in its high confidence ordains"[70] (*Agamemnon*: 10-11). As she loses her determinate form in the gendered economy of Argos, as the nexus of power relations by which she was constitutively constrained is unsettled, Clytaemestra begins to dematerialize. But what can that mean? Does this mean, as the term seems to suggest, that her body undergoes some "real" change? Or is it merely a change in the way we think about her? These are questions that should remain unanswered. To respond is to reinforce Cartesian grammatical forms that deny the indissolubility of materiality and signification. When Agamemnon's robe moves out of the realm of things that care for the body and toward that occupied by things that harm it, it wavers uncertainly between opposed categories. The same is true of Clytaemestra's right hand. Before, it was an instrument of her wifely affections; now it is a partner in a heinous crime. But which is it "really"? The undecidability of that question explains why Clytaemestra now stands before the old men of Argos as the concrete incarnation of so much gender trouble:

> You try me out as if I were a woman and vain;
> but my heart is not fluttered as I speak before you.
> You know it. You can praise or blame me as you wish;
> it is all one to me. That man is Agamemnon,
> my husband; he is dead; the work of this right hand
> that struck in strength of righteousness. And that is that.
> (*Agamemnon*: 1400-1406)

vi. *Nature/Experience/Language*

THROUGH MY CRITICISMS OF ARENDT, RORTY, AND BUTLER, I HAVE SHOWN HOW VARIous forms of residual Cartesianism compromise their efforts to think about the materialization of specifically human artifacts and, more particularly, the role of discourse in that process. With the help of Butler, I have also suggested that one way to overcome this residue is to shift from an idiom of cause and effect to one of form and matter. The idiom of form and matter is intended as an ontological complement to the understanding of agency I have called the dialectic of projection and reciprocation. The latter denies the pretensions of the Cartesian subject by suggesting that the human agent is as much creature as creator. The former denies the pretensions of that subject's metaphysical correlate, the Cartesian cause, by suggesting that the materialization of bodies that matter is never an affair of unilinear imposition, always one of teasing more determinate shape from bodies never altogether without form or without history.

In this section and the next, I begin to explore the artifact of sense. How do we explain the capacity of the materialized artifacts we call human to make sense of the shaped affairs that emerge within experience? (Part 3, recall, is devoted to an examination of the gender-specific ways various characters, some more fully fictional than others, struggle to make sense of three extraordinary artisanal artifacts.) My response to this question is derivative on what has gone before insofar as the conduct of sense making is, I believe, well understood in terms of the dialectic of projection and reciprocation, and insofar as such conduct is a matter of eliciting more adequate form from already articulated matter. To get at the nature of this distinctive sort of human artifact, I complicate the vocabulary I have thus far recommended by entwining it with a pair of related conceptual triads. The first is nature/experience/language, and the second is feeling/body/meaning. In each case, the middle term is to be understood as a sort of hinge or gateway between its first and third members; and in each case, the final term is to be understood as a more complete formation of the matter afforded by the first.

One last prefatory note before I begin this section in earnest: The argument of the present section, which is principally concerned with articulating a defensible conception of experience, is intended as an introduction to the next section's contention that human bodies are vital participants in the work of sense making, and hence that they are not well regarded as unqualified creatures of their discursive constitution. Recall that in part 1, I refused to posit the priority or superiority of either of the partners to the dialectic of projection and reciprocation. An analogous argument can be made about the relationship between human bodies and human languages. Unwilling to reify and then abstract language from its embeddedness in embodiment, I want to suggest that the body is, to use Scarry's phrase again, the "recoverable referent" of the distinctions language articulates.[71] In order to defend this claim, I argue for the partial meaningfulness of a particular sort of extradiscursive experience—specifically, the sort of embodied awareness that takes shape as so much inchoate (as in rudimentary or incipient) feeling; and I suggest that the meaningfulness of what is discursively articulated cannot be grasped apart from its relationship to such embodied feeling.

In order to relocate the embodied dimensions of sense making, it is necessary to recover some intelligible account of experience. That in turn requires a detour through the pragmatism of John Dewey and William James (as opposed to that of their illegitimate son, Richard Rorty). Indiscriminately poaching from their writings, without attributing specific passages to either and so without acknowledging their temperamental differences, I will quote liberally from both over the course of the next two sections. (If you have some familiarity with Dewey and James, this will serve as a test of your ability to distinguish each from the other. To determine how well you have fared, repair to the citations.)

Rorty advances what might be called a doctrine of radical constructivism. This doctrine is informed by the logically impeccable claim that there is nothing beneath language that can be said to serve as its object (e.g., nature or experience), since anything alleged to be so is itself a creature of discourse. That, recall, is the first shot Butler fires across Kristeva's bow: "(T)o 'refer' naively or directly to such an extra-discursive object will always require the prior delimitation of the extra-discursive. And insofar as the extra-discursive is delimited, it is formed by the very discourse from which it seeks to free itself."[72] From this premise, Rorty draws the conclusion that *"language* is a more suitable notion than *experience* for saying the holistic and antifoundationalist things which James and Dewey had to say."[73] Language, on Rorty's account, subsumes all possible meaning, and so the category of experience is left with nothing much to do.

One response to this argument, formulated by Richard Shusterman, is to ask whether Rorty can in fact make do without any concepts that do the work conventionally done by those like "experience" and "nature."[74] If everything meaningful is discursively articulable, then what sense can we make of the phrase "discursively articulable"? If, as Rorty insists, concepts only bear meaning through tacit reference to the terms they oppose and/or exclude, and if the concept of the discursively articulable swallows up literally everything intelligible, then what is the differential term in terms of which we can make sense of *that* concept? If there is no such term, then don't the totalistic claims made on behalf of radical discursivism evaporate into so much tautological silliness?

Alternatively, and perhaps more productively, we might respond to this argument by acknowledging its truth. That is, perhaps we should grant, first, that any reference to nature and experience invokes discursive constructs that are thick with histories we grasp only in part and, second, that it is only ironically that can we distinguish "language" from these others in order to inquire into their interrelationships. But does the need to speak ironically mean that we should renounce these terms altogether, as Rorty recommends? Or should we do with them what Butler would have us do with the term "women"? "(T)he category of women does not become useless through deconstruction, but becomes one whose uses are no longer reified as 'referents,' and which stand a chance of being opened up, indeed, of coming to signify in ways that none of us can predict in advance. Surely, it must be possible both to use the term, to use it tactically even as one is, as it were, used and positioned by it."[75] It is in this spirit that I speak of "nature" and "experience."

To get started on my first triad, return once more to the metaphor of the web. With that metaphor, I mean to suggest in its most comprehensive sense the ways human and nonhuman things are mutually implicated. To get at this sense, I might ask how human beings incorporate the nonhuman within experience. Or, to reverse perspective, I might ask how the nonhuman incorporates human beings within experience. While either of these questions is better than most a Cartesian might generate, both represent one-sided abstractions from the mutually constitutive relational totality at issue here. Be that as it may, if we are to make sense, we cannot help but abstract things from that totality; and so, opting for the second of my two questions for the moment, I will refer to the realm of the nonhuman, independent of such incorporation, as "nature."

We can never, I repeat, gain unmediated access to the *what* of nature, which I will gesture at via the metaphor of the sea, apart from *how* it is incorporated within the web of experience. Just as there is no way to step outside the logic of artisanal projection and reciprocation in order to know reality in the buff, since "reality" cannot be known apart from the artifactual transformations that render it an intelligible thing, so too there is no way to step outside of language to know nature as it truly is, since "nature" cannot be known apart from the discursive forms that constitute it. Hence only speculatively—

or, perhaps better, only poetically—can we begin to imagine the distinguishing features of that sea's inhabitants on the basis of what appears within the web of experience. For example, the historicity of experience, its capacity to engender tragic incompletions as well as consummatory fulfillments, intimates that nature is composed of an infinitely varied conflux of existents, each of which is marked by the trait of temporality. Because all beings are so qualified, every existent is at the same time an event; and each event is simultaneously a concurrence, an event shaped to individuated form by the complex of relations in which it is implicated. Nature's sea, a pragmatist partial to Nietzsche might say, is a pregnant site of dynamic becoming, of temporally qualified emergents, of intertwining events out of which some beings are born and into which others vanish.

The beings engendered by the intercourse of such moving events are neither perfectly formed nor perfectly formless, neither pure flux nor pure structure, neither unchanging substance nor random accident, neither monistically unified nor radically disjoined. Nature's sea is not the book in which Galileo and Newton dreamed of reading the deterministic, immutable, and universal laws of the Christian god's reason; nor is it the radically amorphous void of Genesis prior to his intervention. Rejecting these alternatives as a pair of ill-conceived twins, I see no good reason to embrace Kathy Ferguson's contention that contemporary philosophy is faced with a choice between "two fundamental and opposing activities: the discovery of truth in an ordered universe versus the imposition of meaning on a disordered one."[76] To embrace the first alternative is to reduce philosophy to the status of a mirror of nature. To embrace its alter ego is to think that in the absence of human will the stuff entering experience is so much shapeless mush.

Were nature to yield only routine, only unremitting sameness, human beings would never be teased into thinking about how this relates to that, and so meaning would never be. Were nature to yield only so much formless flux, experience would never bear within it the rhythms and recurrences that furnish the enduring context in terms of which the genuinely novel is appreciated. As unwittingly insinuated by the philosophical tradition's distinctions between accident and necessity, particular and universal, mutable and eternal, nature is inherently ambiguous, of uncertain import. It harbors within it the conditions of, the potential for, meaning; but it never guarantees that promise's fulfillment.

Woven together in comparatively rudimentary ways, nature's events generate beings such as rocks. When we Cartesians call such things "inanimate," we do them the injustice that is done whenever a class of beings (think of women) is defined in terms of its lack of that which marks a superior class. It is better to say that within this domain the encounters between nature's events assume the form of interactions in which the "accidental" conjunction of antecedent events is the external transitive condition of another's immediate qualities. However, even at this rudimentary level, as Butler intimates when she ascribes the properties of temporality and potentiality to matter, nature's events display a not insignificant sort of agency. "Even atoms and molecules show a selective bias in their indifferencies, affinities, and repulsions when exposed to other events. With respect to some things they are hungry to the point of greediness; in the presence of others they are sluggish and cold. In a genuine although not psychic sense, natural beings exhibit preference and centeredness."[77] Even here, where rock meets rock, the distribution of energies among nature's events is capable of producing changes whose effects are something other than mere repetitions of what went before. A glance at something as majestic as the earth's tectonic plates or as minute as the electrons circling about the nuclei in an atom of tungsten is sufficient to suggest that nature is an unfolding affair, a matter of tensions and potencies pressing to discharge their energies, and so resolve their dynamic possibilities within states of temporary equilibrium.

Interwoven in more elaborate ways, nature's events give rise to beings such as marigolds. Although dependent for their existence on the sorts of physiochemical events that make rocks the unfeeling things they are, the generation of this more intricate form of being releases new forms of causation, forms only potentially present within the realm of the "inanimate." The difference between the animate and the inanimate, if we are to retain this problematic distinction, is not that the former is imbued with some special substance that is its essence. Rather, the difference lies in the ways in which physiochemical energies are interconnected, and hence in the relational possibilities to which each is susceptible and of which each is capable. In contrast to the relative indifference shown by inanimate beings toward the outcomes generated via their relations with other beings, the constituent parts of a marigold reach out toward, actively incorporate, what their sustenance requires. "The root-tips of a plant interact with chemical properties of the soil in such ways as to serve organized life activity; and in such ways as to exact from the rest of the organism their own share of requisite nutrition. Thus with organization, bias becomes interest, and satisfaction a good or value and not a mere satiation of wants or repletion of deficiencies."[78]

Leaving aside earthworms and their ilk, when intertwined in still more fabulous ways, nature's events beget those artifacts we call human beings. Such beings are vitally dependent on the more elementary forms of causation that sustain the existence of rocks, marigolds, and worms through time. To affirm this is not to reduce human beings to these other life forms. But it is to contend that there is no essential ontological gulf between the former and the latter. What I call the web of experience, that sublime manifestation of the potentialities resident within the sea of nature, implicates less complex inorganic and organic transactions, and so cannot be understood apart from them. Granted, our capacity to speak of this web equips us to do more than merely flounder about in the sea of nature. But that capacity, enabling us to reflect on experience's causes and consequences, its implications and significances, is teased from an extrahuman realm that is itself pregnant with this possibility.

With the concept of experience, I mean to challenge Cartesian representionalism and radical discursivism alike; and I mean to do so by inserting a middle term, an intermediary, between nature and language. As we have seen, Cartesian epistemology argues that language, purified by scientific method, can mirror the truth of nature without distortion. As we have also seen, radical discursivism rejects this representationalist account, insisting that there is no nature independent of language's construction of it. To step outside this bipolar debate, I introduce the deliberately paradoxical (in the sense of self-deconstructing) category of experience. With it, I indicate (literally: point at) what does not—indeed, cannot—appear within discourse as such, but which is the condition of any thing's appearance as a materialized artifact of this or that sort.

One of pragmatism's two founders (excluding C. S. Peirce who, I think, can only be included in this company with some difficulty) tried to get at the character of this condition when he claimed that "experience" is a "double-barreled"[79] word. Asked what this could possibly mean, the second answered: "'Experience' denotes the planted field, the sowed seeds, the reaped harvests, the changes of night and day, spring and autumn, wet and dry, heat and cold, that are observed, feared, longed for; it also denotes the one who plants and reaps, who works and rejoices, hopes, fears, plans, invokes magic or chemistry to aid him, who is downcast or triumphant."[80] This passage, if I understand it, is intended to suggest that experience burrows beneath the distinction between *what* is experienced and the *how* of experiencing. Metaphorically speaking, we might say that within experience the relationship between the entities eventually discriminated as human and nonhuman, self and world, is not unlike that between a mackerel and the salty medium it unreflectively inhabits. The term "experience," in other words, challenges the Cartesian ascription of antecedent reality to the discursive constructs it calls "subjects" and "objects." Cartesian epistemology dissects the relational whole of experience into the two individuated structures identified by these terms. Then, forgetting their derivative status, it claims to find these abstractions given in the nature of things. But because each party to this hypostatized dualism is a moment of a more inclusive (but not necessarily harmonious and certainly not homogeneous) whole, experience cannot be identified with, or located in, either or both of its terms.

On this account, it is a mistake to ask what portion of our belief reflects the world in itself, and how much is our conceptual contribution. Such a Kantian inquiry presupposes the very dualism that is rendered questionable by the appeal to experience. Similarly, it is a mistake to ask how it is possible for a human mind to come to know the external world. Such a Cartesian question only makes sense if one first assumes that the knower has somehow extricated himself from experience. And, finally, it is a mistake to endorse the sort of collective subjectivism implicit in Rorty's radical constructivism. Such constructivism forgets that whatever meaning human beings are capable of enjoying is generated *within* the dialectical exchange between nature's events, the extra-discursive textures of experience, and the articulations of language.

The term "experience," as I mean it, is not intended to gesture at some ineffable substance located who knows where. It is crucial that this term be understood in relational terms, that is, as an articulation of the way nature's dynamic events come to be incorporated within the equally mobile realm of human being. Neither epiphenomenal nor incidental, the relations constitutive of experience are ascribed full existential reality by the "radical empiricism" that defines pragmatism's "mosaic philosophy":

> In actual mosaics the pieces are held together by their bedding, for which bedding the substances, transcendental egos or absolutes of other philosophies may be taken to stand. In radical empiricism there is no bedding; it is as if the pieces clung together by their edges, the transitions experienced between them forming their cement. Of course such a metaphor is misleading, for in actual experience the more substantive and the more transitive parts run into each other continuously, there is in general no separateness needing to be overcome by an external cement; and whatever separateness is actually experienced is not overcome, it stays and counts as separateness to the end. But the metaphor serves to symbolize the fact that experience itself, taken at large, can grow by its edges. That one moment of it proliferates into the next by transitions which, whether conjunctive or disjunctive, continue the experiential tissue, cannot, I contend, be denied. Life is in the transition as much as in the terms connected.[81]

In a way, this metaphor suggests something very much akin to Saussure's understanding of language. Recall, once more, his contention that language is a structure of differences, in other words, that any given term bears distinct semantic import only by virtue of its differential relations with others. What distinguishes pragmatism from Saussurian discursivism, however, is the former's stubborn insistence that language's meaningfulness is not self-contained, and hence that it is ultimately grounded in something other than itself.

Rocks, marigolds, and worms do not possess the capacity to draw nature's relational events, as these are incorporated within experience, through the filter of language and so engender the transformative effects that are articulated meanings. Nature achieves more complete articulation of its potentialities when its affairs, drifting into the net of experience, become matters that matter. That happens not because some enigmatic "spiritual" substance is breathed into something merely "material," but because human beings exhibit the peculiar capacity to convert experience's immanent connections and distinctions into relations of meaning; experience, in short, is thick with the materials of inference. Granted, absent the art of language, we could never conceive of ourselves as beings distinguishable from nature. But acquisition of this art, while clearly making us remarkable beings, does not lift us out of the sea. Should one of our number come to believe that the capacity to speak affords privileged access to nature's essences, we will dub him a metaphysician. Should another of our number, rebelling against such hubris, come to identify what is said with the complete existential reality of things that matter, we will dub him a radical constructivist. Both, we will suspect, are out of their element.

Language, Nietzsche once wrote, is "like a spider web" that "capture(s) what we need to know."[82] Yet Nietzsche also insisted that at present we do not possess the language we need in order to make sense of the experience we now undergo. Such a claim is intelligible only if one assumes that experience can sometimes portend more than we can say, that matters can sometimes enter experience in ways not reducible to the terms of established discourses, perhaps even that sensible bodies can sometimes grasp more than words can acknowledge. Giving determinate form to what matters in experience, language helps us make our way from here to there. But in doing so, it always abridges the relational connections and disjunctions that make experience what it is.

From the perspective of pragmatism's radical empiricism, the "multiverse . . . is more like a federal republic than like an empire or a kingdom. However much may be collected, however much may report itself as present at any effective centre of consciousness or action, something else is self-governed and absent and unreduced to unity."[83] No language, in other words, can do justice to a world of experience whose partly determinate and partly indeterminate affairs are always pregnant with emergent meanings pressing beyond the margins of what is discursively articulable and in that sense knowable:

> What is really "in" experience extends much further than that which at any time is *known*. From the standpoint of knowledge, objects must be distinct; their traits must be explicit; the vague and unrevealed is a limitation. Hence whenever the habit of identifying reality with the object of knowledge as such prevails, the obscure and vague are explained away. It is important for philosophic theory to be aware that the distinct and evident are prized and why they are. But it is equally important to note that the dark and twilight abound. For in any object of primary experience there are always potentialities which are not explicit; any object that is overt is charged with possible consequences that are hidden; the most overt act has factors which are not explicit.[84]

To acknowledge the measure of unrealized possibility that is ever resident within experience is to understand why humility is an epistemological virtue, why the activity of making sense is necessarily tragic, and why any philosophy that aspires to be democratic must never give way to the quest for certainty:

"The philosophic attempt to define nature so that no one's business is left out, so that no one lies outside the door saying 'Where do *I* come in?' is sure in advance to fail. The most a philosophy can hope for is not to lock out any interest forever. No matter what doors it closes, it must leave other doors open for the interests which it neglects."[85] Qualifying our inveterate tendency to believe that language is adequate to our sense-making needs, the appeal to experience reminds us that any story can be told in this way or that, but that no one of these tellings can ever conclude with an emphatic "the end."

The preceding account of the relationship between nature, experience, and language is susceptible to various misreadings designed to get it back onto more familiar terrain. Permit me to anticipate one. Via the category of experience, am I committing the sin of foundationalism by other means? (I will return to this issue when I enter the quarrel within feminist theory concerning this category.) The term "experience," some have argued, is typically invoked by those who hope it can do some of the epistemological labor its discredited fellows—for example, reality, nature, fact—are no longer up to. Joan Scott, for example, holds that the appeal to experience "is one of the foundations that has been reintroduced into historical writing in the wake of the critique of empiricism." Such invocation, she continues, always "works in much the same way: it establishes a realm of reality outside of discourse and it authorizes the historian who has access to it."[86] So authorized, the inquirer can then forgo genealogical investigation into the political relations constitutive of experience: "The appeal to experience as uncontestable evidence and as an originary point of explanation . . . take(s) as self-evident the identities of those whose experience is being documented and thus naturalize(s) their difference."[87]

Such, no doubt, is indeed the case when experience is taken to be some sort of indubitable fact, a source of primordial truth located either in the subjective consciousness or in the external world. However, when I argue that experience should not be evacuated of all sense by collapsing it into or identifing it with discourse, I do not mean to suggest that it is either brute or self-certifying, at least not in the way a naive empiricist might intend. Granted, early pragmatism's talk of "pure experience" and "immediate experience" invited such a positivist construction. To wit:

"Pure experience" is the name which I gave to the immediate flux of life which furnishes the material to our later reflection with its conceptual categories. Only new-born babes, or men in semi-coma from sleep, drugs, illnesses, or blows, may be assumed to have such an experience pure in the literal sense of a *that* which is not yet any definite *what*. . . . (T)he flux of it no sooner comes than it tends to fill itself with emphases, and these salient parts become identified and fixed and abstracted; so that experience now flows as if shot through with adjectives and nouns and prepositions and conjunctions.[88]

The grammar of this passage appears to imply that experience is the sort of thing that subjects can "have" (as one might "have" a chunk of property?) rather than a mode of being antecedent to this very discrimination. Futhermore, it seems to imply that experience, "shot through" with language, is still "experience." In contrast, I want to suggest that while experience is a condition of language's articulation, it becomes something other than experience (although it remains continous with experience) once its matters pass through language's formative articulation. And I want to contend that because experience is always a relational affair, what is in experience is always complexly mediated by cultural histories, political institutions, artisanal artifacts, and so forth. For this reason, I consider all talk of "pure" and "immediate" experience a throwback to a metaphysical tradition we should now move beyond. I am, in sum, quite willing to grant that we never eat experience raw. What I will not grant is that the intelligibility of what we eat is exhausted by its discursive digestion.

A more subtle version of this same charge is advanced by Butler when she, echoing her criticism of Kristeva (and sometimes Foucault), argues that the appeal to experience often serves to locate the source of resistance to hegemonic norms in an ontological space located somewhere beyond or outside culture. But, as Butler insists in *Bodies That Matter*, there is no such outside: "(T)here is an 'outside' to what is constructed by discourse, but this is not an absolute 'outside,' an ontological thereness that exceeds or counters the boundaries of discourse; as a constitutive 'outside,' it is that which can only be thought— when it can—in relation to that discourse, at and as its most tenuous borders."[89] Or, as she puts much the same point in *Gender Trouble*, what is "'unsayable' within the terms of an existing cultural form is not necessarily what is excluded from the matrix of intelligibility within that form; on the contrary, it is the marginalized, not the excluded, the cultural possibility that calls for dread or, minimally, the loss of sanctions."[90] I, however, have no desire to appeal to some "absolute outside," if that phrase is intended to point toward something radically external to what enters experience; the erection of such impenetrable borders is quite inconsistent with my affirmation of the ontological continuity (but neither the identity nor the reducibility) of nature, experience, and language. Nor do I wish to deny that the constitution of hegemonic norms necessarily entails some construction of that which it forbids, nor that the intelligibility of the former turns on the latter. However, if these two quotations are intended to suggest that all meaning, whether inside or outside a dominant discourse, is a creature of its discursive articulation, then I do take exception. My aim, once more, is to suggest that there are sensible conditions of meaning other than the discursive, that these conditions take shape as so many embodied feelings, and that absent these conditions meaning could not be. That, though, is a matter for the next section.

To close this section, I want to tell a quick bedtime story. This tale, I hope, will prove a helpful metaphorical complement to the argument of this section as well as an anticipation of what is to come. Once upon a time, the story goes, there lived a patriarch in archaic Greece. After ten years' warfare and ten years' wandering, he finally returns to his home, Ithaka, disguised as a beggar. Uncertain who he is, suspecting that he may be her long-absent husband, Penelope contrives to trick this "strange man, if man you are,"[91] into disclosing his true identity. Offering him accommodations for the night, she orders her servant, Eurykleia, to move the bed she once shared with her husband into the hallway. At these words, the stranger finds himself "tried to the breaking point" (23:206). Odysseus knows that he made this artifact, quite unlike the impermanent bed of leaves he fashioned in Phaiákia, in a way such that only a god could remove it from its original location:

> An old trunk of olive
> grew like a pillar on the building plot,
> and I laid out our bedroom round that tree,
> lined up the stone walls, built the walls and roof,
> gave it a doorway and smooth-fitting doors.
> Then I lopped off the silvery leaves and branches,
> hewed and shaped that stump from the roots up
> into a bedpost, drilled it, let it serve
> as a model for the rest. I planed them all,
> inlaid them all with silver, gold and ivory,
> and stretched a bed between—a pliant web
> of oxhide thongs dyed crimson. (23:216-227)

This thing: "What shall I call it and be right, in all eloquence?" Were Odysseus a student of Plato, no doubt he would assert that he has fashioned something superior to the poet's bed, that bed of mere words; but, taught that matter is recalcitrant to divine logos, he would also feel obliged to concede that what he has made is "a particular bed and not what we call the real bed, the form of a bed."[92] To his credit, however, Odysseus is not a student of Plato. Consequently, he answers this question by insisting that out of nature's embryonic possibilities, he has fashioned something fully real, a materialized artifact, that nature could never have engendered absent his projective conduct. This sturdy consolidation of so many still vital natural events was drawn into the web of experience as certain of its potentialities were explored, while others were left behind. Although now incorporated within experience, this bed remains quite literally rooted in the earth, and so it qualitatively conserves the distinctive hardness of olive tree trunks, much as the fleece comforter atop that bed retains the warmth of the sheep from which its wool was fashioned.

Although recalling the nature from which it is wrought, this trunk also points toward the human relationships in which it is now, as it were, embedded. Until Penelope instructs Eurykleia to remove this artifact from its accustomed site, this is a thing whose materiality is constitutively affirmed by the familiar relations it sustains to various artisanal and human artifacts, and that familiarity is in turn confirmed by a name that appears unquestionably true to its nature. But, now, Penelope has graphically demonstrated that words possess the rhetorical power to tear this thing from that relational whole, to transform it into an accomplice to a ruse. To call it such is not to uproot it from its ground in nature, nor to remove it from the realm of experience, nor even to deny its identity as a bed. But it is to articulate yet another of this artifact's polymorphous possibilities, possibilities whose range cannot be antecedently specified in the language available to either Odysseus or Penelope.

When Odysseus bellows, "Who dared to move my bed?" (23:209), he capitulates to Penelope in their battle of wits. Now no longer party to a trick, this artifact is restored to its original home. In an atrophied sense, perhaps Rorty is right to claim that when Penelope utters the word "bed," this phoneme makes sense to Odysseus because of its differential relation to other sounds in their shared vocabulary. But this word could not bear even that measure of sense were their bodies and this bed not unreflectively bound together within the textures of extradiscursive experience. Acknowledging the weariness of their limbs, their desire to mourn so many lost years, this artisanal helpmate invites Penelope and Odysseus to weep the night away. Deeply implicated within their overlapping histories, this bed gestures toward a past they cannot forget as well as a future into which they fall, to the outside from which they are sheltered as well as the inside to which they are summoned.

It is much too thin to say, as an English major might, that this bed "symbolizes" the love Odysseus feels for Penelope. For this bed renders durably sensible the passion he felt when he first met Penelope, much as her uterus still bears within its lining the marks of pregnancy years after she gave birth to Telemachus: "There is our pact and pledge, our secret sign, / built into that bed" (23: 213-14). Their bodies, each dancing to a melody remembered by the other's limbs, "know" more about how that bed will respond to this recollection than their words can ever say.

To bring my little story to an end, let me simply note that when I insist that the relationship between language, experience, and nature is continuous, a matter of re-forming that which is never wholly without form, I do not mean to equate the causal conditions of sense with the meanings that emerge in discourse. The porpoises of the Mediterranean respond to the mackerel Odysseus uses for bait as so many mute stimuli. But Odysseus will respond to the shrimp Penelope prepares for dinner tomorrow night not as so many insensible physiological triggers but as active contributors to a meal that, because he shares it with her, is fraught with meaning (even though they say not a word). Should they now break their silence, should they complain about the suitors who exhausted their stores of meat, their talk of shrimp will bear sense because their words are relationally implicated within the qualitatively rich experience of their feast. Just as these shrimp will come to be digested within the tissues, nerves, and cells that make Penelope and Odysseus speaking beings, so too will the extradiscursive matter of this experience come to be absorbed within their common sense of this reunion's bittersweet reality.

vii. *Feeling/Body/Meaning*

WITH GOOD REASON, THE CARTESIAN BODY HAS BEGUN TO DECOMPOSE. NO LONGER ARE we quite so likely to locate the body squarely on the nature side of the nature/ culture dualism, figuring it as the inert instrument through which an autonomous immaterial will secures its expression. However, as one would expect in a world whose logic remains Cartesian even as its substance fades away, the principal challenger to this understanding typically represents the body as a docile site that derives its intelligibility exclusively from the various cultural practices that etch their disciplinary imperatives onto its surface.

But perhaps these are not our only options, and perhaps it is possible to extract the kernel of truth from each without giving way to the error of either. Perhaps the body is neither a thing of nature, nor a thing of culture, but a materialized artifact situated beyond the terms of this dualism. If we are to approach that beyond, Elizabeth Grosz tells us, what we need is

> an account which refuses reductionism, resists dualism, and remains suspicious of the holism and unity implied by monism—a notion of corporeality, that is, which avoids not only dualism but also the very problematic of dualism that makes alternatives to it and criticisms of it possible. The narrow constraints our culture has imposed on the ways in which our materiality can be thought means that altogether new conceptions of corporeality . . . need to be developed, notions which see human materiality in continuity with organic and inorganic matter but also at odds with other forms of matter, which see animate materiality and the materiality of language in interaction, which make possible a materialism beyond physicalism (i.e., the belief that reality can be explained in terms of the laws, principles, and terms of physics), a materialism that questions physicalism, that reorients physics itself.[93]

Perhaps, to use the language of part 2, the human body is an open but never perfectly plastic artifact, a complex of more or less recalcitrant potentialities that may be fashioned into this or that materialized form. Perhaps, to use the language of part 1, the body is neither an unfettered agent of artifactual projection nor so much raw material awaiting artifactual reciprocation, but rather a Promethean creator as well as a creature of Prometheus.

Much of my argument in part 1 was intended to show how, to quote Merleau-Ponty, the body is the "fabric into which all objects are woven."[94] Working from that premise, I argued that artisanal artifacts are not, first and foremost, puzzles to be made sense of, but rather the resources of sense making. (Recall Merleau-Ponty's discussion of the blind man's stick as well as my discussion of Walla Walla's synagogue.) If that is so, then to explain how the body is a creature of artisanal artifice is at one and the same time to affirm that the body can participate in the fashioning of sense. Absent its status as a creature, it could not be a creator. Absent its formation as a determinate materialized artifact, it would have nothing to work from or with when it comes to the matter of making sense. Agents, in sum, construct meaning by appropriating and reworking the terms in terms of which they are constructed.

In part 1, I emphasized the artisanal artifact's contribution to sense making; in this, the second half of part 2, I will emphasize the body's contribution. Do recall, though, that it is the dialectic of projection and reciprocation that transforms protohuman beings into human beings proper, and hence that the distinction between human and artisanal artifacts is analytic in character. With that in mind, I now want to reject the radical constructivist contention, best exemplified by Rorty, that the human body is unable to offer any independent contribution to the project of sense making, any contribution that is not itself a manifestation of the body's antecedent discursive constitution. On the alternative account advanced here, human bodies furnish the ill-formed but indispensable materials of discursive intelligibility.

In *The Roots of Thinking*, Maxine Sheets-Johnstone argues that philosophy's linguistic turn must now be complemented by a "corporeal turn," an acknowledgment of the ways meaning grows out of and remains anchored in living bodies. Much as Elaine Scarry argues that artisanal artifacts find their "recoverable referents" in the parts and capacities of human bodies, so too does Sheets-Johnstone contend that linguistic artifacts find what she calls their "semantic templates"[95] in the structures of human embodiment. To render this claim plausible, she offers what is admittedly a difficult-to-substantiate account of language's anthropological origins. Most who are given to the linguistic turn, she suggests, leave the birth of language unexplained, treating it as something akin to an uncaused cause. To counter this omission, she reminds us that human beings are primates, and she insists that this fact must figure centrally in any account of language's origins. Most anthropological evidence suggests that the upright posture of hominids is at least three million years old, that the practice of tool making dates to about two and a half million years ago, and that language appeared on the scene somewhere between a half million and a million years after that. If these dates are accurate, can we infer an order of causality on this basis? Can we guess that the emergence of language was contingent on the work done by so many creatures of Prometheus, as tools were employed to dig into experience and so uncover the relations between this and that? Can we guess that speech was at first primarily a kinesthetic/aural phenomenon, so many sounds whose portent was firmly rooted in and responsive to how things smelled, tasted, looked? Is it possible that speech was originally a way of negotiating the palpable reality of events that demanded immediate attention to their qualitative textures and felt relations? To imagine that language was once so urgently implicated in the immediacies of experience is not to reinstate a representationalist account of language, one that denies the contingent connection between this sound and that meaning. But it is to say that the connection between language and the pressing realities of everyday life was not arbitrary, if that term is taken to signify an absence of any intrinsic relation.

Sheets-Johnstone illustrates these speculations by asking us to imagine discovery of that archetypal artisanal artifact, the hammerstone. It is her guess that the possibility of this tool's invention turned on a prelinguistic form of analogical imagining. Such thinking, she supposes, involved extrapolation of an inarticulate awareness of the capacity of teeth to break off bits of this or that to the capacity of a stone to do the same. A creature who finds itself grinding something to pieces with its teeth is at the brink of a generalizable recognition—specifically, realization of its embodied capacity to transform some thing into something else. In this sense, an actualized corporeal power is the condition that opens up, but does not guarantee materialization of, the possibility that a creature may come to recognize itself as an agent, as a being endowed with certain open-ended potencies. When one of those potencies is actualized, for example, when this agent comes to employ a stone *as* a hammer, that in turn may disclose the possibility of making a stone *into* a hammer. When awareness of the transformative capacity of teeth is thus projected into a freestanding artifact, the ground necessary to articulation of the discursive concept of hardness is already well tilled. That emergent concept takes shape as a grasp of a causal capacity, the capacity of hard things to transform matter from this shape into that; and that concept's content *is* that creature's grasp *of* that relationship. Language, however, is not the sole condition of this grasp. Latent in inarticulate habits, this concept's linguistic elaboration grows out of antecedent realization of a stone's potential efficacy, and that in turn grows out of a primitive apprehension of the capacity of teeth to alter the form of things given in experience. (Note, incidentally, that if this line of reasoning is plausible, then perhaps the most dramatic manifestation of the excess of artisanal reciprocation over projection is language itself.)

Even if Sheets-Johnstone is wrong in her account of language's origins, it seems to me that we are nevertheless well-advised to explore the corporeal matrices of what is discursively intelligible. To do so, if only for a moment, let us revive Hegel's baby, who, you will recall, made a brief appearance in part 1. Well before that baby says a word, her tongue begins to fashion sense, often through literal incorporation, of what is found in the world. That baby will in time come to think of her body *as* a body only because, long before, a gnostic system of tactile-kinesthetic sensibilities was forged through so many sense-making forays conducted by her organs of corporeal engagement. The experience of touch, more specifically, is the primordial condition of Wilhelmina's emerging sense of selfhood, a sense that first materializes as a resonant feel for its standing as so much animate potentiality. (Were this baby named Renée, no doubt she would think her sense of selfhood contingent on abstract recognition of her nature as a disembodied locus of immaterial consciousness; we would find this precocious creature quite unlike any to emerge from a woman's womb.) Should Hegel's baby eventually become one of Piaget's subjects, he will no doubt note that her lips make the shape of an "O" when she struggles to pry the lid off a matchbox. That oral gesture we will understand as her embodied anticipation of the result she seeks, her spontaneous but acquired grasp of what in time she will intend when she speaks the word "open." Should Piaget remain attentive, he will see how little Wilhelmina teases other sorts of extradiscursive spatial awareness out of what might be called her corporeal logos. Putting things in her mouth, expelling matters from her anus, clutching and releasing Hegel's pinkie, sticking out her tongue at her psychologist, she will in time come to grasp the conceptual distinction between inside and outside, a distinction that will make sense only because it has been actively nurtured by a myriad of embodied incidents of "in" and "out."

In arguing for the rootedness of what is discursively articulated in corporeal sense, I am not arguing for a reduction of the former to the latter. Nor am I denying that the latter is irreducibly shaped by the former. However, to borrow Richard Shusterman's persona for a moment, "I am here urging recognition of a category of experienced practice which grounds and guides intelligent activity but which is not at the discursive and epistemological level of the logical space of reasons nor is simply reducible to the physical conditions and causes described by natural science."[96] Sufficiently refined, the sense of which I speak is a matter of embodied capacity, of knowing how to make one's way through the situations of everyday life. The Cartesian privileges propositional meaning, while the radical discursivist privileges the grammatical rules that inform all such propositions. But knowing how to swim is irreducible to either. My arms' circular motions "make sense" of the liquid resistance they meet, even though I cannot afford that sense conceptual articulation. By the same token, knowing how to speak Japanese is not reducible to what we can say in Japanese, nor to what we can say about what it is to speak Japanese. As with swimming, speaking is a dispositional skill, a capacity to project accustomed habits beyond the range of their past realizations, and whatever sense is made thereby makes sense because it is rooted in the embodied sensibilities out of which discourse grows. Such habits furnish resources in the form of funded meanings serving, not as external means of identification, but rather as atmospheric media whose pervasive implication within each lived situation provides the ill-defined yet meaningful field within which specific things are brought forward as matters of express articulation. Should those habits become the sub-

ject of explicit discourse, should they move from the background to the foreground of sense making, they will become something other than what they
were absent such elaboration.

To relate this notion of corporeal sense to the speculative ontology of the
preceding section, recall the pragmatist contention that "(w)hat is really 'in'
experience extends much further than that which at any time is *known*" or, to
rephrase the point so as to render it more suitable to my ends, discursively articulable. The sensible body, I now want to contend, is the agent through
which human beings secure access to that indistinct but not insignificant
what. My premise here is the following: Simply because we can never speak of
any thing's existence absent linguistic mediation, that in and of itself does not
require us to believe that matters can never enter experience extradiscursively,
nor that the meaningfulness of such things is entirely conditional on their discursive mediation. Embodied "feelings," I wish to suggest, furnish the qualitative materials without which discursively articulated distinctions would be so
many ethereal phantasms. Ambiguously situated between world and word,
testifying to the true nature of neither, feelings are found at the shadowy junc-
tion between the what and the how of experience, between those conjoint moments that the Cartesian confuses with the antecedent reality of object and
subject. As such, and as was the case with "experience," to speak of "feelings"
is to engage in an inherently ironic, even paradoxical, endeavor. To do so is to
participate in their discursive reformation, and that is to make them into
something other than what they essentially are. To translate this paradox into
a denial of the reality of feelings is to permit the logical imperatives of professional philosophy to ride roughshod over one of the more subtle manifestations of embodied experience.

When nature's mobile existents are caught up within and transformed via
their incorporation within experience, what Dewey calls "qualities" are engendered. Qualities are located neither in the existents themselves, nor in human
agents, but in the relationship between the two. Moreover, and consistent
with Nietzsche's contention that every thing is essentially constituted by its
differential relations with all other things, a feeling is always a registration of
some sensed distinction between one relational matter and another. What is
felt is the sensed difference between matters of experience, not the discrete
essence of some unitary stuff. Were matters otherwise, were thinking "no
more than registering abstract identities, it would be a most superfluous performance. Things and concepts are identical with themselves only in so far as
at the same time they involve distinction."[97] The sensory-kinetic experience of
qualitative differentiation, in sum, is the fertile soil out of which discursive
concepts are eventually awakened: "Knowledge of sensible realities thus
comes to life inside the tissue of experience. It is *made*; and made by relations
that unroll themselves in time."[98]

"Without immediate qualities those relations with which science [or language] deals, would have no footing in existence and thought would have nothing beyond itself to chew upon or dig into. Without a basis in qualitative events, the characteristic subject-matter of knowledge [or speaking] would be algebraic ghosts, relations that do not relate."[99] Our living bodies, in other words, are the indispensable conditions of our minds. The latter grows out of the former in the sense that vital configurations of felt sense, so many relations of implication and inference present within experience, furnish thinking and speaking with the "terms" whose connections and disjunctions, once untangled, become the stuff of articulated significance. "Prepositions, copulas, and conjunctions, 'is,' 'isn't,' 'then,' 'before,' 'in,' 'on,' 'beside,' 'between,' 'next,' 'like,' 'unlike,' 'as,' 'but,' flower out of . . . the sensational stream, as naturally as nouns and adjectives do, and they melt into it again as fluidly when we apply them to a new portion of the stream."[100]

Although qualitative discriminations furnish the rudimentary materials of sense making, they are not to be considered so many inferior or inchoate cognitions. Arguably, as I noted in my preface, the Western philosophical tradition is defined by its inveterate conviction that the materialized accomplishment we call cognition is the only way to secure access to what is real; and, arguably, the radical discursivist proves to be that tradition's most recent offspring when he contends that language's categories furnish our sole means of intelligible entry into the world. I reject such logocentric voracity. The felt qualities of experience are not so many Lockean "sensations," so many protoepistemic atomic bits that gradually coalesce into so many simple ideas. Nor are feelings the medium through which epistemology's neutered objects cross from the realm of the purely physical to that of the purely psychical. Rather, feeling is an extracognitive mode of participation in the web of experience, an embodied conduit through which the qualitatively textured world passes into us, and we into that world. Perhaps, as the sons of Plato have always insisted, meaning at its most sublime is indeed an epistemic accomplishment. But even should this intellectual conceit prove defensible, this achievement always emerges out of and remains dependent on a background of feeling that is never left behind, that is always actively but inarticulately implicated in what is known and said.

For much the same reason, what I am labeling "feelings" should not be confused with emotions. When I tell the dualistic sons of Descartes that feeling is not a mode of cognition, not a mode of access to the objective world, they quickly conclude that this term must therefore refer to so many subjective promptings located within the psyches of so many private egos. But to interpret feeling in this way is to set it up for easy dismissal by those who consider such business the peculiar affair of women. Equally important, it is once again to represent a relational matter, a matter of con-fusion (in the literal sense of pouring together), as a well-bounded and so determinate object. To situate the term "feeling" on terrain defined by the subject/object dualism is to locate and lose it at one and the same time.

Felt qualities, although real, never identify themselves by name. Because they are relatively undifferentiated, they bear the capacity to assume many discursive forms. "Without language, the qualities of organic action that are feelings are pains, pleasures, odors, colors, noises, tones, only potentially and proleptically. With language, they are discriminated and identified."[101] Right now, the vital reality of bodily pain, of dis-ease, consumes my body. Out of the difference between this feeling and that of health, the articulated category of disease is teased. Once elicited, that category fundamentally informs what I find real. But such articulation would have nothing to stand as an articulation of, and so would make no sense, were I not first to hurt.

"Apart from language, from imputed and inferred meaning, we continually engage in an immense multitude of immediate organic selections, rejections, welcomings, expulsions, appropriations, withdrawals, shrinkings, expansions, elations and dejections, attacks, wardings off, of the most minute and vibratingly delicate nature."[102] How matters enter experience, accordingly, is never fully exhausted by, or equivalent to, our articulation of their felt qualities. To speak *of* a feeling is to bound an ill-formed matter whose tentacles reach out in many directions, mingling promiscuously with many other equally ill-formed matters; to say "its" name is to halt that intercourse by partitioning participants otherwise thoroughly entangled. Any term, therefore, represents a contingent stabilization of the relations it consolidates, a materialized artifact whose appearance of self-subsistent identity is always contested by what it excludes:

> The essence of life is its continuously changing character; but our concepts are all discontinuous and fixed, and the only mode of making them coincide with life is by arbitrarily supposing positions of rest therein. With such arrests our concepts may be congruent. But these concepts are not *parts* of reality, not really positions taken by it, but *suppositions* rather, notes taken by ourselves, and you can no more dip up the substance of reality with them than you can dip up water with a net, however finely meshed. When we conceptualize, we cut out and fix, and exclude everything but what we have fixed. A concept means *that-and-no-other*. Conceptually, time excludes space; motion and rest exclude each other; approach excludes contact; presence excludes absence; unity excludes plurality; independence excludes relativity; "mine" excludes "yours"; this connexion excludes that connexion—and so on indefinitely.[103]

If "what really *exists* is not things made but things in the making," and if it is equally true that "(o)nce made, they are dead, and an infinite number of alternative conceptual decompositions can be used in defining them,"[104] then to confine sense to what can be discursively articulated is to turn the enterprise of philosophy into so much necrophilia.

Like hammers and human beings, what is made of sense is a materialized artifact. Just as hammers are made of wood, and just as human beings are made of bodies, discursively articulated meanings are made of qualitative sense. Just as hammers and human beings are more or less stable articulations of the relational matters of which they are composed, so too are the linguistic events that comprise established discourses. To apply the language of artisanship to sense-making in this fashion is to suggest that meanings, like hammers and human beings, are not created *ex nihilo*. Perhaps more important, it is to suggest that the adequacy of meaning is not a matter of its accurate representation of whatever is given in experience as so much sensed feeling. To believe that mimesis is the criterion of adequacy is akin to believing that the value of a hammer turns on its bare reduplication of the qualities evinced by its constitutive materials. But not every hard thing is a hammer, and so a hammer cannot be any old thing that displays the quality of hardness. Rather, a hammer is a transformation of the materials bearing this quality into something that, although conserving this property, is not identical with it. By the same token, the articulation of felt sense into discursive meaning involves the qualitative transformation of insufficiently formed materials into a more sufficient realization of their evocative possibilities. Hence the adequacy of such meaning cannot be determined by asking whether it corresponds to, simply replicates, the materials from which it is made.

Rorty is quite right to insist that "we have no prelinguistic consciousness to which language needs to be adequate," if the term "adequate" is taken to mean accurately representational. But if the criterion of adequacy is one of sufficient response to the imperatives of sense making, then the answer is not so clear. The meaning of discourse is always partly contingent on its relationship to extradiscursive experience, and so its adequacy is always partly a matter of how well it responds to the call of inarticulate desires, frustrations, hopes, and anxieties. That Rorty understands this on some level is intimated when he writes: "If you want your books to be read rather than respectfully shrouded in tooled leather, you should try to produce tingles rather than truths."[105] But he can make nothing of this potentially productive insight because he must consider that tingle intrinsically meaningless, a brute response occasioned by a verbal stimulus that is itself the sole bearer of meaning.

A better account of Rorty's tingles might suggest that the relationship between sensed feeling and discursive significance is always dialectical. The former furnishes the ill-formed but never senseless materials that are subject to discursive exploration and reformulation in the process of making the latter. The distinction between "sense" and "significance" is not, then, a distinction between what is natural and what is cultural. Rather, it is a distinction between two different (but always interdependent) ways of incorporating the stuff of experience. To say that one furnishes the condition and context for the other is not to ascribe it ontological superiority; it is only to say that absent the sensible bodies that ground our talking heads, we would live in an (un)world of so much immaterial nonsense.

In opposition to those who collapse one into the other, in this section and its predecessor I have suggested that the relationship between language and experience is always problematic as well as paradoxical. The meaning of what language enables us to say cannot be fully grasped until we resituate discourse within the extradiscursive context of embodied experience. Yet what is "in" experience always spills over the boundaries of our concepts, and so that context can never be exhaustively known as a discursive object. The word "experience," recalling that overflow, reminds us of the partiality of all discursive frames as well as of the error of any Cartesian epistemological framework that assumes the transparency of world to word. More important from the standpoint of politics, the term "experience" reminds us of the import of those inchoate intimations that, because they have no recognized status or fit within available discursive frameworks, sometimes well up and press against a dominant culture's hegemonic discourses. Denial of the reality of such intimations is, I suspect, a luxury restricted to those who, as a rule, find currently available linguistic resources adequate to their sense-making needs.

viii. *Black Widows*

IMAGINE THAT A BAND OF WOLF SPIDERS WERE TO MANUFACTURE A WEB AND, UPON COMPLETION, employ their guile in persuading a company of black widows to join them as so many helpmates on this prefabricated site. Contending that they alone know how to fashion and so refashion its essential structure, the former convince the latter that their nature renders them incapable of doing the same. Because they must work within its antecedently established confines, the widows never quite feel "at home" in this web. Were they members of the Zygiella family, and were they to find themselves in a web spun by members of, say, the Araneus clan, without hesitation they would scramble to the web's periphery, drop from its frame, and set to spinning a home of their own. But, unable to do what they cannot imagine, our company of widows must make the best of a problematic situation.

The Cartesian paradigm of use is a fit discursive web for the contemporary sons of Hephaestus. As I suggested in part 1, that paradigm is bound up with a particular notion of autonomy, with a representation of the agent as a being who sits apart from the world of things and who, for that reason, is secure in the knowledge that he can command what he makes. This notion of autonomy is in turn bound up with a repudiation of the body, for its needs are all too firmly mired in the grubby affairs of the world. As such, this paradigm presupposes and reflects a gender-based division of labor, one that designates women as caretakers of bodies and men as beings who, because the burden of such care has been foisted on others, can afford to pursue loftier matters. Although the minds of men are thus dependent on the bodies of women, that dependence must be disavowed if the myth of masculine self-sufficiency is to remain secure. Accordingly, we have good reason to suspect that the Cartesian paradigm of use, although revealing as an articulation of the acquired sensibilities of those who monopolize the means of interpretation in patriarchal cultures, is propped up by a tissue of fictions. Were Descartes to acknowledge that absent the work done by women, his philosophical labors could not be, surely he would find cause to fret about his masculinity.

"(W)oman makes man and man makes the world."[106] To unpack Wendy Brown's epigram, let me paraphrase an argument advanced by Dorothy Smith in her book, *The Everyday World as Problematic*.[107] Consider women's work or, more modestly, what we know of such work within the West. While I do not mean to ignore the work done by many women outside the household, whether extended or nuclear, and while I do not mean to overlook the fact that many women have been able to escape work within the home because it has been foisted onto the backs of their less fortunate sisters, and while I do not mean to deny that many subjugated men have been required to engage in "women's work," it is nonetheless true that *as a categorical matter* the identity of woman has been generally defined in terms of the forms of labor constitutive of what Aristotle called the sphere of necessity: reproduction, child rearing, and household maintenance.

Because the forms of labor typically practiced by the daughters of Athena are deemed indispensable but unworthy means to ends that cannot be fulfilled within the household, to be a woman is to be a thing whose conduct cannot engender the forms of reality that are fully human. Because her work in making and maintaining the artisanal artifacts that sustain daily life is conventionally relegated to the sphere of instinct, because that work is habitually excised from dominant conceptions of what counts as culture, it has left few traces within the discursive categories generated by and within that culture. Women's work, in short, has remained largely invisible from the perspective of concepts fashioned out of the experience of those who must shun banal labor in order to preserve their dignity as men.

For these reasons, much of what women do evaporates into the unworld of the inexpressible, and there it assumes the quality of a paradox. That work, which disappears all the more completely the more successful it is, can only be spoken of within the confines of discursive schemes that deny its meaningfulness. As such, the situation of woman proves factually problematic. Under conditions of what Iris Young calls "cultural imperialism," those in subordinate positions

> find themselves defined from the outside, positioned, placed, by a network of dominant meanings they experience as arising from elsewhere, from those with whom they do not identify and who do not identify with them. The group defined by the dominant culture as deviant, as a stereotyped Other, *is*

culturally different from the dominant group, because the status of Otherness creates specific experiences not shared by the dominant group, and because culturally oppressed groups also are often socially segregated and occupy specific positions in the social divison of labor. . . . Cultural imperialism involves the paradox of experiencing oneself as invisible at the same time that one is marked out as different.[108]

With this quotation in mind, recall my earlier argument regarding the dangers involved in abstracting language from the relational complex in which it is embedded and of which it is an articulation. Smith and Young, it seems to me, give us additional cause to reject any simple equation of available discursive means with the experience of gender. So long as women remain caught within the logic of a sense-making order teased out of the lives of others, like so many black widows inhabiting alien turf, experience will pose questions that cannot be answered from within its confines.

With this last claim, I tread on much-contested terrain. The term "experience" has proven one of principal foci of debate in Anglo-American feminism over the course of the past three decades. As I read this debate, "experience" was initially invoked in the late 1960s and early 1970s as a way of countering the absence of talk about women's oppression within the discourse of the American Left. That void was countered through formulation of the slogan, "The personal is the political," which effectively contested the Marxian assumption that oppression was to be looked for in the workplace and in the state, but not in the bedroom and the kitchen. The appeal to the "personal" was an appeal to the "subjective experience" of women, and the operative assumption was that by virtue of their common relationship to men all women suffered more or less identical forms of oppression. The 1969 manifesto of the Redstockings put the point well: "We regard our personal experiences and our feelings about that experience as the basis for an analysis of our common situation. We cannot rely on existing ideologies as they are all products of male supremacist culture."[109] As this quotation indicates, inquiry into women's lives soon generated the more radical contention that mainstream conceptual categories are an expression of the experiences of men alone and so are ideological in the sense that, although partial in fact, they claim universal validity. From this, there followed the conclusion that feminist inquiry can open up the possibility of fashioning concepts that are true in the sense that they are faithful to the unique character of women's experience.

Feminist standpoint theory, which Judith Grant aptly describes as "an epistemological argument that tries to describe a distinctly 'female' or 'feminine' knowledge through recourse to the experiences of women,"[110] is perhaps the most prominent contemporary heir to this history. From the premise that common features of women's experience elicit distinctive ways of knowing, standpoint theorists characteristically conclude that such ways are superior to those bred by the experience of men, and hence that women have a special capacity to grasp the truth of social reality. What links premise to conclusion here is the contention that members of a dominant group have neither cause nor capacity to question the myths that legitimate their superiority, whereas members of a subordinate group, by virtue of their status as outsiders, have both.

For a familiar example of such an argument, consider Nancy Hartsock. In her essay, "The Feminist Standpoint: Developing the Ground for a Specifically Feminist Historical Materialism," Hartsock argues that because men deny the needs of their bodies, they develop a dualistic consciousness that rigidly disconnects all things cultural from all things natural, thus encouraging a posture of instrumentalism toward the latter. Women, by way of contrast, are daily reminded of their continuities with the natural world. The experiences of menstruation, intercourse, pregnancy, and lactation, all of which throw into doubt the Cartesian separation of self from world, induce a sense of connection with nature as well as a nonmanipulative attitude toward its matters. At least in principle, Hartsock concludes, such experiences make "available a particular and privileged vantage point on male supremacy." Fashioned into an epistemology, this vantage point can provide access to a "deeper level or essence" of reality, a level that "both includes and explains the 'surface' or appearance, and indicates the logic by means of which the appearance inverts and distorts the deeper reality." Knowledge of this reality, to complete the circle, furnishes the "ontological base for developing a non-problematic synthesis, a social synthesis which need not operate through the denial of the body, or the death struggle between the self and others."[111]

In large measure, quarrels among standpoint theorists have concerned the source of the distinguishing features of women's experience and so of their epistemic privilege. Consider, for example, Catharine MacKinnon. In her essay, "Feminism, Marxism, Method, and the State: An Agenda for Theory," MacKinnon echoes Marx's assertion that the structure of a capitalist economy is ultimately derivative upon the expropriation of workers' labor. Seeking to adopt the epistemological form but not the substantive content of this argument, MacKinnon argues that in fact it is a principle of sexual dispossession that governs "the totality of social relations." To show how women might come to know this principle, she submits a brief on behalf of consciousness-raising as *the* method of feminist science: "In consciousness raising, often in groups, the impact of male dominance will be concretely uncovered and analyzed through the collective speaking of women's experience." Because its epistemic efforts are grounded in such experience, feminist science can affirm its "special access" to "reality,"[112] and so justify its claim to know the single principle that defines that reality.

Finally, consider Sara Ruddick. In her essay, "Maternal Thinking," she argues that women, as mothers, develop certain "generic" capacities in caring for their children; that these acquired forms of skilled conduct qualify as so many ways of knowing; and, finally, that these cognitive capacities furnish the basis for reconstruction of a patriarchal world built by those who, for the most part, are not intimately implicated in the conduct of child rearing. That Ruddick can offer her characterization of these capacities without significant cultural qualification turns on her adaptation of Habermas's argument in *Knowledge and Human Interests* concerning the existence of irreducible imperatives common to all who are human. Following this lead, Ruddick argues that "there are features of mothering experience [e.g., extended gestation, protracted infant fragility and dependence, etc.] which are invariant and nearly unchangeable, and others which, though changeable, are nearly universal"; and from these features she derives an account of the interests that "govern maternal practice throughout the species."[113]

I recognize that in lumping together these thinkers, I am glossing over important differences between and qualifications of their respective arguments. Be that as it may, it is nevertheless true that each derives considerable rhetorical power from her appeal to experience. For each, the phrase "women's experience" points either to a reality that, because it remains more or less immune to time, provides the touchstone from which women's permanent interests can be derived; or to an identity that, because it proves more or less invariant across space, unifies the lives of those living in so many heterogeneous contexts. Equally important, for each, experience is considered either a form of knowledge (Ruddick), or a form of potential knowledge (Hartsock and MacKinnon). In the former, the epistemic authority of such knowledge is internal to its very being. In the latter, the claim to epistemic authority emerges only after such potential knowledge has been disciplined and refined by feminist method.

Such appeals to experience have been subjected to extensive criticism in recent years, and that criticism has generated a debate that is saturated with residual Cartesianism. That this is so is indicated by the fact that such criticism waffles indeterminately between the charges of objectivism and subjectivism. Those who criticize standpoint theory on the grounds that it is subjectivist contend that it presupposes what Kathleen Jones calls the "transparency of experience," the "assumption that the meaning of any experience is somehow already present, already constituted and internal to that experience in advance of the articulation of it through language. The assumption seems to be that experience needs only to be 'tapped' or 'taped' (listened to) in order for it to yield up its secrets (meanings) to its owners (those who 'have' it)."[114] Taking experience as an irreducible and self-authenticating voice, a source automatically productive of discursive meaning, such a psychologistic construction forgets that what that inner voice utters may be nothing other than what it has been told to say. Moreover, for those who endorse the transparency of experience, there is no way in principle to adjudicate a debate between women who find that experience whispers rather different things into their respective ears. Ultimately, when feminist discourse becomes caught between such experts, either the multiplicity of subjective perceptions must be conceded; or the superiority of one over all others must be dogmatically affirmed; or a mythical universal Woman must be invented in order to arbitrate between these rival renditions.

Those who criticize standpoint theory for its objectivist pretensions argue that any attempt to ground feminist claims to knowledge in something common to all women, whether that be the practices of mothering, the distinctive qualities of female sexuality, the expropriation of women's reproductive capacities, or whatever, is essentialist and for that reason ideological. For example, replicating Butler's critique of Kristeva, Teresa Ebert takes Hartsock to task because she "grounds her theory of social relations, in the last instance, on a biology and erotics of reproduction: on the menstruation, pregnancy, lactation of the female body as if these were self-evident, invariable, essential processes."[115] Such a move represents as universal features of women's experience that, at the very least, are culturally variable and that, more often than not, are extrapolated from the lives of those who are Western, white, middle-class, and heterosexual. If crosscutting interests and salient allegiances rooted in class, racial, religious, and other differences are to be given their due, these critics continue, the category of experience must be subjected to vigorous genealogical investigation. To do otherwise is to smuggle into one's theoretical apparatus a conceptual surrogate whose unacknowledged task is to do much the same work conventionally done by "Nature" or "God" within masculinist philosophies.

After reviewing these criticisms, Grant correctly notes that "feminist theory has vacillated between inventing an experience of Woman writ large, and attempting to summarize those of all particular women."[116] Unwilling to paddle interminably between the sinkholes of subjectivism and objectivism, Grant concludes that feminists should scrap the concept of experience altogether. For reasons suggested in the preceding two sections, I think Grant's exhortation should be rejected.

When Ruddick, Hartsock, and MacKinnon invoke the term "experience," their aim is to designate the substantive *content* distinguishing the experience of women from that of men. This content is then used to explain the generation of certain ethical attributes allegedly displayed by women—for example, why they are empathetic rather than egotistical, why they prefer harmony to conflict, and so forth. More important for my purposes, that content is also used to explain the generation of certain epistemological capacities allegedly displayed by women—for example, why they see things as organic wholes rather than as mechanical aggregates, how it is possible for women to grasp structural contradictions that escape men, and so forth. But my aim is not to specify the content of anyone's experience. As I explained earlier, the experience of which I speak is to be located neither in the "subjective" psyches of individual knowers, nor in certain "objective" features of the known world; what I mean to get at with this term is antecedent to that very distinction. Hence I cannot be accused of assuming "the transparency of experience," if that phrase means something like "taking for granted the epistemic authority of that which resides in the consciousness of individual women." Nor can I be accused of "essentialism," if that term means something like "rooting claims to knowledge in something more universal or permanent than the contingencies of human affairs."

Most modestly, the term "experience" is simply a mnemonic device, reminding us that all discursive articulations—for example, that between subject and object, mind and body, male and female, theory and practice—are abstracted from a more comprehensive web, a web whose relational matters come without the neat borders specified by these nouns. As such, the term "experience" is an inquiry perpetually put to us, inviting us to ask what is marginalized and/or excluded by dominant modes of discursive articulation (e.g., the Cartesian paradigm of use). So conceived, experience cannot ground anything; it cannot afford epistemic privilege to anyone; it cannot promise to unify the members of any putative group. To speak of experience is to pose an open-ended question; it is not to mandate any particular response to that question.

I should not, however, be guilty of false modesty in speaking of what this category can and cannot do. Although aware of all the appropriate caveats, I nonetheless want to offer a qualified endorsement of standpoint theory's contention that women characteristically inhabit a significance-laden web that is, in important respects, unlike that inhabited by men; and I want to offer a qualified endorsement of its claim that women's residence there can (but never must) bring to appearance contradictions within that web, contradictions that are neither recognized nor articulated within the discursive forms teased out of the conduct of men. The first of these claims follows from my account of the dialectic of projection and reciprocation, which suggests that to be differentially situated within that dialectic by virtue of one's position in a gender-specific division of labor is to differentially undergo the excess of reciprocation over projection. The second follows from my account of the relationship between bodies and feelings, which suggests that it is possible to have some extradiscursive but nonetheless sensible intimation of structural tensions that are occluded by a dominant constellation of articulated meanings.

These two claims are internally related. If women can sometimes grasp contradictions that elude men, if women are more likely than men to sense the limitations of the Cartesian paradigm of use, if women sometimes display ethical virtues absent from their more brutish counterparts, this is not because their bodies bleed even when uncut, not because their wombs are occasionally colonized by little aliens, not because they are by nature smarter or nicer. Rather, it is because they are distinctively formed creatures of Prometheus, human artifacts whose habituated sensibilities are fruits of the work performed by re-current intercourse with gender-specific configurations of artisanal artifacts. To the extent that such sensibilities are themselves gender specific, they open up the possibility that women and men will tease different matters from the web of relations constitutive of experience.

Although relations are not directly perceptible as such, all things partici-pate *in* them and so all things partake *of* them. What is discursively articulable are those materialized realities that have come to appear *as if* they were deter-minately bounded and so self-contained. But that appearance, the tacit claim of existing articulations to completeness and finality, is always belied by the web of relational connections and disjunctions that crisscross these apparently self-sufficient realities, making them what they are and are not. When these relational connections become the stuff of feeling, they appear as an indefinite call to explicate, to unravel and then reweave, some of the implicit relations between this and that, relations that will remain unacknowledged so long as received discourses remain uncontested.

When a woman responds to such a call, her aim is not to determine the meaning of this situation *to* her, or to anyone else for that matter. What she seeks, instead, is the meaning *of* the relational reality in which she is embed-ded as a vital part; and in this qualified sense, what I am calling "feeling" does indeed testify to the objectivity of the situation in which she finds herself. But to affirm such objectivity is not to affirm feeling's grasp of so many clear and distinct objects; such, by definition, are absent from experience. Nor is such objectivity to be confused with the achievement of a bird's eye view of this rela-tional tangle as it "really" is. Because these mutually imbricated relations al-ways spin off to places that can never be comprehensively traced in space or time, she can never secure an exhaustive grasp of what enters into her present situation. Moreover, and paradoxically, to begin to fashion discursive sense of that tangle is of necessity to reweave its threads, and so to engage in imma-nent transformation of what the Cartesian contends is statically re-presented in the act of knowing. In sum, a woman who seeks to step beyond the web of experience in order to grasp it in what Hartsock and MacKinnon call its "total-ity," an arachnid who wishes to go by the name of Archimedes, is sure to fall headlong into an abyss of absurdity.

Exactly what transpires, then, when a woman searches for the right words to express a felt dissatisfaction, only to recognize the inadequacy of the terms ready to hand? What happens, more specifically, when the fact of gender loses its status as a materialized reality and assumes that of a contestable artifact, a man-made fiction? What are the conditions of the possibility of that event?

Sense making is impossible absent materials to work on, to elicit form from. Accordingly, if gender's appearance of facticity sometimes crumbles, the conditions necessary to that possibility must be latent in experience; or, per-haps better, experience must be pregnant with those conditions. For a concrete example of one such condition, recall that in large measure the identity of woman has been defined in terms of the routine tasks necessary to child rearing, bodily sustenance, and domestic maintenance; in equal measure, the identity of man has been defined in terms of his distance from such tasks. Were this the end of the matter, were reciprocal gender identities perfectly constituted by and through such terms, then it would be difficult to know how to account for the emergence of modern feminism. To account for that eventuality, borrowing from Smith once again, we might note that with the expansion of a capitalist economy more and more women have found it necessary to become something other than, or rather in addition to, home and baby makers. Many women, more exactly, have taken jobs where their principal task is to give tangible form to the disembodied world of Cartesian men. As secretaries, for example, women manufacture the written texts that afford business transactions palpable documentation. As nurses, women perform the routine tests (e.g., determining temperature and blood pressure) that mediate between a patient's body and the professional expertise of predominantly male physicians. As social workers, women pass back and forth between the concrete circumstances of the welfare state's wards and the impersonal administrative codes of the bureaucratic state:

> Participation in the "head" world is accomplished in actual concrete settings making use of definite material means. Suppression of interest in that setting is organized in a division of labor that accords to others the production and maintenance of the material aspects of a total process. To those who do this work, the local and concrete conditions of the abstracted mode are thematic. The organization that divides the two becomes visible from this base. It is not visible from within the other.[117]

The women of whom Smith speaks are categorically situated within one world, the world of domesticity, while at the same time occupying a marginal position within the extradomestic world of men. In large part, moreover, their marginalization in the latter is made palpably real through the complex of artisanal artifacts giving it determinate structure. Work in what Daphne Spain calls "open-floor occupations,"[118] for example, is typically characterized by an absence of the walled spaces called offices, and so an absence of the second skin that protects masculine bodies from unwanted intrusions. If at home, walls articulate the site where she is defined by her availability to one man; at work the absence of walls marks the space where she is available to many.

To do essential work in a realm deemed marginal (the home), while at the same time doing marginal work in a realm deemed essential (the workplace), is to occupy an internally ambiguous relational site. Should that ambiguity become a matter of so much feeling, that feeling will open up the possibility of moving from such ill-formed sense to a discursively articulated grasp of its significance. But there is never any guarantee that this latent potentiality will in fact be realized; to point to structural contradictions implicit in a web of experience is not in and of itself to explain why they are sometimes recognized as such. In order to do that, we must explain how critical agency is possible. That is, we must explain how it is that the status of woman as a distinctive sort of artifact, as so much matter shaped to materialized form, does not preclude her from refashioning the conditions of her own intelligible constitution.

Any feminism that cannot answer this question cannot specify the conditions of its own possibility. To establish the terms of my response, let me first indicate the relevance of my earlier discussion of Butler and, more particularly, her shift from a Cartesian to a neo-Aristotelian conception of causality. To abandon the former in favor of the latter is, I concede, to deprive us of certain ways of speaking that are not without political utility. When the conduct of discursive constitution is framed in Cartesian terms, the body is typically figured as an antecedently existent blank surface; that, recall, is the representation Butler sometimes ascribes to Foucault. When the agencies of that body's consititution are located external to it, as hands are external to the clay they shape into a vase, their efficacy is taken to be a matter of so much literal and figurative manipulation. Conjuring up connotations of coercion and constraint, such imagery invites a representation of subjects as so many heteronomous effects manufactured by causes not of their own making, and that in turn justifies a politics of outrage. Feeding off liberal understandings of what it is to be an autonomous self capable of meaningful consent, that outrage furnishes the foundation for rhetorically effective claims concerning the injustice of such victimization.

The issue grows more complex, however, when we shift to the idiom of form and matter. As noted above, when joined to Butler's ascription of the qualities of temporality and potentiality to matter, the neo-Aristotelian language of form and matter effectively brings the body back from its Cartesian grave. If, moreover, neither materiality nor signification is the independent cause of the other, if their relationship is indeed one of immanent interconstitution, then the embodied beings designated as women must in some sense participate in the processes by which they are discursively formed as intelligible subjects. Their bodies are not, on this construction, so many chunks of inert Galilean matter hammered into shape by incessant blows of the patriarchal tool. Rather, their bodies are the already shaped sites where discursive form, which is neither unambiguously within nor without those sites, achieves more or less complete (as in ontologically weighty) materialization. Neither her own autonomous cause, nor a purely heteronomous effect, each woman is a materializing emergent.

If that be so, then identification of a clear and distinct villain to animate feminist outrage, a distinguishable first cause of women's oppression, is a deeply problematic, perhaps even impossible, endeavor. What is lost on this strategic front may, however, be gained on another. Granted, it smacks of blaming the victim to claim that because bodies actively participate in the processes by which they are discursively constituted, the creatures known as women are in some sense complicitous in their own subordination. But to contend that the body vitally incorporates the form by which it materializes also entails ascribing to it a sort of agency that is absent when it is taken to be an inert thing wholly determined by external forces. And if the body does indeed exercise such agency, might "it" also occasionally play a role in contesting the processes by which it is intelligibly informed?

Butler has various explanations for the possibility of resistance to the norms of compulsory heterosexuality, all of which presuppose her contention that "we can attribute meaning only to that which is representable in language,"[119] as well as her correlative contention that "the constituted character of the subject is the very precondition of its agency."[120] On her account, for example, the need to draw boundaries around the regime of compulsory heterosexuality necessarily entails specification of a constitutive "outside." Consisting of the forms of abjected subjectivity that are deemed "unthinkable" within this regime, the very existence of such an "outside" contests heterosexuality's hegemonic pretensions. Moreover, the imperatives of discursive constitution are never monolithic or noncontradictory; the multiplicity of their injunctions—for example, the demand that women be sexually alluring and simultaneously chaste—renders their fulfillment an intrinsically impossible ideal. Finally, the very fact that incessant repetition is essential to the success of performativity demonstrates that subordination to the prevailing norms of gender identity is never complete or permanent.

While perhaps sufficient to account for the conceptual possibility of agency, can these explanations tell us when and why this potentiality is sometimes actualized? The relentlessness of performativity and reiteration may explain why women and men so often act as they "should." But does conceptualization of resistance as "the possibility of a variation on that repetition"[121] account for how and when they do not? The notion of abjection may account for the production of those "deviant" identities that contest established notions of normalcy. But can it explain why those identities sometimes become the stuff of which political resistance is made, whereas at other times they become the stuff of which suicides and incarcerations are made? The inconsistent demands of discursive constitution may account for the impossibility of achieving a seamless self-identity. But can they explain why the working out of these contradictions sometimes enables a reconfiguration of cultural and political relations, whereas at other times it spawns ever more desperate denials of their discordance?

The question, once again, is "how one accounts for the agency that exists. Is it to be inferred from the structure of the self apart from its constitutive social and discursive relations, or will it be implicated from the start in the social and discursive relations which both condition and limit the making of any such claims?"[122] With Butler, I concede the impossibility of locating an extra-discursive guarantor of resistance's eventual emergence. With Butler, I repudiate the voluntarist subject whose essence is somehow antecedent to and independent of the relations by which it is constituted. With Butler, I agree that the paradox of agency consists in the fact that the subjects deemed capable of critical engagement with the powers that be are engendered within and by the very network of power relations they would reweave. For all these reasons, and again with Butler, I contend that agency is never a given fact, but always a fragile potentiality, a potentiality that may be crushed or summoned forth, frustrated or dynamically released.

Butler, however, cannot account for the actualization of this potentiality because her explanation of individual agency is so thoroughly linguistified, so dependent on her conviction "that an 'I' is founded through reciting the anonymous linguistic site of the 'I.'" It may be true, as she contends, that repetitive citation of the personal pronoun is "the invocation by which a subject comes into linguistic being."[123] But to identify the act of invocation with what it invokes, to think that "linguistic being" is the only intelligible sort of being, to forget that such being's capacity to bear meaning turns on forms of sense making irreducible to the linguistic, is to commit yet another version of the intellectualist fallacy.

When a woman says "I," or better still "I can," her claim to agency is a fruit whose vital roots can be traced to the embodied habits that situate her within a world of corporeal sense. Her capacity to take materials given in experience and transform them into a question, to grasp gender as an imposition rather than a naturalized fact, is simply the most evident manifestation of acquired tactile-kinesthetic sensibilities. The sense-making capacities of those sensibilities, so many creatures of her sustained intercourse with gender-specific classes of artisanal artifacts, cannot be exhaustively articulated within reflective beliefs, expressible in propositional form. Such beliefs disclose only the explicitly formulated elements of embodied meanings whose involvement with and implication in the world is, for the most part, tacit. Entering into relations with things given only partial articulation via received linguistic forms, the habits borne by a woman's body often "grasp" far more than clumsy words can say.

To compel the somatic conditions of meaningful experience to disappear because their work problematizes universalistic affirmations of the discursive constitution of reality is to leave the agencies of that constitution homeless. Granted, what Butler calls the "resignification" of received discursive resources (which Rorty calls "metaphorical redescription") is a vital moment of resistance. But it is not the only moment. To hold otherwise is an intellectual conceit that confuses the heady work of genealogical inquiry with the embodied rage, the frustration, the pain, that renders such work an urgent imperative. In sum, should we heed Butler's call to explore the "modalities of materialization," including the various ways bodies become bodies that matter (in both senses of this phrase), that exploration must in time lead us to reject the residual Cartesianism implicit in her contention that all things, if they are not discursively intelligible, are so much nonsense.

To bring this section of my argument to an appropriate metaphorical close, think once more of the various spiders wandering across the pages of this book. From the same organic materials, web weavers produce two very different sorts of silk thread. The first, wetter than the other, able to stretch four times its original length without snapping, is principally responsible for capturing prey. The second, dryer than the first, more like a steel girder than a rubber band, makes up the radial spokes converging at the web's hub. Bound together by glue droplets sprinkled over the surface of each catching thread, these two ways of teasing form from matter generate an enduring structure that is at once supple and sturdy. That structure takes on a new twist when, as in the case of theridisoma spiders, an additional thread is attached laterally to the web's hub. Once tightened, the entire structure bulges, much like an umbrella turned inside-out by an unanticipated gust of wind. When some guileless prey flies into this three-dimensional edifice, even should that potential foodstuff be another spider, a theridisoma will release its front legs, causing the entire web to snap back to a flattened plane, capturing its victim within a trap of another's devising.

Such is the situation of the black widow who opened this section. Although she has taken no college courses in feminist theory, she knows much about what it is to be female in a world made primarily by males. She does not know the word "patriarchy," but she participates sensibly in its reality each time her abdomen shudders in response to her mate's intimations of violence. To her, "patriarchy" is not an abstraction, but a life of little degradations that hint at, but never express outright, the hollowness of his protestations of affection. The sense carried in her abdomen is partial to the extent that she does not recognize that its qualities are what they are because of a structure of congealed relations whose tentacles extend well beyond her local situation. Should she come to explicate that structure, she will move not from a condition of nonsense to transparent intelligibility, but from a condition of insufficient to more adequate sense, as inadequately discriminated qualities come to stand as so many signs pointing beyond themselves. When at last she does learn to speak the term "patriarchy," that knowledge will prove profound only because it first emerged out of and remains anchored in her belly.

Alternatively, if spiders give you the creeps, think once more of Susie and Calvin. If Calvin grows up to be a card-carrying member of the National Rifle Association, that may be explained in large measure by noting the affinity between, on the one hand, this organization's instrumentalist construction of the relationship between guns and their employers and, on the other hand, the sedimented sense-making habits he has acquired by virtue of his standing as a man in a world whose most consequential artifacts routinely confirm his pretensions to autonomy. If Susie, now a mother of two and a case worker for the Division of Youth and Family Services, finds that slogan problematic, this may be explained in large measure by noting the incongruity between the NRA's instrumentalism and the sense-making habits she acquired while being fashioned as a girl, a woman, and now as a mother. This is not to say that such fashioning is the mechanical cause of the effect that is her uneasiness. Rather, it is to say that such habituation, teaching Susie how to care about matters without posturing as their sovereign, showing her how to value things without regard for their utility, reminding her that the nurturance of persons is inseparable from the cultivation of things, has prepared the soil out of which grows her animosity toward this bastion of unrepentant Cartesianism.

To confine Susie to the discursive, as do Rorty and Butler, is to miss the embryonic presentiments from which feminist understandings are sometimes born. Present at the margins of semantic availability, a feeling of the gap between experience and conventional articulations of it is a vital condition of whatever conduct may in time respond to that summons. To urge receptivity to such feeling is to invite women to attend to the inklings of anger, the traces of insufficiency, the hints of fear, that once in a while well up in the bodies of those who live within a discursive order that denies much of what they do the capacity to bear meaning. To act on such intimations, to seize the measure of unrealized possibility resident in any structure of materialized reality, is never an easy matter. The objectivity of artisanal artifacts, the density of the relational knots woven into the web of experience, the harm done those entangled in its sticky strands, the sanctions imposed on those who dare to tear those tangles asunder, all mock the disembodied fantasy of perpetual self-invention. Should Susie one day become a creator, that will testify not to her achievement of Cartesian autonomy, but to her standing as a creature whose instigation of gender trouble is simultaneously constrained and enabled by the gifts of Prometheus.

ix. *A Pregnant Pause*

WHEN ADRIENNE RICH GAVE *OF WOMAN BORN* THE SUBTITLE *MOTHERHOOD AS EXPERI- ence and Institution*, she implied that her capacity to criticize the latter turned on her sense of the former. The distinction between experience and institution is essential to her argument, which she states as follows: "Throughout this book I try to distinguish between two meanings of motherhood, one superimposed on the other: the *potential relationship* of any woman to her powers of reproduction and to children; and the *institution*, which aims at ensuring that

that potential—and all women—shall remain under male control."[124] In this section, my aim is to ask whether Rich's invocation of "experience" is congruent with the account recommended here; to (re)diagnose the rash she contracted when pregnant with her first child; and to explain how the issue of reproduction can be understood in terms of the dialectic of projection and reciprocation.

What is the "institution" of motherhood? It is not difficult to answer this question in terms of the Cartesian paradigm of use. The medicalization of pregnancy and labor in the West, accelerating since invention of the forceps, is now a familiar story, in part thanks to Rich's book. This domain of experience, graphically demonstrating the excess of reciprocation over projection, has been effectively colonized by various agencies of specialized expertise seeking maximal instrumental control. As their praxically cumulated intelligence was displaced, midwives were supplanted by male obstetricians, and homes were forsaken for the bureaucratically structured centers of supervision known as hospitals. There, at about the time Rich was due to deliver, these historical processes found their fulfillment in the construction of childbirth as an event whose indispensable participants were to be rendered literally senseless through liberal doses of analgesics and anesthesia. As so many specimens of unrefined nature, women in labor thus validated the Cartesian representation of the body as an inert object bearing no necessary relation to the thinking ego imprisoned within it: "No more devastating image could be invented for the bondage of woman: sheeted, supine, drugged, her wrists strapped down and her legs in stirrups, at the very moment when she is bringing new life into the world."[125]

Assessing this history, Rich concludes that the "many fragments of lived experience belong to a whole which is not of our creation."[126] How exactly are we to understand this appeal to "lived experience"? The answer is implicit in Rich's account of what happened when, at the age of twenty-six, she responded to pregnancy with all the symptoms of a severe allergic reaction:

> I was effectively alienated from my real body and my real spirit by the institution—not the fact—of motherhood. This institution—the foundation of human society as we know it—allowed me only certain views, certain expectations, whether embodied in the booklet in my obstetrician's waiting room, the novels I had read, my mother-in-law's approval, my memories of my own mother, the Sistine Madonna or she of the Michelangelo *Pietà*, the floating notion that a woman pregnant is a woman calm in her fulfillment or, simply, a woman waiting. . . . In my own pregnancy I dealt with this waiting, this female fate, by denying every active, powerful aspect of myself. I became dissociated both from my immediate, present, bodily experience and from my reading, thinking, writing life.[127]

Via this appeal to the "fact of motherhood," Rich seeks to root women's identity and so their unity in the promptings of a "real body," which presumably exists apart from, antecedent to, all specific cultural constructions of it. It is out of that body's "immediate experience," moreover, that she seeks to tease the critical resources that will enable her to contest the "institution" of motherhood.

Rich, I submit, has misread her rash. Neither the reality of the female body, nor the conduct of motherhood, can be distinguished from the history making each what it is. There is no way, in other words, to definitively segregate the "fact" from the artifact of reproduction. Correlatively, it is a mistake to abstract reproduction from the constellation of artisanal artifacts that make the world distinctively human. Human hands are the first tools, the initial means with which we dig into the relational tissues of qualitative experience, and so initiate transformation of the defenseless creatures whom Prometheus pitied into the armed creatures whom Zeus feared. Those hands, recall, are the recoverable metaphorical referents of a host of artisanal artifacts, including those located at the far end of the crossed arms of a forceps. To acknowledge this relational continuity is not to deny that these manufactured hands are surrogates for appendages now effectively amputated from the arms of midwives. But it is to recall that any effort to neatly distinguish what is "natural" from what is "artificial" within reproduction will falter on the fact that beings become distinctively human only by becoming creatures of Prometheus.

To fold reproduction into the larger category of artifactual production, to insist on the mutually constitutive relationship of artisanal and human artifacts, is not to lose sight of the distinctive features involved in generation of the latter. In certain respects, it is true, human artifacts are not unlike the motors I discussed in part 1. Recall that a motor is a distinctive sort of artifact in the sense that what is projected within its structure is not a specific capacity or part of the human body, but rather the undifferentiated capacity of a body to do work. Correlatively, to fashion a new human being is to produce a materialized creature in whom the generalized capacity to engage in the dialectic of projection and reciprocation is itself realized.

However, what distinguishes baby making from motor making is the way in which form and matter are related in each. When a human being makes a motor, the form of the latter is antecedently present as a conceptual project entertained by that maker, and that form is made concretely real via the durable organization of the parts it informs. But when human beings make a new human being, achievement of that end is not contingent on antecedent conceptualization by its participants; the parties to such making are themselves embodiments of the form to be realized in another; and the union of form and matter is immanent within that other as the power of spontaneous growth. While motors and babies both embody the generalized capacity to engage in work, only in the latter can that capacity grow more articulated over time as a result of the tendency of form to realize itself, to mature. Motors move but do not grow, age but do not die. (I realize that, with the development of cyborgs, this generalization is increasingly problematic.) The labor performed within women's wombs, in sum, involves a distinctive sort of artifactual production, a sort that is both like and unlike that involved in the generation of artisanal artifacts.

With these general claims in place, let us read Rich's rash once more, but this time absent her residual essentialism. In writing *Of Woman Born*, I would argue, what Rich does is to articulate discursively what she could only sense years before. She now comes to understand her allergic reaction not as the symptom of a disease but as a protopolitical protest against the cultural representation of pregnant women as beings who suffer with grace and without question. What was originally experienced in and by her body as an uneasy sense of helplessness, as a craving for expertise, a desire to say something she could not express, is now read as an incipient invitation to revolt. If, some two decades later, Rich finds herself in a position to accept that solicitation, this is only because its inchoate message was a matter of qualitative sense long ago. That rash, in short, was not "had" as some external stimulation, some Rortyan mechanical cause, assaulting her otherwise witless body. Meaning-impoverished but not dumb, her body had just enough sense to rebel against its complicity in the obstetric practices conspiring to turn her pregnancy into an affair in which she was only incidentally implicated.

But how are we to account for the existence of that sense? Did Rich's dermatitis express the epistemic import of a body whose capacity to bear healthy babies reveals the error of the professional construction of pregnancy as a medical condition akin to a disease? Was her skin disclosing the transhistorical and crosscultural reality of the project that is men's expropriation of women's reproductive capacities? If neither of these answers seems plausible, as they do not to me, then what were the conditions of the possibility of this event?

To be pregnant, Rich tells us, is to be neither one nor two. Whether this ambiguity will be taken as a source of anxiety to be denied or as an opportunity to question the Cartesian dualism of subject and object turns on two conditions: first, the presence of embodied habits that dynamically seek to project conduct into an intelligible future; and, second, a structural context whose immanent tensions are severe enough to render the work of such habits a productive enterprise.

A pregnant woman brings to experience whatever sense-making habits she has acquired in time as a result of her artifactual engagements. Understood not as mere reflexes but as so many responsive capacities, these habits comprise what Rich calls "the corporeal ground of our intelligence."[128] Replying to the affairs of experience without speaking about them, such habits guide conduct even though they are almost never deliberately invoked. *What* a particular pregnancy is, therefore, turns in large measure on *how* such habits take hold of the ripening affair in which they are concretely implicated.

What renders the sense of childbirth deficient, to abstract one moment from the more comprehensive whole that is a pregnancy, are learned habits of bodily engagement that sabotage its capacity to sustain a tense equilibrium between doing and undergoing, projection and reciprocation. Meaning is enriched to the degree that the dialectical relationship between these two phases is sensitively grasped. In its active phase, agency is characterized by a reaching forward into a future not yet known. But such stretching squanders the resources of sense when women, taught to fear their bodies, confuse such projection with the achievement of control. Responsiveness to what experience brings, and hence receptivity to the excess of reciprocation over projection, is a matter of suffering. That suffering, though, is not to be identified with affliction. Affliction, the condition of a slave, is what despoils meaning by stripping persons of the power of agency. Suffering that is generative of meaning occurs, Rich writes, only when "pain can be transformed into something usable, something which takes us beyond the limits of the experience itself into a further grasp of the essentials of life and the possibilities within us."[129] To suffer, in other words, is not to withdraw in fear but to yield. Never to be confused with passivity, such yielding takes place only when acquired habits call a woman to meet what experience metes out.

Embodied habits will go for nought, however, unless what they are to grasp has been rendered tangible by interrelated transformations in the structure of the family, of the economy, of the state. What Rich's rash expressed, albeit indistinctly, was an inchoate articulation of relational realities brought into the space of materializable appearance by alterations in received ways of connecting and disconnecting various artisanal and human artifacts. Absent structural mutations—for example, in the relationship of public and private spheres in the years immediately following World War II—Rich's discontent would have found nothing to grab hold of and so could not be real-ized. Decades later, her words spoke to many others because their bodies, multiple sites on which these changes had also left their mark, endured these incoherences as well.

To her credit, and unlike some standpoint theorists, Rich does not argue that the institution of motherhood has a unique generative root that, once located, can be yanked out with a mighty tug. Nor does she argue that women's "real" or "true" experience can be crafted into an epistemological criterion that will successfully adjudicate between competing ways of giving motherhood cultural shape. Her appeal to "lived experience," freed from its essentialist pretensions, is not a claim to knowledge but a question about what matters. Never claiming to deliver the true path to women's liberation, never claiming to know its determinate terminus, Rich rouses her readers to an ongoing project of experimental practice predicated on nothing surer than a sense of the potentialities the institution of motherhood now occludes, frustrates, and denies: "In a sense, female evolution was mutilated, and we have no way now of imagining what its development hitherto might have been; we can only try, at last, to take it into female hands."[130]

But how are we to know which of these potentialities are worthy of exploration and which are to be shunned? Reason is not adequate to this question. Inquiry into the relations between the imperatives of late capitalism, the commodification of women's bodies, the struggle to regulate the quality of reproduction's "product," the ideological legacy of Cartesianism, the perpetuation of patriarchal institutional structures, may help explain why pregnancy now assumes this materialized form rather than that. It cannot, however, usurp the praxical task of recrafting embodied sense from experience's offerings, of taking these ill-formed matters out of the hands of Calvin and placing them into those of Susie. Whether such conduct will succeed in situating women within so many confluent streams of vital sense cannot be known till after its work is done.

x. *Venus Files for Divorce*

IN THIS FINAL SECTION OF PART 2, I CONCLUDE MY FORMAL EXPOSITION OF THE MATERIALized artifact that is gender. Specifically, via a brief discussion of the unhappy marriage of Venus to Vulcan, I seek to wed part 1's contention that gender identity is well understood as a complex fruit of the dialectic of projection and reciprocation to part 2's discussion of the relationship between experience, embodiment, and the conduct of sense making. That done, the conceptual web informing part 3's analysis of three specific artisanal artifacts will be as complete as I know how to make it at the present time.

The speaking spider must never be confused with the Cartesian cogito, that epistemological monad who seeks to know who he is by abstracting from his identity everything other than the formal capacity to cogitate. Undistinguished by skin color, sex organs, religion, ethnicity, wealth, political affiliation, such a being is unlike any I have ever encountered. Within the web of experience, inhabitants are differentiated as individuals via the distinctive configuration of relations in which each participates. To think that there is an identifiable being antecedent to its relational incorporation is to reinvent the humanist subject Nietzsche considered fit only for the hangman's noose. There is no independent subject who bears these relations or who is situated amidst these relations; rather, the site of their interarticulation *is* the individual. Accordingly, just as the artisanal artifact, which appears so obdurately self-identical, can be dis-integrated into the dynamic relational fields from which it emerges, so too can the human artifact.

The term "gender," which abstracts one set of relations from that field, is inherently problematic. This is so for at least three reasons. First, while other relational forms can be elicited from this field using terms like "race," "class," and "ethnicity," in experience no single form remains un(in)formed by the others. That alone is sufficient to render suspect the apparently self-contained classes of "women" and "men," and hence the category of gender itself. Too often, we assume that we can meet this concern by specifying how these other relational forms modify what it is to be a woman or a man. But to inquire into the differences between, for example, African-American women and European-American women is to assume that each of these hyphenated adjectives modifies but does not essentially transform the underlying nounlike reality of womanhood. And that is to forget the point of my pragmatist reformulation of Nietzsche's relational ontology: If subjects cannot be unambiguously distinguished from the relations making them what they are, then no single attribute can be said to stand as the antecedent ground that is adjectivally modulated in this way or that.

Second, the problematic character of this category is compounded by the fact that gender, like patriarchy, assumes no universal or transhistorical form. In part 3, I refer to the mother of Achilles, the bride of Frankenstein, and the anonymous narrator of Christa Wolf's *Accident* as "women." But each of these three beings, as a creature of Prometheus, is what she is by virtue of the reciprocative work performed by very different artifactual forms. On what grounds do I ride roughshod over such historical variability, ignoring the very real differences between what it is for each to be a "woman"?

Third, consider Butler's claim that the signifier "women" "does not describe a preexisting constituency but is, rather, part of the very production and formulation of that constituency, one that is perpetually renegotiated and rearticulated in relation to other signifiers within the political field."[131] To this claim, add yet another good Butlerian question: "To what extent does the category of woman achieve stability and coherence only in the context of the heterosexual matrix?"[132] In other words, given that the category of woman only makes sense by virtue of its tacit reference to woman's other, and given that the discourse of gender is a vital contributor to the relationships of which it speaks, to what extent does deployment of this category help to consolidate a binary structure of compulsory heterosexuality?

Putting my second qualm on hold for a moment, let me respond to the first and third by noting that the vice of "gender," as with any comparable abstraction, is also its virtue. Imagine that we were to try to fashion a concept that, in all the requisite detail, adequately articulated the inflection of gender by all other intersecting structures of stratification. Such an effort would be doomed from the very beginning. Predicated on the mistaken assumption that the purpose of concepts is to depict reality, that effort would be forever absorbed in a Sisyphean struggle to exhaust the heterogeneity of social reality. Even if such a concept could be fashioned, it would prove no more useful to critical political engagement than is a mirror. To the extent that such engagement is a matter of praxical exploration of the import of concepts, those concepts are valuable precisely because they do *not* re-present reality, precisely because they *do* abstract from its entanglements in order to furnish something more like an orientational map than an exact duplicate. Let us therefore grant that all conceptual articulations of gender are necessarily selective, provisional, and contestable; and let us grant that, because their meaning cannot be known apart from the conduct they inform, such articulations cannot help but take part in constituting the reality they are said to portray. With that done, we can meet the third of the criticisms cited above by shifting discussion away from questions concerning the representational adequacy of particular formulations of gender and toward questions concerning their specifically political import.

The perils intrinsic to conceptual abstraction can be mitigated, at least in part, by recalling that the term "gender" speaks not of a determinate attribute possessed by singular entities, but of an internally complex relationship between various materialized and materializing things. Giving form to those relations, gender is the semiautonomous medium within which sexual differentiation is elicited (as opposed to created out of nothing) from the stuff of embodied experience, teased forth as an intelligible reality distinct from other forms of difference. That structure typically involves the assymetric division and ascription of mutually exclusive traits and capacities to its constituents. As such, gender is an oppositional relation whose standing as a materialized artifact is stabilized by its apparent necessity.

If gender identity is a materialized artifact fashioned and refashioned in time, then no account of its reality at any given moment can be considered complete absent an account of the specific processes through which women and men are engendered. Had Susie been born in archaic Athens, for example, her father would have marked the occasion by hanging a tuft of wool above the door of his home, signifying her future as a woman and, more precisely, as a woman destined to spin. (Were Susie Calvin, an olive branch would take the place of wool.) But Susie, at the moment of her birth, is not yet a woman. She must become one through her incorporation of various woman-making labors, just as Calvin must do the same through his incorporation of various man-making labors. Gender, therefore, is not a fixed identity or a destiny dictated by anatomy, but a materialized reality elicited from bodies via their differential engagement in continuously rearticulated fields of artifactual engagement.

This claim can be made more concrete by recalling that the division of labor constitutes one of the primary structures of stratification in most, if not all, human communities. As with that derived from Marx, my understanding of the division of labor is comprehensive in the sense that it presupposes no unambiguous differentiation between labor, the artisanal artifacts giving labor its specific form, and the relations between persons engaged in such labor. It is more comprehensive than its Marxian analogue, however, insofar as it is not compromised by a gender-blind conceptualization of class or by a restriction of the category of labor to the production of commodities destined for sale in an ostensibly free marketplace. Including the labor involved in the bearing and rearing of children, caring for the sick and elderly, maintaining a household economy, my conceptualization does not contribute to making "women's work" more invisible than it already is.

In all of the cultures with which I am familiar, labor is divided along gender-specific lines.[133] On the one hand, to return to my second criticism of the category of gender, these lines differ from time to time, place to place, and so there is no stable referent of the term "women." On the other hand, insofar as the division of labor produces so many binary oppositions between two sorts of beings, defined in relation to one another and betokened but not dictated by anatomical differences, we are entitled to bridge space and time with the terms "women" and "men." Putting our hands together, adapting Teresa Ebert's account of patriarchy, we might say that the continuity of gender stratification is "not so much the continuity of the same but rather *different* reconfigurations of an ongoing socioeconomic structure of gendered oppression. [The gendered division of labor] is continuous on the level of the structure or organization of oppression and discontinuous, that is, heterogeneous, in its historically specific and conjunctural practices."[134] Theoretical orientation to the gendered division of labor thus invites us to note the historically persistent reality of gender stratification, as well as the continuity of inegalitarian control over and access to the artifactual instrumentalities of such stratification, but it does not commit us to the view that the condition of women is forever the same.

The discursive abstraction of "gender" is never experienced as such. Its reality is fully incorporated within the concrete loci of lived practice, and the gendered body is a fruit of the work done within and by such loci. To illustrate this point, let us consider a single locus in comparative perspective. Recall part 1's discussion of the suburban home in which I was raised and my mother was confined. In a nutshell, I argued that the walls of that edifice help fashion intelligible gender hierarchies by giving determinate form to the movements of bodies passing through space and time. While it may be true that the ultimate recoverable referent of these walls is the vulnerable skin of human bodies, to say that alone is to occlude the ways these walls are informed by but also constitutive of a structure of relations that makes those bodies specifically feminine or masculine. Thus, the four exterior walls that, for Calvin, define a site where he is free to say what he pleases are the same walls that, for Susie, define a site where she does what she is told.

Such walls sustain the boundaries of an artifactual site, the home, that is vital to daily reproduction of a gender-specific division of labor. That gendered division of labor *is* a matter of regulating access to and deployment of the artisanal artifacts presently in circulation. As those artifacts are transformed in time, so too are the relations in which they participate and hence the creatures they shape. In a not atypical preindustrial Roman household, to offer but a single example, the artifactually articulated division of labor mandated a sort of palpable reciprocity between members of each gender. In this regard, Virgil is as good a guide as any Greek:

The hour when early rest drives sleep away,
when in the circle of the passing night
the housewife, her first task to sustain life
by weaving and Minerva's humble arts,
awakes the embers and the sleeping fires,
as she adds on the night to her day's work
and keeps her housemaids toiling on at some
long chore by lamplight, that her husband's bed
be chaste, and that she raise her children well:
Just so, and just as eagerly, the Lord
of Fire rises up, at that same hour,
from his soft couch to labor at the forge.[135]

Venus rises to fuel the fire that will respond to the unrelenting need of warm-blooded creatures to maintain a constant body temperature. The heat Venus summons is a condition of Vulcan's liberation from that need, and hence of his freedom to forge artifacts that will last far longer than any fire she can build. Although her more ephemeral arts are never considered anything other than means to the ends of others, the work of "housewife" and "husband" concretely complement each other. Venus makes and mends garments made of cloth, while Vulcan makes and mends those made of leather. She nurses infants, while he fashions the cradles in which they sleep. Venus scrubs the floors, while Vulcan prepares the lye. She bakes bread, while he builds the hearth, chops wood for the fire, and pounds grain into meal.

To point to such complementarity is not to romanticize this divine relationship; on some level, Venus and Vulcan both understand that their exchange of labors is hierarchically structured and legitimated by the prerogatives of patriarchal right. Be that as it may, the mutual intelligibility of their marital relationship is largely a function of its concrete incarnation in the relations sustained between various artisanal artifacts. Their respective labors can be grasped as integrated parts of a more comprehensive whole, a whole that is more akin to an economic partnership than to what we now consider a marriage rooted in romantic sentiment, because the intelligent habits through which each makes sense of the world are creatures of such artifactual engagement. If their relationship appears as a given, a materialized artifact, that is to be explained in large measure through reference to the artifacts whose reciprocational work affords that relationship palpable and enduring form.

Should Venus and Vulcan somehow be transported to an industrialized context, say, to eastern Pennsylvania in the middle part of the present century, the materiality of gender and hence the routinized subordination of the former to the latter will grow ever more problematic. Marx and Engels contend that in the face of capitalism's resolute march "(a)ll fixed, fast-frozen relations, with their train of ancient and venerable prejudices and opinions, are swept away."[136] This is certainly so, but we must not forget that the concrete terms of those relations are so many refashioned linkages between human and nonhuman artifacts. As Vulcan's forge is reincarnated as a Bessemer converter, as Vulcan himself is reborn as a wage earner laboring in the shadow of Bethlehem Steel, the gender-producing machine that is the household is transformed as well. No longer, for example, does Vulcan do any of the preparatory work associated with the baking of bread; the burdens associated with such "unproductive" work fall to Venus alone. Consequently, the kitchen comes to be defined as her special domain, a domain from which those unfamiliar with its distinctive artisanal artifacts are ever more completely excluded. As the link between Venus's self-conception and this site grows ever tighter, the sense-making habits derived from engagement with its constitutive artifacts increasingly differentiate her world from that of her husband. If what one does *is* what one becomes, and if what one does is largely a matter of *how* artisanal artifacts articulate such conduct, and if all such conduct is a matter of teasing form from matter, and if different ways of teasing form from matter inculcate different ways of making sense of what appears in experience, then each time Venus flips Vulcan's flapjacks with a stainless steel spatula, she is engaged in making herself (and being made) into the sort of being we recognize as a woman. Recall, moreover, that no artisanal artifact ever exists in isolated splendor. The spatula Venus holds is what it is by virtue of its tacit reference to, and relationship with, a host of other artifacts, ranging from the Bisquick she purchased at the local market, to the cast-iron griddle manufactured in a Pittsburgh mill, to the potholder that protects her chafed hands, to the sink in which she will wash that griddle, to the sewer that will carry away her dirty dishwater, and so forth and so on. While no doubt Venus thinks she is merely performing a simple culinary service for her husband, in fact she is calling on an army of artifacts, all of which conspire to fashion and confirm her status as a member of that "damnable race."

With consolidation of the artifactual conditions necessary to what in time will become the doctrine of separate spheres, the home comes to be ever more closely associated with a specific gender, with a protected zone of privacy, with specific emotional tones, with not fully human but necessary forms of labor, with the guardianship of morality. The distinguishing characteristics of Venus's sphere are what they are by virtue of their mutually exclusive relationship to what they are not, that is, the distinguishing features of Vulcan's world. Whereas his work in a steel mill is specialized, remunerated, and conducted in the company of others, her domestic work involves a multitude of more or less unspecialized chores, is unpaid, and is performed in isolation from others similarly situated. As Vulcan becomes a citizen, a being defined by his right to join with others in a political sphere from which all bonds of kinship are now erased, intergenerational ties wither away within the once-extended household, leaving Venus solipsistically trapped in the company of her linoleum counters. When she escapes their petty tyranny, she does so either to purchase the prefabricated commodities needed to perpetuate the private sphere, or to move children outside and back inside its confines. Suspecting that she will never be chosen queen for a day, Venus awaits the return of the man whose home is his castle.

Under these circumstances, it should come as no surprise when Venus finally files for divorce. Although still sharing a bed, their ever more desperate protestations of love can no longer bridge the gulf between their worlds. Perhaps when they were younger the pleasures of Cupid were sufficient to hold their bodies fast. As those delights fade, however, they find that they have little in common and less to speak of. Their relationship unconfirmed by the artisanal artifacts with which each is engaged, their labors specialized and separated rather than divided and complementary, only a vague sense of obligation to the children now keeps them under the same roof. Once those maturing artifacts flee what they know is a charade, the burden of maintaining an appearance that finds no substantiation in the world's durable goods proves too much to bear.

Notes

1. Ovid, *Metamorphoses*, vol. 1, trans. Frank Miller (Cambridge, Mass: Harvard University Press, 1971), 6:78-82.

2. Ovid, *Metamorphoses* 6:131-32, 140-45.

3. Hannah Arendt, *The Human Condition* (Chicago: University of Chicago Press, 1958), 5-6.

4. Hannah Arendt, *On Revolution* (New York: Penguin, 1965), 59. Although taken from a different text, this quotation is congruent with the representation of labor Arendt advances in *The Human Condition*.

5. Arendt, *Human Condition*, 212.

6. Arendt, *Human Condition*, 94.

7. Arendt, *Human Condition*, 52.

8. Arendt, *Human Condition*, 155.

9. Arendt, *Human Condition*, 179.

10. Arendt, *Human Condition*, 183-84.

11. Arendt, *Human Condition*, 190.

12. For another account of some of my reservations about Arendt, see my *Politics/Sense/Experience: A Pragmatic Inquiry into the Promise of Democracy* (Ithaca, N.Y.: Cornell University Press, 1991), 59-60.

13. Arendt, *Human Condition*, 305-6. The two embedded quotations here are taken from Henri Bergson's *Creative Evolution*.

14. Arendt, *Human Condition*, 230, 7.

15. Arendt, *Human Condition*, 25, 182, 183, 95.

16. Arendt, *Human Condition*, 173.

17. Arendt, *Human Condition*, 194-95, 198.

18. Arendt, *Human Condition*, 22, 9.

19. Arendt, *Human Condition*, 184, 9.

20. Arendt, *Human Condition*, 182-83.

21. Arendt, *Human Condition*, 178-79.

22. Arendt, *Human Condition*, 9, 176-78.

23. Richard Rorty, "Feminism and Pragmatism," *Michigan Quarterly Review* 30, no. 2 (1991): 244.

24. Richard Rorty, "Pragmatism and Philosophy," in *After Philosophy*, ed. Kenneth Baynes, James Bohman, and Thomas McCarthy (Cambridge, Mass: MIT Press, 1978), 57.

25. Rorty, "Feminism and Pragmatism," 256 n32, 233.

26. Richard Rorty, *Contingency, Irony, and Solidarity* (New York: Cambridge University Press, 1989), 9.

27. Ernesto Laclau and Chantal Mouffe, *Hegemony and Socialist Strategy* (New York: Verso, 1985), 108.

28. Saussure, quoted in Frederick Jameson, "The Linguistic Model," in *Language and Politics*, ed. Michael Shapiro (New York: New York University Press, 1984), 176.

29. Richard Rorty, "Inquiry as Recontextualization: An Antidualist Account of Interpretation," in Rorty, *Objectivity, Relativism, and Truth* (New York: Cambridge University Press, 1991), 93, 98, 97.

30. Rorty, "Inquiry as Recontextualization," 93, 107.

31. Rorty, "Inquiry as Recontextualization," 93.

32. Rorty, *Contingency*, 88, 7.

33. Rorty, *Contingency*, 88.

34. Rorty, *Contingency*, 97, 27-29. Rorty is quoting Harold Bloom when he refers to the act of giving birth to oneself. Cf. 29: "The paradigm of such a narrative is the life of the genius who can say of the relevant portion of the past, 'Thus I willed it,' because she has found a way to describe that past which the past never knew, and thereby found a self to be which her precursors never knew was possible." In his more circumspect moments, Rorty acknowledges that self-creation is never a matter of *creatio ex nihilo*, always a matter of re-creation: "But if we avoid Nietzsche's inverted Platonism—his suggestion that a life of self-creation can be as complete and as autonomous as Plato thought a life of contemplation might be—then we shall be content to think of any human life as the always incomplete, yet sometimes heroic, reweaving of such a web" (43). Were Rorty to follow through on the implications of this claim, he would find it considerably more difficult to maintain that the advance of feminism is peculiarly dependent on the quasi-miraculous appearance of those exceptional individuals who are able to break through the crust of received linguistic convention.

35. Rorty, *Contingency*, 13.

36. Murray Edelman, *Constructing the Political Spectacle* (Chicago: University of Chicago Press, 1988), 104.

37. Spivak, quoted in Kathy Ferguson, *The Man Question* (Berkeley: University of California Press, 1991), 124.

38. Joan Scott, "Experience," in *Feminists Theorize the Political*, ed. Joan Scott and Judith Butler (New York: Routledge, 1992), 34. Given the vigor of her criticism, I am not sure why Scott concludes this essay by arguing for retention of the category of experience. Nor, correlatively, do I understand what she means when she suggests that "experience is at once always already an interpretation *and* is in need of interpretation" (37). Given that she collapses experience into the conditions of its discursive production, what is it that is in need of interpretation? How, on her account, are we to give this "what" any significant specification apart from discourse? And if we cannot do so, then why should we retain the concept of experience?

39. John Dewey, "Experience and Nature," in *The Later Works*, vol. 1, ed. Jo Ann Boydston (Carbondale: Southern Illinois University Press, 1981), 26-27.

40. William James, *A Pluralistic Universe* (Cambridge: Harvard University Press, 1977), 26.

41. Rorty, *Contingency*, 5, 40.

42. For these claims, see Rorty, *Contingency*, 7, 12-13, 15.

43. Judith Butler, *Gender Trouble* (New York: Routledge, 1990), viii.

44. Butler, *Gender Trouble*, 88.

45. Butler, *Gender Trouble*, 90, 80-81.

46. Butler, *Gender Trouble*, 91, 7, ix.

47. Butler, *Gender Trouble*, 17.

48. Butler, *Gender Trouble*, 145.

49. Butler, *Gender Trouble*, 2, ix, xi, 147.

50. Butler, *Gender Trouble*, 74, 25.

51. As an aside, it is worth noting that, on Nietzsche's account, any conception of causality that presupposes the neat distinguishability of cause and effect is not merely problematic, but also bound up with the very metaphysics of the subject Butler opposes. Our belief in the autonomous cause, Nietzsche maintains, is the epistemological correlate of the substantive subject who, allegedly standing apart from the totality of its deeds, is the sine qua non of slave morality. If individual selves are to be deemed responsible and so punishable for the immoral deeds they commit, we must posit the existence of autonomous subjects who are capable of freely willing, or not willing, the blameworthy effects whose enduring causes they are said to be. When such subjects are metaphorically extrapolated into the world, suggests Nietzsche in *The Will to Power*, trans. Walter Kaufmann and R. J. Hollingdale (New York: Random, 1967), the result is our familiar notion of cause: "Our 'understanding of an event' has consisted in our inventing a subject which was made responsible for

something that happens and for how it happens. We have combined our feeling of will, our feeling of 'freedom,' our feeling of responsibility and our intention to perform an act, into the concept 'cause'" (296). More caustically, in *The Twilight of the Idols*, trans. Anthony Ludovici (New York: Russell & Russell, 1964), Nietzsche suggests that our familiar grammar of causality is inseparable from "the metaphysics of the hangman" (42).

52. Butler, *Gender Trouble*, 145.

53. Butler, *Gender Trouble*, 136.

54. To see how our ontotheological heritage dogs the thinking of even those most pointedly aware of its failings, consider the following: When Butler is pressed by one strand of her argument to deny the reality of anything apart from its discursive constitution, she makes a move that is suspiciously reminiscent of that made by medieval Catholic theologians in their struggles with residual paganism. In order to guarantee the divinity's omnipotence, these theologians found it necessary to argue that the creation of the universe, as recounted in Genesis, was indeed a *creatio ex nihilo*. To acknowledge the reality of anything prior to that act, let alone anything that might constrain it, would be to cast doubt on the divine patriarch's standing as the singular source of all being. While I don't want to push the parallel too far, I do want to suggest that in certain respects *Gender Trouble*'s category of discourse, although irreducible to the status of a single cause, nonetheless resembles the Catholic god, especially insofar as affirmation of its exclusive capacity to create the real entails denial of the existence of anything other than it. Unlike Plato's demiurge, who works on antecedent materials that resist the impress of Form, if the god of discourse is to be all he claims to be, he must silence anything or anyone who dares to question his monopoly on being.

When pressed by another strand of her argument to suggest that the relationship between discourse and the body takes shape as the mechanistic conjunction of things otherwise disjoined, Butler unwittingly draws on the conception of causality that early modern science, especially that of physics, presupposed as a condition of its practice. Ironically, that representation also has Judeo-Christian roots. What chiefly distinguishes ancient pantheistic religions from their Judeo-Christian counterpart is the latter's insistence on the creator's transcendence, his radical separateness from all mundane things. Working through the implications of this conviction was a condition of early modern natural science insofar as elaboration of its Cartesian conception of causality presupposed elimination of all traces of animism from the objects of the natural world. Only when all hints of soul had been removed from these objects did it become possible to conceive of nature as a scene where so many discrete inertial objects bang into one another in so many monotonous sequences of involuntary motion. Traces of this conception of causality, I would suggest, sneak into Butler's work when she abstracts "discourse" from the web of relations in which it is existentially implicated in order to ascribe it independent status as a cause (or, better, a system of causes) whose power compels chronic performance of the acts that in time generate the self-identical being I mistakenly take my self to be.

55. Butler, *Gender Trouble*, 8, 70.

56. Butler, *Bodies That Matter*, 8-9 (emphasis added), 6. Cf. 9: "In such a view, the grammatical and metaphysical place of the subject is retained even as the candidate that occupies that place appears to rotate. As a result, construction is still understood as a unilateral process initiated by a prior subject, fortifying that presumption of the metaphysics of the subject that where there is activity, there lurks behind it an initiating and willful subject. On such a view, discourse or language or the social becomes personified, and in the personification the metaphysics of the subject is reconsolidated."

57. Aristotle, *Generation of Animals*, trans. A. L. Peck (Cambridge: Harvard University Press, 1943), 738b:22-30.

58. Butler, *Bodies That Matter*, 67, 30.

59. Butler, *Bodies That Matter*, 31-32.

60. Butler, *Bodies That Matter*, 244-45 n8.

61. Aristotle, *Physics*, trans. Hippocrates Apostle (Bloomington: Indiana University Press, 1969), 192a31-32.

62. Butler, *Bodies That Matter*, 33.

63. Butler, *Bodies That Matter*, 68.

64. Butler, *Bodies That Matter*, 69.

65. Butler, *Bodies That Matter*, 33-34.

66. Butler, *Bodies That Matter*, 34-35.

67. Butler, *Bodies That Matter*, 9.

68. Butler, *Bodies That Matter*, 251 n12.

69. Butler, *Bodies That Matter*, xi-xii.

70. Aeschylus, "Agamemnon," in *Oresteia*, trans. Richard Lattimore (Chicago: University of Chicago Press, 1953).

71. When I use the phrase "recoverable referent," it should be clear that I do not mean the second term in this phrase in its conventional epistemological sense. I do not mean to suggest that words are the passive vehicles through which we point to things nonlinguistic. My aim instead is to invoke several pre-epistemological senses of the term, senses that the *Oxford English Dictionary* gets at as follows: "to bring into relation to a thing or person," and "to matter, to be of consequence to a thing." My aim, in other words, is to specify language's relationship to the body, not to show how the former somehow mirrors or grasps the reality of the latter.

72. Butler, *Bodies That Matter*, 11.

73. Richard Rorty, "Comments on Sleeper and Edel," *Transactions of the Charles S. Peirce Society* 21, no. 1 (Winter 1985): 40.

74. Richard Shusterman, *Pragmatist Aesthetics* (Cambridge: Blackwell, 1992), 129.

75. Butler, *Bodies That Matter*, 29. John Dewey made much the same point in "Experience and Nature": "We cannot permanently divest ourselves of

the intellectual habits we take on and wear when we assimilate the culture of our own time and place. But intelligent furthering of culture demands that we take some of them off, that we inspect them critically to see what they are made of and what wearing them does to us. We cannot achieve recovery of primitive naivete. But there is attainable a cultivated naivete of eye, ear and thought, one that can be acquired only through the discipline of severe thought" (40).

76. Kathy Ferguson, *The Man Question* (Berkeley: University of California Press, 1993), 8-9.

77. Dewey, "Experience and Nature," 162.

78. Dewey, "Experience and Nature," 256.

79. William James, *Essays in Radical Empiricism* (Cambridge: Harvard University Press, 1976), 7.

80. Dewey, "Experience and Nature," 18.

81. James, *Radical Empiricism*, 42.

82. Nietzsche, quoted in Tracy Strong, "Language and Nihilism: Nietzsche's Critique of Epistemology," in *Language and Politics*, ed. Michael Shapiro (Albany: State University of New York Press, 1984), 87.

83. James, *Pluralistic Universe*, 145.

84. Dewey, "Experience and Nature," 27-28.

85. James, *Pluralistic Universe*, 19.

86. Joan Scott, "The Evidence of Experience," *Critical Inquiry* 17, no. 4 (1991): 790.

87. Scott, "Experience," 24-25.

88. James, *Radical Empiricism*, 46.

89. Butler, *Bodies That Matter*, 8.

90. Butler, *Gender Trouble*, 77.

91. Homer, *The Odyssey*, trans. Robert Fitzgerald (New York: Vintage, 1990), 23:197-98. Subsequent citations from this text will be indicated by book and line number only.

92. Plato, *The Republic*, trans. Richard Sterling and William Scott (New York: Norton, 1985), 10:597.

93. Elizabeth Grosz, *Volatile Bodies* (Bloomington: Indiana University Press, 1994), 22.

94. Maurice Merleau-Ponty, *Phenomenology of Perception*, trans. Colin Smith (London: Routledge & Kegan Paul), 235.

95. Maxine Sheets-Johnstone, *The Roots of Thinking* (Philadelphia: Temple University Press, 1990), 19, 121.

96. Shusterman, *Pragmatist Aesthetics*, 286 n27.

97. James, *Pluralistic Universe*, 47.

98. James, *Radical Empiricism*, 29.

99. Dewey, "Experience and Nature," 75.

100. James, *Radical Empiricism*, 47.

101. Dewey, "Experience and Nature," 198.

102. Dewey, "Experience and Nature," 227.

103. James, *Pluralistic Universe*, 113.

104. James, *Radical Empiricism*, 114.

105. Rorty, *Contingency*, 21, 152.

106. Wendy Brown, "Where Is the Sex in Political Theory?" *Women & Politics* 7, no. 1 (Spring 1987), 10.

107. Dorothy Smith, *The Everyday World as Problematic* (Boston: Northeastern University Press, 1987), especially 49-105.

108. Iris Marion Young, *Justice and the Politics of Difference* (Princeton, N.J.: Princeton University Press, 1990), 60.

109. "The Manifesto of the Redstockings," in *Notes from the Second Year*, ed. Shulamith Firestone and Anne Koedt (New York: Radical Feminism, 1969), 113.

110. Judith Grant, *Fundamental Feminism* (New York: Routledge, 1993), 92.

111. Nancy Hartsock, "The Feminist Standpoint: Developing the Ground for a Specifically Feminist Historical Materialism," in *Discovering Reality*, ed. Sandra Harding and Merrill Hintikka (Boston: D. Reidel, 1983), 284-85, 304.

112. Catharine MacKinnon, "Feminism, Marxism, Method, and the State: An Agenda for Theory," *Signs* 7, no. 3 (1982): 519-20, 537, 516.

113. Sara Ruddick, "Maternal Thinking," *Feminist Studies* 6, no. 2 (1980): 346-47.

114. Kathleen Jones, *Compassionate Authority* (New York: Routledge, 1993), 202.

115. Teresa Ebert, "Ludic Feminism, the Body, Performance, and Labor: Bringing Materialism Back into Feminist Cultural Studies," *Cultural Critique*, no. 23 (Winter 1992-93): 23.

116. Grant, *Fundamental Feminism*, 112.

117. Smith, *The Everyday World as Problematic*, 84-85.

118. Daphne Spain, *Gendered Spaces* (Chapel Hill: University of North Carolina Press, 1992), 227. In 1990, 31 percent of the women employed in the compensated work force of the United States were engaged in only three occupations: teaching, nursing, and secretarial work. Ninety-eight percent of all secretaries, incidentally, are women.

119. Butler, *Gender Trouble*, 88.

120. Judith Butler, "Contingent Foundations," in *Feminist Contentions*, ed. Linda Nicholson (New York: Routledge, 1995), 46.

121. Butler, *Gender Trouble*, 145.

122. Butler, "For a Careful Reading," in *Feminist Contentions*, 137.

123. Butler, "For a Careful Reading," 135.

124. Adrienne Rich, *Of Woman Born* (New York: Norton, 1986), 13.

125. Rich, *Of Woman Born*, 170-71.

126. Rich, *Of Woman Born*, 276.

127. Rich, *Of Woman Born*, 39.

128. Rich, *Of Woman Born*, 40.

129. Rich, *Of Woman Born*, 158.

130. Rich, *Of Woman Born*, 127.

131. Butler, *Bodies That Matter*, 195.

132. Butler, *Gender Trouble*, 5.

133. See Spain, *Gendered Spaces*, 84-85, for a table that charts the gender-specific allocation of basic artisanal activities in 185 different cultures. In only a very few areas (e.g., fuel gathering; the preparation of animal skins; basket and mat making; and crop planting, tending, and harvesting) are such activities not neatly segregated by gender.

134. Ebert, "Ludic Feminism," 21.

135. Virgil, *The Aeneid*, trans. Allen Mandelbaum (New York: Bantam, 1981), 8:534-45. It is worth noting that the term "housewife" in this passage is anachronistic. The Latin, which Mandelbaum translates as "housewife," is *"femina,"* a term that bears the more general sense of "woman." In her *More Work for Mother* (New York: Basic Books, 1983), Ruth Cowan points out that the term "housewife" does not appear in English until the thirteenth century. As such, its invention is roughly contemporaneous with capitalism's transformation of the preindustrial household into a site of nonproductive labor performed exclusively by the mother.

136. Karl Marx and Friedrich Engels, *The Communist Manifesto* (New York: International Publishers, 1984), 12.

3

EXEMPLARY ARTIFACTS

i. *Shield*

She looked over his shoulder
For vines and olive trees,
Marble well-governed cities
And ships upon untamed seas,
But there on the shining metal
His hands had put instead
An artificial wilderness
And a sky like lead.
                    W. H. Auden

THE PAIN OF LABOR, I AM TOLD, SLIPS QUICKLY BEHIND MEMORY'S SHIELD. WHAT DOES not is the realization that a moment is enough to steal the breath from a mother's treasured prize. Perhaps, for some, the dread of losing what is dearest ebbs as a child ages. But for one who knows that her flesh and blood is fated to perish while she remains alive, that terror will relax its grip only when destiny's work is done.

Something is terribly wrong. Though separated by an ocean's abyss, Thetis hears the wail of her only son. Recalling her womb's first stirrings, she quits her father's sanctuary beneath the sea and hurries to Achilles' side.

As he groaned from the depths his mother rose before him
and sobbing a sharp cry, cradled her son's head in her hands
and her words were all compassion, winging pity: *"My child—*
why in tears? What sorrow has touched your heart?
Tell me, please. Don't harbor it deep inside you."(18.82-86)[1]

Thetis once hoped to secure her baby's immortality, legend has it, by soaking his still-soft limbs in the preservative waters of the river Styx. Several years later, knowing that Achilles would in time be summoned to join the expedition against Troy, Thetis dressed her boy as a girl and hid him among the women of Lykomedes' court. There, the story goes, Achilles seduced the king's daughter, Deidamia, and so she found herself pregnant. When Odysseus and Diomedes at last came to fetch Achilles for war, smelling gender trouble, they unveiled a shield and lance before this incongruous creature. Betrayed by his unwomanly fascination with these artifacts of war, Achilles abandoned his child and set off to play the part of a real man.

Never, Thetis now concedes, can she erase the curse of her union with Peleus, a mortal whose body decays while she remains unmarked by time. Even so, what panic must grip her soul when she learns that Achilles' beloved Patroclus, sent to drive the Trojans from the Achaean ships, has now fallen beneath Hector's blade. Tenderly buckled about Patroclus only hours before, her son's armor now graces the shoulders of his most bitter foe. Not quite yet, though, will she let him hurry to his appointed end, not quite yet will she sacrifice him to the bittersweet cause of heroic fame. Nestled in her arms, Achilles is once again her baby. Thetis knows it cannot be, but her heart whispers that he may still be spared.

> *Wait—*
> *don't fling yourself in the grind of battle yet,*
> *not till you see me coming back with your own eyes.*
> *Tomorrow I will return to you with the rising sun,*
> *bearing splendid arms from Hephaestus, god of fire!* (18.158-62)

Should the divine craftsman fashion for Achilles a mighty shield, then perhaps, if only for a little while, she can shelter him as she did when he was still unborn.

Thetis's appeal to Hephaestus is that of mother to artisan, of creator to creator. What she wants from him is a second skin, some compensation for the thinness, the penetrability, of the only armor her maternal craft was able to fashion for Achilles.

> *So now I come, I throw myself at your knees,*
> *please help me! Give my son—he won't live long—*
> *a shield and helmet and tooled greaves with ankle-straps*
> *and armor for his chest.* (18.534-37)

Hephaestus cannot deny Thetis's request because his own life is a gift he owes to her. When Hera gave birth to Hephaestus, she was disgusted by his disfigurement, by the failure of his body to correspond to the norm of divine mascu-

SHIELD   193

linity. Thrown into the sea, he was rescued by Eurynome, daughter of Ocean, and by Thetis, daughter of Nereus. Surrogates for his biological but unnatural mother, Eurynome and Thetis nursed this castaway back to health. "What shattering anguish I'd have suffered then / if Thetis had not taken me to her breast" (18.465-66). At least in part, his arms are massive now because, as an infant, his mouth drew in the warm milk her breasts silently manufactured.

🔥

WHAT ARE WE TO MAKE OF THE HOBBLED GOD, HEPHAESTUS? WE KNOW THAT HIS CULT, of Asiatic origin, is associated with the fury of volcanic fire. One legend, playing on these chthonic associations, identifies him as the son of Gaia, the earth mother. Hesiod's *Theogony*, in contrast, tells of Hephaestus's parthenogenetic release from the womb of Hera after she, not to be outdone by her foremost rival, witnessed Athena's delivery from the forehead of Zeus. Other accounts, twisting the order of time, suggest that Athena's birth was itself a feat made possible only by the well-timed blows of Hephaestus's hammer.

Hephaestus's association with wondrous creation is confined neither to his own birth nor to his service as midwife to Zeus. Still more remarkable is his capacity to fashion animate things from seemingly inanimate materials. In the beginning, to recall a tale told in my introduction, Zeus kept "hidden from men the means of life. Else you would easily do work enough in a day to supply you for a full year even without working; soon would you put away your rudder over the smoke, and the fields worked by ox and sturdy mule would run to waste." When the compassionate Prometheus stole fire from the god of gods, remember, Zeus retaliated by ordering Hephaestus to "mix earth with water and to put in it the voice and strength of human kind, and fashion a sweet, lovely maiden-shape, like to the immortal goddesses in face."² Educated in the arts of Athena and the wiles of Aphrodite, the manufactured creature called Pandora was discharged as the curse on whom men depend for their very lives.

That the fruits of Hephaestus's labors do not fall neatly on one side or the other of the Cartesian divide between animate and inanimate is additionally indicated by the fabulous beings who inhabit his workshop. When Thetis arrives at his doorstep, the divine craftsman is hard at work

> sweating, wheeling round his bellows,
> pressing the work on twenty three-legged cauldrons,
> an array to ring the walls inside his mansion.
> He'd bolted golden wheels to the legs of each
> so all on their own speed, at a nod from him,
> they could roll to halls where the gods convene
> then roll right home again—a marvel to behold. (18.434-40)

At the end of the day, when these self-propelled utensils have completed their labors, when the time for cleaning up has come, Hephaestus turns to his female automata, "all cast in gold but a match for living, breathing girls. / Intelligence fills their hearts, voice and strength their frames" (18.489-90). These girls are more than a match for their animate counterparts precisely because they owe their existence to the hands of man. Perpetually beautiful, never showing any traces of age, always attendant to their duties, these "artificial" daughters of Hephaestus shame Pandora and her ilk, those "natural" creatures who derive such pleasure from the mischief they work in a world they did not make.

How exactly are we to think about the art of which such materialized artifacts are the products? Hannah Arendt insists that what an artisan takes from nature, work's material, "is already a product of human hands which have removed it from its natural location, either killing a life process, as in the case of the tree which must be destroyed in order to provide wood, or interrupting one of nature's slower processes, as in the case of iron, stone, or marble torn out of the womb of the earth. This element of violation and violence is present in all fabrication." But surely Hephaestus will take at least partial exception to this characterization of his work as well as to Arendt's representation of *homo faber* "as lord and master of the whole earth."³ It is certainly true that when Hephaestus draws Pandora and her artifactual sisters out of the body of Gaia, his flame generates matters that would not otherwise be. But whether such generation necessarily presupposes an act of killing or abortion, as Arendt insists, is not so clear. Is it not possible, Hephaestus asks, that his flame is the impregnating principle that reveals the earth's capacity to give birth not just to fruits but also to artifacts? So conceived, to be a smith is not to be some Cartesian Calvin, but rather a midwife who assists in the delivery of possible beings by shaping the earth's offerings to determinate form within that artificial womb, the furnace. That the relationship between the earth and such handiwork is problematic in light of the former's traditional association with female fertility, Hephaestus will grant. That his labor as mother to the creatures of craft is an unnatural aberration, he will not.

Correlatively, Hephaestus continues, he cannot pretend to be the earth's lord since a true master, before issuing his command, knows just what will count as its successful execution. But that Hephaestus does not know. Better to say that his artisanship is a matter of establishing a dialog with materials whose shape unfolds in time in accordance with potentialities he grasps as he proceeds. To contend, as Arendt does, that fabrication always involves two distinct moments—"first, perceiving the image or shape (*eidos*) of the product to be, and then organizing the means and starting the execution"⁴—is to substitute an intellectualist conceit for the reality of skilled craft. When Hephaestus tells us that over time he has acquired a feel for his materials, he is not telling us that he knows the determinate ends for which these materials serve as so many passive means. Rather, he is telling us that his sentient limbs "know" how leather will respond when stretched just so far, what it means when ore changes from this color to that, how much pressure his cupped hands must apply to fashion a vase whose neck tapers to this point but no further, just how hard to hammer the cold silver worked into the surface of a bronze shield. To think that such "knowledge" takes shape as an idea antecedently articulated in finished form within and by a brain that commandeers the body's docile hands is to represent the dialectical conduct of craft as the imposition of an epistemic tyrant.

The roughness of Hephaestus's hands is deceptive. Unreflective but far from witless, the sense embedded in the musculature of his fingers takes shape as so many acquired habits, so many more or less generalized ways of responding to the partly congruous and partly incongruous situations of everyday life. Rooted in the capacity of memory to abstract prosaic inferences from the commonalities latent in experience, these habits are the dynamic potentialities that locate Hephaestus's conduct in the world he sensibly inhabits. Pace Arendt, Hephaestus can let his tools do their work, leaving his "mind" free to explore their implications, only because the movement of his hands is *not* ruled by an already completed idea of their eventual end, only because their attentiveness to particulars is *not* fettered by cognition's reductive abstractions. To think otherwise is to confuse the struggles of an apprentice, one who must deliberately think *about* what he is doing, with the *thinking-as-doing* of the master craftsman.

The work done by the embodied habits of Hephaestus is not a matter of linear causation, of simply moving some thing from one place to another, as in the case of a spear thrown from one end of a field to another. What distinguishes Hephaestus's causality from such rudimentary manipulation is its transformative effect. Typically, we speak of that effect in either of two ways. Tilting our attention toward what craft works with, we say that some new thing is fashioned *out of* something else; out of hot iron a bridle maker hammers a bit. Alternatively, orienting ourselves toward making's culmination, we say that craft changes some thing *into* another sort of thing; chipping away at a block of stone, the sculptor fashions it into the *Kouros from Anavyssos*. Should our reflection on craft begin with what is given, we might say that Hephaestus's making is rooted in "nature." But if we say that, we must remember that nature, as rationalist philosophy will come to deploy this term, is never encountered in experience; the cosmos furnishes no timeless ideals that may be employed in appraising the adequacy of Hephaestus's works. Borrowing from Heidegger, we might better say that *technē* is an affair of pro-duction, of leading the emergents of *physis* toward some end; and of con-struction, of drawing various things together so as to fashion a whole whose sense is greater than the sum of its parts.[5] Taking what is already growing out of nature as so many immanent potentialities, *technē* fashions its intimations into something that will make manifest qualities hitherto unrealized within experience. Just where one is to cut into this tangle of relations, to discursively discriminate this from that participant in the conduct of craft, is never simply given in the nature of things. Such talk about *technē* blurs the line we are accustomed to drawing between the arts of manufacture and the arts of agriculture. Granted, the conduct of Hephaestus is not identical to that of a farmer who makes more bountiful olive trees that will bear fruit even in the absence of cultivation; and yet, when speaking of these trees' "natural" fecundity, Hesiod uses the same word (*automata*) Homer employs in speaking of Hephaestus's robotic helpmates.[6] Although working with materials that lack a similar capacity for self-motion, Hephaestus must nonetheless respect the immanent potencies distinguishing this material from that; he can only draw from them what they are capable of yielding. Like the bed Odysseus fashioned from the trunk of an olive tree, the shield Hephaestus makes will qualitatively conserve the attributes of the metals from which it is made, manifesting a solidity it would not have were it made of oxhide.

To note that Hephaestus's conduct muddles many familiar conceptual distinctions is no doubt important. But this account will remain incomplete unless its gender-specific dimensions are noted as well. To do so, think once more of the female automata peopling Hephaestus's workshop. As the limping god grows inured to their presence, his relationship to the more mundane instruments of craft subtly changes. No longer does he need his broom, and so in time he loses his feel for the way its handle extends the reach of his arms, how its tightly gathered twigs enlarge the sweep of his hands. Now Hephaestus brings each day to a close by barking commands to the girls he fashioned from gold, girls whose talents are more than a match for a squadron of Hoover uprights. Hephaestus may in time come to forget how the monotonous story of these servants differs from that of the woman he calls his wife, given the similarity of their animate forms; indeed, in time, Hephaestus may well come to think of Charis as a defective prototype of those creatures, as a being whose most vital responsibility is to keep his living dolls in good working order. It will not surprise us, accordingly, when Charis too finds it ever more difficult to say just what it is that makes her a daughter of Pandora rather than a cyborg baked in the furnaces of man.

THE LABORS OF HEPHAESTUS WILL DISAPPEAR IN THE ARMS OF ACHILLES. ALTHOUGH THE history of their accomplishment, how they are made and what they are made of, will be disguised by their apparent objectivity, that story will never be left behind. To illustrate, consider Pandarus, just as he is about to fire an arrow destined to break the tenuous truce between Achaean and Trojan forces:

Then and there he unstrapped his polished bow,
the horn of a wild goat he'd shot in the chest
one day as the springy ibex clambered down a cliff.
Lurking there under cover, he hit it in the heart
and the fine kill went sprawling down the rocks.
The horns on its head ran sixteen hands in length
and a bowyer good with goat-horn worked them up,
fitted, clasped them tight, sanded them smooth
and set the golden notch-rings at the tips. (4.121-29)

Although perhaps inanimate, the bow of Pandarus is not lifeless. Weaving the tale of its origin into an account of its future import, Homer discovers the re-siliency of the goat's horns resident within this artifact. Fitted with a "shaft of black pain" (4.137), this weapon is the agency with which Pandarus's appetite for trouble is projected beyond the confines of his body. When this arrow splits open Menelaus's flesh, doing the work his enemy's teeth or fingernails might if they could with impunity, that bloody wound will sing of this goat's vitality, now reincarnated within the taut spine of Pandarus's bow.

What will save Menelaus is another artifact of war. "The sharp arrow is not stuck in a mortal place, but the shining / war belt turned it aside from its course" (4.185-86).[7] Because the belt is made of metal, we are disinclined to embrace Menelaus's account of the agency it exercised in coming to his res-cue. But perhaps we should not be quite so Cartesian. Granted, it was Athena who directed the arrow's trajectory away from Menelaus's chest and toward his thigh. Yet she would not have dared do so had she not been confident that this belt incorporated its maker's skill in the art of shielding bodies from pain. Made well, that belt "knows" how to respond when a spear, "lusting to sink in flesh" (21.191), hurtles toward it. Should that knowledge prove deficient, this missile's capacity to cause suffering, demonstrating the excess of reciprocation over projection, will radiate throughout the household Menelaus is duty-bound to preserve from harm.

In the company of Auden and over the left shoulder of Thetis, let us watch Hera's son at work. The vitality of artisanal artifacts is most vividly manifest in the shield Hephaestus crafts on Achilles' behalf. A conventional Homeric shield is made from a number of layers of oxhide whose circumference increas-es as one moves to its outer edge. Hephaestus's invention, by way of contrast, is composed of five layers of metal. The two inner plies are made of tin, the two outer of tin, and sandwiched in between is a single layer of gold. What makes this shield still more remarkable, and what invites us to think it alive, are the scenes erupting on its surface:[8]

Figure 3: Shield of Achilles. F. Melian Stawell, *Homer and the Iliad*
(London: J. M. Dent, 1909), 198.

The shield's surface, as you can see, is divided into five concentric bands. The innermost, recalling the creation myth of Hesiod's *Theogony*, depicts the earth, sky, sea, moon, and sun, along with various constellations central to agricultural practice. Within the borders of the outermost band, circling the shield as a whole, flow the life-giving waters of the River of Ocean. Considered together, we might say that the shield's center and periphery depict "nature." Perhaps it is better, though, to say that these two bands articulate conditions of order that, because relatively immune to the ravages of time, temper the flux of experience. Unmoved by mortal desires and schemes, the serenity of this cosmic context deepens the drama of everything transpiring between its inner and outermost rings.

Surprisingly, and quite unlike the more orthodox shield carried by Agamemnon, Hephaestus's creature bears no "Gorgon's grim mask— / the burning eyes, the stark, transfixing horror" (11.39-40). Instead, the three interior bands present so many paradigmatic scenes of everyday activities. Should each of these scenes be considered in relation to the others, and should all be considered as parts of a more comprehensive whole, it will prove no exaggeration to say that on this two-dimensional surface "the god creates a world of gorgeous immortal work" (18:564). But to say that this world is immortal is not to say that it is harmonious or constant. Each individual scene is remarkable because Homer, translating static images into unfolding narratives, presents in a succession of words what is given to Thetis's eyes in instantaneous perception. Testifying to the past from which each scene emerges and the future into which each passes, Homer's poetry etches onto the circular surface of the shield the temporality that will be contradicted by the completed artifact's indestructibility. Leaving key scenes unfinished, in a state of tense irresolution, the shield is pregnant with possibilities that it, precisely because it is timeless, cannot deliver.

The penultimate band, bordered by the River of Ocean, presents a group of young boys and girls, made of finely wrought metal, caught up in a blaze of "rapturous dancing": "A breathless crowd stood round them struck with joy / and through them a pair of tumblers dashed and sprang, / whirling in leaping handsprings, leading out the dance" (18.705-7). The middle band depicts an archetypal agricultural year, divided according to the seasons and the activities appropriate to each. There, under the silent but rejoicing eye of a sceptered king, Hephaestus "forge(s) a fallow field" (18.629). As crews of plowmen labor back and forth across its course, "off to the side, beneath a spreading oak" (18:649), women pour generous portions of barley mead in anticipation of the midday meal. And, just beyond their range of vision, the father of all craftsmen manufactures "a herd of longhorn cattle, / working the bulls in beaten gold and tin, lowing loud / and rumbling out of the farmyard dung to pasture" (18.670-72). That such bucolic splendor is not all it might appear to be, that undercurrents of violence are at work even here, is intimated by the rich blood spewing forth from a bull whose flesh has just been lacerated by a lion's keen claws.

Although seductive, it is not these images that capture the attention of Thetis. Instead, she is drawn to the band immediately adjacent to the shield's celestial center, and it is from here that she begins her gender-specific struggle to determine what this artifact is and, correlatively, what it means. How will she do so given that she is neither the shield's maker nor its intended recipient? How will she do so given that the domain of war, this artifact's most obvious context, is one in which she is a marginal participant at best? As a woman for whom all shields are alien in the sense that they remain unincorporated within the habits of her sensible body, it seems not unreasonable to speculate that Thetis's ways of sense making will be partly, but not entirely, congruent with those of others similarly situated. Think, for example, of the war's alleged cause, Helen. Early in the *Iliad*, we are told, Helen fashions a great red robe, "working into it the numerous struggles of Trojans, breakers of horses, and bronze-armoured Achaians" (3.126-27). Because she is merely mortal, however, Helen cannot grasp the relationship between this particular conflict and the larger cosmic context in which it is situated, and her appreciation of its import is circumscribed in consequence. As a goddess, Thetis can grasp that relationship, and so it seems not unreasonable to speculate that her ways of sense making will be partly, but not entirely, congruent with those of Hephaestus. Like Helen, Hephaestus seeks to render intelligible the relational context into which the shield is to be inserted by securing some distance from its brutal immediacy. But, instead of telling its history in thread, as does Helen, Hephaestus relates the conflict at Ilion to a tale of two other cities, each of which he now founds before the watchful eyes of Thetis.

Neither city exists anywhere in time or space, neither has a history, neither has a name. Each furnishes the only context the other knows. Most commentaries refer to the first as a city at peace, and the second as a city at war.

But that account is far too neat. A more subtle understanding is unwittingly suggested by Hesiod. In the opening lines of "Works and Days," Hesiod advises that the human condition is subject to the workings of a natural force, strife, which can assume two forms. The first, most obviously apparent in the city under siege, reveals itself in war: "So they clashed and fought like living, breathing men / grappling each other's corpses, dragging off the dead" (18.627-28). The second, most obviously apparent in the city centered around the agora, reveals itself in the public struggle to resolve a quarrel between two men concerning the blood price for a recently murdered kinsman:[9]

> One declaimed in public, vowing payment in full—
> the other spurned him, he would not take a thing—
> so both men pressed for a judge to cut the knot.
> The crowd cheered on both, they took both sides,
> but heralds held them back as the city elders sat
> on polished stone benches, forming the sacred circle,
> grasping in hand the staffs of clear-voiced heralds,
> and each leapt to his feet to plead the case in turn.
> Two bars of solid gold shone on the ground before them,
> a prize for the judge who'd speak the straightest verdict. (18.583-92)

While these two forms of strife can be distinguished for analytic purposes, never does experience betray such a tidy dichotomy. Hence, in the city at war, the second form is apparent in the debate conducted amongst the besiegers: Is it better to plunder the city or to share its wealth with those soon to be conquered? In the city at peace, the first form is present as an unspoken but very real question: Will not an unending cycle of bloodshed, of uncivil war, erupt should it prove impossible to sublimate this conflict within a rule-governed contest? What distinguishes these two cities, in other words, is not the presence or absence of strife, but rather the predominant form it assumes in each.

What does Thetis think when she gazes upon these two cities in the making? Homer does not say, and so we cannot know for certain. But we can be confident that in fashioning meaning from what Hephaestus crafts, she does not do so de novo. Of necessity, she will begin her work by relating what she sees to her sense of the situation in which she is now proximately implicated, a situation that takes shape as yet another question: How am I to secure a creature of Prometheus for my boy, a surrogate willing to absorb the blows aimed at his unshielded body? Like all good questions, this one does not stand alone. It has its history, an informing context whose principal ingredient is the still unresolved conflict between Achilles and Agamemnon.

When Agamemnon seized the captive Briseis from Achilles, in retaliation for the latter's failure to show proper respect for the Achaean commander, the chief of the Myrmidons elected to defend his honor by withdrawing from the war. Only when the devastating fruits of that decision bring the Achaeans to the edge of defeat does Achilles, playing mother to the doleful Patroclus, dress his friend in the garb of a true man and send him off to die.

> Why in tears, Patroclus?
> Like a girl, a baby running after her mother,
> begging to be picked up, and she tugs her skirts,
> holding her back as she tried to hurry off—all tears,
> fawning up at her, till she takes her in her arms. (16:7-11)

This much of the tale Thetis can surely tell. But what she can say, I would argue, is less than what she can make sense of. Just as Hephaestus cannot put into words all that his skilled hands can do, so too Thetis cannot articulate all that the sensible habits of her body can tease from experience.

Thetis never finds cause to wonder just why Achilles has reacted to Agamemnon's slight with such fury, and that alone is sufficient to indicate her grasp of the gender-specific performances mandated by the patriarchal world into which her son has been born. What it means to play the part of a woman within that world's extended household is etched into the memory-laden tissues of her body. When Zeus became alarmed by a prophecy concerning the strength of the son Thetis would one day bear, he cast her into the *oikos* of Peleus, where she was first wedded and then raped.

> *Me out of all the daughters of the sea he chose*
> *to yoke to a mortal man, Peleus, son of Aeacus,*
> *and I endured his bed, a mortal's bed, resisting*
> *with all my will. And now he lies in the halls,*
> *broken with grisly age.* (18.504-8)

Within this household, where Achilles would succeed Peleus were he not fated to die, the master rules without challenge, ensuring the provision of security, the administration of justice, and the satisfaction of basic needs. Peleus's authority to do so is proximately grounded in the nobility of his birth; less immediately, his rule is sanctioned by the patriarchal *monarchia* of Zeus, whose command is the sustaining condition of the hierarchy of powers ordering the cosmos. But neither of these claims adequately captures the quotidian foundations of Peleus's authority in the unstated rules governing the relations between human and nonhuman things, between human artifacts and the axes, knives, andirons, pots, scissors, vats, looms, and lugpoles that shape bodies to intelligibly gendered form.

Rule within this household is complicated by the relations it sustains to others, and so the *oikos* is not quite the self-contained and seamless web Peleus would have us believe. Bonds of kinship and class, whose boundaries

are not precisely coextensive with those of the household, intrude upon its au-
tarchy. Agamemnon's responsiveness to Menelaus's plea for help in securing
the return of Helen testifies to the power of kinship, while Peleus's own enlist-
ment in that cause testifies to the chain of obligations affiliating those of noble
birth. Thus, horizontal ties between members of a ruling aristocracy are woven into a world that, at first blush, appears to be structured exclusively along
vertical lines of domination and subordination. In addition, within as well as
across these households, horizontal ties are fashioned between those who, silent but not quite invisible, are daily subject to the will of their betters. To the
extent that these animate tools are thereby linked to one another, what Peleus,
Agamemnon, and Menelaus take to be their unchecked authority within the
household is constrained still more.

Agamemnon's status as leader of the Achaean troops, and so his standing
as a man, is perpetually unstable. For he must now dictate to those who, within their respective households, are accustomed to consider themselves unchecked patriarchs. The insecurity of his position becomes apparent to all
when, in the opening passages of the *Iliad*, Achilles calls an assembly to contest Agamemnon's refusal to accept a ransom in return for yet another woman
caught up in the disposition of captives. To this point, we may suppose, Agamemnon has simply taken for granted his right, as king, to distribute the
spoils of war in the same unilateral way he apportions the goods of his estate.
In this sense, he has treated the issue as if it were private, as if it were a concern of the *oikos*. But when Achilles complains about Agamemnon's allot-
ment, he questions this "as if" and so transforms this matter into an affair
that cannot be definitively resolved through appeal to the household's customary principles of justice.

> My honors never equal yours,
> whenever we sack some wealthy Trojan stronghold—
> my arms bear the brunt of the raw, savage fighting,
> true, but when it comes to dividing up the plunder
> the lion's share is yours, and back I go to my ships. (1.193-97)

Implying that military valor rather than formal authority to command ought
to serve as the criterion of distribution, Achilles places an unstated question
before the assembled lords. But neither he nor his peers know quite what to do
with that inquiry. Accustomed to thinking of authority as a monolithic possession monopolistically exercised by a single father, no one of their number is
able to imagine the possibility of distinctively political, as opposed to patriarchal, power.

Just as Thetis understands why Achilles must withdraw in response to
Agamemnon's insult, so too does she understand why Agamemnon can only
respond to her son's scorn by reaffirming his status as bearer of the scepter
that, fashioned by Hephaestus and given to Zeus, transmitted to Pelops and

then to Atreus, was finally bequeathed to the commander of the expedition against Ilion. But Achilles does not find Agamemnon's appeal to the king of the gods convincing. "What a worthless, burnt-out coward I'd be called / if I would submit to you and all your orders, / whatever you blurt out" (1.343-45). However, incapable of articulating an alternative account of justice, Achilles cannot enlist the aid of his fellows in contesting the authority of Agamemnon. Like some barely civilized Polyphemus, Achilles is confronted with a simple choice: accede to his rival or fight to supplant him. His rage prevents him from doing the former, while Athena denies him the latter. Reduced to wordless fury, "down on the ground / he dashed the scepter studded bright with golden nails, / then took his seat again" (1.287-89). Unable to think beyond the discursive confines of the *oikos*, Achilles and Agamemnon are necessarily at odds, caught between irreconcilable affirmations of authority based, respectively, in military prowess and heavenly entitlement. "Once the two had fought it out with words, / battling face-to-face, both sprang to their feet / and broke up the muster beside the Argive squadrons" (1.356-58).

No doubt, Thetis does not understand the conflict between Agamemnon and Achilles in precisely these terms. But surely she senses, however intuitively, the points of convergence between their confrontation and the incident unfolding in the city built around the shield's agora. Each concerns a dispute framed in the language of justice; each involves the transformation of a private concern into a public affair via an appeal to those not immediately implicated; and each at present remains unresolved. These situations differ, though, insofar as the quarrel between Agamemnon and Achilles is without any apparent means of resolution. Animated by the sort of strife pitting those outside against those inside the city under siege, they are effectively at war.

In contrast, the shield's townsmen acknowledge their impasse and so, exchanging one form of strife for another, call "for a judge to cut the knot" (18.585). Fashioning for themselves the judicial institutions Aeschylus will later ascribe to Athena, these rival patriarchs plead their cases before a council of elders, swearing to abide by the verdict that seems most just. The assembled elders sit on stone benches in a circle deemed "sacred" because it is Zeus who, ultimately, presides over all conflicts of justice. As each stands in turn to state a proposed settlement, he takes in his right hand the symbol of public authority, the scepter. When held by Agamemnon, this artifact affirms the divinity of his authority and so his exclusive title to rule. But in the elders' hands, the scepter is first and foremost a mark of *themis*, of orderly procedure among those wishing to speak their peace. That scepter is the artifactual materialization of their common sense that determination of the just is not the prerogative of any single man, and its objectivity enforces their mutual determination to hear the opinions of all entitled to speak before judgment is rendered.

The very possibility of calling such arbitration into play, especially in a case of murder, testifies to the palpable but uncertain reality of a form of communal identification transcending the boundaries of the aristocratic household. In its absence, homicide remains an essentially private affair, involving only the kin of those immediately involved, and demanding either retaliation in kind or exile of the murderer. (The latter was the fate of Patroclus, who, after killing a companion during a childhood game of dice, fled his home and was eventually taken in by Peleus.) But when the parties concerned ask this informally constituted body to decide whether revenge or ransom is appropriate in this instance, as well as what the limits of each should be, they gesture toward a new way of teasing form from the ambiguous matters of experience. Just as weddings sometimes unite families previously disparate and so confuse the integrity of exclusive kinship allegiances, so too the emergence of orderly procedures of adjudication anticipates a day when the common cause of equitable mediation will prevail over the uncertain imperatives of familial vengeance. On that day, the human artifacts called "citizens" will fully materialize, as all free male creatures claim equal share in what, according to Plato, is Prometheus's most valuable gift, the art of politics (*politikē technē*).[10]

The reality of this art, and so of the cause of public justice, is inseparably bound up with the artisanal artifacts articulating its sense. For example, the hope that internecine conflict can be kept at bay, that strife can be regularized, is embedded within the gold contributed by each party. That prize is to be awarded to the elder whose "straight" speech most adequately does justice to the claims of all parties involved.[11] The equation of right doing with "straight" talk is itself a metaphorical abstraction from so many concrete disputes concerning land ownership. The original sense of *dikē* is "boundary," used most commonly in reference to the dividing lines drawn between two pieces of land; the employment of this term in speaking of a legal controversy's resolution is derived from the practice of drawing such lines, which may of course be either "straight" or "crooked." Judith Butler, accordingly, may be right to contend that when a judge invokes the authority of the law, "what is *invoked* by the one who speaks or inscribes the law is *the fiction* of a speaker who wields authority to make his words binding, the legal incarnation of the divine utterance"; and she may be right to contend that the conventions constitutive of this fiction "are grounded in no other legitimating authority than the echo-chain of their own reinvocation."[12] But to say that and no more is to neglect what gives this fiction its ontological density. It is to forget that absent a courtroom, whether marked by stones or set in concrete, no amount of reinvocation will suffice to make this fiction real. Correlatively, absent a public space secured by artisanal artifacts, no citizen will ever tangibly grasp just what it is to affirm the principle of publicity, of what it is to bring a political matter to a place where it, simply by virtue of being so located, is available to all.

The reality of the public space now being carved out by the shield's elders is also contingent on its relationship to what it is not. Its appearance requires that the received structure of difference, specifically that appropriate to a world of aristocratic patriarchs, become problematic. If patriarchs are to become citizens, the walls of the *oikos* must crumble. No longer can those walls conflate the emerging distinction between public and private concerns, arrogating to the space they enclose all matters regarding the making and unmaking of human artifacts. Some affairs, leaking through their cracks, must seep toward the center of the city, materializing there as so much matter available for reformation within and by the discourse of citizens. The recognizability of such affairs, their intelligibility as the stuff of specifically political strife, will depend on their identification as not-household matters, just as the recognizability of democratic citizens will turn on their distinguishability from aristocratic patriarchs.

But what about those beings who are not able to take part in such matters, who are compelled to remain enclosed within the now destabilized walls of the *oikos*? What happens to those who must attend to its necessities in order that others may leave them behind? To answer this question, let us return to the shield. Within the city at peace, two scenes unfold. The second, as we have seen, concerns an incipient legal issue. But that transitory issue is what it dramatically is only because it is situated against a mundane backdrop of enduring intelligibility, of received ways of relating various sorts of artifacts to one another.

> With weddings and wedding feasts in one
> and under glowing torches they brought forth the brides
> from the women's chambers, marching through the streets
> while choir on choir the wedding song rose high
> and the young men came dancing, whirling round in rings
> and among them the flutes and harps kept up their stirring call—
> women rushed to the doors and each stood moved with wonder.
> (18:573-79)

Here the traffic in women takes shape as their apparently timeless movement out of the households of fathers and into those of husbands. What these men do out of doors, within the circle of elders, is possible only by virtue of the confinement of women behind those same doors (except, of course, when they are escorted through them for the purposes of exchange); and, once shut tight, each of these doors remanufactures the palpable distinction between what is public and what is private.

At one level of analysis, regardless of whether men are aristocratic patriarchs or democratic citizens, the work done by these doors does not fundamentally change; women will remain so many daughters of Pandora in any case. On another level, however, not merely the work but the very nature of these doors is transformed as egalitarian sensibilities encroach. If an artisanal artifact, like its human counterpart, is what it is by virtue of the relationships in which it participates, then to alter the relationship between Peleus and Thetis is to refit the door through which he dragged her on their wedding day. Even then, we know, she resisted his sexual aggression. But, at that time, she interpreted her struggle exclusively in terms of the threat her future son allegedly posed to Zeus. Now we have reason to think she knows better.

Thetis is a marginal being. Spatially, she is caught between the divine and the mundane. Temporally, she is caught between, on the one hand, a fading aristocracy embodied for her in the persons of Peleus and Achilles; and, on the other hand, an emerging egalitarian order in which her husband and her son will prove equally anachronistic. Is it possible that Thetis, on the basis of her marginality, her inarticulate feel for qualitative differentiations very much in the making, can sense that the door separating inside from out is now a bit ajar? To possess prophetic powers, as she does, is not simply to peer into the future; it is also to endure the present in a distinctive way. Knowing her son must die at Ilion, she is forever discovering intimations of what is to come in what is now. Can she see in the shield's circle of elders a faint portent of what one day in Athens will become the Council of the Areopagos? Can she anticipate that this council will in time be enlarged, subdivided, and then reconstituted as the *dikastēria* and *ekklēsia*? Can she imagine that one day even the club-footed commoner who goes by the name of Thersites, an outcast like she and Hephaestus, will stand as an equal next to the sons of the patriarchs? In some way, however ill formed, does she realize that the culture of patriarchal aristocracy and so the cult of heroic masculinity, most perfectly exemplified by her "swift-footed" son, is now on its last legs?

Inlaid on the shield's curved wall, like the embryo once planted in the lining of Thetis's uterus, resides a seed that in time will give birth to so many boys destined to wrest control of collective affairs from their fathers. Bearing the names of Draco, Solon, and Cleisthenes, these sons will stake out and plow a new field of agency. On that field, matters previously left within the *oikos*—homicide, marriage, property—will be recultivated on specifically public ground. At first glance, the shield is silent about such matters; its apparently self-contained cosmos, neatly demarcated by bands circling endlessly round one another, presents the sort of comprehensive vision that is only available to the gods. A closer look, however, reveals that the shield is in tension with itself. As the paradigmatic artifact of an order predicated on the supremacy of a warrior aristocracy, as the most visually striking piece of a hero's armor, the shield proclaims Achilles' *oikos*-identity on the battlefield. And yet, moving hither and thither on its surface are some creatures who confirm the reality of that identity and others who beckon beyond it. Does the king of the middle band sense his eventual superfluity when, looking across the border into the next, he spies a pair of litigants before a leaderless council? As a harbinger of the day when politics will stand as an autonomous arena of conduct, as a sign of the time when the heroic prowess of Achilles will be supplanted by the collective power of armed male citizens, the shield says more than its maker ever intended.

"(T)HIS THING: WHAT SHALL I CALL IT AND BE RIGHT, IN ALL ELOQUENCE?" THIS QUES-
tion cannot be answered in any definitive way. The philosophical import of the
shield consists of its refusal to stand as a neatly bounded object susceptible to
unequivocal specification. We may be tempted to privilege Hephaestus's answer to this question. But whatever his intention in making the shield it will
play only a bit part in the subsequent biography of this artifact, and so he cannot dictate its identity. Nor, for that matter, can anyone else. There is no thing
in itself. There are only things-in-contexts; and so to know what this particular thing is, we must explore the shifting relations by which it is constituted.
To say that it is so constituted is not, however, to deny that it is also an active
participant in the construction of these same relations. When Glaucus, ally to
the Trojans, exchanges armor with Diomedes, the Achaean, they do not merely pass so much inert stuff back and forth between them. As yet another manifestation of the excess of reciprocation over projection, this exchange is a
performative act, a vow of friendship, a rematerialization of a relationship first
fashioned by their fathers. By the same token, when Thetis delivers the fruit of
Hephaestus's labors to Achilles, that act is (re)productive of a relationship between creator and creature, a knot tied round the heart of each. The shield
now bears this tangle as surely as it supports the dancers leaping across its surface.

To dissolve the shield's objectivity in this way is to affirm its referential instability. To say that, however, is not to say that its meaning is whatever so
many privatized Cartesian subjects say it is. Granted, the shield is an expression of skill for Hephaestus, a symbol of hope for Thetis, an emblem of identity for Achilles, a thing of terror for Hector. But it is also party to the fashioning
of a palpable web of relations whose sense is shared precisely because it and its
kin create a differentiated space that is some place as opposed to no place.
Think, by analogy, of the sword Achilles now holds. As Achilles thrusts this
projection of the human arm's capacity to do harm toward the thin margin
separating Hector's helmet from breastplate, he simultaneously anticipates
his opponent's parry. Steadying himself for that counterthrust, Achilles shifts
his weight slightly to the left. Hector, in turn, anticipates Achilles' anticipation and responds accordingly. Wholly engrossed in this furious dance, each
grasps how the sword functions in the other's experience and, as a result, in
his own as well. Their capacity to assume the standpoint of the other is inseparable from their knowledge of how to wield their swords, just as their capacity
to wield their swords is inseparable from their knowledge of how to assume
the other's standpoint. The sword is a thing of mutual significance precisely
because it participates so vitally in the shared conduct of killing.

Returning with her gifts, including shield and sword, Thetis finds Achilles
embracing the corpse of Patroclus. The arch of his arms, resembling the cradle

she fashioned for his head not long ago, reports her failure to ease his suffering. Disentangling the living from the dead, she directs her son's attention elsewhere: "*Accept this glorious armor, look, / a gift from the god of fire—burnished bright, finer / than any mortal has ever borne across his back*" (19.12-14). As "the gear clashed out in all its blazoned glory" (19.16), the eyes of Achilles are drawn to the shield. Its surface summons from him an ensemble of qualitative responses, responses that Homer reduces to one. "The more he gazed, the deeper his anger went, / his eyes flashing under his eyelids, fierce as fire" (19.19-20). As a hero who lives each moment as if it were his first and last, the depthless Achilles cannot do what we can. Locating the rounded shield within an elongated context, we know that his rage, like the shield itself, is a creature of its history. We know, for example, that Hephaestus's gifts recall the armor Peleus gave his son before embarking for Ilion. Haunting that recollection, we remember Peleus receiving that armor as a wedding gift from Hephaestus; Patroclus donning that armor before going out to die; Hector adopting that armor as his own after slaying Patroclus; Thetis knowing that soon after Achilles strips that armor from Hector's shoulders, her son will die. Achilles, by way of contrast, is effectively confined to the shield's surface, and so cannot begin to explore the viscera of its relational reality.

No doubt Achilles appreciates the solemnity of the innermost and outermost bands. No doubt he is struck by the animosities gripping the two cities. No doubt he enjoys the scenes of ordinary people taking part in prosaic activities. But beyond that, unable to see except through the eyes of a commander, he probably cannot go. Achilles is unlikely, for example, to sense the irony of his own situation, a doomed hero bearing into battle moving representations of all that makes everyday life sweet, of all he left behind in Phthia. Moreover, because he subscribes to an ethos that identifies the battlefield as the locus of immortality, because he shares the contempt of that ethos for the common, his grasp of the opposition between the shield's exhortation to peace and this war's horrors cannot be as acute as it must be for Thetis. As a woman who has been ejected from the divine house of Zeus, as a goddess who has felt the force of the mortal patriarch, Thetis can detect in the shield what Achilles cannot— a compressed declaration of the perversity of an order that asks a mother to rejoice at the prospect of her son's imminent death.

To say that Achilles' grasp of the shield is comparatively superficial is not to say that he finds it unintelligible, a brute thing. Achilles' way of weaving the shield into a web of meaning is not ours. To render the shield a thing of sense, what Achilles does is this: First he puts on the greaves, followed by the breastplate. He then picks up sword and shield, each of which he grips with the aid of cross-belts slung over his shoulders. Finally, placing a crested helmet on his head, he raises into position the spear Patroclus found too heavy and so left behind. He is now ready for battle.

And brilliant Achilles tested himself in all his gear,
Achilles spun on his heels to see if it fit tightly,
see if his shining limbs ran free within it, yes,
and it felt like buoyant wings lifting the great captain. (19.453-56)

As a boy, Achilles learned the man-making arts of war not so much through explicit instruction, but by watching his father. As a young man, that learning was gradually effaced within the corporeal structures of so many realized skills. Initially orienting his conduct *to* the acquisition of these skills, today he acts *from* them, responding expertly but unreflectively to the nuances of this situation and that.[13] If Peleus could see the incarnation of these skills at just this moment, twirling about like one of the shield's graceful dancers, he would know that the vigor that once flowed within his own limbs now courses through the arms of his son.

Because these arms are made so well, the skill of Hephaestus is readily integrated into the habits of Achilles. Yet in assimilating these artifactual materializations of Hephaestus's craft, Achilles' cultivated dispositions for war undergo subtle but significant reconstitution. Unlike the armor lost to Hector, this helmet balances a bit farther back on his skull, these greaves grip his calves a bit more firmly, this breastplate demands a bit more from his shoulders. As the training recollected by his muscles imperceptibly acknowledges these peculiarities, he becomes a slightly different warrior. As Peleus's education fuses with Hephaestus's craft on the mobile site that is Achilles' body, the relational web joining each to the other two becomes something other than what any one intended.

His "whole body cased in tremendous bronze" (13.228),[14] Achilles dons an artifactual membrane whose toughness expresses the tenderness Hephaestus feels for Thetis and her son. In a way, this shell of metal is an agency of Achilles' disembodiment and so a boast in the face of his mortality. Removing from his body some measure of its vulnerability to pain, it divests him of preoccupations that would hound him were he naked. Doing so, this brazen suit expands the range of Achilles' corporeality, challenging him to thrust his arms into situations where they would otherwise never dare to go. Still, no matter how perfect, the gifts of Hephaestus cannot overcome the circumstances of his mongrel generation. When death at last takes him, the imperishable armor he wears as a shroud will mock the finitude that is his lot.

Like an artificial limb, the sword Achilles grips complements this swelling of his bodily compass. Is this sword an extension of Achilles' arm? Or is his arm an extension of the sword? The issue is intrinsically indeterminate. What is true of Hephaestus's hammer is equally true of Achilles' sword. At the sword's far end, pointing away from Achilles' body and toward an undifferentiated class of prospective victims, the tip of its blade expresses an appreciation of one specific sort of harm to which human flesh is vulnerable. At its near end, pointing back toward Achilles' body and away from those who would harm it, the sword's oval handle articulates an understanding of how beings with opposable thumbs can grasp things otherwise certain to draw blood. Gesturing in two directions at once, the arc described by this weapon's agency draws Achilles into the world and it into him.

The contestability of the boundary we ordinarily draw between human artifacts and their artisanal complements is demonstrated most graphically when the distinction between body and weapon collapses altogether. Because the clash of sentient arms is so thoroughly bound up with the clash of their nonsentient counterparts, Homer sees no need to distinguish between the crash of body against body and that of sword against sword: A "wall" of warriors "bulked together, / spear-by-spear, shield-by-shield, the rims overlapping, / buckler-to-buckler, helm-to-helm, man to man massed tight" (13.154-56). Still more dramatically, consider Achilles, who, while waiting for Thetis to return from Hephaestus's workshop, strides atop the rampart built to protect the Achaean ships. From his head pours forth a river of fire, striking enemy charioteers dumb. Three times he lets fly with an enormous cry, and the Trojans "whirled in panic— / and twelve of their finest fighters died then and there" (18.264-65). Here voice is the blade and body the handle of the animate weapon called Achilles.

If Achilles' armor is a new skin, and if his sword and spear are the agencies by means of which his wrath is extended beyond arms' reach, then what exactly is his shield? Mimicking the action of his left forearm in blocking the blow of a clenched fist, Achilles and shield collaborate to deflect a torrent of arrows, freeing his right arm to attack. But the shield is more than just a defense mechanism. Bearing into battle its displays of civilized delights, as well as those of war's agonies, the shield is Homer's most poignant statement about the terrible ambiguity inherent in the fire Prometheus stole from Zeus. On the one hand, this artisanal artifact signifies the capacity of human beings to construct a world of durable goods that, individually and collectively, shelter them from the harm that would otherwise befall creatures so ill equipped by nature. On the other hand, the shield signifies the capacity of human beings to obliterate the benign logic of projection and reciprocation in a frenzy of world destruction.

From the volcanic furies churning deep within Gaia's bowels Hephaestus forges a gift for Achilles, and it is these same elemental fires that now blaze forth from the warrior's eyes. As the shield's all consuming inferno "calls up the wild joy of war" (19.179), the powers summoned by its maker are welded to the rage of the destroyer.

> Achilles now
> like inhuman fire raging on through the mountain gorges
> the wind swirling the huge fireball left and right—

chaos of fire—Achilles storming on with brandished spear
like a frenzied god of battle trampling all he killed
and the earth ran black with blood. (20.553-59)

Born not of the union of human and divine but of the "salt gray sunless ocean"
and the "towering blank rocks" (16.39-40), Achilles erupts as an anarchic automaton, a hellish counterpart to Hephaestus's metal girls. His daemonic
wrath, relentlessly generating corpse after corpse after corpse, obliterates the
fragile boundaries separating beast from human, mortal from divine, culture
from nature, madness from reason. Swallowing the dancers, the wedding cele-
brants, and the plowmen within the undifferentiated abyss of war without respite,

the powers collided! A mammoth clash—the wide earth roared
and the arching vault of heaven echoed round with trumpets!
And Zeus heard the chaos, throned on Olympus heights,
and laughed deep in his own great heart. (21.440-43)

WHEN ACHILLES' RAMPAGE IS COMPLETE, ZEUS TELLS THETIS SHE MUST ORDER HER SON
to accept a ransom for the body of Hector, slain hero of the Trojans, and so she
hastens to her son's encampment one last time. When Odysseus, Ajax, and
Nestor approached Achilles' quarters earlier, they saw before them an imposing declaration of Achilles' stature among men, an artifactual monument to
his prowess as Achaea's preeminent warrior:

the tall, imposing lodge the Myrmidons built their king,
hewing planks of pine, and roofed it high with thatch,
gathering thick shaggy reeds from the meadow banks,
and round it built their king a spacious courtyard
fenced with close-set stakes. A single pine beam
held the gates, and it took three men to ram it home. (24.529-34)

What Thetis sees as she approaches is something else. Not in any literal sense
does she think of Achilles' shelter as an enlarged womb. But the experience of
pregnancy, still impressed on her vital organs, takes part in making of this
thing something akin to a refuge. Its walls, like Hephaestus's armor, protect
her son as she no longer can. Wrapping around Achilles, enveloping him within their silence, they offer fleeting moments of respite from the brutalities
transpiring not far from its door.
    Passing through the mouth of his asylum, Thetis finds Achilles once
again choking on his tears. Scanning its interior, her eyes light upon the elabo-
rately decorated chest she gave him when he embarked for Ilion. She knows

exactly what this vessel of hope contains, for she had "filled it to the brim with war-shirts, windproof cloaks / and heavy fleecy rugs" (16.264-65). But does she appreciate the irony stitched into their seams? Does she recognize that it is only their funded warmth that enables Achilles to disregard his body's otherwise imperious need to maintain a stable temperature? Does she note how these treasured servants are the conditions of his participation in the ritualized form of male violence called war? Does it occur to her that, just as Achilles gave Patroclus the armor that prompted him to wager his life, so too has she dressed her boy well for death?

> *My child—*
> *how long will you eat your heart out here in tears and torment?*
> *All wiped from your mind, all thought of food and bed?*
> *It's a welcome thing to make love with a woman. . . .*
> *You don't have long to live now, well I know:*
> *already I see them looming up beside you—death*
> *and the strong force of fate.* (24.155-61)

Beside these phantoms rests the funeral vase that will soon house the bones of Thetis's flesh and blood. Made by Hephaestus, the golden amphora she received from Dionysos whispers the dread secret she will never confess to her boy: Only his death, making Achilles one among so many "after images of used-up men,"[15] can finally release her from the anguish of knowing his fate.

ii. *Cyborg*

> O why did God,
> Creator wise, that peopled highest Heav'n
> With spirits masculine, create at last
> This novelty on earth, this fair defect
> Of nature, and not fill the world at once
> With men as angels without feminine,
> Or find some other way to generate
> Mankind?
>
> John Milton

No young woman, I am confident, is eager to conclude that her betrothed is a liar. Far more damaging, though, to suspect but not to know for certain whether his words are so many counterfeit goods. To uncover an undeniable falsehood is to come into possession of a clear and distinct ground for confrontation. But unconfirmed traces of deception leave the accusing finger unsure of its target. Marriage, she was once told, is a sacred bond fashioned from so much transparent sincerity. Surely, therefore, his vow is enough to show that she is mistaken. She must be the guilty one, for never would he mislead her.

When Victor was thirteen, vacationing with his family at the baths near Thonon, he happened on a work composed by the alchemist, Cornelius Agrippa. Fascinated by the philosopher's forays into the occult, Victor communicated his enthusiasm to his father. But Alphonsus, a creature of the Enlightenment, wished his son to grow free of all superstitions, of all infatuations with the supernatural: "Ah! Cornelius Agrippa! My dear Victor, do not waste your time upon this; it is sad trash."[16] Crushed but unrepentant, Victor collected all of Agrippa's works, as well as others by Paracelcus and Albertus Magnus, when the family returned to Geneva. Afraid to speak openly of these tales of transmutation, Victor turned to his stepsister, a child adopted by his parents when he was only four: "I disclosed my discoveries to Elizabeth, therefore, under a promise of strict secrecy."[17] Elizabeth, though, showed little interest in the wonders of alchemy. What really mattered to her was Victor's eagerness to confide in her, his "more than sister" (41). Their guilty confidence, violating the command of father, cemented their special relationship.

Because of what they were to each other as children, Elizabeth cannot imagine that Victor, now a man, would withhold anything from her. Yet, twice in recent years, she has found reason to call Victor's frankness into question. The first occurred some time after he left home to attend university at Ingolstadt. In the beginning, Victor recalled his father's parting injunction: "I know that while you are pleased with yourself, you will think of us with affection, and we shall hear regularly from you" (56). But now, four years later, Victor rarely communicates with either his father or Elizabeth. They receive partial explanation for his silence only when Henry Clerval, Victor's boyhood friend, secures permission to attend Ingolstadt as well. There, Henry is met by a Victor who, emaciated from overwork, slips rapidly into a feverish state of nervous exhaustion. Reluctant to trouble the aged Alphonsus and the fragile Elizabeth, Henry's letters to Geneva minimize the severity of Victor's illness.

Victor's secret and Henry's half-truths are never found out. Yet, perhaps because "a man is blind to a thousand minute circumstances, which call forth a woman's sedulous attention" (131), Elizabeth is attuned to clues that escape Alphonsus. To Victor, she writes:

> We cannot help imagining that your friend Clerval conceals the extent of your disorder: for it is now several months since we have seen your hand-writing; all this time you have been obliged to dictate your letters to Henry. . . . Dear Victor, if you are not very ill, write yourself, and make your father and all of us happy; or—I cannot bear to think of the other side of the question; my tears already flow.[18]

On the mend, Victor responds at once. We never learn just what he writes, but it is not difficult to guess. Surely, his desire to comfort Elizabeth and Alphonsus, as well as his reluctance to discredit Clerval, incline him to make light of his disease. Poring over that letter, Elizabeth, we may also guess, is caught between her desire to be reassured, which requires that she embrace as true what she suspects is a lie; and her suspicion that Victor is far sicker than he says, which requires that she read his words as so many fabrications.

Elizabeth's confidence is shaken once again when Victor returns from Ingolstadt to Geneva. When Alphonsus urges Victor to marry Elizabeth, he responds with enthusiasm: "I love my cousin tenderly and sincerely. . . . My future hopes and prospects are entirely bound up in the expectation of our union" (129). Yet when Alphonsus presses his son to set a date for the wedding, Victor demurs: "I expressed a wish to visit England; but, concealing the true reasons of this request, I clothed my desires under the guise of wishing to travel and see the world before I sat down for life within the walls of my native town."[19] Taught that men are creatures who, by nature, resist domestication, Elizabeth reluctantly accedes to Victor's plan for a journey of not more than two years. But, beginning to grasp the unintended truth of Victor's childhood reference to her as "the inmate of my parents' house" (41), she also quietly registers her regret "that she had not the same opportunities of enlarging her experience, and cultivating her understanding."[20]

Toward the close of his voyage, now in Paris, Victor receives another letter from Elizabeth. The composition of this letter, I would guess, is the fruit of her lingering confusion and unexpressed resentment. How is Elizabeth to make sense of the apparent contradiction between Victor's repeated protestations of love and his chronic "flying to solitude" (157)? She cannot respond to this rift between word and deed with overt anger. That would challenge her self-conception as a woman who equates fulfillment with the achievement of domestic harmony. Instead, the seeds of recrimination yield so many self-effacing doubts:

> You know well, Victor, that our union has been the favourite plan of your parents ever since our infancy. We were told this when young, and taught to look forward to it as an event that would certainly take place. We were affectionate playfellows during childhood, and, I believe, dear and valued friends to one another as we grew older. But as brother and sister often entertain a lively affection towards each other, without desiring a more intimate union, may not such also be our case? Tell me, dearest Victor. Answer me, I conjure you, by our mutual happiness, with simple truth—Do you not love another? (157)

Because it would be too threatening, too stark, Elizabeth cannot simply ask: "Do you love another?" The obliqueness of her phrasing takes the edge off what Victor might otherwise read as an indictment. Elizabeth thereby transforms a possible accusation into an expression of anxiety, of worry that she may be undesired by the man she is to love. Yet, because Elizabeth knows it will crush her if he does indeed confess his love for another, she invites him to sidestep her question. If you are to refuse me, she pleads, let me dictate the terms of that rejection. Tell me that you forsake me out of respect for the boundaries appropriate to a relationship between siblings. If your affirmations of love have been so many lies, then deceive me when at last you speak the truth.

Victor's response, in a letter that is "calm and affectionate" (159), addresses Elizabeth as if she were not a sister but a child, a creature whose worries are so many groundless phantasms: "Chase away your idle fears; to you alone do I consecrate my life, and my endeavours for contentment" (159). Whatever reassurance these words may convey are immediately swept away, however, as Victor continues:

> I have one secret, Elizabeth, a dreadful one; when revealed to you, it will chill your frame with horror, and then, far from being surprised at my misery, you will only wonder that I survive what I have endured. I will confide this tale of misery and terror to you the day after our marriage shall take place; for, my sweet cousin, there must be perfect confidence between us. But until then, I conjure you, do not mention or allude to it. This I most earnestly entreat, and I know you will comply. (159)

What effect must this brief note have on Elizabeth? Recalling their childhood bond, Victor draws Elizabeth into his confidence, reminding her that he tells her things no one else knows. But the secret they are now to share is unlike any they held as children. Only Victor knows its content, and only after she has spoken the words that will bind her to him forever will this nightmare be revealed. Sensing that Elizabeth finds the terms of this bargain unsettling, Victor appeals to her feminine sympathies. Were she now to know what he cannot say, she would immediately realize that her concerns pale when compared to the immensity of his suffering. If she truly loves him, she will nurse him without inquiring into the nature of his disease.

Victor's request for "perfect confidence" requires no reply from Elizabeth; he knows she "will comply" (159). Returning to Geneva within the week, Victor greets an Elizabeth who has "lost much of that heavenly vivacity that had before charmed me" (159). Whether Elizabeth senses his disappointment, whether she begins to wonder if his agreement to marry is rooted in anything other than a desire to placate Alphonsus, we do not know. What we do know is that Victor, without speaking a word, asks Elizabeth to conspire in cultivating the semblances appropriate to this occasion. "As the period for our marriage drew nearer, whether from cowardice or a prophetic feeling, I felt my heart sink within me. But I concealed my feelings by an appearance of hilarity, that brought smiles and joy to the countenance of my father, but hardly deceived the ever-watchful and nicer eye of Elizabeth" (160). Elizabeth, by way of contrast, is only partly successful at concealing her dread of what is to come. On the morning of her wedding day, "she was melancholy, and a presentiment of evil pervaded her" (161). Inadequately veiled, her trepidation does not escape Alphonsus. But, because he is desperate to believe in the web of illusion they spin together, he reads her agitation as nothing more than "the diffidence of a bride" (161).

"What is it that agitates you, my dear Victor? What is it you fear?" (163). Elizabeth's question is unfeigned, at least in part. Put to her husband on the first night they are to share a bed, Elizabeth does not know in any literal sense to what she refers (although she was quite close to the mark when she asked whether he is involved with an-other). Although unknown, that "it" is nevertheless some-thing to her, and Elizabeth has little difficulty discerning its general import for their future. "Something whispers to me not to depend too much on the prospect that is opened before us; but I will not listen to such a sinister voice" (162). Just as the eyes of Alphonsus must be blind to what they see, so must the ears of Elizabeth remain deaf to what they hear. If either were to do otherwise, neither could go on playing the parts assigned them by the compulsory rituals of matrimony. Obeying Victor, Elizabeth goes dutifully to bed. She takes no action to arm herself against the voice she silences. Were she to do otherwise, after all, how could Victor remain confident of his ability to protect her from harm?

JUST WHO, OR WHAT, WHISPERS TO ELIZABETH? TO ANSWER THIS QUESTION, WE MUST retreat to Victor's years at Ingolstadt. Persuaded that Victor should become acquainted with customs other than those peculiar to Geneva, Alphonsus is the one who chooses a university so far from home. Victor's departure is delayed by the death of his mother, Caroline, who succumbs to scarlet fever while nursing Elizabeth back to health. As she resigns herself "cheerfully to death" (47), Caroline makes explicit what Victor and Elizabeth had always sensed of their parents' designs: "My firmest hopes of future happiness were placed on the prospect of your union. This expectation will now be the consolation of your father" (47). To Elizabeth, Caroline adds the injunction to "supply my place to my younger children" (47). Already skilled at being a sister to those who are not her siblings, Elizabeth must now learn to be a mother to those who are not her children. And, to Victor, Elizabeth must be what she cannot: surrogate for a mother whose death has demonstrated that love given without stint is sometimes suddenly withdrawn.

Victor approaches his departure from Geneva with ambivalence. His childhood, he insists, had been idyllic:

My mother's tender caresses, and my father's smile of benevolent pleasure while regarding me, are my first recollections. I was their plaything and their idol, and something better—their child, the innocent and helpless creature bestowed on them by Heaven, whom to bring up to good, and whose future lot it was in their hands to direct to happiness or misery, according as they fulfilled their duties towards me. With this deep consciousness of what they owed toward the being to which they had given life, added to the active spirit of tenderness that animated both, it may be imagined that while during every hour of my infant life I received a lesson of patience, of charity, and of self-control, I was so guided by a silken cord, that all seemed but one train of enjoyment to me. (40)

Yet sometimes that cord felt like a noose tightening around Victor's throat. Boarding the chaise that will take him to Ingolstadt, Victor recalls how often, as an adolescent, he felt "cooped up in one place, and had longed to enter the world, and take my station among other human beings" (49). Although he cannot bring himself to say so, Victor senses that his father can afford to wrap his fist in velvet only because his authority goes unchallenged. And, with equal prescience, Victor senses that the affections showered upon him first by Caroline and, more recently, by Elizabeth aim to tame as well as nurture him: "She was the living spirit of love to soften and attract: I might have become sullen in my study, rough through the ardour of my nature, but that she was there to subdue me to a semblance of her own gentleness" (43). These efforts at domestication, hiding their true purpose beneath a veneer of submissiveness, must now be cast aside. Just as Achilles had to shed the dress Thetis draped over his shoulders at Lykomedes' court, so too must Victor repel the arms of Elizabeth to earn the name given him at birth.

At Troy, Achilles pursued a distinctively masculine ideal of heroism via warfare. At Ingolstadt, Victor pursues a tempered version of that same end via natural science. That pursuit is well understood as an effort to live the truth of Cartesian metaphysics, along with its artifactual correlate, the Cartesian paradigm of use. Victor's eventual failure to verify that paradigm testifies, not to the weakness of his will, but to the impossibility of the project he seeks to make real. Relentlessly drawing him back within the world he seeks to escape, Victor's work mocks his pretensions to autonomy. The struggle to sustain that pretense will in time demand Elizabeth as its most precious sacrifice.

In his *Discourse on Method*, Descartes tells of the epistemological crisis that followed his early education in the works of Scholastic philosophy. Discovering that "there is nothing about which there is not some dispute," Descartes concluded that never can he build "anything solid upon foundations having so little firmness." For a time, he conceded, the prospect of glory tempted him to turn from medieval philosophy to the sciences of the occult. But, already well washed in the waters of skepticism, he remained undeceived "by the promises of an alchemist, by the predictions of an astrologer, by the importures of a magician, or by the artifices or boasting of anybody who makes a point of claiming to have more knowledge than he actually has." So disillusioned, Descartes abandoned his schooling and set about traveling, thinking it "good to know something of the customs of various peoples." In his wanderings, however, once again he "found hardly anything about which to be confident," for there is "about as much diversity" in the customs of various cultures as there is "among the opinions of philosophers."[21]

Concluding that no teacher and no culture could furnish the security his soul craved, Descartes determined to cut himself loose from the uncertain web of human dependencies. As his army unit settled into its winter quarters, you will recall, Descartes retired to a small stove-heated room in order to explore the conditions of individual autonomy. To begin, he knew, he would have to raze all the haphazardly accumulated contents of his mind. Radical abstraction from the past is a necessary antecedent to discovery of the indubitable first principle from which a self-contained world might be spun from the single fact of self-consciousness. This work, by its very nature, cannot be shared with any other human being. The unity of the world under construction here, its comprehension of all entities within the terms dictated by the presence of consciousness to itself, can only be compromised by the company of others. As Descartes explains by analogy: "Often there is less perfection in works made of several pieces and in works made by the hands of several masters than in those works on which but one master has worked. Thus one sees that buildings undertaken and completed by a single architect are commonly more beautiful and better ordered than those that several architects have tried to patch up, using old walls that had been built for other purposes."[22]

Splendid in his chilly isolation, Descartes reasons that his ability to doubt everything other than his capacity to think means that he must be a being essentially defined by this immaterial activity. "I knew that I was a substance the whole essence or nature of which was merely to think, and which, in order to exist, needed no place and depended on no material thing." Requiring nothing else to confirm the truth of his existence, Descartes effectively renounces his identity as a son whose corporeal frame was once fashioned within another's womb; for "this 'I,' that is, the soul through which I am what I am, is entirely distinct from the body."[23] Emerging from his bare room as an autonomous monad, a clear and distinct sovereign, Descartes is reborn as father to himself.

For two years after his discovery of Agrippa, Victor "was occupied by exploded systems, mingling, like an unadept, a thousand contradictory theories, and floundering desperately in a very slough of multifarious knowledge" (45). Then one day, at the age of fifteen, he witnessed a remarkable event. In the midst of a violent storm, Victor watched as a lightning bolt incinerated an ancient oak, reducing its majestic trunk to a charred stump. Told that this scene of utter devastation was caused by an invisible and little-understood force named electricity, Victor was pitched headlong into an abyss of uncertainty. Repudiating his alchemical inquiries because they could not account for this spectacle, Victor concluded that "nothing would or could ever be known" (46) with confidence about the things of the external world. Whatever defense he might secure against such skepticism, he now calculated, was to be found in "mathematics, and the branches of study appertaining to that science, as being built upon secure foundations, and so worthy of my consideration" (46).

Victor's departure for Ingolstadt two years later is a logical extension of his rejection of the alchemists. However inarticulately, he has now come to understand that, for a male child, the household is a site where father's command is wedded to multiple sources of feminizing dependence. As an aspiring Cartesian dualist, he concludes that the achievement of autonomy demands wholesale detachment from this suffocating site of human relatedness. However, unlike Descartes, Victor recognizes that he need not shun the company of others to secure the soul's isolation. Granted, he must extricate himself from the network of ascriptive ties into which he was of woman born, without choice and without reason. But, once freed from that, it matters not how many people surround him so long as he remains apart. Because the seclusion of his childhood years endowed him with an "invincible repugnance to new countenances" and so rendered him "totally unfitted for the company of strangers" (48), Victor is confident that residence amongst his fellows at Ingolstadt will not compromise his solitude.

But Victor is not quite ready to move into Descartes's toasty chambers. Just as Descartes found it necessary to begin his project of self-creation by rooting from his mind "all the errors that had been able to creep in undetected,"[24] so too must Victor complete the extermination of his past. "My dear sir," explains M. Krempe, professor of natural philosophy, "you must begin your studies entirely anew" (49). From his father, Victor had learned to spurn the dream of transmuting base metals into gold. Now, from his surrogate fathers, Victor learns that the alchemist's magical incantations and secret rites must give way to the painstaking experiments of the disenchanted chemist and physiologist. At first, Victor is repelled by a mechanistic science that seems to evacuate the world of all spiritual powers, leaving behind nothing more than a quest to multiply the means of material comfort. "I had a contempt for the uses of modern natural philosophy. It was very different, when the masters of the science sought immortality and power; such views, although futile, were grand: but now the scene was changed. . . . I was required to exchange chimeras of boundless grandeur for realities of little worth" (50). Disgust turns to zeal, though, when Victor learns that abandonment of the quest to discover the alchemist's elixir of life does not entail withdrawal from the campaign to outwit death. "I will pioneer a new way, explore unknown powers, and unfold to the world the deepest mysteries of creation" (51). If mortality is the mark of all women-born creatures, then perhaps that curse can be erased by one destined to discover the "principle of life" (53).

Of course, Victor must in time leave behind his teachers as well; dependence on them is no less emasculating than was dependence on family. Within two years of his arrival at Ingolstadt, Victor has devoured all that his instructors can offer, and so at last he is ready to consummate Descartes's dream. That achievement, he understands, requires unswerving adherence to the method prescribed in Descartes's "Third Meditation": "Now I shall close my eyes, I shall stop my ears, I shall disregard my senses. I shall even efface from my mind all the images of corporeal things; or at least, since that can hardly be done, I shall consider them vain and false. By thus dealing only with myself and considering what is included in me, I shall try to make myself, little by little, better known and more familiar to myself."[25] Like Descartes, Victor seeks to guarantee the success of his project by isolating himself from all that might compromise its purity. "In a solitary chamber, or rather cell, at the top of the house, and separated from all the other apartments by a gallery and staircase" (56), Victor carves out a space from which all reminders that he owes his being to others, all desires that might prove unattainable, are utterly excluded.

Fortification of this space involves complementary processes of contraction and expansion. Denying his senses their accustomed nutriment, Victor's world is dramatically condensed. "It was a most beautiful season; never did the fields bestow a more plentiful harvest, or the vines yield a more luxuriant vintage: but my eyes were insensible to the charms of nature. And the same feelings which made me neglect the scenes around me caused me also to forget those friends who were so many miles absent" (56). However, as Victor's idyll closes in on itself, his ego simultaneously begins to balloon. Convinced that the *sum* of *cogito ergo sum* is the only emphatic reality, Victor's "I" must inflate until it presses tightly against the walls of his cell. If his ego is to create its own self-sufficient world, all that is external must be subjected to his command or, more accurately, consumed by his will. Victor, in short, must come to think himself omnipotent, a creature whose conduct is pure projection without a trace of reciprocation. "I ceased to fear, or to bend before any being less almighty than that which had created and ruled the elements" (86).

As Victor and world collapse into one another, his body struggles to tease some sense, however insufficient, from this experience. "My cheek had grown pale with study, and my person had become emaciated with confinement" (55). Yet, desperate to believe that the unconscious facts of embodiment are so many contingencies, irrelevant to his true identity, Victor cannot acknowledge what his body language says so clearly and distinctly. Emerging from his bare room as a haunted incarnation of Descartes's autonomous monad, Victor's person unwittingly intimates that the heroic project of self-creation must ultimately terminate in asphyxiation of the being whose essence it is to think.

The Cartesian ideal of autonomy is not, however, the only image informing Victor's self-identity. Hephaestus, recall, fashions a magnificent shield that exemplifies the patrician ethos of the archaic cosmos, even as portions of its design foreshadow disintegration of that same world.[26] Victor is similarly caught within the creases of history. Vying for control over the disposition of his soul are various constructions of heroic masculinity, each of which can be traced back to specific sociohistorical contexts, each of which has its appropriate artifactual accompaniments. What we call "Victor," more specifically, is the site where the archaic warrior, the Platonic philosopher, the Cartesian ego, and the Baconian scientist collide.

That Victor is a contemporary Achilles, a creature of the hypermasculine warrior ideal, is easily shown. The words he speaks to those who would retreat before impossible odds are exhortations addressed to himself: "Oh! be men, or be more than men. . . . Do not return to your families with the stigma of disgrace marked on your brows. Return as heroes who have fought and conquered, and who know not what it is to turn their backs on the foe" (178). Victor, however, is not to earn an immortal name by pitting his body against others in a rage of reciprocal killing. His glory, instead, is to be won through performance of epic deeds of the mind, the discovery of truths whose permanence will conquer the transience of mortal existence. Unlike Clerval, who is fascinated by the "moral relations of things" (43), Victor strives to pass beyond such fluctuating phenomena, to come to know the underlying substance that is their true reality. Unlike Elizabeth, who contemplates "with a serious and satisfied spirit the magnificent appearances of things," Victor's quest is "directed to the metaphysical, or, in its highest sense, the physical secrets of the world" (42-43). Seeking a site that will yield a simulacrum of the solace he identifies with such metaphysical accomplishment, Victor climbs to the summit of Montanvert. Exalted by the glacier's exquisite silence, this Genevan Plato knows that only at these heights can his winged soul, shedding his body's sensuous ties to matters prosaic, "soar from the obscure world to light and joy" and so "forget the passing cares of life" (88).

Posing the question to which god is a not uncommon response, Victor seeks to abstract the unique generative property that, because it is essential to all living beings, defines them as such. In one way, this is a good Platonic endeavor. To search for *the* universal substance that is differentially manifest in all living things is to presuppose the adequacy of a Platonic logic of identity. That logic, recapitulated in the Cartesian cogito's reductionist definition of itself in terms of the self-presence of disembodied consciousness, stipulates that all things can be thought of as so many parts of a comprehensive whole, and hence that in the last analysis the problem of alterity is an illusion. Victor departs from Platonic transcendentalism, however, insofar as he believes that this universal substance, taking shape as an invisible and ethereal fluid, can be located within the world of mundane experience. No doubt familiar with Sir Humphry Davy's early nineteenth-century *Elements of Chemical Philosophy*, Victor has learned of the interconvertibility of electrical and chemical forces, and so of the contention that the vital magnetism of galvanic electricity is the bridge that overcomes the gulf between animate and inanimate. By taking possession of this bridge, he hopes to demonstrate that life and death are "ideal bounds" (55), bounds that need no longer define what it is to be a human being. Seeking to make the body itself immortal, as opposed to freeing the immortal soul from the perishable body, Victor's gamble is far more daring than any entertained by Plato.

Moreover, with the Baconian scientist and against the classical philosopher, Victor has learned that one can know with certainty only that which one makes. At first, it is true, Victor's aim is not to fashion some palpable thing. His absorption of the aristocrat's prejudice against the labor of craftsmen is initially sufficient to deter him from such a grubby occupation. Yet only for the briefest of moments can he maintain that discovery of the principle of life is "the summit of my desires," "the most gratifying consummation of my toils. . . . When I found so astonishing a power placed within my hands, I hesitated a long time concerning the manner in which I should employ it" (54-55). The fact that Victor's hesitation is eventually overcome by a compulsion to "employ" this principle as a means to some other end signals his exit from the world of classical contemplation and entry into that of modern utilitarianism. Driven by the unlovely logic of a bourgeois age, Victor sets out to create an artifact that will experimentally confirm what he already knows is true. But as soon as he commits himself to this project, much like Athena in her competition with Arachne, Victor becomes a spider caught within a web not of his own making. Victor's "internal being" is in a perpetual "state of insurrection and turmoil" (51) because his Cartesian dream is in reality a nightmare, and the "monster" he creates is not that terror's cause but rather the vehicle of its de-monstration.

If Victor is to succeed, he must quit his elevated study, the rarefied locale appropriate to pursuit of what he calls "metaphysical" knowledge. Although aspiring to supplant the divine, Victor cannot create *ex nihilo*, and so he reluctantly acknowledges that making something new "does not consist in creating out of void, but out of chaos; the materials must, in the first place, be afforded: it can give form to dark, shapeless substances, but cannot bring into being the substance itself" (22).[27] To grant that his work is reliant on antecedently existing materials is, however, to find cause to worry whether those materials may prove recalcitrant, whether their obdurate properties may participate in dictating the character of what is created; and that in turn is to find cause to wonder whether the achievement of Cartesian mastery is ultimately an illusion. The self-assured posture of this would-be sovereign can be sustained, in other words, only by disavowing or denying creation's dependence on that which cannot be generated out of the creator's own being.

This difficulty is compounded by the fact that Victor can no longer unproblematically endorse the idea of a god who, in his transcendence, is the uncaused cause of the principle he locates. As his father's son, as a creature of the

Enlightenment, Victor is persuaded that he cannot know the principle of life apart from its realization *in* matter. The methods he must therefore employ—those cultivated by the atheistic sciences of chemistry, physiology, and anatomy—are of the sort a classical metaphysician would sneer at. To the vaults and charnelhouses of Ingolstadt, in short, Victor must go; for only there can he scrutinize "all the minutiae of causation, as exemplified in the change from life to death, and death to life" (54). Yet to carry rotting organs from the grave back to the study is to engender a stark confrontation between the pathetic nobility of Victor's "metaphysical" aspirations and the hideous disreputability of its carnal conditions. To seek to transcend death by means of the mortal, as he does, is to transform Descartes's refuge of self-consciousness into Victor's unhallowed "workshop of filthy creation" (56).

That Victor must return to earth in order to secure the conditions of his epistemic adventures is still more troubling because he is keenly aware of the conventional association of nature with things female. Paracelsus, author of one of Victor's adolescent primers, once wrote: "He who would enter the Kingdom of God must first enter with his body into his mother and there die."[28] Embracing Paracelsus's exhortation to invade the earth but rejecting death as its necessary consequence, Francis Bacon later encouraged "the studious to sell their books and build furnaces," to forsake "Minerva and the Muses as barren virgins, to rely upon Vulcan."[29] But the prospect of using Vulcan's tool to know Gaia, of putting Bacon's prying fingers in place of Plato's disengaged eyes, terrifies Victor. Even so, he cannot help but confess his "fervent longing to penetrate the secrets of nature," to enter nature's "citadel" (44-45).

Victor's vacillation between extremes of self-assertion and self-loathing is, at least in part, the fruit of his unsuccessful negotiation of the war between ancient and modern. His faith that he may in time discover the secret of eternal life is based on his conviction that modern science offers "continual food for discovery and wonder" (53), and so the prospect of perfect freedom and boundless progress. But from the ancients, and derivatively from the alchemists, Victor has also absorbed the nagging suspicion that a science set free of the moorings provided by cosmology and theology is a science free to pursue ends that are "unlawful, that is to say, not befitting the human mind" (57). Hence he can never quite forget Agrippa's warning that inquiry into nature's wonders goes teleologically awry when, abandoning "moderate bounds," it shows "us so many devices to make strange plants, so many portentous graftings and metamorphoses of trees; how to make horses copulate with asses, wolves with dogs, and so to engender many wondrous monsters contrary to nature."[30] Desperate to escape the finitude of embodied existence, yet sensing the transgression this desire entails, Victor can neither ignore nor acknowledge the guilt gnawing away at the core of his being.

Victor feels the full force of these overlapping contradictions when, "by the glimmer of the half-extinguished light," he sees "the dull yellow eye" (58) of

his creation open wide and return his wild stare. Victor responds not with ex-
hiliration, as one might expect, but with horror. But why does this thing elicit
dread only now? "I had gazed on him while unfinished; he was ugly then; but
when those muscles and joints were rendered capable of motion, it became a
thing such as even Dante could not have conceived" (59). At this pivotal moment, the sense of Victor's world suffers wholesale dislocation, and the sense
of that dislocation takes veiled shape as a nightmare: "I thought I saw Elizabeth, in the bloom of health, walking in the streets of Ingolstadt. Delighted
and surprised, I embraced her; but as I imprinted the first kiss on her lips, they
became livid with death; her features appeared to change, and I thought that I
held the corpse of my dead mother in my arms; a shroud enveloped her form,
and I saw the graveworms crawling in the folds of the flannel" (58). To want
the touch of Elizabeth's lips, to desire Elizabeth as a woman, is to be reminded
of his emergence from the womb of another, of the fact that he ultimately owes
his life to his mother. At first, it might appear that the threat posed by such
dependence can be stopped cold if both become corpses, beings no longer able
to capture him within their sticky webs. Yet even this, in the last analysis, will
not suffice. For Victor's own body is an ever-present reminder of his dependence on things over which he cannot exert perfect control; its imperious
needs, its transient desires, testify to his deep embeddedness within the world
he despises. If, therefore, he is to escape such implication, Victor must finally
disembody himself.

What Victor fashions in his workshop, I would argue, is the corruptible
body his Cartesian ego must expel in order to be assured of its purity and self-
sufficiency. It is the incarnation of what Victor must shed in order to complete
what Butler might call his "phallogocentric project of autogenesis."[31] But when
Victor looks at that body, and as it gazes back at him, what he sees is not the
soulless mechanism Descartes promised, but rather a some-body. What Victor
sees in those eyes are so many glimmers of self-consciousness, so many traces
of the ethereal substance he alone should now possess. And if this alienated
body displays self-consciousness, it must enjoy a will as well. And if it possesses a will, then it must in time seek its own autonomy and so reject whatever
subordination it now reluctantly concedes. Should that corporeal thing one
day reach toward him, should its arms someday come to encircle his ego, on
that day Victor will surely die.

"AND THIS THING: WHAT SHALL I CALL IT AND BE RIGHT, IN ALL ELOQUENCE?"[32] AS DOES
Victor, one might answer Orestes' question by applying some familiar noun to
the creature of his workshop. At first referring to this thing as "a being" (58),
the salutary vagueness of this generic label quickly gives way to others more

determinate. These others Victor finds reassuring because they unambiguously indicate how he should act with respect to it. If this thing is indeed a "daemon" (34) or a "monster" (58),[33] as Victor frequently proclaims, then he knows it is evil; and, if he is certain that it is evil, then he knows that he can destroy it with impunity.

But perhaps we should resist the temptation to which Victor too readily succumbs. Recall, once again, how the shield made by Hephaestus subverts its own tacit claim to stable identity. Belying its appearance of artifactual facticity, the shield dissolves into a strained site of contestation over the future and its import. Much the same is true of the thing Victor releases into the world. However, whereas the shield's internal stresses are present but subdued, the thing Victor makes loudly announces the unresolved tensions passing through the arms of its creator and into its body. Its composition as a factitious totality, a disunited whole assembled from various parts of various beings of various sorts, offers a standing challenge to the tidy boundaries we conventionally draw around what we take to be self-evident artifacts. Better, consequently, to consider this thing not as a well-defined object but as a testament to experience's capacity to pose questions for which language is inadequate. To do otherwise, to diminish this thing's uncanniness through premature ejaculation, is to lose sight of precisely what makes it simultaneously horrifying and intriguing, that is to say, monstrous.

What renders this thing especially vexing for Victor is its destabilization of virtually every one of the dualistic categories found within Descartes's conceptual tool kit. From the standpoint of those categories, this thing is unthinkable, an impossibility. Its existence violates the neat divisions Descartes erects between inside and outside (its ill-stitched seams of skin allow internal organs to peek through); human and animal (its parts are taken not merely from the cemetery and the laboratory but also from the slaughter house); life and death (it is animate, yet composed of so many corpse fragments). Most fundamentally, though, its existence violates the distinction between creator and creature, between this "modern Prometheus"[34] and the artifacts he makes. Victor must assume that he can touch without being touched, make without being made, project without suffering the consequences of artifactual reciprocation. But if the creature awakes and speaks, if this artifact proves able to participate in determining its own signification, if this being's capacity for agency dramatically reveals the ability of things made to incarnate the sentient intelligence allegedly restricted to human beings, then Victor's conception of what counts as a subject and what counts as an object must fall apart. Unable to repudiate the sense-making grid of Cartesianism, but all too aware of its inadequacy to this thing, Victor cannot help but fail to comprehend, let alone master, the fruits of his labor.

Unsurprisingly, as its maker, Victor wants to contend that this thing can be understood through reference to the activity by which it was fashioned as well as the materials entering into its composition. Yet Victor cannot offer a definitive characterization of either. To see why this is so, recall Hephaestus. In speaking of his work, Homer promiscuously mingles terms a good Cartesian will apportion to the mutually exclusive vocabularies of manufacture and agriculture. Homer can do so because he thinks of Hephaestus's flame as a magical source of impregnating power; that flame takes ores growing within the earth and shapes them into forms intimated but, as yet, unrealized in experience. Granted, what Hephaestus makes is distinct from what nature engenders, but it is not for that reason to be located in the opposed category of the conventional. For Hephaestus, moreover, since all things are wrought from a common mother earth, there can be no sharp distinction between the animate and the inanimate.

As a devotee of Descartes, Victor cannot speak as does Hephaestus. For him, this thing must be either natural and capable of self-movement, or it must be artificial and mechanically propelled. At times, Victor opts for the first horn of this dilemma. Sometimes, that is, he conceives of his work on the model of biological gestation, and so he likens the relationship of artificer and artifact to that of father and child. "A new species would bless me as its creator and source; many happy and excellent natures would owe their being to me. No father could claim the gratitude of his child so completely as I should deserve theirs" (55). Granted, Victor is not without reason in adopting this vocabulary. If his quest for autonomy is compromised by his labor's dependence on materials he did not create, still more problematic is the fact that he owes his own existence to one of Pandora's intriguing daughters. But if Victor can substitute his work for the labor assigned to Pandora, if reproduction can become an orderly process of self-spawning, like Zeus giving parthenogenetic birth to Athena, then he can deny his body's status as an artifact made by another. By the same token, if Victor can postpone the "horror" of "immediate union" (130) with the chaste Elizabeth, then he can forgo the deed that is sure to sully his pretensions to Cartesian disembodiment.

But, of course, the language of biological generation does not really do justice to what Victor has done, and he knows it. Hence at other times he opts for the second horn of this dilemma. Sometimes, that is, he conceives of his work on the model of manufacture, and so thinks of the relationship of artificer and artifact as akin to that of industrialist and machine. This is most readily apparent when Victor considers the life principle that transforms a hodge-podge of bones, flesh, and organs into a self-moving artifact. When Victor first encountered electricity, it burst forth as a miraculous source of devastating power. Now, though, he grasps its work in the secular terms of cause and effect. Electricity, as cause, does not impregnate this thing. Rather, in accordance with the demythologized laws of galvanism, the mechanical alternation of positive and negative charges within electricity's current generates convulsive motions; and those motions set to work the organ that, just like a pump, is this thing's beating heart.

There is good reason for Victor to speak this vocabulary as well. Victor wishes to affirm his mastery over all things external, and that can be guaranteed only if the things he makes are so many will-less tools rather than so many stubborn children. But this vocabulary serves Victor's interest for another less obvious reason. Unlike the palpable reality that is Hephaestus's flame, invisible electricity is "artificial" in the sense that it does not appear as such in unscientifically reconstructed experience. Affirmation of its existence as a universal force appearing under multiple guises (heat, light, magnetism) was impossible prior to articulation of its theoretical presuppositions. Once materialized, belief in this caloric fluid's reality undermines confidence in the capacity of the unaided senses to grasp the tangible truth of things. As such, electricity displays all the characteristics that Victor the Cartesian aspires to exhibit as well: abstraction, disembodiment, and immateriality. It effectively serves as a metaphor for, an exemplar of, the ego he thinks he is, as well as that ego's unity with the metaphysical knowledge he imagines he has discovered.

Neither vocabulary, though, is quite adequate to Victor's sense-making purposes. Robert Boyle, one of Victor's predecessors, once referred to nature as "God's great pregnant Automaton."[35] The incongruity our ears hear in that phrase must be akin to the strangeness Victor feels when he wonders whether he has given birth to a machine, or perhaps manufactured a child. Victor's Cartesian world grows still more unsteady when he discovers that the inconstancy of his speech has infected his tools as well. Are his instruments, like Hephaestus's hands and hammers, so many midwives attending at the birth of nature's offspring? Or are they so many inert devices wholly subordinated to the will of their extranatural user? If they are the former, then Victor may well conclude that the labor of his tools, like the work of a nurse, ties creator to creature in a web of ethical relations from which neither can escape. If the latter, then Victor may rest assured that tools establish no essential connection between the two, and so render moral claims irrelevant. Victor, however, can neither definitively exclude nor definitively embrace either of these characterizations and, in consequence, his tools collapse into so much referential instability. Watching things once solid dissolve into so many shifting phantasms, Victor discovers that the mere "sight of a chemical instrument" is now sufficient to "renew all the agony of my nervous symptoms" (66). Indeed, in time, mere talk about these instrumentalities proves sufficient to elicit visions of horror. Praised for his invention of several implements, Victor feels as if his admirer is placing, "one by one, in my view those instruments which were to be afterwards used in putting me to a slow and cruel death" (66). Affording expression to the spiritual substance that is the Cartesian mind, immaterial words now torture a body to which they bear no essential connection. Conflating the distinctions between creator, the tools of creation, and the words used to speak of both, Victor's agitation unwittingly testifies to the mutual embeddedness (but not reducibility) of some (but not all) of the participants in the materialization of things (deemed) real.

THE PROBLEM REMAINS: HOW SHALL WE SPEAK OF THIS THING? SO FAR, WE HAVE FOUND that no single noun, nor any singular account of its origins, is adequate. Turning elsewhere for a clue, as have many schooled in Freud, we might read this thing as Victor's alter ego, as his way of giving expression to fantasies and aggressions otherwise repressed. Such interpretations err, I believe, insofar as they construe this thing exclusively in terms of its relationship to Victor. Once completed and situated within the world, however, we can no longer rightly call this thing "Victor's creature." On the one hand, this thing remains an incarnation of Victor's vital powers, and so an expression of his capacities as a maker. On the other hand, like all artifacts, this thing quickly becomes something other than the sum of its materials, its principle of animation, and the intention of its maker. As an unpredictable source of reciprocative energy, this creature speaks more truly about the world-transformative import of artifacts than do Hephaestus's tripods and metal dancers, those obedient creatures who never miss a step.

To do justice to the sense in which this artifact remains related to and yet stands apart from Victor, perhaps we should call it "Victor/Victoria." To simplify matters, let us abbreviate that to "Victor(ia)." If, as I have suggested, this creature is Victor's alienated body, and if Victor's body is a principal source of the dependence he seeks to conquer through the achievement of immortality, and if mortality is itself a sign of Victor's emergence from the body of his mother, then we have good reason to consider Victor's creature female. To do justice to the sense in which this artifact wears the body of a man, but is simultaneously an expression of the quality of embodiment that Victor wishes to displace onto women, let us refer to Victor(ia) using the suitably ambiguous pronoun "s/he." Like Clytaemestra, Victor(ia) is the incarnation of so much gender trouble, a discordant thing that cannot be deemed real within the confines of compulsory heterosexuality. Showing that gender identity is not necessarily rooted in, mimetic of, or dictated by, anatomical sex characteristics, the creature's failure to conform to the norms that stabilize and legitimate the gendered division of labor unmakes the world in which Victor and Elizabeth, till now, have found themselves at home.

As with any artifact, Victor(ia)'s entry into the world exhibits the excess of artifactual reciprocation over projection. In more familiar instances, a single body part or capacity is projected into an artifact (e.g., blanket mimics skin), and that artifact reciprocates by freeing the body from an otherwise pressing concern. In the case of Victor(ia), however, the capacity to engage in artifactual projection is itself projected into an artifact, and that explains why it is no more correct to call this thing a "creature" than to call it a "creator." To do either is to substitute a pernicious Cartesian distinction between active and passive, a distinction that itself carries considerable gendered baggage, for a sensitive appreciation of the ongoing dialectic between making and being made.

The musculature of Achilles' left hand becomes differently reticulated as it accommodates the heft of his new shield. If the same is true of Victor, if Victor is effectively remade by that which he makes, then the boundary between things human and things artifactual must be far more permeable than he, as a good Cartesian, can afford to acknowledge. Occasionally, Victor dimly grasps this truth. For example, while living in a remote Scottish village, he notes that his presence would have occasioned surprise "had not all the senses of the cottagers been benumbed by want and squalid poverty" (139). Denied rich engagement in the dynamic of projection and reciprocation, such beings have become so many pale incarnations of the dreary labors performed by a monotonous company of barren artifacts. Correlatively, while conversing with his rescuer, Victor laments that human beings, regardless of class status, are so many "unfashioned creatures, but half made up" (36). However, blinded by the Cartesian ideal of masculine autonomy, Victor cannot follow up on this insight by asking whether these creatures might become more fully human by becoming more completely remade.

If the distinction between person and thing is ambiguous, then the qualities we conventionally ascribe to one can sometimes become qualities of the other, and vice versa. There is no essence distinguishing one from the other; and so, as I noted in part 1, a thing in time may become personified (the slave emancipated), just as a person may in time become thingified (the human being enslaved). The latter is best illustrated by Victor's own biography, which, paradoxically, exemplifies the logic Descartes extols as the road to rational autonomy. Cut loose from the world's web, Victor's years at Ingolstadt plunge him ever more deeply into solitary confinement. That withdrawal involves a slow slide into several forms of object-ivity. Victor's inchoate grasp of these forms is indicated when he represents himself as a victim of fate, of chance, and of an untamed passion or fury;[36] when he responds to various crises by fainting, falling ill, feigning the helplessness of a child, and climbing aboard a boat drifting to nowhere; and finally, showing that he is not altogether unaware of what it is to be a thing of the household, when he considers himself a being akin to a woman: "I became as timid as a love-sick girl, and alternate tremor and passionate ardour took the place of wholesome sensation and regulated ambition."[37]

At such moments, Victor becomes a sort of automaton, something not altogether unlike one of Hephaestus's golden girls. True, he continues to wear "the human form" (120), but he is not what he appears to be. On occasion,

Victor understands this fact as well: "(T)hrough the whole period during which I was the slave of my creature, I allowed myself to be governed by the impulses of the moment" (131). And, on other occasions, Victor expresses the desire that he might become still more of a thing. "Oh! stars and clouds, and winds, ye are all about to mock me: if ye really pity me, crush sensation and memory; let me become as nought" (127-28). Here, ironically, the being whose essence it is to think prays for obliteration of the capacity that makes him something more than so much insensate matter in mechanical motion. Surreptitiously confessing that he can no longer bear the burdens imposed by the Cartesian account of autonomy, Victor (in typically dualistic fashion) hungers for an un-world in which the task of sustaining a self simply melts away.

The reverse path, that leading from thinghood to personhood, is best illustrated by Victor(ia). What makes this artifact remarkable is not its acquisition of a biography; all artifacts do that. Rather, what makes it exceptional is its ability to tell its own story. Unlike those less articulate, Victor(ia) can contest the judgments of those too quick to stabilize its meaning. Unlike those less intelligent, Victor(ia) can explain how the logic of projection diminishes the alleged insentience of the nonhuman world. Unlike those too much given to Cartesianism, Victor(ia) can show why destruction of an artifact, while perhaps not an act of murder, is not a matter to be thoughtlessly undertaken.

"Who was I? What was I? Whence did I come from? What was my destination?" (112). Victor(ia) might well answer these questions by contending that s/he is the sort of artifact Victor aspires to become. Victor wishes to escape the gentle tyranny of his father; Victor(ia) is called child by no parent. Victor wishes to abstract himself from all social relations; Victor(ia) has no relations to uproot. Victor wishes to rid himself of his past; Victor(ia) discovers that the past is an unrecallable "blot, a blind vacancy" (107). Victor wishes to secure perfect autonomy; emerging into the world as a fully formed adult; Victor(ia) is utterly independent. "I was dependent on none, and related to none. 'The path of my departure was free'; and there was none to lament my annihilation" (112).

But matters are never quite so simple. Unlike Victor, Victor(ia) wants nothing more than to be something other than an embodiment of the metaphysics of Cartesianism. From the moment its eyes open till it disappears into the polar night, the biography of this thing can be read as a lived revelation of Cartesianism's misunderstanding of the project of making sense. In the beginning, Victor(ia) tells Victor, the world was so much extradiscursive chaos. Knowing no distinction between self and world, what s/he felt was a synesthesia of shadowy textures. "It is with considerable difficulty that I remember the original era of my being; all the events of that period appear confused and indistinct. A strange multiplicity of sensations seized me, and I saw, felt, heard, and smelt, at the same time; and it was, indeed, a long time before I learned to distinguish between the operations of my various senses" (92). Prior to that discrimination, the bodily medium through which experience passed was not Descartes's body, that reified thing explicitly thematized by the scientific intellect as a complex structure of mechanically interacting wheels, pulleys, and levers. Rather, Victor(ia)'s body was first and foremost a locus of qualitative experience, of ill-defined pangs of hunger, fear, fatigue, and so forth. So long as s/he remained motionless, so long as eyes alone took in the world, Victor(ia)'s principal sensations were those of light and dark. Only when s/he began to walk, only when the latent capacity for locomotion began to realize itself, only when this body began to act as something akin to tool, did the world begin to acquire significant definition. "I walked, and, I believe, descended; but I presently found a great alteration in my sensations. Before, dark and opaque bodies had surrounded me, impervious to my touch or sight; but I now found that I could wander on at liberty, with no obstacles which I could not either surmount or avoid" (92). Challenging a metaphysical tradition that privileges the sense of vision in speaking of knowledge and its acquisition, Victor(ia)'s conduct demonstrates that in the absence of the body's kinesthetic movement, nothing would ever appear as anything. Only after several days of tactile maneuvering through an inchoate sea does Victor(ia) prove able to see "plainly the clear stream that supplied me with drink, and the trees that shaded me with their foliage" (93). The stream, as an intelligible thing whose waters are distinguishable from the banks leading to it, comes into being as such only because the legs fashioned by Victor have already endured the qualitative distinction between dry and wet.

As these differentiations become sedimented within Victor(ia)'s flesh and bone, s/he acquires habits that draw the future into a present that is no longer wholly without sense. Each situation lived through acts back upon this artifact, expanding and transforming what are now becoming so many more or less refined skills. Already, in other words, does this creature of Prometheus engage in a project of self-making; and that project in turn prepares the ground for discursive thinking, as conduct begins to uncover recurrent relationships between the questions and answers, the structures of tacit implication, embedded within the textures of experience. To this point, though, Victor(ia) has no conscious ideas, let alone any that might qualify as clear and distinct. The event that is meaning, the transformation of sensed connections into articulated relations, remains for now an unrealized potentiality.

Victor(ia)'s cumulative fund of corporeal meanings is dramatically expanded when, one day, s/he discovers a still-glowing fire abandoned by several beggars. "Overcome with delight at the warmth I experienced from it . . . I thrust my hand into the live embers, but quickly drew it out again with a cry of pain" (94). This incident, although not itself an instance of knowing, is nonetheless a condition of knowledge. Its travels down the epistemic path proper begin when Victor(ia) exclaims: "How strange, I thought, that the same cause should produce such opposite effects!" (94). Beginning to grasp the relationship between fire, its generation of heat, and its capacity to produce pain, this thing tentatively steps beyond the barely significant world of qualitative immediacy and into one of incipient intelligence. Appreciation, however partial, of the relational network in which fire is sometimes implicated intimates the possibility of tending to a fire; and that in turn evokes Victor(ia)'s first deliberate projection of artifactual capacity within a tool standing apart from its body. "It was morning when I awoke, and my first care was to visit the fire. I uncovered it, and a gentle breeze quickly fanned it into a flame. I observed this also, and contrived a fan of branches, which roused the embers when they were nearly extinguished" (94).

Absent the capacity to make a fire from scratch, Victor(ia) remains in a world that is more inhuman than not. Spending most days searching "for a few acorns to assuage the pangs of hunger" (94), the brute imperatives of survival overwhelm experience's intimations of matters richer in significance. Only much more thorough immersion within the artifactual will enable this thing to cultivate the qualities peculiar to being human. Such immersion takes place when Victor(ia) acquires a second skin, a layer of protection that lightens the afflictions otherwise preoccupying the first. Taking up residence within a "low hovel," a shelter "from the inclemency of the season, and still more from the barbarity of man" (95), Victor(ia)'s barely awakened capacity to move beyond the elemental and into the meaningful begins to issue forth as an articulated world.

Overhearing the speech of those in the cottage next door, Victor(ia) realizes, albeit not in so many words, the fallacy of any naive representationalist account of language. "Their pronunciation was quick; and the words they uttered, not having any apparent connection with visible objects, I was unable to discover any clue by which I could unravel the mystery of their reference" (100). Does this discovery, though, transform Victor(ia) into a disciple of Saussure or of Rorty? Recognizing that the meaningfulness of language does not turn on designation, the unmediated passage from signifier to signified, does Victor(ia) now conclude that language is an arbitrary and self-contained system of free-floating phonemes? Quite the contrary. Because s/he never forgets the ground of human being in embodiment, Victor(ia) knows what Saussure and Rorty do not: Absent tactile engagement in a web of palpable affairs, affairs whose qualities intimate distinctions between this and that, the words s/he struggles to fashion by moving tongue, teeth, and lips this way and that would have nothing to latch onto, and so s/he would never acquire the "godlike science" (100) of language.

Although language is thus tethered, Victor(ia) nonetheless feels a gap between the words s/he learns and the situation s/he inhabits. Noting the contexts in which particular words and specific phrases are typically spoken, Victor(ia) comes to appreciate what such language fragments characteristically do, how they customarily work. But the experience s/he has of language is akin

to that of a voyeur who cannot quite identify with any of the parties under surveillance. She watches as the integrated exchange of words and deeds is undertaken by persons who know, for example, what it is to be masculine or
feminine; s/he sees how these engendered identities are grounded in conventional postures, in habitual intonations, in subtle rituals of domination and
subordination. But Victor(ia) has no such reliable identity. Granted, the body
parts s/he sports are not altogether unlike those of the men she spies on. Yet
the sentiments of sympathy that well up within those parts seem to ally
Victor(ia) more with women. Like women, Victor(ia) finds that s/he lives in a
world whose words, fashioned by others, never quite seem right, never quite
enable her to say just what s/he wants to say. Yet if indeed s/he is a woman,
then surely the morphology of "her" body is all wrong.

Victor(ia)'s sense of indeterminate gender identity, of falling short of mod-
els s/he played no part in fashioning, is aggravated when s/he learns to read.
What s/he manages to grasp of the texts s/he pores over s/he understands because s/he is able to relate their words to already acquired sense-making habits. Studying the lives of Solon, Numa, and Lycurgus, for example, s/he notes:
"The patriarchal lives of my protectors caused these impressions to take a firm
hold on my mind; perhaps, if my first introduction to humanity had been
made by a young soldier, burning for glory and slaughter, I should have been
imbued with different sensations" (113). Even so, no matter how much
Victor(ia) wishes it were otherwise, the gulf between what s/he reads and what
s/he senses remains: "As I read . . . I applied much personally to my own feelings and condition. I found myself similar, yet at the same time strangely unlike to the beings concerning whom I read" (112). Recognizing that what s/he
wants to say cannot be exhaustively articulated in the vocabularies furnished
by Milton, Plutarch, and Goethe, the artifact hungers for a thicker sense of
identity, a sense more completely confirmed by the structures of the world, artisanal as well as linguistic. But not even Victor(ia)'s discovery of Victor's diary, which includes an account of his work at Ingolstadt, can satisfy that need.
Written by a Cartesian who believes the human organism, absent the soul, is
merely so much matter in mindless motion, Victor's diary cannot begin to
speak to the pain suffered by a being whose body proclaims its intimate connection to the mind housed within: "I sickened as I read" (113).

Clytaemestra murders Agamemnon in fury at a patriarchal order that
sanctions the murder of a daughter for the sake of a war undertaken to rescue a
woman she considers a whore. Her response to that order, in spite of her wrath,
is ambivalent. On the one hand, she detests that world and wants nothing to
do with it. On the other hand, she is filled with rage at her marginality, and so
wishes to assume her rightful place within it. The artifact fashioned by Victor
is similarly torn. On the one hand, s/he despises a world that would bring into
being, only to abandon, a being who never asked to be. On the other hand, s/he
is desperate to enter the company of humanity, to be accepted as kin to those

who now turn away in terror. Clytaemestra resolves her ambivalence by committing a deed she can never undo. Victor(ia)'s response takes shape as so much vacillation between the poles of personhood and thinghood.

Sometimes, Victor(ia) proves more human than Victor. The artificer raves like a demon; the artifact speaks like a philosopher. The artificer appears incapable of any emotions other than self-absorbed pity and rage; the artifact, lamenting the harm s/he has done, begs Victor for his pardon. The artificer can think of nature only as something to be either concretely manipulated or abstractly contemplated; the artifact delights in wooded glens, finding their enchantments so many salves for a wounded soul. Victor(ia)'s most poignant expression of the qualities of being human, however, comes when s/he struggles to make Victor acknowledge the ethical import of the excess of artifactual reciprocation over projection. Victor(ia) understands that the deeds through which humans realize their capacity to care for one another can overcome their fragility, their impermanence, only when situated within the more enduring framework of an artifactual world. That truth, Victor(ia) contends, imposes on those who make that framework an obligation to attend to its legitimate needs. Spurning the neutered amoralism implicit in Cartesian utilitarianism, Victor(ia) insists that artificer and artifact are equally entitled to claim that the other is guilty of injustice when either fails to do what it ought. "Oh, Frankenstein, be not equitable to every other, and trample upon me alone, to whom thy justice, and even thy clemency and affection, is most due. . . . (L)isten to me; and then, if you can, and if you will, destroy the work of your hands" (90-91).

Acknowledgment of the responsibilities entailed in the project of making, Victor(ia) insists, should have been evident when s/he was first created. At that time, Victor should have considered how, if at all, this artifact might enter into, become part of, the larger company of made things. But it is too late for that now. Fashioned in a state of motherless abstraction, this being can find no place in the web of relations sustained by the world's artifacts. To the extent that it remains without such a place, to the extent that it is by nature what Victor aspires to be by design, to that extent is its existence meaningless. Recognizing that it is only relatedness that enables some thing to mean something, Victor(ia) asserts a "right" to a companion artifact, one that will link its biography "to the chain of existence and events" (127). S/he responds to the experience of gender trouble, in other words, by embracing the imperatives of compulsory heterosexuality, by demanding that Victor fashion something akin to one of Hephaestus's golden girls.

Victor must refuse all such demands, especially when claimed by a thing which/who is supposed to be a no-thing. Just as Achilles abandoned his illicit child, so too must Victor desert his. "Begone! I will not hear you. There can be no community between you and me; we are enemies. . . . Cursed (although I curse myself) be the hands that formed you!" (90-91). Should these hands

fashion a second artifact to accompany the first, Victor knows that their intercourse will soon make a mockery of his pretensions to mastery. He can check
the logic of artifactual reciprocation, the capacity of intertwined artifacts to engender effects anticipated by no one, only by denying Victor(ia) a mate. To justify that refusal, Victor invokes what he takes to be a higher obligation. "My
duties towards the beings of my own species had greater claims to my attention" (180). But, as Victor(ia) surmises, this is an obligation without concrete
content; its abstract universalism, predicated on a strict disjunction between
his species and all others, justifies ignoring all duties to specific entities,
whether taking the form of persons, things, or person-things.

Victor(ia) knows that the Cartesian dualism of self and world is so much
nonsense, and s/he knows that this dualism is part and parcel of a larger metaphysic that, in order to deny the interconstitution of each with its other, categorically distinguishes between animal and human, created and creator,
woman and man, madness and reason. S/he knows, moreover, that this metaphysic informs Victor's ambition, and hence that retribution for the injustice
s/he has suffered will remain incomplete until both are vanquished. Achievement of that triumph, s/he understands at last, demands a return to undifferentiated chaos, a condition in which all vestiges of the Cartesian
discrimination between subject and object are obliterated. No longer able to
bear the world's failure to furnish the discursive categories necessary to a
meaningful self-identity, Victor(ia) becomes a thing possessed by "an insatiable thirst for vengeance" (182):

> When night came, I quitted my retreat, and wandered in the wood; and now,
> no longer restrained by the fear of discovery, I gave vent to my anguish in fear-
> ful howlings. I was like a wild beast that had broken the toils; destroying the
> objects that obstructed me, and ranging through the wood with a stag-like
> swiftness. . . . I, like the arch-fiend, bore a hell within me; and, finding myself
> unsympathized with, wished to tear up the trees, spread havoc and destruc-
> tion around me, and then to have sat down and enjoyed the ruin. (118)

With this wish's fulfillment, the fire Prometheus gave to human beings in a
self-sacrificing act of charity turns against its original purpose. The blaze
whose warmth revives this artifact's chilled members, whose energy softens
the nuts s/he eats in the evening, whose gathering power dares Victor(ia) to
draw ever closer to the hearth of strangers, becomes the fire of the holocaust:

> As the night advanced, a fierce wind arose from the woods, and quickly dis-
> persed the clouds that had loitered in the heavens: the blast tore along, like a
> mighty avalanch, and produced a kind of insanity in my spirits, that burst all
> bounds of reason and reflection. I lighted the branch of a tree, and danced with
> fury around the devoted cottage, my eyes still fixed on the western horizon,

the edge of which the moon nearly touched. A part of its orb was at length hid, and I waved my brand; it sunk, and, with a loud scream, I fired the straw, and heath, and bushes, which I had collected. The wind fanned the fire, and the cottage was quickly enveloped by the flames, which clung to it, and licked it with their forked and destroying tongues. (120)

Like some electrified Achilles, Victor(ia) welds the powers of the maker to the rage of the destroyer. But, unlike Achilles, Victor(ia) cannot vent her/his wrath against human beings directly, and so s/he turns to their artifactual surrogates, those artisanal artifacts whose recoverable referents are to be found in the bodies she would destroy if only she could.

ONLY FOR SO LONG WILL VICTOR(IA) REMAIN "UNABLE TO INJURE ANY THING HUMAN" (120). As we have seen, s/he enters the relationship between Elizabeth and Victor wearing the guise of Victor(ia)'s secret. Specific knowledge of this secret's content is confined to Victor, and so Elizabeth can only guess why he has now become so strange. Not surprisingly, as a woman educated to estimate her value in terms of her desirability to men, she worries that the mutations in his character signify some failure, some deficiency, on her part. But this is not the only way Victor(ia) enters Elizabeth's world. S/he also does so as an anonymous killer whose first victim is Victor's younger brother, William. Cradling William's corpse, much as Thetis does with Achilles, Elizabeth exclaims: "O God! I have murdered my darling child!" (69). But Elizabeth is not William's mother, nor is she his murderer. Why then does she assume responsibility for his death? On a superficial level, the answer is simple: That morning, Elizabeth placed about William's neck a locket that has now disappeared; the murder occurred, she is convinced, while a thief sought to make off with this treasure. A more profound reason for her self-accusation, however, has to do with her artifactual formation as a woman.

If Victor's biography demonstrates what it is to embark on a project of radical self-creation, Elizabeth's biography demonstrates what it is to become a creature of immaculate self-sacrifice. Following Caroline's untimely death, recall, Elizabeth "determined to fulfil her duties with the greatest exactness; and she felt that that most imperious duty, of rendering her uncle and cousins happy, had devolved upon her. She consoled me, amused her uncle, instructed my brothers. . . . (S)he was continually endeavouring to contribute to the happiness of others, entirely forgetful of herself."[38] In stark contrast to Victor, Elizabeth defines her being exclusively in terms of her relationship to others, and in every case, those others are male. For Elizabeth, there can be no extrafamilial understanding of her identity as a woman. A woman, after all, is a being whose nature is to minister to the concrete needs and desires of those within the household, and she does that via her incessant engagement with the artifacts whose reciprocational powers render her a creature fit for nothing but that household. Unlike the golden girls of Hephaestus, Elizabeth requires no express command to set her to work. Indeed, whenever possible, she anticipates and responds to the needs and desires of those whom she services long before they are articulated. Ironically, to the extent that Elizabeth succeeds in this project of self-objectification, to the extent that she becomes something akin to the perfect psychological anorexic, to the extent that she actively produces the appearances appropriate to a disappearing subject, she becomes the ideally docile Cartesian artifact Victor cannot make; "no one," Victor announces, "could submit with more grace than she did to constraint and caprice. . . . I loved to tend on her, as I should on a favourite animal."[39]

Victor wishes to construct a world of autonomous creation. Yet when he discovers that nothing he creates is truly subject to his will, he is quick to deny responsibility for what he has wrought. Elizabeth lives in a world that is not of her creation, yet she automatically assumes responsibility for all things. Having learned that she is answerable for the well-being of the men about her, Elizabeth quite sensibly concludes that she is equally liable should matters go awry. When that assumption is joined to her standing as surrogate mother to the Frankenstein household, Elizabeth cannot help but infer that she is culpable for William's death.

But Elizabeth is not quite the superficial creature this portrait suggests. It is misleading to represent her, as have virtually all interpreters, as nothing more than an imperfect version of Hephaestus's automatons. Earlier, we heard Elizabeth express regret that she, unlike Victor, had no opportunity to explore the world beyond Geneva. She raises much more profound questions about the engendered quality of the opposition between public and private spheres when Justine, devoted servant to the Frankenstein family, is discovered with William's locket in her possession and arrested for the crime of murder. Victor is confident that the rules of court procedure will exonerate Justine. Surely, he concludes, the circumstantial evidence found on Justine's person is not enough to convict her, and so he need not reveal what he alone knows, the true identity of William's killer. Although his faith in his servant's probity is now sorely tested, Alphonsus is equally persuaded that right will ultimately prevail: "If she is innocent . . . rely on the justice of our laws, and the activity with which I shall prevent the slightest shadow of partiality" (76).

Knowing in her heart that Justine is no killer, Elizabeth is less sanguine about the judicial process, and so she pleads with Victor to do what she dares not: *"You perhaps will find some means to justify my poor guiltless Justine"* (75). But Victor does not. Consequently, and quite remarkably, at Justine's trial Elizabeth exits the private and enters the public realm: *"It may . . . be judged*

indecent in me to come forward on this occasion; but when I see a fellow-crea-
ture about to perish through the cowardice of her pretended friends, I wish to
be allowed to speak, that I may say what I know of her character" (78). Elizabeth's tribute to Justine's virtues, the testimony of a woman swayed no doubt
by emotional attachment, goes for nought. Aware that "public indignation was
turned with renewed violence" (79) against this ungrateful servant, the judges
sentence Justine to death by hanging. Threatened with excommunication and
eternal damnation should she remain unrepentant, Justine confesses her
"crime." Submitting "in patience to the will of Heaven" (81), putting on a
cheerful face to comfort the anguished Victor, proving herself a better "woman" than even Elizabeth, Justine fabricates a fiction in order to corroborate the
falsehood fashioned in court.

    Elizabeth cannot bring herself to be quite so obeisant. If only for a mo-
ment, the cumulative weight of the thousand little cruelties she does to herself
to sustain the appearance of gendered virtue proves too much to bear. When
Justine's topmost vertebra snaps at the bottom of the executioner's rope,
something cracks within Elizabeth, too. Unable to take "delight in her ordinary occupations," she is "no longer that happy creature" (84) of Victor's
youth. She now knows something, something she cannot quite articulate,
something she desperately wishes to unknow:

> *When I reflect . . . on the miserable death of Justine Moritz, I no longer see the*
> *world and its works as they before appeared to me. Before, I looked upon the*
> *accounts of vice and injustice, that I read in books or heard from others, as*
> *tales of ancient days, or imaginary evils; at least they were remote, and more*
> *familiar to reason than to the imagination; but now misery has come home,*
> *and men appear to me as monsters thirsting for each other's blood. . . . Alas!*
> *Victor, when falsehood can look so like the truth, who can assure themselves*
> *of certain happiness? I feel as if I were walking on the edge of a precipice, to-*
> *wards which thousands are crowding, and endeavoring to plunge me into the*
> *abyss.* (85)[40]

Immediately, though, Elizabeth steps back from this ledge. *"Yet I am certainly
unjust"* (85). After all, she concedes, everyone in Geneva is persuaded that Justine committed a heinous crime against an innocent, and so her sentence cannot be altogether without reason. *"I could not consent to the death of any
human being; but certainly I should have thought such a creature unfit to remain in the society of men"* (85). That Elizabeth can draw little comfort from
such specious reasoning becomes all too apparent when she injudiciously
characterizes Justine's execution as an *"assassination"* (85). Yet if that be so,
then how should she represent those who condemned Justine to die? And how
should she depict the legal order that cinched the noose around Justine's neck?
Elizabeth speaks neither of these questions. Were she to dare to do so, were she

to speak of murderers and kangaroo courts, she knows that Victor would deny her the reassurance she so desperately requires right now: *"I know, I feel, she was innocent; you are of the same opinion, and that confirms me"* (85).

What exactly does Elizabeth, this almost outlaw, glimpse in the shadows of the chasm from which she withdraws so quickly? What is it that she must leave unsaid, even unthought, if her world is to remain intact? The crisis Elizabeth endures at this moment is a crisis of sense making, of the adequacy of received discursive forms to the unsettling materials of experience. Always before, Elizabeth's understanding of legal matters, however slim, was unproblematically situated within the context of her more comprehensive faith in the legitimacy, the materialized reality, of Geneva's political order. In this case, however, she vaguely senses that Justine has been killed not because she is guilty, but because reconsolidation of a troubled patriarchal order requires an occasional human sacrifice. Justine on the scaffold is Iphigeneia at the altar.

Justine is the scapegoat for a system of justice whose origins can be traced to the archaic adjudication depicted on Achilles' shield, as that system has been reshaped to meet Apollonian and Cartesian imperatives. The aim of archaic justice was to preserve peace within the city when kinship allegiances threatened to tear it asunder. The shield's elderly arbiters gathered in a circle seek a resolution that will accommodate the legitimate claims advanced by each of the aggrieved families and so reduce the likelihood of a bloody feud. The meting out of such justice challenges established authority within the *oikos* by undermining the claim of the patriarch to reign without rival. Acknowledgment of the reality of distinctively political justice, of justice served by the community in the interest of its own preservation, tempers the absolutism of Agamemnon, Peleus, Menelaus, and Odysseus. The unsubstantial being of the protopolitical justice administered on Hephaestus's shield is significantly solidified, moreover, when Athena establishes determinate institutional forms for dealing with homicides. With specification of the role of juries, with codification of general rules regulating the production of testimony and evidence, with transformation of the elders' circle of stones into a courtroom set in concrete, the supremacy of public justice over the claims of private vengeance more fully materializes. But what patriarchal rule loses thereby is restored by other means. For the public arena demarcated by the courts is defined as a realm that, although ultimately relying on fear of female Furies to ensure obedience, excludes women as well as their claim to participate in fashioning the legal identities of future citizens. Orestes, recall, is acquitted of the crime of murdering Clytaemestra because, as Apollo points out, the "mother is no parent of that which is called her child, but only nurse of the newly-planted seed that grows" (*The Eumenides*: 667-68).[41] Unauthorized to speak the language of public justice, women are relegated to the private sphere, and there citizen-patriarchs rule as they will.

In Elizabeth's day, the relationship between public and private spheres is not altogether the same. Most particularly, with the rise of the modern state and the emergence of capitalism, the conduct of economic as well as political activities has in large measure been removed from the domain of the *oikos* and hence from the kinship relations that households organized. The domestic sphere, in other words, is no longer principally responsible for either the creation of goods or the administration of justice, both of which are now more neatly distinguished as realms of specifically masculine activity. Even so, and although it is now Erasmus Darwin rather than Apollo who demonstrates that a woman's role in reproduction is to contain and nourish the embryonic substance divinely implanted within Adam's seed, and although it is now John Locke rather than Aristotle who justifies exclusion of women from the political sphere on the ground that it must not be tainted by the irrationality of feminine desire, identifiable traces of the archaic regime remain incarnate in the system of justice Elizabeth now finds without its accustomed moorings.

When Elizabeth's body is suddenly given to vertigo, it does so because the strands supporting the web of her world give way. The law is a sense-making artifact. Its categories assign roles (e.g., juror, witness, defendant); prescribe discourses for its participants (e.g., the language of evidence, of sentencing, of impartiality); distribute authority (e.g., judge over juror, officer over prisoner). As such, the law offers one way of fashioning sense, in this case, from the corpse of a strangled child. Till now, Elizabeth regarded that way as natural, as given in the nature of things. But when Justine dies, without warning, the majesty of the legal order reveals itself as a fiction, a made-up thing, an artifact made by and for men; *"when falsehood can look so like the truth, who can assure themselves of certain happiness?"* What she senses but can only partly articulate is the rootedness of that order in so much sublimated violence between male citizens who still hanker after the unchallenged prerogatives of patriarchy; *"men appear to me as monsters thirsting for each other's blood."* It is as if, before her mind's eye, the participants in the solemn rituals of this court were to fade away, only to be replaced by Achilles and Agamemnon squabbling over disposition of a slave girl.

Elizabeth knows in her bones why Justine cannot be set free. The court and its proceedings give institutional form to a peculiarly Cartesianized rendition of Apollo's justice. Just as Victor turns to science in order to escape dependence upon concrete others (read: women), so too the law establishes a norm of impartiality in order to keep personal particularities at bay. Just as Victor isolates himself at Ingolstadt in order to ensure that nothing out of control (read: women) can intrude on his work, so too the law seeks to contain criminality so that an established regime will not be engulfed by chaos. In typically Cartesian fashion, the law strives to achieve these ends by establishing a binary opposition between guilt and innocence. No longer is it possible, as with the council of archaic elders, to justify a proposed resolution by arguing that it more or less adequately answers the need of a community to forestall disintegration into so many warring clans. If a child has been murdered, someone must be guilty, and that someone must be found and punished. To admit that a criminal remains free is to mock the sanctity of the law, to readmit into the world the very insecurity that is to be banished by the dualistic logic of the legal order. If the law cannot discover a perpetrator, accordingly, one must be fashioned. The law operates without respect to persons, and so it is not essential that Justine serve this end. However, the circumstantial evidence implicating her, combined with her standing as a domestic servant, renders her the ideal candidate.

Of course, if the Cartesian account of the self-conscious ego is correct, if the radical constructivist's denial of all extradiscursive sense is true, then we must conclude that Elizabeth knows none of this. But neither Descartes, nor Rorty, nor even Butler, can account for Elizabeth's terrifying insight; nor can they explain why Victor, who knows of Justine's innocence better than does Elizabeth, does not suffer a like torment. As a man who may sleep and eat within the home but who will never be exclusively defined in terms of his role within it, Victor will never step to the edge of Elizabeth's abyss. His status as a civil being, a being who is free to leave the home in order to take part in science and politics, requires his unyielding confidence in the legal order that confers this status upon him. Elizabeth, by way of contrast, stands as that order's marginalized presupposition rather than its vital participant. As with Thetis, her ambiguous position with respect to that order is the condition of her horrible vision. And, in this regard, Elizabeth is kin to that most profoundly marginal creature, Victor(ia). Pleading with a Victor who refuses to listen, Victor(ia) sarcastically exclaims: "The guilty are allowed, by human laws, bloody as they are, to speak in their own defence before they are condemned. . . . Oh, praise the eternal justice of man!" (91). Victor(ia), not Victor, is Elizabeth's better half.

"I shall be with you on your wedding night" (142). As Victor(ia) had promised, the secret Victor has kept for so long is finally revealed to Elizabeth. By evening's end, and only because his wife has now assumed the form of a perfect *res extensa*, Victor can afford to suspend, if only for a moment, his relentless pursuit of unqualified independence: "(W)hat I now held in my arms had ceased to be the Elizabeth whom I had loved and cherished" (164). But what exactly has "Elizabeth" now become? Perhaps, she is the ideal free-floating signifier, a sign without power to contest the meanings ascribed to her by others. Or perhaps her lifeless body is an indeterminate metaphor, a revelation of some obscure truth about the self-contradictory quest to secure autonomy with the aid of artifacts who/which invariably take on lives of their own. Or perhaps her mute remains speak all too clearly about the import of artifacts that, fabricated by men, enter the experience of women who suffer their effects without grasping their causes.

iii. *Reactor*

Out of the libraries
Emerge the butchers.
Pressing their children closer
Mothers stand and humbly search
The skies for the inventions of learned men.
                                        Bertolt Brecht

RAPE, I HAVE COME TO UNDERSTAND, CAN WEAR MANY DISGUISES. TO CONTEND THAT forced penetration defines rape is to say as much about the definer as about the defined. For one accustomed to projecting his embodied agency into the world, but unaccustomed to thinking of his capacity to act as itself a creature of that world, for one who considers the appearance of blood the definitive sign of injury, no doubt coercive transgression of the body's clear and distinct boundaries is what rape paradigmatically is. However, for one more accustomed to acknowledge the interimplication of body and world, rape can draw no blood, leave no marks on the body's surface, but prove no less brutal for that reason. For her, to define rape exclusively in terms of demonstrable penetration is itself a violation.

Mother to Achilles, Thetis knows well enough why her son cannot refuse to battle Hector. "More than sister" to Victor, Elizabeth understands well enough why her fiancé cannot remain within the suffocating confines of Alphonsus's household. At other times, however, a woman can neither see nor touch the men who shape her destiny, and so cannot so readily grasp the reasons for their conduct. At these moments, she must rely on less palpable resources in order to fashion sense from situations still in the making. Such, I suspect, was the case for legions of women in northern Europe who, early one morning in 1986, awoke to find a host of invisible assailants, borne by the breezes of a late spring, bursting through their closed doors.

What exactly happened at the V. I. Lenin Nuclear Power Station on April 26, 1986? As a rule, we do not find this question problematic. We do not find ourselves groping for words, struggling to figure out how best to respond. We answer without hesitation, using terms like "reactor," "explosion," "accident." These familiar nouns, threads of a more comprehensive discursive web, are woven together in ways that afford our talk coherence and direction. To call this artifact a "reactor" is to affirm that an "explosion" is not essential to what it is. What it essentially is is a matter of the end for which it was designed by its makers. Were that purpose otherwise, we would call it something else—a "bomb," perhaps. Accordingly, when this thing does in fact erupt, we situate that event in the sphere of the contingent. What happened was an "accident." And once that determination has been made, the drift of our conceptual resources invariably leads us to conclude that, if we are to bring this matter to a close, we must root out and punish those responsible for this thing's violation of its appointed telos. Today, the single word "Chernobyl" is sufficient to invoke this altogether Cartesian web of common sense.

This way of speaking about Chernobyl, of rendering comprehensible this extraordinary incident, is not the only way. Its apparent adequacy to this event reveals little of the truth about Chernobyl. What it does reveal is the enduring authority of a network of institutionalized relations of power whose legitimacy relies, in large measure, on the persistence of received discursive strategies. Some of the strands woven into that network are readily identified; we academics know how to tease out the threads labeled "command economy," "nuclear energy," "bureaucratized state." Others are not so readily apprehended, and the work they do in affording that network its distinctive textures is all the more effective precisely because of their relative invisibility. Such, I suggest, is true of the thread we isolate for analytic purposes using the term "gender." To show how that strand is related to the sense-making discourse that categorizes Chernobyl as an "accident," to discover that this discourse is itself a fiction, is to destabilize the meaning of the artisanal artifact we call a "reactor," to recover some measure of its referential instability. And that in turn is to breathe new life into the question: What happened at the V. I. Lenin Nuclear Power Station in the early morning hours of April 26, 1986?

GRIGORI MEDVEDEV, AUTHOR OF *THE TRUTH ABOUT CHERNOBYL*, IS A CHARACTER INHABiting a text of his own devising, a Victor whose foremost creature is himself. Elaborating his account of the events leading up to and following the explosion at Chernobyl, Medvedev fashions a being fit to make an appearance on the world's stage. What do we learn of this self-made man, and what remains unsaid?

Medvedev, Medvedev informs us, is a Russian physicist who served as deputy chief engineer when construction of the first reactor at Chernobyl began in 1970. In 1979, when radioactive gases and liquid wastes escaped from the reactor at Three Mile Island, he was a section chief in the Ministry of Energy department responsible for the operation of all Soviet nuclear power stations. After reading a confidential account of the accident in Pennsylvania, Medvedev elected to challenge the Soviet state's repeated affirmations of the unqualified safety of its nuclear plants. However, he could find a publisher for only one of the four short stories he wrote to dramatize his concerns, and so the others were relegated to his desk drawer. Discharged from his position in operations because of radiation poisoning, Medvedev was subsequently appointed deputy director of the Central Directorate for Power Station Construction, another branch of the Ministry of Energy. Shortly after the conflagration at Chernobyl, he was ordered by the Politburo to head an official investigation into its causes and consequences.

Medvedev's autobiographical comments are essentially confined to these details. He identifies himself exclusively in terms of his status within the overlapping and overwhelmingly masculine worlds of technology, industry, and the state. We may guess that Grigori was of woman born, but that is not confirmed in the text. This is not to say, though, that no women inhabit Medvedev's world. Virtually without exception, however, such beings appear as keepers of the hearth, as wives fearful for their husbands' safety, as mothers anxious to shield their children from harm. For them, Medvedev expresses sincere, albeit paternalistic, concern: "Mothers are giving birth in the Pripyat maternity clinic at this very moment! Their babies must come into a clean world!" (GM, 48).[42] Such solicitude notwithstanding, Medvedev does not consider either gender relationships in general or his more particular relationship to the private sphere relevant to his analysis of Chernobyl. Like his fellow Cartesian, the electrifying Frankenstein, Medvedev abstracts himself from his past, from the network of dependencies out of which he emerged as a boy, in order to present himself as a being who is autonomous, a creator of power rather than its creature. Grigori, we might say, is Victor gone fission.

Medvedev's appearance of autonomy is a vital component of his present authority to stand as author of *The Truth about Chernobyl*. Objectivity, the ability to see matters from a distance, is a virtue that presupposes extrication from the network of particularistic ties that might otherwise contaminate the capacity to judge impartially. But this is not the only condition of his right to speak truth to power. Like Hephaestus in his day, Medvedev is the paradigmatic exemplar of the modern maker. He is a degree-bearing engineer, a professional whose knowledge is inseparable from its realization in the construction of durable artifacts. Unlike Hephaestus, though, Medvedev's skill is not carried within the musculature of his hands and arms. His specialized understanding of the conditions under which radioactive materials will disintegrate in a controlled manner is theoretical rather than practical in the sense that it is not the sort of knowledge that can ever become the stuff of embodied habits. It cannot become so incorporated because it is, by nature, abstract. Its concern is not with the qualitative properties of tangible materials but with the statistical regularities that obtain between an undifferentiated mass of atoms whose interactions his untutored senses will never apprehend.

Medvedev takes his status as a physicist, his work as an engineer, and his position as a high-level bureaucrat and folds all three within the confines of a nuclear identity. This unproblematic self can affirm its special qualification "to reconstruct in authentic detail . . . a picture of the full horror of the Chernobyl nuclear disaster" (GM, x) because it once served as midwife to this artifact and now stands as its Archimedean witness: "No one person knew the whole picture, as each of the participants or eyewitnesses was familiar only with his own small piece of the tragedy. It is my duty, however, to give as complete and accurate a picture as possible. Only the full truth about the biggest nuclear disaster ever to happen on this earth can help people analyze this tragedy in depth, learn from it, and rise to a new level of understanding and responsibility for the future" (GM, 216). Set apart from the events he is to describe, Medvedev's rhetoric effectively distinguishes his epistemic position from that of those ill equipped to grasp it comprehensively; he, for example, is quite unlike the two foolish fishermen who, dangling their lines into the reactor's cooling pond on the night of April 26, had no clue that they, "just like the fry they hoped to catch, had themselves been caught in the powerful trap of a nuclear disaster" (GM, 87).

Medvedev's remoteness from those caught up within the sweep of everyday concerns is the condition of his standing as an Enlightenment hero, a modern Prometheus, a bearer of "the wind of purifying truth" (GM, 1). Well before 1986, Medvedev repeatedly reminds us, he alone dared to steal knowledge from the state, from those petty Zeuses who preserve their status by keeping the inflammatory secrets of nuclear power hidden away in so many sealed files. As the author of "red-hot radioactive fiction," he alone was willing to suffer at the hands of "the sinister corps of censors," the vast majority of whom are women: "In this way, the system used the hands of mothers to choke the flow of spiritual oxygen to their own children." "(D)ragging my cross uphill," he alone did not falter in the quest to wrest from these infanticidal daughters of Pandora a truth destined "to explode one day, like dynamite." He alone understood that this "is the time to think not of wife or children, but of Russia. If we save Russia, no one will kill any children or rape any wives."[43] He alone, finally, grasped that the primary duty of a truth teller is not to this or that fisherman, not to this or that class, not even to mother Russia, but to the statistically significant but undifferentiated abstraction that is all mankind.

The conceptual abstraction of Medvedev's knowledge of physics, like his account of ethical obligation, mimics his narrative detachment from the web of human relations. The materialization of that knowledge within a nuclear reactor, under the direction of multiple bureaucratic agencies, involves a complementary sort of deracination. Recall Descartes's praise of urban planners who recognize that if the rationality of a city's design is to be assured, all that history has bequeathed to the present must be razed. Preparation of the site for the V. I. Lenin Nuclear Power Station required analagous abstraction from the past. Only after the transfer by government decree of twenty-two square kilometers of land from collective and state farms to the Ministry of Energy, only after the displacement of peasants from land they had farmed for decades, could the engineers of Chernobyl begin their work. "I saw it built almost from the ground up" (GM, 31). Flying high above, gazing down upon the community constructed atop this tabula rasa, Medvedev sees that it is marred by none of the disorderliness, the senseless juxtaposition of unrelated things, that ordinarily characterizes unplanned creations. "It was comfortable, convenient, and very clean" (GM, 31). In stark contrast to the meandering course of the Pripyat River, the reactor's perfectly circular turbines housed in perfectly rectangular halls testify to the truth of the reason that wrests boundless power from nature's anarchy.

Medvedev finds untroubled the relationship between what he wishes to say and the linguistic resources available to him. In this self-assured world, words stand as polished mirrors perfectly reflecting their intended objects, and so he finds it easy to name the artifact of present concern. This thing, of course, is a "reactor." But what exactly does it mean to call it that? For Medvedev, as a good Cartesian, to do so is to define this artifact in terms of the organization of its material parts in light of its intended purpose. The aim of this thing is to generate electricity by harnessing the energy emitted when radioactive elements decay. That aim is accomplished through the work of a boiling water pressurized tube reactor. Its core consists of a 2,000-ton pile of graphite blocks shaped into a cylinder 23 feet high and 46 feet in diameter. Each of these blocks contains a tubular channel. Inserted into those channels are 1,680 fuel tubes spaced 9.8 inches apart. Those tubes are made of zirconium alloyed with a trace of niobium, and they contain 190 tons of uranium oxide. The disintegration rate of this radioactive fuel is controlled by the insertion and removal of 211 control rods; because these are made of boron carbide, they absorb neutrons and so prevent them from colliding with other fuel atoms. If all the control rods are simultaneously and fully inserted, the reactor shuts down. As the rods are withdrawn, the chain reaction of nuclear fission begins, and the power of the reactor increases.

What sort of a definition is this? Essentially, Medvedev has characterized this artifact in a way that complements his own Cartesian self-identification. Like its maker, this thing is temporally and spatially autonomous. As we saw, Medvedev's autobiography extends in time only as far as is necessary to establish his professional qualifications; beyond that, his past remains invisible. By the same token, defining the reactor in functional terms, in terms of its present production of electrical power, Medvedev furnishes no account of the historical conditions that engendered its possibility. For example, its relationship to a bureaucratic state, committed to accelerated industrial productivity as well as maximal generation of plutonium and tritium for a nuclear weapons program, is deemed irrelevant to its identity. In addition, Medvedev finds the spatial boundaries of his self clearly demarcated; were he not unambiguously distinguished from the things of which he speaks, were he but one event caught up within a promiscuous swirl, his commitment "to tell the truth, the whole truth, and nothing but the truth" (GM, 259) would prove quite untenable. Correlatively, Medvedev is persuaded that the reactor's boundaries are neatly defined by its concrete walls as well as by the 500-ton "biological shields" affixed to those walls at top and bottom. He thus neglects the reactor's situation as a localized joint within a vast network of relations, a network of interdependence extending well beyond the ends of the high-voltage wires radiating in every direction from atop Chernobyl's turbine halls.

$$\text{\small ❧}$$

MUCH AS THE HANDS OF VICTOR(IA) COME TO CLOSE ABOUT ELIZABETH'S NECK, SO TOO will one link of the chain initiated at Chernobyl come to encircle the narrator of Christa Wolf's *Accident*. In a sense, as with Medvedev, Wolf is a character in and of her own literary creation. What we learn of that narrator can be said equally well of Wolf. She is a novelist who, at the time of *Accident*'s composition, is alone at her family's summer home outside of Mecklenburg in what, in 1986, was still called the German Democratic Republic. The event that prompts this woman to engage in the first-person interior discourse that is this novel is the same event that prompts Wolf to write *Accident*. Yet, unlike the character "Medvedev" in Medvedev's *The Truth about Chernobyl*, Wolf does not expressly identify herself with *Accident*'s narrator. Indeed, she insists on the latter's fictionality: "None of the characters in this book is identical with a living person. They have all been invented by me" (CW, unnumbered page).[44]

Including transparently self-referential detail while simultaneously denying that detail any claim to veracity, Wolf renders author and narrator at once the same and not the same. Such "autobiographical fiction" offers a challenge to Medvedev's belief in the unproblematic facticity of his relationship to the world as well as to the declarative prose he employs to articulate that relationship. Medvedev presents his textual self as a literal re-presentation of its author, an effect whose cause is he. But for Wolf, it is impossible to neatly distinguish authors from characters, speakers from the things of which they speak, discrete causes from their determinate effects. This does not mean that the distinction between word and world dissolves into an insubstantial ether of free-floating signifiers. But it does mean that the mutually constitutive relationship between experience and linguistic articulation, never removed from the ever-shifting web of circumstance, renders it impossible to say with perfect confidence that this is fancy while that is not. This does not mean that everything collapses into so much solipsistic subjectivity. But it does mean that all things fall into the category of ambiguous artifacticity. To Medvedev, that collapse must signify epistemological chaos. For Wolf, it hints at new ways of fashioning significance from the matters given to sense.

The narrator of *Accident* has neither first nor last name, no label that will announce her clear and distinct self. She is one of the anonymous many whose fate is now intertwined with events anticipated by no one in particular. But the absence of a patronym does not mean, as it surely must for Medvedev, an absence of identity. First and foremost, she identifies herself as a woman, and that means affirming her heteronomy, the intrinsic interconnection of her life with that of specific others. Most immediately pressing is her relationship to her brother, whose anesthetized body, on this late day in April, is stretched beneath the knife of a surgeon working to excise a cancerous brain tumor. Like Thetis, her identity is palpably bound up with her "maternal" responsibility to assure the well-being of the men closest to her: *"It may be that your will to live is crumbling a bit. That's why this additional line has been installed, two heads are better than one, as our mother used to say (Take good care of your little brother!)"* (CW, 14). Like Elizabeth, she has learned that a sister's duties sometimes involve the telling of little lies, of half-truths designed to shield men from their vulnerabilities: *"I sat down and wrote you a letter, brother, in large print for the sake of your still weakened eyes, using expressions like 'new beginning' and 'rebirth,' making myself believe in them, although I wondered whether I don't keep insisting on them out of defiance or out of my incapability to truly face the new situation, or whether I merely thought it appropriate to strengthen your will to recover, even through a bit of deception"* (CW, 85).

Less immediate but far more encompassing is her identification with the company of women to whom she is related by blood, by the ties of kinship that Athena sought to enfeeble when she first fashioned citizens out of patriarchs. Reaching forward and backward in time, she thinks of herself as a plurality of complementary beings, each delineated in relational terms, each called forth within different but not discrete contexts. Sometimes sequentially, sometimes simultaneously, she is grandmother, granddaughter, daughter, and mother. The depth of her identification with those who have played these parts before her and those who will do so after she is gone is most apparent when her tongue speaks their words. *"Never say never, I said, and heard my mother speaking through me; saw her standing there and heard her speaking on the telephone with her granddaughter, my daughter"* (CW, 95). Such confusion of identities, parties Medvedev will cleanly distinguish, is a vital resource of her present sense making. Perhaps it was just a dream. Even so, it brings comfort to recall the day when Grandmother Marie, seated on an old wooden bed, explained *"that we all have to die and that we can accept it. For the space of a moment I understood that our lives lead up to such simple truths and I felt gratitude toward my grandparents and all the forebears who had struggled through life before me, and before them, but that feeling disappeared very quickly"* (CW, 66-67).

Why does that feeling vanish so abruptly? It does so because today the thread of her life becomes entangled with that of an-other she will never know. Her relationship to Medvedev is mediated by an artifact that, as in the case of Victor and Elizabeth, of Thetis and Achilles, will challenge their respective capacities to make sense. Medvedev's reading of what he calls this "universal tragedy" (GM, xi) remains untouched by any knowledge of what she endures, while her anxieties remain uninformed by the knowledge that qualifies him as a nuclear engineer. To him, despite his absence from the scene, what transpires on April 26 can be described in terms of the evidence of the body's five senses: "Smoke, fumes, black ash falling in flakes, hot oil being ejected from smashed pipes, the severely damaged roof about to collapse at any minute, the protective paneling hanging perilously over the edge of the turbine hall—and noise, the crackling of fires raging above" (GM, 95). To her, this Promethean inferno is a news item, dispassionately communicated via the disembodied words of an unknown radio announcer, concerning something she can neither smell, touch, hear, see, nor taste.

Till today, the braided multiplicity of her identity never appeared incoherent. But on this day, the strands holding her steady begin to fray. Like Elizabeth upon learning of Justine's death at the end of a rope, she stands on the edge of senselessness:

> What a word. Are you listening in, brother: rebirth. Yes, I could quite well remember the times when I myself used such words and they had a meaning for me. A quick, sharp pain of longing tore open all those times before me, together with the abyss into which they had disappeared. I realized that at some point—perhaps not all at once, perhaps definitively only today—the ropes fastening our life net to certain fixtures had snapped. Ropes which could be called not only safeguards but also bonds. Those before us would forever be supported and bound by them; those after us have cut the ropes and consider themselves released, free to do and not to do as they please. (CW, 79-80)

No longer do the voices speaking through her bear the reassuring intonations of familiar others. "Just then, as I was squeezing some toothpaste onto my toothbrush, I heard someone say: So, it had to come to this! The woman who had spoken was myself" (CW, 7). For the first time, today, she discovers strangers within herself, alien(ated) beings who appear not as friends and relatives but as so many unpredictable discharges springing from places she cannot locate. "How strange that a-tom in Greek means the same as in-dividuum in Latin: unsplittable. The inventors of these words knew neither nuclear fission nor schizophrenia" (CW, 29).[45] In Accident's narrator, Medvedev's Cartesian self encounters its disintegrating alter ego.

Yesterday, what she found most terrifying was what threatened to pin her, to crush her, beneath its massive bulk. Today, she worries whether invaders too tiny to be apprehended penetrate her unshielded pores. Yesterday, she knew that if she were harmed, the signs of violence would be immediately apparent in the wounds of her flesh. Today, she learns that injuries done may not show themselves for decades; indeed, as in the house of Atreus, the curse of the mother may not reveal its horror for generations. Yesterday, she thoughtlessly repeated her mother's maxim about the importance of milk to a child's plastic bones. Today, this most prosaic source of nourishment may be so much poison.[46] Or it may not. How can her daughter, now grown with children of her own, possibly know which milk is safe and which is contaminated? In this world, which of her sense-making habits can possibly show her how to play well the part of a (grand)mother? *"Seeing hearing smelling tasting touching— and that's all there is? Who believes that, anyway. We can't have been sent on our way with so little sensitivity back then. Although the demand for a built-in Geiger counter does sound rather pretentious, even humorous. Who could have predicted all those millions of years ago that it would one day enhance our species' chances of survival?"* (CW, 15).

As wayward radioactivity tears at the genetic structure of living cells, it shreds the materialized media of prosaic meaning. The artisanal artifacts fashioned to counter the precariousness of naked human bodies now turn against themselves. So many things customarily associated with the labors of women—darned socks, washed dishes, made beds—now appear as (possibly) lethal vessels, as hollows where unseen particles gather to await their unsuspecting prey. *"I informed that authority who was critically examining everything I ate that the eggs in my refrigerator had grown in the bellies of chickens before the accident. . . . Definitely not yesterday fresh"* (CW, 8-9). Things that once joined persons together via the world-sustaining power of artifacts—a kitchen table, a soccer ball, a volume of fairy tales—now drive them apart, as each seeks the security of an uncontaminated haven. Things that once melted effortlessly into the structures of everyday routine suddenly come aglow with unresolvable contradictions, posing questions that cannot be shaped to intelligible discursive form. *"Everything I have been able to think and feel has gone beyond the boundaries of prose"* (CW, 58).

Some—her elderly neighbor Gutjahr, for example—will deny, or perhaps remain oblivious to, the radical novelty of what has happened today. For him, the old saws of past generations will do for now as well: "What's done is done. And weren't these things always blown way out of proportion? . . . What I don't know won't hurt me" (CW, 13). For her, such platitudes ring hollow. *"The radiant sky. Now one can't think that anymore, either. . . . Calling it 'cloud' is merely an indication of our inability to keep pace linguistically with the progress of science"* (CW, 21-22, 27). Should she therefore learn the language of science? *"So the mothers sit down by the radio and attempt to learn the new words. Becquerel . . . Half-life is what the mothers learn today. Iodine 131. Cesium"* (CW, 27). But that will not do either. Trivially, it will not do because this chaos of esoteric signs mocks her struggle to make sense: chemists speak of "becquerels," physicists of "curies," geneticists "sieverts," doctors "grays," radiologists "röentgens." Less trivially, it will not do because what one expert proclaims another denies, sapping her impulse to righteous anger. Most fundamentally, it will not do because to learn such terms is to accede to the trivialization of everyday life, to grant the insignificance, the inferior reality, of the rhythms of being that emerge from lives devoted to daily detail. *"Life as a se-ries of days. Breakfast. Measuring out the coffee with the orange measuring spoon, turning on the coffee machine, savoring the aroma which envelops the kitchen. . . . Boiling the egg for exactly five minutes, managing the trick, day in day out, in spite of the faulty egg-timer. Imperishable pleasures"* (CW, 8). She would rather go silent than acquire a tongue that denies such creature com-forts their vernacular sense.

A crisis of identity is a crisis of language is a crisis of time. For Medvedev, time proceeds in straightforward linear fashion, and so its passage can be re-constructed as a succession of events marching relentlessly forward. "We can learn the lessons of Chernobyl . . . only by rigorously analyzing the causes, na-ture, and consequences of the disaster at the nuclear power station in the Byelorussian-Ukranian Woodlands. I shall now try to do just that by recording events as they occurred, hour by hour, day by day, before the accident and while it was actually occurring" (GM, 28). For *Accident's* narrator, nothing could be more problematic than the present and, by extension, the counterfeit realism of conventional narrative. *"On a day about which I cannot write in the present tense, the cherry trees will have been in blossom. I will have avoided thinking, 'exploded,' the cherry trees have exploded, although only one year earlier I could not only think but also say it readily, if not entirely with convic-tion"* (CW, 3). To write in early May about that day in late April is to look back-ward in time. But the import of that past no longer ceases at the present. It now hurries toward an indefinite future, and that future must be read into the meaning of the present if sense is to be made of what happened in the past. Yet, even for one blessed with the powers of Cassandra, what can it possibly mean to think 24,360 years ahead, to fold one's understanding of the half-life of plutonium 239 into present sense? Not even future perfect tense can paper over the incapacities of linguistic categories fashioned when the future was a matter of imminent consequence rather than an abstract thing of limitless ex-tension.

FOR MEDVEDEV, TIME IS NOT AN ISSUE WORTH TARRYING OVER. HIS AIM IS TO DO WITH words what Frankenstein did in fact, "to revive the dead and the maimed, and have them return to the control room to relive those tragic hours" (GM, x). Medvedev's account of the events leading up to Chernobyl, considerably abridged, goes something like this: On April 25, a routine safety test was initi-ated. The aim of the test was to determine whether, in the event of a complete power failure, the residual inert force generated by the decelerating turbines would produce enough energy to ensure continued operation of the reactor's automatic monitoring devices. In preparation for this test, control rods were gradually inserted into the core throughout the late morning. By early afternoon, as expected, the reactor was generating about half its usual power. The emergency core cooling system was then disconnected in order to prevent it from cutting in automatically as the turbines slowed. At 2 P.M., continuation of the test was delayed because of an unexpected surge in the demand for electricity from Kiev. When resumed, about nine hours later, the reactor had slipped into what is known as an "iodine well." Under these circumstances, the iodine and xenon gases naturally produced during a reactor's operation, having insufficient time to decay, join with the control rods to slow the rate of fission. The reactor in this condition is highly unstable because its various coefficients—temperature, steam production, water pressure, and neutron flux—no longer rise and fall in relation to each other in straightforward linear fashion. To balance the reactor and so make it possible to proceed with the test, several control rods were withdrawn. This action produced a surprisingly large escalation in power, prompting the operators to attempt an immediate shutdown of the reactor. That effort proved unsuccessful because so many manually operated control rods had already been withdrawn, and because their automatic counterparts jammed halfway into the core. The reactor then surged from 5 percent to about one hundred times its normal output in the space of two seconds, generating an explosion at 1:23:44 A.M. on April 26. The force of that blast tore apart the concrete casement surrounding the reactor's core, blew the biological shield off its top, and spewed radioactivity, along with massive blocks of burning graphite, into the night sky.

The incident at Chernobyl jeopardizes the intelligibility of Medvedev's Cartesian world, and it does so in a way that threatens the self-representation he fashions for public consumption. The specific nature of that threat is intimated when, describing his return to Chernobyl as part of the government's investigative team, Medvedev confesses: "All of us in the nuclear power industry, including me, were to blame for what had happened to those perfectly innocent people. . . . I found these sentiments sweeping over me, try as I might to resist them" (GM, 215). To keep such sentiments at bay, under ego's control, Medvedev must shield himself from Chernobyl's epistemological fallout. His effort to do so is successful in the sense that his cognitive equipment does not disintegrate into so many irradiated pieces. But that success is dearly won, for it comes at the price of an impoverished, indeed an incoherent, grasp of the truth about Chernobyl.

"Chernobyl came at us like a bolt from the blue" (GM, 27). Like Victor casting about for an account of the destructive power of lightning, Medvedev cannot leave this extraordinary event unexplained without betraying his standing as a scientist. In this quest, he must overcome a difficulty not unlike the fundamental dilemma of Cartesian epistemology. Descartes presupposes the existence of a strict and mutually exclusive distinction between material things that operate according to the lawful principles of mechanical causality and immaterial things that, like the Judeo-Christian god and the human soul, are capable of free agency. The oft-repeated epistemological question generated by this ontological dualism is this: How is it is possible for the mind to come to know anything with certainty about matters of the external world, given that such things are essentially unlike the knowing soul? Descartes's answer is implicit in his representationalist account of truth, an account that regards the mind as something akin to a mirror. Suitably buffed by the rules of scientific method, that mirror can supply accurate reflections of objects outside and fundamentally unlike it.

Thinking like a Cartesian, Medvedev is persuaded that a nuclear reactor is a complex tool designed to achieve specific ends by human makers who are autonomous in the sense that they stand essentially apart from, and hence can control, the things they create. When that tool goes awry, when it acts like a "reinforced-concrete nuclear beast,"[47] he must find some way to link artificer and artifact without undercutting the essential distinction between autonomous subjects, which are capable of significant agency, and heteronomous objects, which are not. The boundary between human beings and the things they make must remain clear and distinct, in other words, if Medvedev is to sustain his conceptual excision of artifactual reciprocation from the arc linking it to projection. Only then can he remain confident that he is not a speaking spider caught within a web that mocks his Enlightenment pretensions.

Medvedev relates creator to creature, while preserving the rule of the former over the latter, by employing the complementary vocabularies of design flaw and operator error. If the accident was due to a flaw in the reactor's design, then insufficient technical knowledge is the problem and additional research is the solution. If the accident was due to operator error, then carelessness is the problem and improved training is the solution. In either case, the question to be asked about Chernobyl is the following: "(S)pecific individuals within those organizations were responsible for such matters. Who were they? Were they capable of fulfilling the responsibility assigned to them?" (GM, 36). For Medvedev, thinking like a physicist, the explanatory task is to find the human cause of the effect that is this disaster. Or, to translate such language into its moral analogue, his task is to identify the agent or agents who, in failing to perform responsibly, are now to be blamed for the explosion. Whether as scientist or as ethicist, Medvedev accepts the account of unilinear causality whose invention Nietzsche ascribed to the hangman.

In the best of all possible worlds, Medvedev's inquiry will culminate in an assignment of culpability that is specific and unequivocal. His charge will be most satisfactorily executed if, step by step, he can trace backward the chain of events until he locates the determinate misdeeds of a particular individual as this disaster's uncaused cause; and, indeed, at one point Medvedev thinks he has located just such a culprit. Meeting with other members of the investigative commission formed by the Politburo, Medvedev pounces on Victor Bryukhanov, director of operations at Chernobyl: "I was seething with rage. I believed that of all the people present, he alone was to blame. Or at least more to blame than anyone else" (GM, 225). As his grudging qualification intimates, Medvedev knows that matters are not nearly so simple. Off duty at the time, Bryukhanov was asleep at home when the accident occurred. He made none of the decisions, gave none of the orders, that triggered this catastrophe; and so, except perhaps as a scapegoat, a Justine in drag, it is hard to see how all blame can be placed at his feet.

At other times, Medvedev gives us good reason to suspect that Bryukhanov is altogether innocent. For he "was nothing more than a pawn manipulated by the ideologues of the period of stagnation, which was now gone forever" (GM, 225). But if Bryukhanov is something akin to an automaton, a puppet moved by forces outside itself, then surely it is wrong to charge him with either moral failure or professional error. Hephaestus's robots may one day break down, but it would be foolish to blame them for that incapacitation. Moreover, if Bryukhanov is in fact a mere pawn, then does it not follow that those in the highest administrative and scientific positions, the "ideologues of the period of stagnation," are the true culprits? That implication is at the very least awkward, of course, given Medvedev's own standing as one of the Soviet Union's leading nuclear engineers; and so, not surprisingly, he is quick to point out that he "had nothing to do with operational questions and therefore was unable to do anything" (GM, 46) about removing incompetent personnel. Perhaps more important, to assign blame to individuals so far removed from the scene is to raise questions about the adequacy of Chernobyl's designation as an "accident." If this event was one of the "unpleasant, but inevitable, corollaries of nuclear technology" (GM, 49), as Medvedev claims many Soviet officials had come to believe, then perhaps Chernobyl was a predictable manifestation of the "sheer insanity of the administrative-command system" (GM, x). But to blame the "system" is to abandon the project of imputing personal responsibility, which in turn is to find no one in particular to blame, which in turn is to raise serious doubts about the adequacy of the Cartesian metaphysic of use and the ethical discourse associated with it.

Unwilling to doubt that metaphysic, Medvedev renews his hunt for a determinate villain, now pointing his finger at the operators on duty at the time of the explosion. As the reactor became a familiar home, a place where operators did their humdrum jobs, they grew increasingly cavalier about its capacity to disrupt their routines. "Over a period of decades, the operators' confidence gradually became greatly exaggerated and made it possible for the laws of nuclear physics and safety rules to be completely overlooked" (GM, 49). In particular, Leonid Toptunov and Alexsandr Akimov, senior engineer and shift foreman at the time of the explosion, "failed to show the proper sense of responsibility and blithely proceeded to commit serious breaches of the nuclear safety regulations. . . . They also could not have been particularly devoted to their work; if they had been, they would have pondered every move thought-fully, showing the vigilance expected of true professionals" (GM, 57).

This ascription of blame, like that directed at Bryukhanov, is untenable for at least four reasons. First, it seems wrongheaded to charge persons with incompetence when there is no good reason to expect them to possess the expertise necessary to sustain a claim to competence. Still searching for *the* cause of Chernobyl, Medvedev wonders whether his prey might be a policy rather than a person. Perhaps the root cause of the explosion was adoption of nepotistic personnel procedures that permitted, even encouraged, the hiring of those untrained in the art of generating nuclear power: "Those seeking such employment had previously been, for the most part, real enthusiasts, with a profound passion for nuclear energy; whereas now all kinds of people were pouring in. Of course, they were attracted primarily not by the pay, which was not particularly good, but by the lure of prestige. . . . I contend that it was this policy . . . that led to the events of 26 April 1986" (GM, 9, 43). But if that is so, then should not those who formulated and implemented this policy be held accountable, not those who were its ambitious beneficiaries? Furthermore, if this policy is in fact the cause of the explosion, then are we not back to blaming the anonymous "administrative-command system," which, as we have already seen, will not bear the weight Medvedev requires of it?

Second, if Bryukhanov is a pawn, and if Toptunov and Akimov are subordinates of a pawn, then it is hard to know how they can be any more culpable than is he. And yet Medvedev does not really consider these agents pawns. Instead, he typically represents Chernobyl's operators as so many autonomous egos who, like simple tool users, can be held responsible for the consequences they engender. But are these operators in fact so many unfettered sources of free causal agency? Or are they more akin to vital organs of a wonderfully intricate automaton? The specifically nonhuman members of this internally complex being, to abstract what in reality is altogether confused with their human counterparts, have usurped much of the skill once incarnated in the thinking limbs of Hephaestus. The tacit responsiveness once located in his hands, his sense of how different materials respond to variations of temperature and pressure, has been effectively expropriated and reincorporated within the reactor's array of electronic sensors. Because that array is so finely articulated, we might even say that Hephaestus's entire central nervous system, thoughtless in its automaticity, has now been surgically removed, only to be reembedded in the skeleton of Reactor #4. Thus disembodied, the animate servants who monitor the reports of this system are more akin to Elizabeth than to Victor, more like Thetis than Achilles. Like women, the dreary task of Toptunov and Akimov is to minister to the vital needs of this concrete body so that it can more efficiently attend to its heroic end, that of generating public power without limit.

Contrary to Medvedev's portrayal, a nuclear reactor is not simply a means of producing energy. It is also a way of engineering relations between persons. The bureaucratic chain of command, giving determinate form to the specialized labors of the reactor's human artifacts, is effectively dictated by the technical requisites of realizing this extraordinary form of power. To the extent that Chernobyl's operators are creatures of these relations, they are not well understood as so many Cartesian fonts of unencumbered volition. This is not to deny that the operators made choices; nor is it to deny that some of those choices qualify as mistakes. But it is to say that the context of action within which those choices were made, a context leaving little room for individual discretion, is such that no operator should be made to bear the measure of responsibility implied by Medvedev's dualistic vocabulary of blame and absolution.

Third, to assign blame to Toptunov and Akimov is to assume that they had access to information that, at least in principle, would have made it possible for them to make better choices. Perhaps if they were wielding hammer and tongs, shaping molten metal into a shield, that might be the case. But the situation of Toptunov and Akimov is not that of Hephaestus. A computer named Skala surveyed the condition of the Chernobyl reactor at 6,234 different points every five minutes, and the information so gathered appeared as a succession of cartograms on various monitors. The sheer volume and complexity of this data challenges the conception of human agency built into the vocabulary of Cartesian responsibility. Based on his own experience, Medvedev reports that when a nuclear accident commences, "you experience a feeling of numbness, of complete collapse within your chest and a cold wave of fright—the main reason being that you have been taken by surprise, and that, to start with, you have no idea what to do—while the needles of the automatic printer drums and the monitoring instruments are swinging in all directions, while you are frantically trying to keep track, and while the cause and precise pattern of the accident remain unclear" (GM, 72-73). If such disorientation is, as Medvedev suggests, an inevitable accompaniment to this sort of crisis, then it is an exercise in bad faith to blame Chernobyl's operators when they fall prey to it.

Moreover, the data appearing on those screens are qualitatively different from those afforded Hephaestus when, for example, the head of his hammer flies off its handle. The intangible information made available to Toptunov and Akimov, if it is to prove meaningful, must be subjected to an act of theoretical interpretation that relates it to matters distant and unseen. Each of the reactor's computer screens transforms invisible three-dimensional events into so much two-dimensional digitalized text. The significance of that data is not assured, as is the case with more prosaic artifacts, by its intimate relationship to organic habits fashioned from materials given to the body's engaged senses, and so the conduct of sense making requires forms of thinking quite unlike those employed by Hephaestus. Whereas his intelligence takes shape as so much incorporated skill, so much inarticulate know-how, that of Toptunov

and Akimov appears as an ever more frantic struggle to apply a technical manual's "if-then" statements to a situation whose signs do not correspond to any
of the "ifs" described therein. Condemned to a hell where they are judged by a
strict code of professional accountability but denied what they need in order to
fulfill its dictates in a nonroutine situation, the bodies and minds of these neo-
Cartesians cannot help but go their separate ways.

Just seconds before the explosion, Toptunov and Akimov wonder whether
the evidence now before their eyes is to be believed; "after all, computers occasionally lie" (GM, 68). Indeed, even after the blast, their actions remain "based
on the false assumption that the reactor was still intact. They were utterly unwilling to believe that the reactor was no more" (GM, 117). It is only when the
effects produced by massive radiation poisoning begin to register in their noses
and throats that they prove willing to ascribe any credibility to the cries of their
dosimeters, now permanently fixed at the maximum reading. Yet, even then,
they still cannot fathom the import of the glowing graphite chunks scattered
about their feet, chunks that could only have come from inside the reactor's
core. Disbelieving what their bodies now know to be true, they respond to this
chaos of signs by deploying sense-making resources uninformed by the para-
doxes of nuclear science; in short, they fight fire with water. Not surprisingly
in this topsy-turvy world, the result is to make matters worse. For as water
mixes with nuclear particles, jets of radioactive steam are produced, yielding
yet another medium for the conveyance of radionuclides into unshielded
lungs.

Fourth, and finally, how can Toptunov and Akimov be held responsible for
the explosion given Medvedev's reluctant admission that "the death sentence
was implicit, to some extent, in the very design of the RBMK reactor" (GM,
56)? Each control rod within the reactor at Chernobyl is a little over twenty
feet long. Its lower end consists of a graphite tip, followed by a hollow segment
a little more than a yard long, followed by the portion that absorbs neutrons
and so slows the rate of fission. Given this design, the rods begin to dampen
the fissioning process only when the absorbent portion reaches the core; indeed, because their entry displaces water in the rods' channels, their initial insertion generates a momentary surge of reactivity. But Toptunov and Akimov
knew nothing of "this exceedingly grave mistake by the reactor designers,"
which, contradicting the charge he already leveled first against Bryukhanov
and second against the flawed personnel policy, Medvedev now deems "the
main cause of the nuclear disaster" (GM, 90). In sum, Toptunov and Akimov
literally do not know what they are doing when they try to bring the reactor to
an immediate halt by inserting all of the control rods simultaneously. "It simply never occurred to anyone that death could come from a device that was
supposed to protect" (GM, 60).

Aleksandr Akimov is not disingenuous when, from the hospital bed where he is soon to die of radioactive poisoning, he tells his wife, Lyubov, over and over again: "I did everything right. I don't understand why it happened" (GM, 61). Schooled in the same vocabulary of moral analysis spoken by Medvedev, Akimov cannot shake the conviction that someone must be responsible for this nightmare. But Akimov is no more successful than is Medvedev in locating that individual. "He had," Lyubov reports to the government commission, "no complaints about the people on his shift, who had all done their duty" (GM, 253). But does that mean that he, as shift foreman, is alone responsible? Again, Lyubov reports: "I was with my husband a day before his death. He was already unable to say a word, but you saw the pain in his eyes. I know he was thinking about that damned fateful night, playing the whole scenario over and over again in his mind, and he was unable to accept that he was to blame" (GM, 253). Protesting his innocence, while simultaneously confessing that his conscience pains him far more than do his rotting intestines, Akimov can be relieved of this unresolvable dilemma only by death.

Occasionally, Medvedev fears he will never locate the clear and distinct villain his Enlightenment rationalism requires. At such moments, he is tempted to jettison his technological instrumentalism in favor of its mirror image, wholesale technological determinism. Speaking of the final two hours prior to the explosion, Medvedev writes: "But developments proceeded as programmed by Fate. The apparent reprieve granted by the Kiev load dispatcher, when he shifted the tests from 2 P.M. on 25 April to 1:23 A.M. on 26 April, actually led straight to the explosion" (GM, 50). Here Medvedev finds himself falling into a world whose workings are controlled by a demonic power, by a perverse being whose inexplicable interventions ensure that actions intended to produce one result actually yield their opposite. In this world, science's promise of redemption from myth and technology's promise of domination over nature appear as so many shams. But, surely, that cannot be. Reconstructing events just sixteen minutes prior to the explosion, Medvedev asks once more: "Could the disaster have been averted in this situation? The answer is yes. All they needed to do was categorically to scrap the experiment, switch on the emergency cooling system, and start up the emergency diesel generators. . . . This chance was let slip" (GM, 68). Like some overburdened *deus ex machina*, the discourse of personal responsibility appears once again in order to extricate human beings from the clutches of Fate, to demonstrate that at least within the realm of the hypothetical they remain masters of their fate.

The ethical discourse Medvedev speaks is perhaps not altogether inappropriate when the consequences of action, in terms of spatial and temporal extension, are more or less bounded. The maxim "Do unto others as you would have others do unto you" can serve as a practicable rule of human relations when it is possible to trace, with some measure of confidence, the results of actions taken by you and your neighbors. It is much less clear that this discourse is apt when it proves impossible to track those consequences back to specific persons—indeed, when no such persons can be identified because agency is so thoroughly segmented amongst an interdependent multiplicity of actors, each of whom has only a partial understanding of the whole in which all are commonly enmeshed, many of whom are absent from the scene where those consequences are immediately felt. In such a world, to speak of the "chain of command," with its image of so many sequential effects neatly lined up with their discrete causal antecedents, is to relate a fable whose power to reassure is directly proportional to its power to deceive.

If the discourse of personal responsibility is vitiated when consequences cannot be traced back to determinate authors, still more must it be impaired when the spatiotemporal range of those consequences cannot be definitively identified. The very point of artifactual projection is to reap the excess of reciprocation. What renders the logic of artisanal artifacts necessarily problematic is the fact that the production of such excess always threatens to outstrip categories of sense making teased from yesterday's experience. The greater the reciprocational excess, in other words, the more quickly will received resources of intelligibility prove incompetent. On April 26, the pushing of a single button, aimed at bringing #4 to a halt, served as proximate cause of the worst nuclear disaster in history. But the exponential multiplication of such consequences did not cease with that explosion. Much of the radioactivity released from Chernobyl, on falling into the sea, became extremely diluted. Paradoxically, when that radioactivity passed through animate forms that filter large quantities of water, these innocuous quantities were quickly reconcentrated. Radionuclides of cesium 137, for example, were absorbed by zoo- and phytoplankton, which were then consumed by shrimp, which were then eaten by larger fish. As a result, measurable radioactivity in the muscle of Baltic perch jumped from virtually zero to 3,100 becquerels by December of 1986.

Think of such glowing perch as a metaphor for the human condition in an age when Prometheus is truly unbound. The capacity of human hands to inflict pain is projected into Achilles' sword, an artifact capable of spilling far more blood than naked fists will ever bring forth; but that sword is made of metal and so it will corrode in time. The capacity of human beings to remake themselves is projected into Victor's creature, an artifact capable of murdering with impunity because it is stronger and faster than its creator; but that thing is an embodied being and so it too can be destroyed. In Medvedev's reactor, the fire of Prometheus is projected into an artifact that, once it assumes a life of its own, mocks every effort to contain its proliferation of effects in space and time. The victory over death that Victor hoped to achieve by learning the secret of immortality is finally realized within an artifact capable of killing without end.

What Medvedev cannot grasp is that the world engendered by Chernobyl, when looked at from the standpoint suggested by the logic of everyday artisanal artifacts, is a world gone mad. That logic holds that human beings are sustained in their everyday affairs by a complex web of made things. Those artifacts, so many realizations of potentialities latent in nature's offerings, make less immediately pressing the burdens of embodiment; their archetype is the bed Odysseus fashions from the trunk of an olive tree in order to cradle Penelope's body next to his. The mimetic relationship between the structure of this artifact and the needs of these bodies is the condition of the former's intelligibility; the frame of that bed, shaped with an eye to the design of human backs, relieves their spines of the fatigue they accumulate by day. Even in the case of the profoundly different artifact that is the reactor at Chernobyl, the human body still offers the metaphorical resources of sense making; thus Medvedev speaks of the reactor's "membranes," its "mouth," its "eye," and its "bowels" (GM, 101, 103, 147, 177). But the sense-giving logic of artisanal artifice disintegrates into so much life-denying nonsense when things designed to shield the human body from harm, to bring it comfort, turn into instruments of torture. When the reactor's mouth becomes a pair of "red-hot jaws," when its membranes appear "like some monstrous flycatching machine, waiting for the chance to drag a living creature into its infernal belly" (GM, 167, 121-22), Prometheus is stood on his head.

Those who survive the onslaughts of this machine can do so only because their bodies, like that of Victor's creature, now incorporate bone marrow extracted from living relatives and blood-producing cells drawn from the livers of fetal corpses. Those who fail to survive do not, in death, cease to haunt the living. Should their bodies be given conventional burials, the still-vital radionuclides nestled in their decomposing flesh will in time be released into the soil where, washed away by the earth's groundwaters, they will renew their destructive work. Should these already blackened bodies be cremated, the smoke issuing forth will carry its deadly load to distant lands. Chernobyl's victims must, therefore, be denied their right to return to dust and ash. Sealed within lead coffins, their lids soldered shut, those who perished in the immediate aftermath of this inferno need no memorials to remind the living of the pain they may yet cause.

Medvedev's repeated invocation of the language of personal responsibility is a sort of conceptual containment project. Its aim is to minimize the sense-making threat posed by the explosion at Chernobyl, to tame this event by enclosing its import within the confines of a familiar discourse. The artisanal counterpart of that boundary project is the concrete shell built around the reactor's remains in order to seal it off from the outside world. That "sarcophagus," insisted an official skilled in the terminology of Cartesianism, will "secure the burial of everything that remains of the radioactive fallout of this entire accident in general, so that it can be reliably contained and supervised and will not give rise to any doubts whatsoever."[48] But this structure, a mammoth mausoleum for the operator whose body was never recovered, cannot contain the uncontainable. When #4's walls collapsed, tossing its contents to the winds, "its" boundaries became coextensive with the ground covered by that discharge. Chernobyl ablaze, one versed in Hegel might say, is humanity's first genuinely universal artifact.

"WHAT SHALL I CALL IT AND BE RIGHT, IN ALL ELOQUENCE?" FOR THE NARRATOR OF Christa Wolf's *Accident*, Orestes' question has a new urgency. When the artifact at Cherobyl explodes and so enters into a wide range of never-anticipated relational networks, its appearance of objectivity is severely compromised. The fragmentation of its walls dislodges human electrons from their accustomed sense-making orbits, inviting them to ask whether this thing's reality is adequately captured by a term that denotes only its manipulation of natural phenomena in the production of electrical power. To continue to call this thing a "reactor" is to partake of a vocabulary that serves all too well the interests of those who are all too eager to have "it" reacquire its standing as an apparently neutral tool, a thing unproblematically absorbed within the fabric of everyday experience.

The question of this artifact's identity opens up for *Accident*'s narrator, whereas it does not for Medvedev, because she lacks his nuclear identity, the identity of one whose self-understanding is essentially congruent with the institutional order it inhabits. She is at once of and not of the world of men. As a daughter and mother, she identifies herself in relation to the concerns of women. But as an author whose words travel far beyond the walls of the household, as a woman who has refused to sacrifice herself in the manner of Thetis and Elizabeth, she expressly identifies herself in relation to more comprehensive concerns. The immediate site where domestic and extradomestic cross paths is her garden. For Medvedev, the cloud of radioactivity expelled by the reactor appears as "an enormous, sinister flower head" (GM, 78). When news of that blossom reaches *Accident*'s narrator, she is tenderly transplanting Japanese peace plants from pots to bed. As these alien species begin to cross-pollinate, their first yield is an inchoate feeling. Her skin, she senses, is "*chafing on a cunningly well-hidden secret. . . . I was reminded of certain documents where the true, the secret writing appears only after chemical treatment, whereby the original, deliberately irrelevant text is revealed to be a pretext*" (CW, 17, 23). Unlike those locked in the drawers of Soviet nuclear experts, this secret has no determinate content. But it is not for that reason to be dismissed as subjective or unreal. For this some-thing is as palpably present in the relations structuring her situation as was the secret that Victor kept from Elizabeth for too long.

This feeling secures initial articulation as so much ill-formed rage. If she is now helpless in the face of events she had no hand in creating, she will show that she too retains the power to destroy. *"At the stroke of the hour I heard on my little radio that one would be well advised to wear gloves today if working in the garden was unavoidable, and I heard a sound escape my throat which resembled a manic clarion call of triumph, while fervently continuing to pull weeds with my bare hands. . . . You, I say to the weeds, I'm going to wipe you out!"* (CW, 24-25). If faceless others have injected so many nameless fears into her world, she will show that she too can cause alarm. *"White leghorns. The only good thing you can say about them is that they react to my clapping and hissing with fear, if also confusion"* (CW, 3). If "inanimate" objects have now come alive, maiming guilty and innocent alike, she will show that she remains master of the artifacts that people her world. *"All at once I observed myself weighing in my hand like a projectile one of the ceramic cups out of which we like to drink tea. And then put it back on its shelf, firmly, but without breaking it, reached for the olivewood salad utensils and, with a precise and accurately aimed throw, whipped them into the corner"* (CW, 48).

As she struggles to find the right words to bridge the semantic gap separating what is felt from the articulations available to her, only in fits and starts does this rage begin to take shape as an express question:

> *Sometimes, brother, you get caught up in such diffuse circumstances that you don't even know what you should actually be thinking about. Physiologically speaking, that must be represented by a flickering in several parts of the brain, I would assume. A precautionary allocation of as yet nondirectional energy which does not flow unswervingly into the prepaved compound network, but rather gropes about in unexplored territory before gathering itself, for example, into a question: Whence this desire for fission, for fire and explosions!* (CW, 46-47)

The term that jars here, that marks her entrance into a sense-making space quite unlike that inhabited by Medvedev, is "desire." Were her brother present, he would once again take exception. *"You forbade me to use the word 'desire' in this connection. Desire, desire . . . you said. That was another one of those exaggerated, partisan expressions"* (CW, 47). "Desire," he might have said more bluntly, is the word of a woman. But that cavalier dismissal will not persuade her to let it go. For this word, she now suspects, furnishes the initial clue that in time will enable her to weave together things that, to Medvedev as well as to her brother, must appear quite unconnected.

Recall, one last time, how Hephaestus etches onto the surface of the shield he fashions for Achilles a dramatic rendition of archaic Greek cosmology. Even in the chaos of battle, that shield eloquently attests to the comprehensive web of meanings that renders vitally significant the heroic ethos exemplified by its hypermasculine bearer. Something analogous happens when *Accident*'s narrator peers into Chernobyl's exposed core. In that clash of conflicting powers, she finds a sign, a manifestation, of a more encompassing order. Isolated from that order, the explosion appears as a random incident, an "accident." Returned to that context, Chernobyl appears as an accident by design—or, better, a symptom of a particular configuration of institutionalized powers, as these are played out on a technological tableau. The reactor's still smoldering corpse, she now comes to suspect, is one of the more telling creatures of an ultimately (self)-destructive cult(ure) of militarized masculinity.

Consider the nuclear experts who now tread, uninvited, on the tender shoots of her garden. Who are they? How do they live? She does not know for sure; but the character of her brother, she guesses, offers a clue. She has never understood the intensity of his passion for computers, which seems strangely at odds with the posture of dispassionate rationality he assumes in his dealings with persons. "*I saw how you relished its obedience when you called up the program*" (CW, 28). Is it possible that her brother's desire to demonstrate his mastery over this artifact is an expression of some unknown loss, of some longing left unsatisfied?

> *What do people want? I guess, dear brother: people want to experience strong emotions and they want to be loved. Period. Deep down, everybody knows that, and if the gratification of their deepest desires is not granted, does not succeed, or is denied, then they—no, we!—create substitute gratification and cling to a substitute life, a substitute for life, the entire breathlessly expanding monstrous technological creation, a substitute for love* (CW, 32).

Might the culture of Chernobyl be an artifact of the anger that wells up in those whose most primordial needs go unmet? Might the experts of Chernobyl be so many Frankensteins who, like Victor, have learned that love is sometimes taken away, without reason, without warning? While we may not wish to endorse the psychoanalytic argument implicit in this last quotation, and while we certainly want to contest the gender essentialism creeping into this account, the fact remains that *Accident*'s narrator is onto something here.

Think again of Victor Bryukhanov. Bryukhanov, Medvedev tells us, is a sullen individual characterized by "an inner stubborness, accompanied by a poor knowledge of people" (GM, 42). Like his Genevan counterpart, this Victor struggled to live up to his given name by distinguishing himself as a young man at the polytechnic institute in Tashkent. His appointment, when he was only thirty-five, as director of the V. I. Lenin Power Station made clear to all the full measure of his ambition; and his designation as a Hero of Socialist Labor when Chernobyl's fourth reactor was commissioned in late 1983 testified to the wisdom of that appointment. Pursuing a glory that can never be secured within the household, much like Descartes in his solitary cell and Frankenstein in his removed attic, Victor and his fraternity of like-minded colleagues came to inhabit *"an isolation ward, without women, without children, without friends, without any other pleasures apart from their work, subjugated to the strictest of safety and security regulations"* (CW, 62). Enclosed within that ward, *Accident's* narrator guesses, these men never experience the routine chores that fill up the days of so many women. *"I resolved to make a list of those activities and pleasures which, more than likely, are foreign to those men of science and technology. To what end? In all honesty: I don't know. I was simply wondering whether the various compartments of our brain didn't perhaps interact with one another in such a way that a woman who has been nursing her infant for months would be prohibited by a blockage in a certain part of her brain from supporting with word and deed those new technologies which can poison her milk"* (CW, 21). If indeed that nursing mother is so prohibited, is that to be explained by something inherent in the maternal body, as Kristeva and Rich might argue? Or is that to be explained by the distinctive complex of sense-making habits she has acquired as a result of the reciprocational excess engendered by the host of artisanal artifacts that define her daily routine?

Victor supervises the construction of an artifact that objectifies the quest of a Cartesian culture to escape the bonds of debilitating heteronomy by establishing its unqualifed domination over nature. This quest must fail for the same reason Frankenstein's effort failed. The means of satisfying that desire is an artisanal artifact whose requisites, indeed whose mere existence, make certain claims on its makers. *"What they do know, these mere children with their highly trained brains, with the restless left hemispheres of their brains working feverishly night and day—what they do know is their machine. Their lovely, beloved computer. To which they are bound, shackled, as only ever a slave to his galley"* (CW, 63). The Cartesian ego struggles to throw off the chains of embodiment. He does so by projecting his body's vulnerabilities into an artifact that, because it incorporates knowledge of those frailties, allows him to neglect their otherwise imperious demands. But that projection creates a new source of dependence—specifically, dependence on this objectified response to the body's infirmities. As such, that thing does tacitly what Victor's creature does expressly; it affirms its makers' obligations to care for *its* needs, to acknowledge *its* just claims. But obligations, so many acknowledgments of relational reciprocity, are so many dependencies, and so this made thing must be unmade. *"At which crossroads did human evolution possibly go so wrong that we have coupled the satisfaction of our desires with the compulsion to destroy? . . . Has the idle, oversized part of our brain fled into manic-destructive hyperactivity, faster and faster and, finally—today—at breakneck speed, hurling out ever new fantasies, which we, unable to stop ourselves, have turned into objectives of desire and entrusted to our machine world in the form of production tasks?"* (CW, 65, 71-72). In sum, when allied to the Cartesian quest for perfect autonomy, the Promethean urge to create becomes bound up with an urge to annihilate the artifactual conditions on which that imagined self-sufficiency depends.

If the technological sophistication incorporated within the artifact at Chernobyl is an unacknowledged expression of impossible desires, then the ritualized appeals to reason emanating from the company of nuclear experts must ring either hollow or sinister. "In Chernobyl," Medvedev writes, "a cosmic tragedy had taken place; and the cosmos can be handled not by brute force alone, but by the force of reason, which is in itself a living and more powerful cosmic force. . . . [M]an, as a being with reason, must ensure that all his scientific and technical achievements, especially nuclear power, are used to make life flourish, not fade" (GM, 260). At first blush, this appeal seems innocuous enough, especially given that its concrete substance reduces to a call for enhancing the professionalism of plant operators and improving the design of reactor control rods. It appears less innocent when one asks whether the very possibility of Medvedev's rationalism entails a sort of conceptual violence, a tearing asunder of things thoroughly entangled. *"Who is it that locates the danger zone within a radius of precisely thirty kilometers, of all things, I thought to myself. Why thirty? Why always these even, round numbers? Why not twenty-nine? Or thirty-three? Would that be an admission that our calculations don't work out? That the natural and the unnatural don't obey our decimal system?"* (CW, 58). And it appears still less so when one asks whether Medvedev's representation of the heroic feats to be accomplished by a deified reason does not turn on continued production of the crises to which it alone can respond. Do you not detect a trace of secret delight, even of perverse pride, when Medvedev proclaims that Chernobyl was "the biggest nuclear disaster ever to happen on this earth" (GM, 216)?

At a press conference held two weeks after the explosion, the chairman of the Soviet Union State Committee on the Use of Nuclear Energy, A. M. Petrosyants, said perhaps more than he intended when he blandly remarked: "Science requires victims" (GM, 5). The anonymity of Petrosyants's categorization of those harmed is the premise of Medvedev's contention that "Chernobyl has harmed everybody."[49] Practiced in the arts of abstractive rationalism, neither understands that the category of "everybody" is a reifying fiction, that the status of victimhood is not democratically distributed, that the pain that attends this status is not homogeneously felt. Consider, for example, the older women who would just as soon not know that they are twice as susceptible to radiation-induced cancer as are their male counterparts. Consider the younger women who, pregnant at the time of the explosion, reluctantly accepted the government's official recommendation to abort. Consider the mothers who, like Thetis deprived of her prophetic powers, still wonder whether each little malady is the initial sign of what in time will take their children away. Consider the wives who, in their capacity as primary caretakers, now minister to those permanently debilitated by Chernobyl's fallout. If humanity is to continue its upward march, perhaps Petrosyants should have said, women must stand tall as so many Iphigeneias, ready for sacrifice on the altar of radioactive reason.

"*Whence this desire for fission, for fire and explosions?*" To suggest that Chernobyl is symptomatic of a more profound cultural disarrangement, to grope toward some more adequate articulation of the felt connections between artifactual projection, the ethos of heroism, and the Cartesian quest for autonomy, is to do a better job of sense making than does Medvedev. But even this answer smacks of too much Medvedev, of a misplaced desire to simplify matters artificially by precisely distinguishing villains from victims. "*It is indescribably satisfying to grab hold of a nettle bush with one's right hand while digging along the length of its root with the index finger of the left hand until the right spot has been found, from which the entire length of the tough, deep, branched rootstock can be pulled out, gingerly and steadily*" (CW, 25-26). What is occasionally possible in dealing with weeds is never possible in politics. An explanation of Chernobyl that confidently accuses some reified monster labeled "patriarchy," an account that makes it far too easy to savor the resentful pleasures that accompany victimhood, will not do. No such account will do justice to the complex of mutual desires, the universal complicity, that sustains the order that produced this catastrophe.

Watching television at dusk, *Accident's* narrator listens to "*one of the countless experts who are now shooting up out of the ground like mushrooms*": "As always with new technological developments," he proclaims, "one would have to take certain risks into account until one fully mastered this technology as well. . . . *Now I should have grown cold. Now I should have been shocked or outraged. No such thing. I knew very well that they knew it*" (CW, 5, 103). But why exactly is she not horrified by this domesticated version of Petrosyants's claim? She is not, in part because this claim is so mundane, so drearily predictable. She is not, in part because she is deeply ambivalent about the import of modernity's technological wizardry: "*When we spoke on the telephone yesterday, I did not tell you what I recently saw on television: a computer, specially developed for operations on the human brain, programmed to make precise incisions down to one-hundredth of a millimeter. Less fallible than the human hand, they said*" (CW, 10). She is not, in part because as a young socialist she once felt something akin to the visionary impulses that appear to animate so many Medvedevs: "*Do the utopias of our time necessarily breed monsters? Were we monsters when we, for the sake of a utopia we were not willing to postpone—justice, equality, humanity for all—fought those in whose interest this utopia was not (is not), and, with our own doubts, fought those who dared doubt that the ends justify the means*" (CW, 30). She is not, in part because it is her desire, as it is everyone's, to remain untroubled: "*I was once more forced to admire the way in which every-thing fits together with a sleepwalker's precision: the desire of most people for a comfortable life, their tendency to believe the speakers on raised platforms, and the men in white coats; the addiction to harmony and the fear of contra-diction of the many seem to correspond to the arrogance and hunger for pow-er, the dedication to profit, unscrupulous inquisitiveness, and self-infatuation of the few*" (CW, 17). And, most fundamentally, she is not because she knows that, however reluctantly, she will answer yes when a friend asks if she too has felt "a certain wanton desire for those evil news reports every hour? A dark, malicious glee leveled at our own selves?" (CW, 54). No matter how much she wishes it were otherwise, she will acquiesce when her friend insists that they must now "examine the whole situation from the point of view of our mutual guilt" (CW, 54).

SO LONG AS CHERNOBYL REMAINED INTACT, IT RECEDED INTO THE UNPROBLEMATIC BACK-ground of everyday politics, and so its contribution to the stabilization of a bureaucratically organized authoritarian order went largely unnoticed. That order is a web sustained by various artifactual forms, forms including things as diverse as persons, institutions, works of craft, and languages. Each sort of ar-tifact is susceptible to the occasional turn of events that challenges our famil-iar expectations: a nail may bend; an election may be circumvented by a coup; a joke may elicit only blank stares; a woman may go mad. In most cases, the effects of such "accidents" are readily contained. But that can never be guaran-teed in advance. Because each creature of Prometheus is mutually implicated in the fate of its kin, a tear in any one may work its way into others. If in time a sufficient number of these relations come to affirm their status as fictions, as things made rather than given, the real world may find itself up for grabs.

When Chernobyl exploded, its latent political qualities became manifest, disclosing a matter of public concern. To the state, which benefitted from this artifact's inconspicuousness, the democratization of this thing was in some ways far more disconcerting than was the radioactivity gushing from its core. For years, much like Victor, the Soviet state had found it relatively easy to keep secret whatever difficulties it encountered in controlling its nuclear creatures. Should some suspicious Elizabeth dare to raise questions about what she could not know, it was enough to say, as did Petrosyants in 1972, that the "continuing skepticism and distrust felt toward nuclear power stations are caused by exaggerated fear of the radiation danger to the personnel working at the station and, in particular, to the surrounding population" (GM, 4). Much the same strategy was deployed, at least at first, in 1986. In fact, the order to evacuate the area around Chernobyl, now dubbed the Zone of Estrangement, was delayed by more than thirty-six hours in the hope that this matter might yet remain the state's private possession. When that proved impossible, the task became one of checking the explosion's capacity to subvert the official reality sustaining the state's already fragile authority.

The first strategy of containment deployed by the Soviet state was an institutionalized version of Medvedev's futile search for the villain(s) of Chernobyl. Medvedev presents himself as a rebel who dares to question the official truth about Chernobyl. That self-representation is perhaps true in the sense that he fingers parties who, no doubt, would prefer to remain hidden behind a shield of bureaucratic anonymity. But in a more profound sense this is so much unwarranted self-aggrandizement. For his reading of this disaster in the terms furnished by the discourse of personal responsibility finds its precise political analogue in the state's trial of Bryukhanov and his subordinates.

Recall how Elizabeth, on the occasion of Justine's trial, began to suspect that the law must either find or fashion a culprit when something beyond its ken occurs. Recall also her sense that the law's assignment of blame must be unequivocal to rematerialize the order thus undermined. On August 12, 1986, along with four others, Bryukhanov was charged with violating a criminal statute concerning the breach of safety regulations at "explosive-prone enterprises." Because his signature was found on a document misrepresenting the levels of radiation shortly after the explosion, Bryukhanov was also charged with the abuse of power for personal advantage. During the trial, questions about the design of this artifact were either suppressed or obfuscated. The flaw in the control rods, for example, was characterized as one of several "peculiarities and shortcomings inherent in the reactor," anomalies that played "not very well-defined roles" in contributing to the accident.[50] On July 27, 1987, to the surprise of no one, all five were found guilty, and Bryukhanov was sentenced to ten years' imprisonment.

The trial of Bryukhanov may be read as an attempt to shore up several tenets vital to the Cartesian paradigm of use. By shutting off questions about the reactor's design, it affirmed the innocence, the inherent neutrality, of this artifact. By implying that better-trained personnel could have prevented its self-destruction, the trial affirmed the separability of human beings from the things they make and hence the latter's subordination to the former. By alleging that Bryukhanov's actions were motivated by an immoral desire for private advantage, it deflected attention away from this artifact's situation within a political/military regime that demanded the expedient production of nuclear power at any price. By conducting a trial aimed at explaining what happened on this particular day in April, it reinforced the rationalist contention that the normal state of affairs is defined by the absence of accidents (as opposed to asking whether accidents may be a predictable outcome of administrative practices that segment Chernobyl's work into so many discontinuous bits). In sum, in convicting these scapegoats, the Soviet state showed itself far superior to Medvedev in the art of playing Descartes. The state's judgment is troubled by none of the qualifying phrases, the uncertainties, the contradictions, that vitiate Medvedev's quest to isolate Chernobyl's singular cause. The second containment strategy employed by the Soviet state is a corollary of the first. The search for Chernobyl's villains implies a search for its heroes. Each is a complementary part of a larger masculinist discourse that represents men as autonomous authors of the identifiable consequences generated by their visible deeds. The manufacture of heroes, like that of villains, presupposes a suitable context, and no context is more useful for this purpose than that of war. The metaphorical militarization of Chernobyl was perhaps inevitable given the emergency mobilization of conscripted soldiers, including chemical warfare units, as well as the deployment of sophisticated military equipment, including helicopters, to "bomb" the reactor with water, sand, boron, and lead. "They were truly at war—and it was a nuclear war" (GM, 190). The inexorability of this analogy, however, should not blind us to its political utility. By transforming Chernobyl into an arena of combat, the military metaphor justifies the sacrifices to be exacted from its latest round of victims. More important, it invites identification of a few of this conflict's protagonists as noble exemplifications of the warrior ethic of Achilles.

The Soviet state and Medvedev are equally eager to lift out of the crowd those who, in the immediate aftermath of the explosion, displayed valor above and beyond the call of duty. Those who best fit the bill, all concur, are the firefighters ordered to quench the blazes burning in and around the reactor. However, abstracted from the fields of Troy, the designation of these men as heroes seems tragic, comic, and above all, utterly anachronistic. Strapping on the armor forged by Hephaestus, Achilles knows all too well, can see all too clearly, the foe that is Hector; the courage he must muster is coextensive with the adrenaline coursing through his veins. But the "truly heroic firefighters" (GM, 83) of Chernobyl are not so many reincarnations of Achilles. Their character is much better suggested by the young conscript who later complained that Chernobyl was far worse than Afghanistan because, at least in Afghanistan, he knew where the bullets were coming from. Thinking this was a fire like any other, these "heroes" literally did not know what they were doing when they attacked their foe with water and so fueled its fury. Nor did they have any grasp of the injuries done to their internal organs as they shoveled chunks of raging graphite, emitting up to twenty thousand röentgens per hour, back into the reactor's exposed core. Only with tongue in cheek can one call heroes those who, armed with weapons that invigorate their opponent, remain oblivious to the wounds they suffer.

That fourteen of Chernobyl's employees were buried with full honors in Mitino Cemetery may bring some consolation to their families. Perhaps, should their relatives read Medvedev's book, they will draw comfort from the meaning he teases from their sacrifice. "Your deaths jolted everybody out of their complacency. . . . Their memories haunt us. We would dearly like to see them again" (GM, 265, 261). But such sentimentality is insufficient to keep at bay the cynical chill that comes over *Accident*'s narrator as she watches the news flit by in black and white: "*I tried to steel myself against the faces of people which might appear—did appear—on television, who would try to force a smile. Whose hair would have fallen out. Whose doctors would use the word 'brave.' A graphite fire which no one could have expected, as we shall be told, is, however, extraordinarily hard to put out once it has started. But someone had to do it*" (CW, 42).

With that chill, to her surprise, comes a peculiar sense of freedom. Chernobyl violates familiar modes of sense making by deriding our capacity to anticipate, if only in imagination, the temporal close of the consequences engendered by artifactual projection. We do not know how to think our way across the gulf separating the half-life of a human being from the half-life of a gram of plutonium 239. Paradoxically, though, Chernobyl's indefinite elongation of time is accompanied by its simultaneous compression. To learn that once-prosaic actions—eating vegetables, bathing children, becoming pregnant—are now fraught with unknown perils is to inject mortality into the fabric of everyday awareness. What is usually forgotten in the mundane business of living now becomes focally immediate. And that, in turn, threatens to dissolve the web of relational obligations binding each to others, known and unknown, in time. To pursue a distant end, to defer present pleasures, to join one's life to another, each of these commitments loses much of its sense when the very notion of a goal is sabotaged by the present's radical uncertainty. "*I was having a new experience with a wicked kind of freedom. I saw that there also exists the freedom to refuse to obey anything, even self-imposed duties. For the first time I faced the possibility that even duties such as these can disintegrate and I realized that no habit would be strong enough to take their place*" (CW, 23).

The realization of such freedom is a political accomplishment of a sort. It is the achievement of one who has come to recognize that all human things are so many artifacts, so many formed matters subject to renegotiation. That recognition does not situate *Accident*'s narrator outside or above the web of human affairs; it does not locate her where Medvedev, the self-proclaimed Archimedean, likes to think he sits. But nor does it leave her squarely within the world of things as they were just yesterday. Her most acute sense, her sense of reality, has undergone decisive dislocation. No more can she suffer fools who have nothing better to do than search for heroes and villains. No more can she tolerate scientific ambitions that require the sacrifice of women to masculine fantasies of disembodied autonomy. No more can she abide the edicts of a state that represents its voice as that of impartial reason. But these refusals, liberating as they are, are also deeply unsettling. They leave her dizzy in the face of the intrinsic ambiguity, the indeterminacy, of all things. They jeopardize her relationships with men, most particularly her brother. And they tempt her to withdraw from the world, to retreat to a place that is not so ugly, to seek solace in the arms of one long gone.

> *Late at night I was startled by a voice and by a crying. The voice had called from far away: A faultless monster! The crying came from me, as I noticed after some time, I was sitting in bed crying. My face was flooded with tears. Just then, very close to me, in my dream, a giant, nauseatingly putrescent moon had swiftly sunk down below the horizon. A large photograph of my dead mother had been fastened to the dark night sky. I screamed. How difficult it would be, brother, to take leave of this earth* (CW, 109).[51]

Notes

    1. Homer, *The Iliad*, trans. Robert Fagles (New York: Penguin, 1990). For this and all subsequent quotations from *The Iliad*, I place the appropriate book and line citation immediately after the passage in question. In all quotations from *The Iliad*, I have italicized the words of Thetis.

    2. Hesiod, "Works and Days," in *Hesiod: The Homeric Hymns and Homerica*, trans. Hugh Evelyn-White (New York: G. P. Putnam, 1920): 43-47, 60-64.

    3. Hannah Arendt, *The Human Condition* (Chicago: University of Chicago Press, 1958), 138.

    4. Arendt, *Human Condition*, 225.

    5. Martin Heidegger, "The Question Concerning Technology," in *The Question Concerning Technology and Other Essays*, trans. William Lovitt (New York: Harper & Row, 1977). On this point, see also Jean Pierre Vernant, *Myth and Thought among the Greeks* (Boston: Routledge & Kegan Paul, 1983), 261:

> Contrary to the view of Espinas, the work of the artisan does not fall within the order of "human manufacture" in which man, becoming aware of his opposition to nature, attempts to humanize it through artificial devices which he can continue to perfect indefinitely. Instead, in his work the artisan sees his own activity becoming "natural." . . . Man is not yet sufficiently distinguished from nature for human activity to be dissociated from what is natural without thereby being placed in the category of what is merely conventional.

    6. Hesiod, "Works and Days," 41.

    7. Because it ascribes a more active role to the belt, for this quotation I have used the translation offered by Richard Lattimore, *The Iliad* (Chicago: University of Chicago Press, 1951). Fagles translates the same lines as follows: "The point's not lodged in a mortal spot, you see? / My glittering war-

belt stopped the shot in front" (4.214-15). All remaining quotations are from Fagles's translation.

8. The passage in which Homer describes the shield and the scenes etched on its surface can be found in book 18 of *The Iliad* at 558-709.

9. For three distinct accounts of the import of this scene, see Robert Bonner and Gertrude Smith, *The Administration of Justice from Homer to Aristotle*, vol. 1 (Chicago: University of Chicago Press, 1930), 31-42; Michael Gagarin, *Early Greek Law* (Berkeley, Calif: University of California Press, 1986), 26-33; and Mark Edwards, *The Iliad: A Commentary*, vol. 5 (New York: Cambridge University Press, 1991), 214-18.

10. For this story, see Plato's *Protagoras*, at 320d-23a, in *The Collected Dialogues of Plato*, ed. Edith Hamilton and Huntington Cairns (Princeton, N.J.: Princeton University Press, 1961).

11. Just who gets to decide what counts as the "straightest" verdict is a subject of some dispute. Fagles's translation leaves the matter ambiguous. For a translation that is overtly democratic in import, see Alexander Pope, *The Iliad of Homer* (New York: Hurst & Co., 1883): "One pleads the fine discharged, which one denied, / And bade the public and the laws decide" (390).

12. Judith Butler, *Bodies That Matter* (New York: Routledge, 1993), 107.

13. I take the distinction between acting "to" acquire a skill and acting "from" an acquired skill from Drew Leder, *The Absent Body* (Chicago: University of Chicago Press, 1990), 30-32.

14. The reference here is to Hector, but it applies equally well to Achilles.

15. Homer, *The Odyssey*, trans. Robert Fitzgerald (New York: Vintage, 1990), 11.561.

16. Mary Shelley, *Frankenstein*, ed. Johanna Smith (Boston: Bedford, 1992), 44. For the most part, quotations are taken from this edition of Shelley's 1831 text, and subsequent citations include page references only. In a few instances, I have taken passages from the first edition, published in 1818. In those cases, which I call attention to in the notes, quotations are taken from *Frankenstein*, ed. James Rieger (Indianapolis: Bobbs-Merrill, 1974). One of the most significant differences between the two editions concerns the representation of Elizabeth. In the 1818 edition, Elizabeth is much more likely to express suspicion of Victor's truthfulness, and she is more detailed in expressing outrage at perceived injustices (e.g., the execution of Justine). By 1831, in large measure, Elizabeth has been remade in the image of the "proper woman." For an exploration of this transformation, see Mary Poovey, *The Proper Lady and the Woman Writer* (Chicago: University of Chicago Press, 1984).

17. Shelley, *Frankenstein* (1818 edition), 33-34. No mention of this shared secret is included in the 1831 edition. It might also be noted that in the 1818 edition Elizabeth is identified as Victor's cousin, whereas in the 1831 edition, she is a foundling.

18. Shelley, *Frankenstein* (1818 edition), 58-59, 62. In the 1831 edition,

Shelley removes all phrases that might indicate any measure of suspiciousness on Elizabeth's part. As with Thetis, I have elected to italicize all of Elizabeth's words, whether written or spoken.

19. Shelley, *Frankenstein* (1818 edition), 150. In the 1831 edition, Victor never offers a substantive justification for this trip. He says only, "I expressed a wish to visit England, but, concealing the true reasons of this request, I clothed my desires under a guise which excited no suspicion, while I urged my desire with an earnestness that easily induced my father to comply" (130).

20. Shelley, *Frankenstein* (1818 edition), 151. Elizabeth's complaint is omitted from the 1831 edition. There, we learn only that she "was filled with disquiet at the idea of my suffering, away from her, the inroads of misery and grief. . . . She longed to bid me hasten my return,—a thousand conflicting emotions rendered her mute, as she bade me a tearful silent farewell" (131).

21. René Descartes, *Discourse on Method*, trans. Donald Cress (Indianapolis: Hackett, 1980), 3, 5-6.

22. Descartes, *Discourse on Method*, 6.

23. Descartes, *Discourse on Method*, 18.

24. Descartes, *Discourse on Method*, 15.

25. René Descartes, *Philosophical Essays*, trans. Laurence Lafleur (Indianapolis: Bobbs-Merrill, 1964), 91.

26. Although it has no obvious place in the main text of my narrative, I do wish to note the parallel between the structure of the shield fashioned by Homer and the structure of the novel fashioned by Mary Shelley. The surface of the shield is partitioned into five concentric rings of decoration. The text of *Frankenstein* is partitioned into five concentric circles of narration. The first and the fifth are told by Victor's Arctic rescuer, Robert Walton; the second and the fourth are related by Victor Frankenstein; and the middle is recounted in the voice of Victor's artifact. Such coincidences, I suspect, are the stuff of which belief in cosmic design is made.

27. This quotation is taken from Shelley's preface to the 1831 edition. Although it refers to her work in writing the novel, I think it offers an implied counter to Victor's pretensions to omnipotence.

28. Paracelsus, quoted in Mircea Eliade, *The Forge and the Crucible*, trans. Stephen Corrin (London: Rider, 1962), 154.

29. Francis Bacon, quoted in Carolyn Merchant, *The Death of Nature* (New York: Harper & Row, 1983), 171.

30. Cornelius Agrippa, quoted in Merchant, *Death of Nature*, 184.

31. Butler, *Bodies That Matter*, 36.

32. A play based on Mary Shelley's novel was first performed at the Royal Cobourg Theatre in London on July 3, 1826. In the list of *dramatis personae*, the identity of the thing created by Victor was indicated by a series of asterisks. Picking up on this clue, Anne Mellor, in her *Mary Shelley* (New York: Routledge, 1989), writes: "As a unique being, an original, the creature functions in

the novel as the sign of the unfamiliar, the unknown. He is a sign detached from a visual or verbal grammar, without diachronic or synchronic context, without precursor or progeny" (128). Mellor is on to something important here, although I think she fails to attend adequately to this thing's stubborn materiality, that is, the sense in which it is both more and other than a linguistic artifact.

33. For the most part, Shelley's interpreters have been no more willing than is Victor to bear the tension that comes with leaving this being's identity indeterminate. In his "*Frankenstein*: Creation as Catastrophe," in *Mary Shelley's Frankenstein*, ed. Harold Bloom (New York: Chelsea, 1987), Paul Sherwin provides a useful catalog of the more familiar readings of this thing's identity:

> If, for the orthodox Freudian, he is a type of the unconscious, for the Jungian he is the shadow, for the Lacanian an *objet à*, for one Romanticist a Blakean "spectre," for another a Blakean "emanation"; he also has been or can be read as Rousseau's natural man, a Wordsworthian child of nature, the isolated Romantic rebel, the misunderstood revolutionary impulse, Mary Shelley's abandoned baby self, her abandoned babe, an aberrant signifier, *différance*, or as a hypostasis of godless presumption, the monstrosity of a godless nature, analytical reasoning, or alienating labor. Like the Creature's own mythic version of himself, a freakish hybrid of Milton's Adam and Satan, all these allegorizations are exploded by the text. (40)

I concur with Sherwin on this final point.

34. Often forgotten, this is the subtitle Shelley gave to her novel.

35. Robert Boyle, quoted in Brian Easlea, *Witch-Hunting, Magic and the New Philosophy* (Atlantic Highlands, N.J.: Humanities Press, 1980), 214.

36. See Shelley, *Frankenstein* (1831), where Victor compares the passion that rules his conduct to "a mountain river, from ignoble and almost forgotten sources; but, swelling as it proceeded, it became the torrent which, in its course, has swept away all my hopes and joys" (44). See also Victor's reference to "(C)hance—or rather the evil influence, the Angel of Destruction, which asserted omnipotent sway over me from the moment I turned my reluctant steps from my father's door" (49). Finally, consider Victor's assertion that his "situation was one in which all voluntary thought was swallowed up and lost. I was hurried away by fury; revenge alone endowed me with strength and composure" (168).

37. Shelley, *Frankenstein* (1818 edition), 51.

38. Shelley, *Frankenstein* (1818 edition), 39.

39. Shelley, *Frankenstein* (1818 edition), 30.

40. Shelley, *Frankenstein* (1831), 85. In the 1818 edition, when Elizabeth speaks with Justine in her cell, she states:

Yet heaven bless thee, my dearest Justine, with resignation, and a confidence
elevated beyond this world. Oh! how I hate its shews and mockeries! when
one creature is murdered, another is immediately deprived of life in a slow tor-
turing manner; then the executioners, their hands yet reeking with the blood
of innocence, believe that they have done a great deed. They call this *retribution*. Hateful name! When that word is pronounced, I know greater and more
horrid punishments are going to be inflicted than the gloomiest tyrant ever
invented to satiate his utmost revenge. (82-83)

I have chosen to omit this passage from my consideration of Elizabeth's revelation for two reasons: First, as Anne Mellor explains in her *Mary Shelley* (64),
many if not all of these words were written by Percy rather than Mary Shelley;
and, second, these words suggest an Elizabeth who is much too certain of the
law's injustice. In contrast, I believe Elizabeth is caught between the conclusion that the law is fundamentally unjust and her equally profound desire not
to come to this conclusion.

    41. Aeschylus, *The Oresteia*, trans. Richard Lattimore (Chicago: Univer-
sity of Chicago Press, 1953).

    42. Grigori Medvedev, *The Truth about Chernobyl*, trans. Evelyn Rossiter
(New York: Basic Books, 1991). All quotations from this book are designated
by the author's initials (GM), along with the appropriate page citation.

    43. Grigori Medvedev, *No Breathing Room*, trans. Evelyn Rossiter (New
York: Harper Collins, 1993), 48, 53, 87, 92, 195. This book is in effect a sequel
to *The Truth about Chernobyl*. In terms of substantive content, it adds little to
its predecessor. As this paragraph suggests, however, it is rich in provocative
gender-specific metaphors.

    44. Christa Wolf, *Accident: A Day's News*, trans. Heike Schwarzbauer and
Rick Takvorian (New York: Farrar, Straus, and Giroux, 1989). All quotations
from this work are designated by the author's initials (CW), along with the appropriate page citation. As with Thetis and Elizabeth, I have italicized the
words of Wolf's unnamed narrator.

    45. Anna Kuhn, in her *Christa Wolf's Utopian Vision* (New York: Cam-
bridge University Press, 1988), notes the difficulty of finding an adequate English equivalent for the term translated as "accident" in Wolf's title. In a
technical context, the German *"Störfall"* suggests a breakdown in some complex system. The term "breakdown" is obviously suggestive because of its con-
notation of psychological/emotional collapse. In a nontechnical sense, Kuhn
notes, the term *"Störfall"* might also be translated as "a cause for concern"
(262). That translation, as I will suggest toward the end of this section, hints
at Chernobyl's acquisition of an explicitly political dimension.

    46. Speaking of poison, it is perhaps worth noting that the Ukranian term
"chernobyl" refers to a bitter herb known in English as "wormwood." Wormwood is mentioned in a passage found in "The Revelation of St. John the Di-

vine," a book of the Ukrainian Orthodox Church Bible. Chapter 8:10-11 reads as follows: "When the third angel blew his trumpet a great star flaming like a torch descended from the sky, falling upon the third part of the rivers and upon the sources of the water. The star is called Wormwood. The third part of the waters turned to wormwood, and great numbers of men died from drinking the waters because they had been poisoned."

47. Medvedev, *No Breathing Room*, 54.

48. Ivan Silayev, quoted in Piers Paul Read, *Ablaze* (New York: Random House, 1993), 208.

49. Medvedev, *No Breathing Room*, 115.

50. Read, *Ablaze*, 231.

51. Those given to such Freudian endeavors are invited to engage in comparative analysis of this dream and the dream Victor Frankenstein endures after he first sees his creature. When that task is complete, you should compare these two dreams with the one Medvedev relates in *No Breathing Room*. About to abandon his effort to find a Soviet publisher for *The Truth about Chernobyl*, Medvedev draws comfort from a dream in which two faces, one male and the other female, appear to him in a black sky. The male face descends to within one hundred feet and, so situated, engages Medvedev in a conversation about his publication difficulties. When the male face retreats to its original position, "(t)he woman's face began to shrink and to descend to the same altitude, where it stopped above me, staring at me probingly and lovingly, without a word. Compassion was visible in its eyes. Soon the face soared back into the sky, and after a moment both faces vanished among the stars" (147-48).

PHILOMELA'S LOOM

S ISTERS TO ERECTHEUS, KING OF ATHENS, PROCNE AND PHILOMELA ARE FIRST SEPA-
rated when the elder of the two marries Tereus of Thrace. When their son,
Itys, turns five, Procne begs Tereus to permit Philomela to visit Thrace, if only
for a little while. "If you give me a chance to see my sister you will confer on
me a precious boon."[1] Tereus agrees and, offering to escort his wife's sister, em-
barks for Athens. However, on reaching his destination, he is "inflamed with
love" for Philomela, "quick as if one should set fire to ripe grain, or dry leaves,
or hay stored away in the mow" (456-58). Telling no one of his designs, Tereus
returns to the shores of Thrace with Philomela. There, before going home to
Procne, he rapes his young guest.

Beaten but not defeated, Philomela vows that one day she will make
Tereus's crime known to all:

> If those who dwell on high see these things, nay, if there are gods at all, if all
> things have not perished with me, sooner or later you shall pay dearly for this
> deed. I will myself cast shame aside and proclaim what you have done. If I
> should have the chance, I would go where people throng and tell it; if I am
> kept shut up in these woods, I will fill the woods with my story and move the
> very rocks to pity. (542-48)

Tereus responds to Philomela's threat by drawing his sword, cutting off her
tongue, raping her again, and imprisoning her within a hut hidden deep in the
forest. To Procne, he explains that his charge fell ill and died on the voyage
from Athens.

"And what shall Philomela do?" (571). Her "speechless lips can give no token of her wrongs. But grief has sharp wits, and in trouble cunning comes"
(574-75). As a daughter of Athena, Philomela knows that craft needs no voice
to speak. Like so many surrogate tongues, her slender fingers will now proclaim what she cannot say. Setting to work on a loom Tereus left behind, in
purple and white, Philomela weaves her story into a web of cloth. Struggling to
draw her pain out of its hiding place, to give it the shape of a tale, to stitch that
tale into the seams of something she can cradle in her arms, Philomela proves
herself the equal of any son of Hephaestus.

When an old woman presents Philomela's gift to Procne, "the savage tyrant's wife unrolls the cloth" and "reads the pitiable tale of her misfortune"

(582-83). Not in any literal sense, of course, does Procne "read" her sister's message. Disclosed before her eyes all at once, like Orestes holding aloft his father's blood-soaked robe, the brutal immediacy of this spectacle shocks in a way speech, unfolding its terms one by one, cannot. At first, Procne's "questing tongue can find no words strong enough to express her outraged feelings" (584-85). But, when outrage yields to rage, Procne frees Philomela from her prison and considers how best to avenge her sister. "I am prepared for any crime," even to "fire this palace with a torch, and to cast Tereus, the author of our wrongs, into the flaming ruins" (613-15). That, though, will not do. Better to make her husband live on in agony than to deliver him too soon into the comforting arms of death.

Thinking in turn of Itys and then of Philomela, Procne asks: "Why is one able to make soft, pretty speeches, while her ravished tongue dooms the other to silence? Since he calls me mother, why does she not call me sister? Remember whose wife you are, daughter of Pandion!" (632-34). With these words Procne knows what she must do. One stroke of the knife is enough to bring the days of Itys to an end; many more are required to fashion his body into meat fit for a stew. "This is the feast to which the wife invites Tereus, little knowing what it is" (647-48). When Tereus calls for his boy to join them at the table, Procne exults: "You have, within, him whom you want" (655).

As Procne flees, clutching the hand of her sister, eluding the arms of her husband, a divinity whose name we never learn intervenes to stem this river of blood. Upon Tereus's head "a stiff crest appears, and a huge beak stands forth instead of his long sword. He is the hoopoë, with the look of one armed for war" (672-74). Philomela is transformed into a swallow, a creature who can do no more than twitter, while Procne assumes the shape of a nightingale, forever mourning in song the son she cherished and murdered.

Because it draws together my two principal concerns—the constitution of gender relations and the politics of artifacts—I find this a fit tale to tell at the close of this book. Less immediately apparent is the fact that my way of telling this story, which largely follows the path marked by Ovid, is untrue to my larger argument. Specifically, the grammar informing my narration tacitly gives top billing to human subjects, their intentions, and their actions. The weight of its discursive emphases implicitly suggests that the tale of Procne, Philomela, and Tereus can be understood, at least in principle, in abstraction from the web of artisanal artifacts that antecedently situate their conduct within an intelligible world. These artifacts, my telling intimates, are so many silent servants to the ends of those subjects who are the only agents truly worthy of mention. The sword of Tereus, for example, is simply an incidental instrument through which what really matters, his will, is made real, just as the tapestry of Philomela is merely a useful means through which what really matters, her desire to communicate, is afforded expression. On this telling, neither sword nor tapestry is considered an agent in its own right, an artifact whose entry into the world remakes the web of experience out of which all creatures of Prometheus, human as well as artisanal, are teased.

To set matters right, perhaps I should now retell this tale, putting its artisanal artifacts in the grammatical loci previously occupied by human artifacts, and vice versa. After all, were he not a creature of his father's household, Tereus would not know what it is to be a patriarch and so would not know what it means to close Procne within its confines. Absent the skills her hands have acquired as fruits of the loom, Philomela would be unable to set in motion a cascade of events that will culminate in the death of her assailant's most cherished good. More generally, absent the labors performed by the artisanal artifacts that have afforded determinate form to the otherwise inchoate matter of their bodies, Philomela and Tereus would not be the significantly differentiated beings we call woman and man, and so could not possibly come to be mistaken for this story's essential actors.

Although the second is the better of the two, neither of these tellings is altogether adequate. In part 1, I argued that neither the discourse of technological instrumentalism nor its parasitical twin, that of technological determinism, will do. In part 2, I argued that neither the epistemologist's representation of language as a passive instrument for the expression of autonomous thought nor the radical discursivist's representation of language as the hegemonic author of all meaning will do. Such binary formulations are always gender-laden, and they find their echo in conventional representations of men as so many freely willing sovereigns and women as so many consummate victims. While perhaps such dualisms serve the interests of Tereus, they are no friend to Philomela.

Better, therefore, to ask how the capacity for human agency is itself a creature of habit, of habits that are what they are by virtue of the ways they have been called into being and consolidated by the artisanal artifacts into which the capacity for agency has itself been projected. Is such an argument circular? It is only if one thinks that agency, to be deemed free, must be something akin to a miracle (Arendt), or something to be explained through recourse to individual genius (Rorty). These appeals to an uncaused cause prove superfluous, however, when one recalls that this capacity, first realized in something on the order of a hammerstone, is itself a metaphorical actualization of a potentiality latent within the body's native capacity to transform some antecedently existing matter into some-thing else. Once that capacity is realized in the fashioning of a few simple artifacts, the dialectic of projection and reciprocation is off and running, and so the capacity for agency needs no other explanation.

To discredit all neat and tidy distinctions between creator and creature, victimizer and victim, as I recommend here, is not to claim that the situation of men and women is the same. Obviously, I also tell the tale of Procne and Philomela because, in its brutality, it offers a condensed metaphor for the ways in which the human artifacts known as men have conspired with a host of artisanal artifacts to constrain and silence women, relegating the latter to a realm where their work in fashioning and sustaining the artifactual conditions of reality is rendered invisible, where that work proves unable to find confirmation in dominant discursive resources. The sword of Tereus, a projection of his arm's ability to cause pain, tells us more about the harsh realities of women's subordination than we may wish to recall. The loom of Philomela, a projection of her capacity to share meaning with others, tells us much we need to know about why women sometimes find it necessary to speak a foreign tongue.

If this is the moral of the tale I tell, then perhaps I should end this work with a series of prescriptions, a solution to the problem posed by the artifactual conditions of gender exploitation. Raised in the culture of the United States, schooled in the philosophy of pragmatism, reared as my mother's son, I find it very difficult to resist the impulse to close by saying something constructive about "*the* problem of gender and technology." But resist that impulse I will, for I do not believe that such a problem exists. To attribute to "technology" or "gender" a specific, coherent, and determinate essence is to substitute an intellectual reification, a pernicious abstraction, for what we more urgently require: nuanced explorations of the various ways different sorts of artisanal artifacts participate in fashioning distinct complexes of gender-specific habits and sense-making orientations out of the body's indeterminate (but not unlimited) potentialities.

In these pages, I have argued that if such explorations are to succeed, they must not focus exclusively on the most recently fashioned of contemporary technologies. It may be true, as Donna Haraway tells us, that the cyborg offers an apt metaphor for what is most significant about the specifically postmodern condition.[2] But to think that this border-crossing alien tells us *all* we need to know about that condition is to forget that the worlds of Thetis and Elizabeth, Achilles and Victor, have not perished but rather are now folded within a present where artifacts of many ages cohabit uneasily. True, for those who can afford to do so, ever greater chunks of time are now spent chatting with anonymous others in cyberspace. True, for those who cannot afford to do otherwise, ever greater chunks of time are now spent performing mindless chores in the faceless company of monochrome monitors. But to define postmodernity in these terms alone is to take for granted, indeed to do an injustice to, all of the more mundane artifactual conditions that make such activities possible, ranging from the clothes that shield Philomela's flesh and blood to the metal shell that safekeeps the internal organs of her microcomputer. To overlook these prosaic artifacts, to render them theoretically invisible, is to do to them precisely what men historically have done all too well to the women who have specialized in the disdained imperatives of home and child making.

To highlight the terms of our artifactual dependency, I have devoted considerable time to things that ordinarily find no place in professional philosophy:

doors, robes, thumbtacks, swords, looms, forges, beds, toothbrushes, hammers, brooms, walls, forks. In doing so, I mean to espouse, even to celebrate, a sort of unphilosophical materialism. Without discounting the work done by capitalist economies in stimulating an insatiable appetite for consumable trifles, without denying the gulf between those who are more and those who are less alienated from the arcane devices of late modernity, I nevertheless want to affirm our common passion for what, just this once, I will call material things. That passion is an expression of our bodies' hunger for intimate connection with the world as well as, perhaps paradoxically, an expression of our desire to displace the imperatives of those same bodies onto things willing to suffer in our stead. Should we sneer at such things, we will never understand what those who are impoverished grasp all too well: to be deprived of a goodly supply of the things of this world, to find one's existence condemned to Descartes's shack and stove, is to be akin to Prometheus bound atop Mount Caucasus.

In according special place to such unheroic artifacts, I do not mean to deny the uniqueness of the present, nor do I mean to argue that the relationship between such artifacts and human bodies is either culturally or historically uniform. Given my embrace of Nietzsche's claim that what a thing is is a matter of the relational webs in which it participates, I must be committed to the view that the ceramic cup spared by *Accident*'s narrator is not identical to the "same" cup spared by Elizabeth or by Thetis. With that said, I do once again want to insist that we are not well served by theoretical exercises that ride roughshod over the unevenly sedimented presence of the past in the present. True, unlike Thetis, I no longer need to attend to an open fire to secure light after dark. True, unlike Elizabeth, I no longer need to keep wood ablaze in the kitchen stove to secure heat throughout the day. For me, to flip two switches is to accomplish what demanded so much more of my ancestors. Be that as it may, so long as toilets need cleaning, clothes need mending, floors need scrubbing, dishes need washing, children need bathing, it will remain necessary for me to perform these chores or, alternatively, to delegate them to some other human or artisanal artifact. For that long will an analysis of gender relations, as well as inquiry into other relational structures of exploitation, remain inseparable from any assessment of the politics of technology.

I am disinclined to close with a call to arms, with a rousing set of rules for action, for another reason as well. Just as I am wary of theoretical speculation that dismisses the burden of the past to affirm the malleability of the present, so too am I wary of speculation that confuses its discursive abstractions with the totality of what is sensibly immanent within experience. Because I am persuaded that experience will always outwit and outrun the fruits of thinking, I have little confidence in the capacity of theoretical inquiry to offer direct or specific guidance to the sort of conduct through which inequalities are undone, injustices are rectified, exploitations are eliminated. When asked to contrast his brand of philosophical thinking with that definitive of the intellectual artifact we call "the Western tradition," William James responded: "As compared with all these rationalizing pictures, the pluralistic empiricism which I profess offers but a sorry appearance. It is a turbid, muddled, gothic sort of an affair, without a sweeping outline and with little pictorial nobility."[3] If all good theory is good by virtue of its sorry appearance, as I believe it is, then such intellectual production is singularly ill equipped to furnish a precise map whose highlighted routes will show us how to march confidently into a future of unfettered emanicipation.

At its best, it seems to me, inquiry that hopes to answer James's call does what it can when it offers new ways of looking at matters otherwise too familiar, things that have, as it were, disappeared from view because they make too much common sense. I have tried to do just that by calling explicit attention to the network of artisanal artifacts that, precisely because they are so commonplace, so often vanish. I have tried to counter the apparent objectivity of such things by insisting on their referential instability, their intrinsic ambiguity. I have tried to contest the ascription of neutrality to artifacts by showing how they are constitutive ingredients of the relational complex we identify using the term "gender." And I have tried to question the Cartesian affirmation of such things' passivity by locating them within the dialectic of projection and reciprocation and, correlatively, by insisting that because the latter always exceeds the former, the creation of artifacts always remakes their makers in ways that no one ever fully anticipates.

My affirmation of theoretical humility is also derivative on this last point concerning reciprocational excess. So long as it is distinctively human, the human condition will always and necessarily take shape as a tragic comedy. With Marx, I would like to think that alienation from the things we make is a historically specific phenomenon, that our artisanal artifacts will one day stand as so many unproblematic sources of self-realization. But if we can never know with certainty just what will become of us as our artisanal artifacts assume lives of their own, if the capacity of Prometheus's fire to ameliorate the press of embodiment can never be neatly distinguished from its capacity to destroy, then Marx's confidence is misplaced. Freud, I suspect, is closer to the mark: "Man has, as it were, become a kind of prosthetic God. When he puts on all his auxiliary organs he is truly magnificent, but these organs have not grown onto him and they still give him trouble at times."[4] If such trouble is part of what it is to be a creature of Prometheus, then a more prescient Zeus would have understood that mere receipt of the divine trickster's gift rendered additional punishment superfluous.

"Prometheus Bound," Aeschylus's dire admonition to those who would rival divine prerogative, finds its logical antithesis in the cocky hubris of "Prometheus Unbound." Neither Aeschylus nor the husband of Mary Shelley, however, do justice to Prometheus himself. Were he to tell his own tale, I suspect he would elect to call it "Prometheus Rebound(s)." Although certain that his transgression would be punished in time, never did Prometheus imagine that he would be made to suffer so. "In helping man / I brought my troubles on me; / but yet I did not think that with such tortures I should be wasted on these airy cliffs, / this lonely mountain top, with no one near" (269-72).[5] Yet Prometheus refuses to repent, refuses to renounce his love for those who, although blessed with his gifts, ultimately remain but "creatures of a day." "Worship him, pray; flatter whatever king / is king today; but I care less than nothing / for Zeus" (937-39).

"The gods named you wrongly when they called you Forethought; you yourself need Forethought to extricate yourself from this contrivance" (85-87), says Might to Prometheus. To know that the gifts of Prometheus rebound in ways even he cannot foresee, to know this but to dare to act nonetheless, demands a sort of salutary foolhardiness. To his credit, humanity's divine benefactor anticipated this need as well. When a chorus of elders asks Prometheus how he "caused mortals to cease foreseeing doom" (250), he cites neither the fire he stole from Zeus, nor the skill he stole from Hephaestus and Athena. Offering an enigma instead of an answer, he says only, "I placed in them blind hopes" (250-52). Philomela's tapestry is one emblem of that hope.

Notes

1. Ovid, *Metamorphoses*, vol. 1, trans. Frank Miller (Cambridge: Harvard University Press, 1971), 6:443-44. Succeeding quotations from this story are identified by line numbers only.

2. I recently ran across a remarkable advertisement for Microsoft's "Natural Keyboard." Arguably, this ad provides indirect support for the argument, advanced by Carol Stabile, in her *Feminism and the Technological Fix* (Manchester: Manchester University Press, 1994), to the effect that Haraway's "technomania" (152) serves all too well the hegemonic interests of multinational capitalism. Part of that ad reads as follows: "An idea is followed by an impulse that shoots down your arm. Your fingers move across a keyboard. Words appear upon a screen. This is how we work, how we think, how we are. Together with a Microsoft Mouse that jumps to highlighted buttons and returns to its original position [not Rawls's, I trust], you are connected, fitted, ergonomically and intuitively one with the machine. To think faster and work faster the physical link between you and the machine must be seamless. The Microsoft Natural Keyboard is that link." No comment.

3. William James, *A Pluralistic Universe* (Cambridge, Mass.: Harvard University Press, 1977), 26.

4. Sigmund Freud, *Civilization and Its Discontents*, trans. James Strachey (New York: W. W. Norton, 1961), 38-39.

5. Aeschylus, "Prometheus Bound," in *The Lyrical Dramas of Aeschylus*, trans. J. S. Blackie (London: J. M. Dent, 1920). All succeeding quotations are indicated by line number only.

INDEX

Saussure, Ferdinand, 97n47, 114, 117, 145, 232
Scarry, Elaine, 7, 48, 52, 74, 140; on the dialectic of projection and reciprocation, 4–5; on objects, 38; on rooms, 40–41; on the sentience of artifacts, 45. *See also* dialectic of projection and reciprocation
schema, 133–36. *See also* Butler, Judith; form; matter
Scott, Joan, 117, 147, 185n38
sense making, 12–14, 139; of Agamemnon's robe, 84–92; contribution of artisanal artifacts to, 47–51; and feelings, 155–59, 170–72; involvement of different senses in, 87–88; and pregnancy. *See also* embodiment; experience; feelings; language
sexual harassment, 9, 113
sexuality. *See* gender
Sheets-Johnstone, Maxine, 152–53
Shelley, Mary, 13, 272n16, 273n26, 283
Sherwin, Paul, 274n33
shield of Achilles, 191–212
Shusterman, Richard, 141, 154
Smith, Dorothy, 160, 167
space, 69–73
Spain, Daphne, 167, 189n188, 190n133
spiders: Arachne's transformation into, 99–101; black widows, 159, 171; continuous with webs, 19–21, 45–46; wolf, 159. *See also* Arachne; webs
Spivak, Gayatri, 117
Stabile, Carol, 283n2
standpoint theory. *See* feminism
steamboats, 82

stethoscopes, 36
Susie, 68, 72–73, 171–72, 179
synagogues. *See* Judaism

tables, 53
tape recorders, 5, 48
tapestry. *See* Arachne
technology: academic inquiry into, 15; and determinism, 28–31, 60, 97n45; and gender, 1–2; invention of term, 28; and nature, 37. *See also* artisanal artifacts; Cartesian paradigm of use; dialectic of projection and reciprocation
teleology. *See* Aristotle
telephones, 58
temporality, 131–32
Tereus, 277–80
Thetis, 13, 191–212, 217
Thomas, Nicholas, 81
Tocqueville, Alexis de, 62
toothbrushes, 21–22, 81, 249
Toptunov, Leonid, 255–58
trial. *See* law; politics

Venus, 180–83
Vernant, Jean Pierre, 271n5
V. I. Lenin Nuclear Power Station. *See* Chernobyl; nuclear reactors
Vulcan, 180–83, 223

watches, 79–80
Weber, Max, vii, 29
webs: as animate, 45–46; Cartesian interpretation of, 19–21; composition of, 171; as metaphor in the work of Hannah Arendt, 104–11; as metaphor in the work of Richard Rorty, 114–16; reverberations within, 63; scientific

ABOUT THE AUTHOR

Timothy V. Kaufman-Osborn is Baker Ferguson Professor of Politics and Leadership at Whitman College, where he teaches political theory and constitutional law. He is the author of *Politics/Sense/Experience: A Pragmatic Inquiry into the Promise of Democratic Politics* (Ithaca: Cornell University Press, 1991) as well as numerous articles on various topics, including feminism, pragmatism, and Japanese politics. He is currently working on a critical history of state-sponsored hangings in Great Britain and the United States.